D1126762

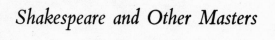
Shakespeare and Other Masters

SHAKESPEARE
AND OTHER MASTERS

BY

ELMER EDGAR STOLL

Professor of English, University of Minnesota

NEW YORK

RUSSELL & RUSSELL · INC

1962

The use of this feigned history hath been to give some shadow of satisfaction to the mind of man in those points wherein the nature of things
doth deny it, the world being in proportion inferior to the soul. . . .
Therefore, because the acts or events of true history have not that magnitude which satisfieth the mind of man, poesy feigneth acts and events
greater and more heroical.   BACON, *The Advancement of Learning*

> Of fate and chance and change in human life,
> High actions and high passions best describing. . . .
> (Of the Greek tragic poets) *Paradise Regained*

> Non satis est pulchra esse poemata: dulcia sunto
> Et quocumque volent animum auditoris agunto.
> HORACE, *Ars Poetica*

Laissons-nous aller de bonne foi aux choses qui nous prennent par les
entrailles, et ne cherchons point de raisonnements, *etc.*
MOLIÈRE, *Critique de l'École*

I think poetry should surprise by a fine excess and not by singularity;
it should strike the reader as a wording of his own highest thoughts, and
appear almost a remembrance.   KEATS

Art can only be explained and interpreted by art; and one art illuminates
another.   J. W. MACKAIL

Half [the sculptor's] touches are not to realise, but to put power into,
the form.   RUSKIN

Comparison and analysis . . . the chief tools of the critic.   T. S. ELIOT

Il n'y a qu'une façon de comprendre un rôle, celle de l'auteur.
FRANÇOIS DE CUREL

PRÉFACE

ELEVEN of these studies have appeared before, as follows: 'The Critic as Sleuth' in the *Saturday Review of Literature*; 'The Dramatic Texture' in the *Criterion*; 'Reconciliation' and 'The Tragic Fallacy' in the *University of Toronto Quarterly*; 'Hamlet the Man' as an English Association Pamphlet; 'Othello the Man' in the *American Shakespeare Association Bulletin*; 'Othello and Oedipus,' 'Phèdre,' and 'Tartuffe' in the *Revue Anglo-américaine*; 'The Tempest' in the *Publications of the Modern Language Association*; 'Art and Artifice in the *Iliad*' in the Tudor and Stuart Club *Journal of English Literary History*. Two of these, as indicated elsewhere, were, four years ago, delivered as lectures at the Johns Hopkins University and at Wellesley College. To the editors of these magazines and journals and to the institutions of learning I express my thanks for permission to print or reprint. An equal debt of gratitude is owing to the Macmillan Company and the Cambridge University Press for the privilege of reproducing here and there some material from my *Shakespeare Studies* (1927) and *Art and Artifice in Shakespeare* (1933).

All of the studies have been revised, most of them considerably enlarged. They are fairly independent and self-contained, and therefore, since they deal with one subject — dramatic and poetic art — and from one point of view — the art of Shakespeare — they involve some repetition. In order to reduce this I have arranged them in what approaches a logical sequence, and now and then in one have merely referred to another. Two studies, 'Kent and Gloster' (*Life and Letters*, December 1933) and 'Shakespeare's Jew' (University of Toronto Quarterly, January 1939), I have omitted because they are accessible and seem to be in less need of revision.

Assuming, with the poet Grillparzer, that the greatest is (what *a priori* he might have been expected to be) 'the most comprehensible of poets,' I have opposed some of the more notable efforts 'to make him incomprehensible.' The only difficulties I find in Shakespeare (apart of course from a badly edited and printed text) are owing to: (1) a technique that is now at some points unfamiliar; (2) the dramatist's hasty rewriting of other people's plays, such as *Hamlet*; and, above all, (3) the incrustations of criticism. Shakespeare himself in turn has been rewritten, not frankly as in the late seventeenth century, for the stage, but insidiously, deceptively, in the late eighteenth, the nineteenth, and the twentieth centuries, for the closet. This cannot be ignored. To show what Shakespeare is one has to show, at points where there is among the more intelligent a widespread misapprehension, what he is not. As with some early Italian paintings the repainting has to be scraped away. This book, therefore, is, in part, a criticism of criticism. The Prologue is devoted to it. Of some of the more technical or collateral controversy, however, I have been able to relieve the less resolute reader by having recourse (and here merely referring) to the learned journals: *Modern Philology*, August 1937, November 1939; the *Shakespeare-Jahrbuch*, 1938; *Modern Language Notes*, February and May 1939; *English Literary History*, March of the same year; *Publications of the Modern Language Association*, December 1940.

In my earliest monograph, *Othello* (1915), p. 63, I quoted the following, with the page reference, from Mr. Shaw's *Dramatic Opinions and Essays*:

The Shakespearean delineation of character owes all its magic to the turn of the line, which lets you into the secret of its utterer's mood and temperament, not by its commonplace meaning, but by some subtle exaltation, or stultification, or shyness, or delicacy, or hesitancy, or what not in the sound of it. In short, it is the score and not the libretto that keeps the work alive and fresh.

This I have repeated several times since, as, for instance, in *Shakespeare Studies* (1927), pp. 115–16, *Poets and Playwrights* (1930), p. 6; and one reviewer who found it wanting in *Art and Artifice in Shakespeare* (1933) will now readily understand that I had begun to take the matter for granted.

Some indebtedness has to be taken for granted, so vast is the corpus of Shakespeare criticism. That which is less obvious to the reader, my indebtedness to more recent writers, I have studiously endeavored to indicate. But memory is often fallible; and when it is we see this, unfortunately, not in ourselves but others. At times I have not made acknowledgments because, though they might seem to be, they were not due.

An indebtedness of a perhaps bigger, certainly more pervasive

sort one cannot acknowledge. Everyone, however rigid and in-
flexible, is a part of all that he has met, both in print and in the flesh.
Only in general am I aware how much profit I have received from
the intelligent and candid approval or disapproval of those scholars
and (above all) men of letters, in this and other countries, who have
troubled themselves to express it.

E. E. S.

CONTENTS

Horace, proud, irascible, ruthless, and lawless. Most classical scholars
agree, not the poets. §3. Retaliation, honor, and booty, and Achilles'
right to withdraw. The classical scholars ethical like Horace; but think
that, though responsible for Patroclus' death, Achilles becomes penitent
and reforms. §4. De Quincey's attitude, like that of the poets, is rather
vague. 'Ideal' has moral implications, and at some points Achilles is
immoral. §5. The poetical treatment of character — the enlarging and
intensifying, simplifying but liberating, method employed by the
greatest poets to secure the maximum of emotional effect. The intervention of deities, to produce a situation and yet diminish the hero's responsibility. §§6–8. The offers of reconciliation in Book IX involve
the matter of honor, the center of the story. Honor chosen in preference
to long life at the outset, the cause of retiring from the conflict, gives
way only to higher honor as he returns, and that to what is higher still.
The conception supported by the attitude and conduct of the other characters. §§9–11. The wrath and atrocity of Achilles in battle the measure
of his love for Patroclus, as the flight of Hector is the measure of the fear
which Achilles inspires. §§12–13. Hector's reputation with us rescued;
Achilles' preserved. §14. The poetical conception of character clearer
when the two heroes are compared and contrasted. Achilles the larger
nature. §15. Other art and artifice — the musical development of
themes and *motifs*, which, as in Shakespeare, lends itself to emotional
effect.

Shakespeare and Other Masters

Prologue: The Critic as Sleuth

It is the nature of commentators to abhor a vacuum.

SAINTSBURY

. . . it is the peculiar and perpetual error of the human intellect to be more moved and excited by affirmatives than by negatives.

BACON

ELIZABETHAN DRAMA, says a contemporary neo-Baconian (that is, a believer in the Earl of Oxford as the author of the Shakespearean plays) — Elizabethan drama 'is not the simple, straightforward thing that Mr. Drinkwater supposes it to be; but is, on the contrary, complex, difficult, symbolic, topical, and double-minded to the last degree.' In that the neo-Baconian finds his satisfaction. The only imaginable way, then, for an audience to find any is themselves to have no inkling of this complexity; and since for them Elizabethan drama was intended, and of Shakespeare's own writing less than half had got into print before his death, his complexity was — incredible in an artist — repeatedly thrown away. Less improbably, something else has been thrown away.

With Baconians or Oxonians we are here not concerned, nor with the believers in Rutland or Derby, either; but the detective spirit by which they all are animated is not peculiar to the heretical nor indeed to the orthodox criticism of Elizabethan drama. It pervades the sympathetic criticism of highbrow novel and poetry and even the writing of recent history: two years ago a reputable American university professor revived the transcendental myth that the British, in Machiavellian subtlety, sank their own *Lusitania*. In part, certainly, 'history is bunk'; and as such it repeats itself. The British did the same thing a little while ago, cunning and cruel beyond belief, to their *Athenia*. And before either *coup* they had (by their efforts in the contrary direction!) inveigled the Germans into war, into that and then into this. Nothing now is what it seems. When financial advisers quitted the President's service the reasons on both sides were not the real ones. When the Prime Ministers at Munich capitulated they were not intimidated; but the repeated conferences, the preceding ultimata and mobilizations were all stage-play, to intimidate the public in England, France, and Czechoslovakia into accepting the pre-arranged terms. There was frankness enough, though, before that. At what previous time in history did ever a conquering 'Leader' flatly tell the world what he had a mind to do? But this one, saying that he would do it, was not believed, and therefore again and again he has been believed as he said he would do it no more. A new Machiavelli, too new for a knowing old world! And war, it is owing to the fear of war. The peaceable peoples — so deep do they now see — craftily ignore the disquieting preparations and gestures of the warlike, because to do otherwise would make them more warlike and themselves less peaceable. Ours, certainly, is not distinctively an age of good sense; not even where that quality might be considered indispensable — in history and psychology, politics or political economics, in legislation or administration, in educational theory or practice. Debt now is a benefit, a liability an asset, economy anti-social folly; and our excellence *is* 'without great labor.' Nor is it an age of poetry, on the other hand.

Good sense, the Romantic Wordsworth and Coleridge both declare, is 'one property of all good poetry.' How much more then should it be of criticism! In art, also, nothing now is what it seems, and least of all in Shakespeare. Scholars having no Baconian or Oxonian incentive go in for the complex and difficult, the biographical and topical, the allegorical or symbolical, in short the double-minded, often as eagerly as if they had one. Despite the royal prohibition Elizabeth trips in on the stage as Titania, and James 'shambles' in as Bottom, Hamlet, or Prospero; and besides Oxford, Bacon, Rutland, and Derby, noblemen such as Essex, Burleigh, Southampton, and Pembroke either enter the stage door or (by way of the allusions) peep from the wings. Shakespeareans of this saner description likewise dearly love an earl. For them, too, the redoubtable Burleigh is Polonius. And how the *Tempest* — Miranda, Caliban, Ariel — has been allegorized, politically or philosophically, psychologically or biographically, we all too well remember. As we come to the last chapter of another study we wonder what incredible discovery in this play it is now to be. In-

terpretation — it is ingenuity. That is the active principle in a
recent elaborate study of *Hamlet*. To take a single instance, the writer
practically reconstructs the scene of the Murder of Gonzago, and
thereupon, contemplating his own handiwork, cries out, somewhat
in the Oxonian's vein, 'The subtlety of this is masterly in the extreme!' Extreme enough, it is not masterly because misplaced.
Extreme subtlety of method or meaning is incompatible with
drama — incompatible with that 'perfect comprehension and profoundest emotion' which, as Arnold remarks, with the practice of
the greatest poets and the precept of the greatest critics to support
him, 'is the ideal of tragedy.'

What of it? What is the harm? Error might be suffered to perish. In criticism, though presumably a science as well as an art, the
word 'error' has little or no meaning; but the thing itself prospers,
and this particular sort undermines. There are fewer and fewer
principles still generally accepted, scarcely a landmark left standing,
little ground common to critic and reader. Criticism itself, as a
body of thought, falls into greater confusion, and that is bad enough;
sound criticism cannot well be composed or comprehended in the
face of what prevails. But the main damage, perhaps, is what detective criticism does to art. It misinterprets what has been written;
it misleads those who write. For want of a sound criticism and
enlightened public opinion the monstrosities of 'metaphysical' ingenuity arose in the seventeenth century; because of unsound criticism and a bewildered public opinion we have monstrosities of
ingenuity and unintelligibility in the 'new poetry' and the *art
nouveau* today. It is a match of wits between critic and artist. Detectives must have crooks or conjurers to work upon; readers of
riddles must have riddle-makers, or pretend to have; and we all can
point to contemporary poets or novelists, painters or sculptors, that
make the pretense unnecessary. Or the Muse growing impatient of
her role as Sphinx, she enters into collusion with her Oedipus, who
plays official interpreter, as Mr. Gilbert has done for Mr. Joyce; or
else becomes her own interpreter — in label, lecture, 'programme,'
preface, or appendix. With novel or poem, picture, statue, or
musical composition, as with an arithmetic, comes the 'key.' Great
pictures, like great symphonies, poems, and stories, can even do
without their titles or names. But a roundish slice of cold boiled

ham with a live human eye set in the center of it, a knife, fork, and bottle of wine beside it? Or two piles of pans supporting a traveler's trunk, upon which is perpendicularly planted an umbrella? That the one surrealist product is a 'portrait,' the other an 'exquisite corpse,' we must, of sheer necessity, be told. And after we are told what, some of us cannot well content ourselves till we are told why — questions, both, that in the best art either do not arise or else are duly answered by the work of art itself.

Which of the conspirators, critic or artist, is more to blame we will not endeavor to determine; but as things now are, the former, when playing fair, thus becomes, as never he was, indispensable. That is, if the unintelligible is not to remain so. The detective or confidant must needs step in when *Ulysses* or still more formidable artistic riddles are to be read. It is to be admitted that greater scope should be given ingenuity and subtlety in what is meant to be perused in solitude, to be meditated, not performed or presented. It is to be admitted also that times have changed and works of real genius may now be more exacting than before this day of scientific and psychological complexity. They may be studied, as our other diversions are. Whist became bridge, then contract bridge; and this, to be continually all-engrossing, must be daily pondered and taught. Yet the critics presume upon their privilege. 'As if it were not enough that living poets should be unintelligible,' says Mr. F. L. Lucas,[1] 'our critics father the same quality in retrospect upon the dead. In a recent work with the Apocalyptic title, *Seven Types of Ambiguity*, it has been revealed to an admiring public that the more ways a poem can be misunderstood, the better it is.' One couplet of Herbert's is made to mean four different things; but as Mr. Lucas thinks, so far from meaning all four at once, the passage does not mean any of them. Shakespeare, if I am to judge from a laborious but limited acquaintance with the writings upon him, is not at a stroke given meanings so numerous; but then he has had so many more critics, each with his ingenious own.

The critic is nowadays so indispensable only because the artist is so incomprehensible; and partly, no doubt, the artist is so through the influence, the provocation or justification, of science. By it

---

[1] 'The Criticism of Poetry,' British Academy, Warton Lecture (1933), p. 25.

since the day of Copernicus and Newton, and still more in that of Darwin and Einstein, *common* sense (if we may make the distinction) has been contradicted or flouted. A brick, alone in space, would not 'fall'; this fixed and immovable earth both rotates and revolves; parallel lines, contradictorily, meet. Even such things are not what they seem. A 'fourth dimension' was, in my youth, a figure of speech, a symbol of the spiritual, but since then it has been declared a reality; and a month or two ago Einstein was reported to have just added a fifth. And time — the tricks played with it of late by both philosopher and novelist! The inconceivabilities of theology now reappear as the truths of science, and there is no longer the edge of satire to Swinburne's

> Two and two may be four, but four and four are not eight.

To many they no longer are! Poetry, however — above all, drama — is not theology, metaphysics, or higher science. It deals with appearances and produces immediate impressions. Hamlet, Othello, Macbeth, Lear, Falstaff, and Iago are what they seem; unlike men of flesh and blood that is all they are. And in their world the sun still rises and sets; or if the higher learning, through familiarity, finally gains an entrance into poetry, it does so only when it comes speaking that language, as when Lucy, now only a pitiful infinitesimal portion of the planet, is

> Rolled round in earth's diurnal course,
> With rocks and stones and trees.

　In the expression, to be sure, lies the main trouble with the extremist new poetry and art — not so much in the fact that things there treated are not what they seem, but that we know not rightly what they are meant to seem. It is not a matter of good sense or of the common but of sense of any sort at all. The artist, in his impatience of simplicity and craving for originality, will have nothing short of a new language, a new medium (whereas the true artist uses, in a new way, the old). Words and phrases, lines and colors, are peremptorily employed apart from their accepted meanings or traditional associations. Associations, traditions, established conventions, which are important adjuncts to expression, are, as obstacles or impediments, broken or ignored; grammar and idiom, syntax and the very sentence structure, are trampled upon; and arbitrary and impossible combinations are made of thoughts or objects, or rather fragments of thoughts or objects — witness the ham and eye! Here science is not the influence but the pretext. Speaking for poet and critic both, Mr. Ezra Pound declares that

we no longer think nor need to think in the terms of monolinear logic, the sentence structure, subject, predicate, object, etc. We are as capable or almost as capable as the biologist of thinking thoughts that join like spokes in a wheel-hub and that fuse in hypergeometric amalgams.[2]

Mr. Pound says nothing of the freer art of music; yet into this chaos and phantasmagoria that art brings only an illusory relief. Often words and phrases, on the one hand, and lines and colors, on the other, are put together as if they were musical notes, but to produce a harmony that is imperceptible because without a connected meaning; and strangest of all, in work really serious, often even the words are, in jabberwocky style, coined for the occasion, without perceptible meaning in themselves.

How different are the ways of true criticism or creation! Even in philosophy unintelligibility is not profundity. In art it is charlatanry and humbug, childish mystification or pedantic gibberish — like the thirty-three syllable conglomeration 'bababadal...' in Joyce's *Finnegan's Wake*. And criticism is no matter of detecting at all but of receiving and responding. If poet or playwright, especially the latter, is so enigmatic and baffling, he baffles also himself. For art is a communication, not to say a communion. The worthies who have spoken of theirs — Milton and Molière, Pope, Coleridge, Wordsworth, and Matthew Arnold — have protested that it is a simple and open, an imaginative matter, and in such a spirit to be approached. The poet or dramatist, when really such, has not been playing a game of cunning; and the critic's business is not to catch him at it. His business is — for a critic, strange to say, one of the most difficult in the world — to read what is written, hear what is spoken, and putting all irrelevant predilections and prejudices, all merely personal ambitions and opinions behind him, react to the

---

[2] *Criterion*, April 1930, p. 475. See the reply of Mr. Belgion, 'What is Criticism?' *ibid.*, October. He has anticipated me at some points in this chapter and also in one or two others. See, below, Chap. III.

words like the normal human being for whom they were intended, yet, unlike him, watch and question himself as he does it. In any event it is not his privilege to rewrite the poem or play, to bring it up to date or treat it as if it were his own.

In connection with good art there may be problems to solve; but they are not set in the work of art itself. There may be the problems of authorship, in the study of dubious or anonymous Elizabethan plays or the Letters of Junius. Or, in the background, those of source, of influence, or of the author's experience. All these, however, are secondary matters, not immediately important to appreciation; and they do not yield to lawyer's learning or the historian's. That may do for the external evidence, but not for the internal — language and style, context and technique, the author's intention. They yield, if at all, to the learning of the literary scholar. Or the internal matters themselves may involve a problem, preliminary and necessary to interpretation, within the work of art, indeed, but still not a problem the author has set. Such a question arises, moreover, only when the work of art is remote from the present, or when the author's intention has not been completely communicated or fulfilled; and even here the literary scholar's learning, which now again comes into play, only removes obstacles in the path. It should invent nothing, supply nothing, certainly not put there obstacles of its own. What questions are really *raised* are, as in Ibsen or Galsworthy, those not of expression but of content, answered (or intentionally left unanswered) by the author himself. And whether the author is always master of his medium or not, he and his critic, when in the right relation, are not pitted against each other, posing or 'smoking' each other. He does not 'set a trap for the reader,' as a recent clever interpreter of Ibsen thinks to have caught him doing in *Little Eyolf*, and 'decide with an almost satanic smile of satisfaction to keep to himself his esoteric knowledge of the hero's real nature.' Many a critic of Shakespeare might, in character, have said of him the same. But Shakespeare did not write detective stories. In the real ones, to be sure, the 'mystery' is in the end laid bare, and you needn't be a sleuth to read the book. So far as Shakespeare and other important authors or artists, dead or alive, are concerned, the detective story is written nowadays, in excitement and exultation, by whom but the critic, with himself in the leading role. He tells how, as he followed this clue or that, he caught the author out. When in the right relation, however, there is no story to tell; author and critic, like poet and public, dramatist and audience, are engaged mainly in open-minded interplay and whole-souled communion; and the critic, in his essential function, is only public or audience in finest form, at highest potency. As such he should have a faculty for analysis and expression, for discrimination and judgment, even for sympathetic imaginative re-creation; but to what faculty he has for invention and detection he should not give the rein.

Long after writing the above I happened upon the following passage in John Churton Collins' *Studies in Shakespeare*, published in 1904, before the day of ingenuity, of dadaism and futurism, of Joyce, Pound, and Stein, and of the criticism demanded by them and consequently inflicted upon their predecessors. Collins, thou shouldst be living at this hour! In 1904, criticism, though irresponsible enough, was comparatively simple and unassuming, indifferent to the truth rather than making elaborate pretensions to it:

Sainte-Beuve has finely said that the first aim of criticism should be the discovery of truth, not, as Goethe contended, the interpretation of the good and the beautiful. . . . But the discovery of truth is about the last thing with which criticism in our day appears to concern itself. There seems to be the same impression among critics as there is among novelists, that it is disgraceful to be seen on the highways. Into what by-paths fiction has wandered, and into what malodorous abysses and squalid deserts those by-paths have led and are leading it is sufficiently notorious. But the seduction of criticism is much more to be lamented. . . . On its competence and sincerity depends more than can be defined or estimated, for it gives the ply to the serious study of literature generally. Whether that study is to be facilitated or retarded, to go straight or to take wrong turns, to be fruitful or barren — for all this it is responsible. It would not be too much to say that never in the history of letters has criticism been so unscrupulously indifferent to its true functions as it is at the present time. It seems to assume that to tell the truth is to thresh the straw; that anything which is new is better than anything which is true; that the more incontestably established the fact, the more obviously sound the accepted view, the greater the necessity for the substitution of sophistry and paradox.

CHAPTER I

The Dramatic Texture in Shakespeare

I

HE dramatic texture? It is in large measure a matter of suspense, and I have elsewhere[1] remarked the lack of this in Shakespeare as compared with Ibsen and even with Corneille and Racine. That is, except now and then, for a scene or an act, he produces no surprise, after the necessary engrossing but baffling preparations. What does he then instead? Like the Greeks before him, who similarly did not keep the secret from the audience, he offers an effect of excited — in tragedy, of anxious — anticipation; but more than the Greeks, and Corneille, Racine, and Ibsen too, he offers also a realization of the thoughts, feelings, and circumstances that rightly belong to a particular dramatic moment and are essential to the illusion. At their best these effects may hold the interest as well as those of surprise. Anticipation is ordinarily required for the arbitrary and artificial situations of his theater and the ancient — for disguise or mistaken identity, deception or slander, feigning or overhearing, the fulfillment of prophecies or oracles. Suspense — a gradual yet surprising disclosure to the audience as well as to people on the stage — is ordinarily required for those situations which, brought about less quickly and peremptorily, involve past conditions or events, present motives or intentions. Shakespeare generally keeps no secret, present or past. The story, an old or a familiar one, is told fairly from the beginning; the motives or the purposes, the moral or immoral, attractive or unattractive natures of the characters, appear at the outset; the characters themselves are numerous, the incidents frequent and various;

---

[1] Particularly in the chapter 'Shakespeare and the Moderns' in my *Poets and Playwrights* (1930). I am there indebted to Mr. Percy Lubbock's *Craft of Fiction* (1921). In the present chapter there are some echoes from my *Art and Artifice in Shakespeare* (1933).

and if Ibsen produces the impression of depth and volume, Shakespeare produces that of extension and expanse. How, then, does he center this extension, give it structure, force, a sort of volume too? He has a bolder, more striking fable than the Norwegian; and in that lies a certain effect (in the sculptural sense) of 'relief.' He has a good narrative method — contrast between scene and scene, interlocking of incidents and interweaving of the threads of story, crescendo and climax, complication and denouement. But so has Ibsen, a method certainly thriftier, though not so flexible or engaging. He has the treasures and incalculable resources of poetry; and there is nothing more marvelous in drama than the style and tone vivifying, unifying, and distinguishing *Hamlet, Othello, King Lear, Macbeth,* and *Antony and Cleopatra.* In each there is a different atmosphere — a characteristic diction, imagery, and verse — for a different world. But the matter in question is more one of framework and impact. How is it that, apart from the poetical intensity and the realization of character and circumstance, he achieves a unity that shall somewhat make up for the force and point of an ultimate startling disclosure?

Anticipation itself, when well aroused and managed, yields a kind of suspense; as when, in the *Oedipus Tyrannus,* the Messenger from Corinth, bringing the news of Polybus' death, thinks to allay the hero's fears by telling him that, though heir to the throne, he is not the king's son. This news is less reassuring — is still more exciting — to the audience, who know what is coming, and dimly see it coming, than to the hero; the hero's own excitement, indeed, does not now directly appear. At other times it does so appear, as well as that of the less important characters; and there are expectations fearful or joyful, to be justified or not. All this is exciting both on the stage and in the house. For though the audience are aware of the outcome they are so only in general terms — of what it will be but not how it will be brought about; identifying themselves with the hero, they live mainly in the moment, notice mainly what the dramatist is actually presenting; and they are particularly affected by joyful expectations (as in the 'moment of last suspense') that they know in their hearts to be fallacious. So true is this that many critics, after Lessing, have hotly declared against the method of surprise, although Shakespeare himself has followed it for an act or

a scene, as at the beginning of *Hamlet* and near the end of *Othello*;
yet in the play as a whole we need not greatly concern ourselves for
its virtues, seeing that we have the practice of Ibsen, Corneille,
Racine, and Lope to support us, as well as the explicit doctrine of the
Spaniard and even of Aristotle. 'Incidents have the very greatest
effect on the mind,' says the Stagirite, 'when they occur unexpectedly
and at the same time in consequence of one another.'[2] In Shakespeare, for the most part, they have such effect as in Aeschylus and
Sophocles rather than in Euripides.

   The difference in practice and criticism both is best explained by
Mr. Charles Morgan's distinction between 'suspense of plot' and
'suspense of form.'[3] Suspense of plot, which has to do with the
disclosure of a fact, like Epicene's sex or Tom Jones's paternity, or
with that of motive or point of view, like Nora's and Helmer's
in the *Doll's House*, has its indubitable value; but suspense of form,
which has to do with the development and establishment of the
emotional illusion, has a greater value, and in the best work of either
Ibsen or Euripides the two sorts of suspense are conjoined. Suspense of form is the excited expectation not of the answer to a puzzle,
or of the disclosure of a mystery, but — under the spell of illusion —
of the rounding out of a harmony, like the rime to come at the end
of a verse or the rest tone at the end of a song. It is the expectation
of the way that Othello will receive the slander and afterwards the
truth, or that Hamlet will baffle his enemies, have his revenge and
meet his death.

   Now with anticipation — this suspense of form — there is greater
opportunity for irony; and in Shakespeare as in the ancients, not so
continually but more variously, the contrast essential to drama,
which holds it together, takes on this more accentuated and poignant
aspect. There is irony in Ibsen, too, as in *Ghosts*, *The Master-Builder*,
and the *Doll's House*, where the expectations of characters and
spectators alike are defeated and appearances are stripped from
reality; but in Shakespeare there is not only irony of this retrospective
sort, as when the eyes of Macbeth, Othello, or Lear, of Gloster or
Edmund, are opened to what they have done, but also irony of the

---

[2] *Poetics*, cap. 9.

[3] Royal Society of Literature, 'The Nature of Dramatic Illusion,' *Essays by Divers Hands* (1933).

prospective sort, in the character's own expectations defeated, which is tragically enjoyed by the spectators from the beginning. As with the ancients, these expectations, whether favorable or unfavorable, are far more abundant and definite than in Ibsen, and because of superstition they give the irony greater force and point. In Shakespeare's earlier tragedies and histories they often take the form of prophecies or curses, omens and portents, whether or not provoked by presumption, or *hybris*; in the later, they oftener take that of fallacious hopes or warranted premonitions or forebodings. And either form, whether Shakespeare himself much believed in its objective validity or not, is as necessary to him for his irony as to the Greeks. Whether in the earlier or the later Shakespearean tragedies or histories, the story is more complicated and, though presented far more fully, generally less familiar to the audience.

And with anticipation — this knowledge of the facts — there is greater scope for sympathy, greater cause for both pity and fear. To sympathize you must know the facts; when you don't know them, your interest is of another sort; and while the incentive of suspense in Shakespeare and the ancients is an anxious sympathy, in Ibsen and the moderns it is an excited curiosity. Not that the difference is merely a matter of keeping the secret. The modern dramatist, disdaining fatal or villainous influence and deriving the action more strictly from the character, much diminishes our pity when the hero commits the Aristotelian 'deed of horror'; and when to keep pity unimpaired the misdeed is made less than horrible, he takes away our fear. To understand is to forgive; but the sympathy that comes of a complete psychological and sociological motivation is rather less whole-hearted and unalloyed than pity for innocence; crimes like embezzlement and forgery, indicating no sizable passion in the perpetrator, arouse little emotion in the spectator; and consequently the dramatist is fain to make less importunate demands upon our emotions, more upon our intelligence, and put curiosity in sympathy's place.

2

Then there is the matter of imaginative and emotional interrelations, which, like irony, tighten the fabric. But the realistic and intellectual ones we must consider first, and these are in Shakespeare somewhat lacking or neglected.

Maeterlinck, long ago, speaking of the greater dramatist's wide dramatic fabric, called it 'loose'; but that was not a reproach, nor should it be now when we bear in mind the practice of Shakespeare's predecessors and contemporaries, the established taste of his audience, which not merely to attract but to move them he was bound to consider, the quantity and variety of the material presented, and (at the same time) the intensity of effect both expected by them and by himself desired. There are many more characters and incidents than in the Hellenic, the Bourbon, or the modern drama, and, whether it be tragedy or comedy, much greater extremes of passion than in the latter two, as well as passions more various than in any of them. The aim of tragedy and comedy, as in the time of Aeschylus and Aristophanes, was to be as terrible or as hilarious as possible, even to or over the verge of what is now called melodrama or farce; but with this Elizabethan multiplicity of material, both tragic and comic, from both high life and low, in one play together, intensity could not easily be secured by way of singleness or strict verisimilitude of impression. It is in some measure, again, a matter of tradition and of a comparatively primitive technique. As in the ancient drama, the passions are expressed directly and amply, though the speech is kept less rigorously to the dramatic question or business in hand than in the ancient, and far less than in Corneille and Racine. The tragic dialogue is not as in Corneille and Racine an emotional debate, a continual balancing of duty against inclination or of duty against duty, a repeated approach to or recoil from the capital deed. The hero (or heroine) being, like the ancient, rather a sufferer than a doer, his utterances partake of the lyrical rather than the analytic or argumentative. But in greater measure it is a matter of artistic limits. The content of these plays is too big for realism, breaks over its bounds. In the abundance of extraordinary and highly contrasted incident and passion to be motived there is, and in part must be, some little neglect of motivation. The result, not the mental process, preoccupies the dramatist, Mr. Bradley notices, when Coriolanus resolves to burn the city; and in general 'he studied more,' as the discriminating author of *Some Remarks on the Tragedy of Hamlet* (1736) observes, 'to work up great and moving circumstances to place his chief characters in, so as to affect our passions strongly, he applied himself more to this than he did to the means or methods whereby he brought his characters into those

circumstances.' Often, as in later chapters we shall have occasion
to indicate, he has recourse to a summary or superficial motiving,
to mere narrative preparation or bare peremptory announcement,
such as Hamlet's

> As I perchance hereafter shall think meet

for his feigned madness.

Except Jonson's, the Elizabethan structure does not at every
point hold together by a causal, logical, or psychological connection.[4] The same has been remarked in Attic tragedy;[5] and it is
obviously true when the story is taken from myth or legend, as in
the matter of Oedipus' marrying, despite the oracle, his own mother
or of Lear's division of his kingdom. Such improbabilities are acceptable, as Aristotle says, only because the story is familiar — not
the author's own invention — and because they are previous to the
action or near the beginning. But of both Attic tragedy and the
Elizabethan that is true (though less conspicuously) also later in
the dramatic movement, the Elizabethan particularly, in which the
action is far more crowded and extensive. Ordinarily this does hold
together in point of mere fact, but less often in the circumstances.
What happens, what is done, and who does it, are made pretty clear,
but not so clear how it is done, or when, or where, or why. The
chief thing done is made plain as day. That, in anticipation of the
nineteenth-century manager's notorious formula (but in unconscious
imitation of the ancients), is announced and even discussed beforehand, then done accordingly, then referred to as done already:
witness the practical jokes upon Falstaff or Benedick and Beatrice,
the intrigues of Richard, Iago, or Edmund. But in the attendant
circumstances Shakespeare avails himself of the advantages and
privileges of a swiftly moving stage performance — without scenery and without pauses in the action — and keeps to momentary,
superficial, but immediately telling effects.

As is well known, there are irreconcilable contradictions in time
and place. Some of these no doubt are the result of carelessness, in
the hasty, impetuous process of putting a history or *novella* on the

[4] See Miss M. C. Bradbrook, *Themes and Conventions in Elizabethan Drama*
(1935), pp. 31-33, to which I am indebted in this paragraph.

[5] J. T. Sheppard, *Greek Tragedy* (1911), p. 19.

stage. But most of them are so contrived that in the theater the mere contradictoriness or incongruity shall not be noticed[6] and yet an elasticity and a larger liberty shall be secured: short time and indeterminate locality mainly for speed and compression, for dramatic interest; long time and definite locality for verisimilitude and illusion; and by the interweaving of mainplot and underplot the latter serves to fill in the interstices of the former. Neither the contradictions nor the references in themselves are to be treated as necessarily having ulterior significance, and, as in the matter of Hamlet's delay, inferences are not to be drawn concerning the character. They are an example of Elizabethan liberty, of which we are to see many others. 'How galling and repressive it is,' says Mr. Galsworthy, 'to have to remember that our fancy man or woman can only do this or that owing to the limitations of a time and space which cannot be enlarged!'[7] Shakespeare enlarged them, somewhat as, in good hands, the screen has done again. And by means of the omens and forebodings he did that in the matter of future time as well — the future which the novelist can avail himself of and the modern dramatist, except as he chooses a familiar story, scarcely can.

And (partly as cause, partly as consequence) the dramatist makes as free now and then with the incidents themselves. How is it that Lear, in Act II, despatches a messenger to Regan, and Goneril one to warn her, both expecting replies, and yet the messengers, as well as Regan and also Lear and Goneril themselves, enter so nearly together before Gloster's house, a night's ride from Regan's?[8] As with time and place, Shakespeare is, like his fellows, writing to be seen and heard, not read and studied; is endeavoring to pay homage both to the outer everyday realities of life and also to dramatic requirements — in this instance, that the chief characters should all speedily be at the same spot with an accumulated grievance; but in doing so he is flying in the face of probability and logic. Sometimes, in his impetuous haste, he is careless of detail or of coherence in action and

---

[6] A. C. Bradley (*Shakespearean Tragedy*, 1908, Appendix, Note I) thinks it is the short-time references that are not noticed, and, naturally, inquires, How can they possibly affect the spectator? As for the time of Hamlet's delay, see below, Chap. IV, pp. 147ff.

[7] John Galsworthy, *The Creation of Character in Literature* (1931), p. 15.

[8] Cf. Bradley, Appendix, Note U.

character gratuitously. There are loose ends, not to say, contradictions. Adam in *As You Like It*, the Fool and the King of France in *King Lear* are dropped, forgotten by both their friends and also the dramatist; Cassio's wife, Lady Macbeth's children, and three or four characters in other plays, similarly made use of for the moment, do not even emerge from the background because there would be no place for them if they did. Hamlet's having 'forgone all custom of exercise' and yet 'been in continual practice,' Portia's holy hermit and her letter about Antonio's argosies are like many of the details of history and geography. And the scene of Polonius' sending Reynaldo to spy upon Laertes, like that in *Antony and Cleopatra* of Ventidius' refraining from conquest, comes or leads to nothing; in fact both, like a fair number of other short scenes in Elizabethan plays that do not observe the unities and are not provided with an underplot, serve to fill the intervals in a continuous performance of a discontinuous action.[9]

And, as in some of the examples already cited, the dramatist often makes as free with the character. Desdemona listening to Iago's indecent witticisms on the quay and Helena engaging in the discussion of virginity with Parolles almost or quite forget themselves. Horatio part of the time is at home in the Danish court, part of the time a stranger;[10] that is to say, he appears to be one or the other as the reader draws inferences, now from his bestowing, now from his receiving information. These inferences the audience, evidently, were not expected to draw, any more than from references to time and place. How could they with any security, in a world where the causal, logical, or psychological connection is so frequently slighted or omitted? In a world of unmotived jealousies like those of Posthumus, Leontes, and Beaumont and Fletcher's Philaster; of love at sight and sudden villainies and repentances, as in Shakespeare every here and there; of conversions to chastity and abrupt but deliberate lapses from it, as in Dekker, Fletcher, and Massinger; of impersonating and disguising, lying and slandering, to the point of taking in everybody who should know better, as in all the Elizabethans,

[9] Cf. T. M. Raysor, 'Intervals of Time,' *Journal of English and Germanic Philology*, January 1938, p. 30, and below, p. 148.
[10] See G. F. Bradby, *The Problems of Hamlet* (1928), Chap. II, and below, Chap. IV, pp. 148, 161.

whether comic or tragic? In a world where the noble Valentine surrenders his true love to gratify a treacherous and lascivious friend, and Romeo, going to the ball 'to rejoice in splendour of my own,' completely forgets Rosaline in the presence of the fairer? In a world where true-hearted gentlemen like Bassanio go wife-hunting to restore their fortunes, and at the denouement of a comedy or romance exquisite maidens such as Celia and Hero, Julia, Helena, and Mariana marry men morally far beneath them, and high-souled matrons such as Imogen and Hermione receive again serious offenders like Posthumus or Leontes if but repentant? These have sinned more in intention (which on the stage counts for less) than in deed; but actual bloodshed in tragedy is abundant, and some of it, by noble characters like Romeo and Hamlet, is wanting in adequate warrant or regret. The bloodshed cannot all be blamed on the old story. The killing of Paris is the dramatist's addition: the desperate but generous emotions thus awakened are all that justifies it. The 'atrocity' of Shakespeare, as of the Renaissance generally and the ancients, must be frankly accepted: high tragedy is not an image of life, the hero's conduct there not the unbroken reflection of his nature. Seneca and the Renaissance tend unduly towards melodrama; but high tragedy is rooted in that, even as all high passion is rooted in sensation, and sexual or maternal love is stronger than the friendly. Anyhow Hamlet's taking so little thought for Polonius and Ophelia, and Romeo's taking so little for Juliet's two friends whom he has killed, are not to be reckoned against the character. Juliet, Desdemona, and Imogen forget their parents after the rupture. Omissions here do not count unless a point is made of them; and still less are questions to be answered that are not raised. Psychology and our knowledge of life or history are not to be invoked; and Othello is not, as of late, to be held guilty of the intrigue with Emilia suspected by her obviously cynical and suspicious husband.[11] The Moor is a healthy and vigorous, unmarried, middle-aged soldier of fortune — but he is a romantic hero, what is unexpected and unwelcome requires a hint that is unmistakable, and a figure in fiction is not subject to inferences as if he were flesh and blood. Still less where these are not invited, and the character resides not so

---

[11] See my article 'Shakespeare Forbears,' *Mod. Lang. Notes*, May 1939.

much in the connections or suggestions of what he says or does as in the thing said or done itself and the prevailing tenor and manner of his conduct; and resides more in what he says — thinks and feels — and how he says it — though not always even there, witness the pure-minded young ladies! — and in what is said about him, than in what he sometimes does or fails to do.

This, so far as ulterior motives are concerned, is true particularly of the leading personages in tragedy, who (as with the ancients, though these have no such plethora of material and show no such recklessness in the presentation) are superior to their conduct, and are led or driven into dreadful deeds by influences human or super-human. Horatio, a minor character, is at times serving the purposes of exposition and the narrative mechanism, and what individuality he has lies mainly in his attitude to Hamlet and in Hamlet's to him; but the individuality of the Prince himself, of Othello, Lear, or Macbeth — full length and in the foreground — so far appears in what he says and how he says it, in what he thinks and feels in his own right rather than in what he does or fails to do, that with his procrastination, or gullibility, or vanity, or ambition the man in his inner being has little in common. Only in part is he the arbiter of his own destiny, the source of the action; and what motivation there is — witness Hamlet's taking to madness and Iago's counting on the Moor's 'free and open nature' — is often merely narrative and (again) superficial. As in all the greatest tragedy, Greek, classical French, or Elizabethan, the passions are developed in their intensity, carried to extremes; and in the Greek and the Elizabethan the motives given are sometimes emotionally insufficient. Upon Hamlet a psychoanalyst recently made one true remark — the emotions are in excess of the occasion; and it is as true of Lear, Macbeth, Othello, and Iago, and above all of Timon. Ambition is apparent in Macbeth, and ambition or vindictiveness in Iago, as several critics have noticed, only at the outset; and their bloody careers run far beyond the cause or provocation. So Lear's passion, reaching beyond thwarted paternal affection, filial ingratitude, and the realization of his own blind folly, covers the hypocritical injustice and cruelty of life in general, and appeals to and reproaches the heavens themselves. Lear, Timon, and Hamlet alike, in their passionate pessimism, cry out upon woman's vanity, perfidy, and incontinence;

but Hamlet alone has had any occasion for it, and he only in his mother's hasty and improper marriage, for that she was vain or affected does not appear. He has had no more cause to complain of woman's painting, lisping, or nicknaming God's creatures than of the oppressor's wrong, the proud man's contumely, the pangs of dispriz'd love, the law's delay, the insolence of office. Or the emotions are in rebound against the occasion. Macbeth and Othello, by the convention of compelling influence, intensify the situation as they experience the horrors of a man who would *not* have committed the murder, heightened in the former by those of an honorable man, in the latter also by those of a loving one. One and all they rise to the loftiest of melancholy meditations upon the mysteries of human existence. One and all, good and bad, heroes and villains, they are, in a sense, like poets, who, in sorrow and happiness alike, transcend the limits of experience and circumstance.

For in general the method is not one of analysis. Shakespeare's leading characters, men or women, may or may not have a '*ruling passion*' but, including Coriolanus, they are not the embodiments of it — not of ambition or hatred, of love or jealousy, of honor or patriotism, not of 'wrath' in Lear or of 'sloth' in Hamlet, not of moral, religious, or artistic aspiration, of a desire for wealth, knowledge, power, fame, beauty, or eternal salvation, whether these singly or as pitted against another. Not one of his characters is a Napoleon or (as in the flesh they were) a Caesar, Antony, or Brutus; is a Cromwell or a Richelieu; is a Faustus or a Francis Bacon; a Byron, a Shelley, or a Keats. Not one is a bad man but good king, like the Richard III and the Macbeth of history; a cruel saint or egoistic martyr; an illicit lover who struggles with his fate; a Cornelian Curiatius or Racinian Titus, whose love bows to duty. Not one renounces love and life for country and the common good, like three heroines of Euripides. But if there is not much analysis there is description — there is presentation — enough. We know all we need to know. As we shall see, the characters vividly, if not clearly, reveal their own natures, and (as arising from the situation) their feelings and purposes. Yet they have passions rather than principles; are guided by impulses, good or bad. They are generally wanting in a clearly defined point of view, a program or problem, a phi-

losophy or sophistry of life, a dialectic of love and honor, such as
that by which the characters of Corneille and Racine are guided or
judged; and their souls are not arenas for freely contending ideas and
emotions. That Brutus is a patriot and Antony is in love with
Cleopatra is convincingly apparent from the presentation and from
the comment of others; but for the rationale of Brutus's conduct
we must turn to Plutarch, for that of Antony's — All for Love and
the World Well Lost — to Dryden.[12]

Where, then, what is important is made so very clear and explicit
and what is less important is neglected, where minor contradictions
of fact or circumstance are eluded or ignored and implications of
fact or circumstance are not certainly to be counted on — in such
plays, surely, the implications of character are to be counted on still
less and the psychologically insufficient motivation is not to be eked
out by the ingenuity of the reader.

For if the method is not one of analysis it is not one of suggestion,
either. 'The eternal unsuggestiveness' of Shakespeare is what Mr.
Shaw complains of; and if others perceived it as clearly without
complaining, Shakespeare criticism would be in a sounder state.
A casual speech on the Danish national vice of drunkenness cannot
legitimately be turned into an unconscious confession of a very different weakness in the speaker himself, the decision to feign madness
into an effort to avoid or cover the reality, the doubt that the Ghost
may be the devil into a sign that 'he has lost the will to believe,' or
the remark about the traveler not returning into a sign that he has
forgotten about the ghost or no longer believes that there was a
ghost at all.

Mr. Allardyce Nicoll holds an opinion directly opposite to Mr.
Shaw's, one which, I take it, would encourage the Hindu scholar
who recently ventured to show that 'almost everything written on
Shakespeare is true.' (Shadow and sunlight are the same!) Making
much of omissions, of silence or absence from the stage, and other
negative matters, which, as Mr. Courtney rightly says, even in our
suggestive art, do not count unless our attention is somehow, however delicately, drawn to them, he declares that 'considered in this
way, the unrevealed or the unknown in Shakespeare is seen to have

---

[12] On the subject of this paragraph cf. H. J. C. Grierson, *Cross Currents* (1929),
pp. 92–93, 114–16.

as great an importance as the known and the revealed.'[13] 'Surely
no stronger proof of the unsoundness of this principle,' Mr. Waldock replies, 'could be adduced than Professor Nicoll's conclusion
that one of the causes of Hamlet's indecision is "his reliance on the
eminently sane, faithful, and sincere Horatio." ' The main difference between Professor Nicoll and most other Shakespeareans,
however, lies in his recognizing and avowing the princ:ple. Professor Firkins speaks out as frankly but sees more clearly. Shakespeare
'drew men,' he finely says, 'largely, plainly, boldly, for the common
untrained eye.'[14] Still, merely on the strength of the implications,
and from what the character does or says rather than what is said
about him, the critic immediately proceeds to make Macbeth out
to be, not only blundering and incompetent, hesitant or precipitate — supposedly like Hamlet — but also (in himself and not
merely through temptation) very wicked and (worse than wicked)
mean and small. And when to that is added the 'epicure in crime'
(because of the apparent self-consciousness when he bids the earth
hear not his steps) he becomes simply incredible as a tragic hero.
For Richard is redeemed by his irrepressible energy and undaunted
courage, by his wit and humor; and Richard is not expected to have
our sympathy as in the earlier part of the play Macbeth is. In the
later he has it through his spiritual sufferings, his marvelous poetry
and far-ranging imaginative vision, however little this may be in
strict psychological keeping. So Banquo, by Mr. Bradley, has
been made out to be guilty of criminal acquiescence; so Hamlet, by
Tieck and Börne — not fantastic philosophers or burrowing
scholars but reputable men of letters — has been made out to have
seduced Ophelia. In both cases justifiably, if implications count.
But her brother's and father's warnings, the hero's own warnings to
Polonius and Ophelia herself, his indecent jesting with her and the
snatches of indecent folk song in her madness, all hold together as
the details of an external, not an internal, story.[15] And the reader
should, like the true Elizabethan spectator, surrender to the story,
following the main trend, heeding the plain, bold outlines; he should

---

[13] W. L. Courtney, *Studies in Shakespeare* (1927), p. 21. Cf. A. J. A. Waldock,
Hamlet (1931), pp. 70–71.

[14] O. W. Firkins, 'Macbeth,' *Selected Essays* (1933).

[15] See my article 'Shakespeare Forbears,' cited above.

not impede the current of interest by looking backward to construct
more of a human figure than is there, or one that would repel him
if it were there. 'Tragedy is essentially an imitation,' as Aristotle
says, and as we shall later consider, 'not of persons but of action and
life, of happiness and misery'; and Shakespeare not only does not
carefully adjust the Scottish hero's conduct in the inherited story to
fit it more perfectly to the character but also carelessly allows him,
under the sway of the Weird Sisters' temptation and his Lady's
reproaches, to express his generous admiration for her dauntless
spirit immediately after her 'revolting and despicable' proposal (as
Mr. Firkins calls it) to take advantage of the king's defenselessness
and then lay the guilt at the door of the sleeping grooms. Yet in
itself it is a finely impulsive and self-forgetful response,

Bring forth men-children only,

so soon after he has been provoked to cry:

Prithee, peace!
I dare do all that may become a man;
Who dares do more is none;

and it serves to measure for us — still along the main trend, in an
imitation 'of action' — the ascendancy she has now established over
him. For verisimilitude it comes about too speedily, and on what
an occasion! But this is drama, not psychology or realism.

As for motives, we, for our part, must not provide the dramatist
with them, even because he omits them. Like most of the other
Elizabethans, Shakespeare is impetuous, prodigal, and often illogical; but, unlike most of them, generally to great effect. Deliberately
or instinctively he keeps to the surface; and, as later we are to see, in
the improbable but spacious situations that he presents, deep-seated
motives would necessarily reduce the proportions of the hero's
passion and our sympathy. An Othello, a Claudio, or a Posthumus
with the predisposition to suspicion or jealousy, a Desdemona, a
Hero, or an Imogen who had given him any cause for it, or an Iago,
Don John, or Iachimo with an adequate motive or grievance for the
imposture, how they would diminish our love and pity for hero and
heroine and our fear or hatred of the villain! In the source at times
the motive is missing, or is fantastic and bizarre, but oftener it is by

Shakespeare omitted when already provided and in itself — though not for the larger or higher needs of his passions — satisfactory enough: as in Iago and Don John, who were rejected suitors; Leontes, whose wife was incautious and indecorous; Macbeth, who had grievances against a weak and unjust king; Coriolanus, who in the flesh acted better and was treated worse; Oliver, who had been slighted in favor of Orlando; Viola, who was already in love with Orsino; Hamlet, who had reasons for his madness and for his treatment of Polonius, Ophelia, and the ambassadors to England. And in the first scene of *King Lear* there is a remarkable instance. Despite the great improbability of the situation the scene has by the best judges of 'good theater' — both Sarcey and Granville-Barker — been greatly admired, and yet most of the motives in the anonymous *King Leir* or the other sources are dropped and none but superficial and obvious ones retained or provided. There are no ulterior ones, such as the King's undertaking to play a trick on Cordelia in order to induce her to marry a British prince and stay at home, or Goneril's and Regan's jealousy and hatred of Cordelia and desire to discredit her, or Cordelia's desire to test her father and rebuke her sisters. Such explanations and complications would interfere with the intensity and momentum of the scene; and a still greater interference would be the motives inferred or invented by modern critics, such as the King's own vanity or senile debility or 'slothful' and 'voluptuous' craving for a life of ease, or Goneril's and Regan's previous 'sufferings from their overbearing and hot-tempered father.'

All art, to be sure, is suggestive — the ancient as well as the modern, the classical as well as the romantic. It is a question now only of method, of direction or degree. And the Elizabethan suggestiveness is primarily poetical. It is imaginative and emotional rather than logical or psychological, immediate rather than inferential, and it has to do not so much with the inner nature or mechanism of the character as with the situation or the structure of the play as a whole. Reasons and motives count for less, as we are to see, than contrasts and parallels, developments and climaxes, tempo and rhythm, or even the identity of the individual utterance. The psychological implications that Othello has the germ of jealousy in him, and that, along with Desdemona and Cassio, he is wanting in perception, count for little against the purely narrative or dramatic one of the honesty of Iago in the eyes of every soul in the play, including the wife of his bosom.

3

The imaginative and emotional interrelations, as we perceive already, are by no means lacking.

In default of the causal, logical, and psychological, they are required; and so is suspense by anticipation. The method of a prepared surprise, as in Ibsen, demands implications that can be counted on. The method of anticipation both demands and lends itself to explicitness and demonstrativeness; and in Shakespeare compared to Ibsen, not only before but after the turns of fortune, the manifestations of feeling on the part of the characters are far more open and pronounced. Thus the audience receive their emotions by contagion. In Ibsen the characters' feelings are given less scope; and the audience receive their emotions in a sense directly — that is, thrown more upon their own resources — but by a process that is indirect. Contagion is replaced by inference, by suggestion. Not privy to the secret, the spectators 'live and learn' like the hero or the other characters on the stage; and it is as, receiving impressions and gathering information, they instantaneously draw conclusions or make the expected and justified conjectures that they are moved and respond. Then, through the preparation and the surprise, the gradual but tantalizing disclosure, the hero or another may, at the great moment, with the highest effect, speak quietly and reticently. But when the audience are to participate less, are to be thrown less upon their own resources, the perceptions and the emotions of leading characters must, accordingly, be more amply displayed; and Oedipus and Cassandra, Macbeth and Othello, visibly shrink from the abyss before they fall. Oedipus descries it from afar:

O Zeus, what hast thou decreed to do unto me?

Unhappy that I am! Methinks I have been laying myself even now under a dread curse, and knew it not.

Forbid, forbid, ye awful gods, that I should see that day.

So Macbeth faces beforehand even the horror of his treason and assassination; Lear cries, 'O let me not be mad, not mad, sweet

heaven!'; Othello has fears for the future simply because of the fullness of his happiness; Iago, as the hero approaches, the poison already working in his veins, mutters and chuckles, 'Not poppy nor
mandragora, nor all the drowsy syrups of the world shall medicine
thee to that sweet sleep which thou ow'dst yesterday.' In Ibsen, more
as in life, there are only misgivings.

This self-revelation or clairvoyance, though for us and even for
the Elizabethans it involves a loss in verisimilitude, is essential to the
dramatic method. The soliloquizing frankness of the villain concerning his purposes replaces as a unifying and exciting element the
tell-tale frankness of the ancient Fate, whose role he fills. Even those
still more unplausible avowals — on the villain's part, of his own
villainy, and on the hero's, of his own virtue[16] — which are ves-
tiges of an earlier technique (not the Hellenic, though, for that had
the chorus) contribute to the effect. Is this not part of the secret, to
be shared? For the immediate arousing of our emotions there must
be authoritative guidance; in the theater there should be no more
question or hesitation with whom we are to weep than at whom we
are to laugh; and for our emotions, if not for our wits, it is more
exciting to know betimes how wicked and dangerous Iago or
Edmund is, which fact, as the tragedy is constructed, either one,
impervious to every eye but his maker's, is alone in a position to im-
part. Without such excitement, indeed, before the event — after
it of course there will consequently be still more — the letting of the
audience into the secret of the conspiracy from the outset would be
a failure. Suspense itself is, ultimately, a matter of arousing emotion
in the audience; and by this method of anticipation, which is imaginative if not suggestive, emotion is aroused forthwith.

Thus, because it contains an absolute, unquestionable moral element, the emotion in the audience is ampler and intenser than in
these days of naturalism, when wickedness keeps its own point of
view, and to itself is not wickedness, nor, consequently, altogether
such to the audience, and Fate is heredity or environment, which
relieves the bad of blame and deprives the good of credit. When the

[16] As in Othello's speeches, I, ii, 19–24, 30–32 — instances even today but slightly
objectionable from the standpoint of realism. Brutus, in the quarrel scene, is a case
much more pronounced; misunderstanding the technique, critics have taken him to
task for his complacence.

moral judgments of the audience fail wholly to agree with those of the character concerned, and still more when with those of the dramatist, the emotion is directly interfered with. That is the weakness in 'problem plays' such as Granville-Barker's *Voysey Inheritance* and Ibsen's *Borkman*, *A Doll's House*, *Rosmersholm*, and *Hedda Gabler*, in which the hero thinks himself a financial *Uebermensch*, or instead of going into bankruptcy pays off his poor creditors at the expense of the rich ones, and the heroine forges signatures to save her husband or, playing with souls, lures them for their good or that of others to their deaths. Even in novel or short story, as Mr. Belgion says, 'only when the moral beliefs of the reader tally exactly with those on which it is based will the reader have the whole of the emotion which it is potentially able to produce in him.'[17] How much truer that is of the drama, which depends on immediate and unanimous response! And hence it is that in moral judgments there is such explicit or implicit conformity with the prevailing conventional and absolute standards on the part of the Elizabethans, the Greeks, and the classical French.

Now this demonstrativeness, this intensity, helps hold the tragedy together. The anticipation unifies, focuses; nor is that all. It is not merely a matter of before and after but of here and there in the tragedy, crosswise as well as up and down its course. In both the Elizabethan and the ancient, particularly in the Shakespearean, the passions are not only more amply depicted but also more fully developed than in the modern, whether the characters be important or unimportant; and in their changes and relations lies as much of the structure as in those of the incidents. The passions being required, whether the motive is sufficient or not, in their extremity, they lead to or spring from a tragic deed that, as with the ancients and according to the expectation of Aristotle, is one really 'of horror,' done 'in ignorance' or through arbitrary external influence, and in the denouement, as with Othello, Lear, and Macbeth, recoiling on the hero's own head; and they rise and fall, swell and subside, both in the individual and also in the scene or the play as a whole, as in the modern they cannot. As in Greek and French classical tragedy, they are not confined within the limits of natural

[17] 'Tchekhov and Dostoievsky,' *Criterion*, October 1936, p. 20. Cf. my article 'Recent Elizabethan Criticism,' *Journal of English Literary History*, March 1939, p. 51.

conversation; drama here approaches the lyric, by way of outcry and apostrophe, repetition and variation; and as Mr. Shaw says of Othello, the words 'are streaming ensigns and tossing branches to make the tempest of passion visible.'[18] Passion has scope, in all its changes. How pronouncedly, too, the characters react upon one another! Five times after he falls into the Ancient's clutches Othello encounters Desdemona, with continually more marked effect upon both himself and her. The relation of the chief characters to the numerous minor ones is emotional as well: they are loved or hated, praised, pitied, or condemned, rather than analyzed or understood, and their fortunes are rejoiced at or deplored. This, again, the audience receive by contagion; and by it, together with the justification for such feelings in the presentation of the characters and the situation, their sympathies are won and guided. How they are safeguarded — against the critics, as because of the improbabilities of the action they often need to be — by the outpourings of admiration and affection upon Isabella and Helena, Romeo and Juliet, Hamlet, Lear, Othello, Coriolanus, Antony and Cleopatra, and, at the beginning, Macbeth! This is the chorus, and art rather than history repeats itself. Like the chorus, moreover, the numerous characters are a sounding-board or amplifier to the heroes' and heroines' joys and woes. For in Shakespeare, as in the ancients, it is a matter of pity and fear, not of psychological revelation; an anxious sympathy is the incentive of suspense, as an excited curiosity is in Ibsen; and the response is immediate, not delayed. In every way imaginable the dramatist takes advantage of his method; and the whole play is a system and a rhythm — what is that but unity? — a contrast and a harmony, of passions.

Play and scene fluctuate as well as the character. Both end quietly; and there are static scenes, like the martlet one before Glamis Castle, as there are also normal — either controlled or unexcited — characters, like Banquo, Horatio, Kent, Cassio, and Ludovico. The art

[18] G. B. Shaw, *Dramatic Opinions and Essays* (1906), II, 279. But with Mr. Shaw this is only half-hearted praise: 'The words do not convey ideas'; 'its passion and the splendour of its word-music which sweep the scenes up to a plane on which sense is drowned in sound. . . .' This last might almost indicate that Mr. Shaw favored the present-day esoteric word-music, without sense; but of the 'superficiality' he complains.

is essentially classical, and includes repose. The principle is that of rhythm and contrast, not unrelenting tension and continual high pressure as today; and by points of repose the balance is kept and the ultimate effect of tension is heightened.[19] The difference between even *Macbeth* or *Othello* in this respect and *Ghosts* or *Mourning Becomes Electra*! It is somewhat that between Tennyson's *Revenge* and his *Rizpah*.

Nowhere (despite the want of a Cornelian or Racinian contention of motives) is there fluctuation so high or so various as in Shakespeare — from the tragic to the pathetic, from the serious to the comic, from passion to reflection, from action to narration, from dialogue to soliloquy, from fast to slow, from the lofty and rhetorical to the humble or simple, from blank verse to prose or to song. This matter of changing tension, indeed, and of changing tempo in the action and the wording is essential to the adequate expression of the passions and to an appropriate awakening of the spectators' emotions. It is a principle observed by the ancients — the chorus may relieve as well as heighten the tension — primarily, perhaps, out of regard for actor's and spectator's mental and physical capacity. In this, as in all other human or natural activity, contraction follows expansion, systole diastole. But in great art the alternation is not so regular or mechanical as even in nature, and limitations are turned to advantage. The changes, the contrasts, are what is noticeable; it is these, more than the appropriateness of tension or tempo to the situation, that bring the passions home. Art being a matter of effect, high tension is the higher because of the low which it has just supplanted, and the same is to be said of differences in tempo. Moreover, tension and tempo do not go perfunctorily hand in hand. Though the tempo in the scene before Glamis is slackened, whether in action or in wording, the tension, underneath, is heightened: Duncan is stepping towards his doom. It is almost as true of the Porter scene, though comic and discursive, though introducing a new character and in the slower vehicle of prose. The dread knocking still goes on; it is hell-gate that is to be opened; the Porter himself is the worse for the same treacherous hospitality as Duncan's grooms. In the other most effective comic interludes — those of

---

[1] Cf. Coventry Patmore's *Principle in Art* (1889), Chap. VI, to which I am here indebted. Cf. also my *Poets and Playwrights*, pp. 79–85.

the Gravediggers in *Hamlet* and of the Country-Fellow in *Antony and Cleopatra* — there is the same continuity, at its finest in the latter, where upon the boor's floundering exit Cleopatra in

> ' Give me my robe, put on my crown . . .

at once resumes the grand style of just before his entrance. This is a decorum above decorum — a queen capable, at such a moment, of curiosity and a gossipy chat! — a harmony that profits by pause and suspension. Soliloquy, again, is *per se* a retardation so far as the action is concerned; and therefore in tragedy it is, to make amends, almost always in verse, swiftly moving too, like Hamlet's

> O, what a rogue and peasant slave am I,

the rapidity of which, as in many soliloquies of Iago, is heightened by the prose preceding,[20] and the tension by the hero's having already given us — 'Can you play the Murder of Gonzago?' — a fleeting glimpse of his hand. Equally marked and emphatic are the ups and downs in the single situation. If a ghost appears as in the first act of *Hamlet*, or at the banquet in *Macbeth*, it is not once but twice that he does so, with room for reaction, for troubled comment and realization, in between.

4

So much at present for the matter of interrelation; there is another (in so far as the two are separable) of comprehension. (Shakespeare's tragedies are mainly not those of fate but of intrigue; the villain partly or almost entirely taking the place of destiny, and the hero engaging or engaged in an action to which he is by nature superior or averse.) As we have seen, it does not at bottom develop out of the character, which in Ibsen it more nearly does. At heart Othello is not jealous; Macbeth, not dishonorable or murderous; and this contrast is kept before our eyes. In the murder scene of *Macbeth* there is no surprising disclosure of fact, motive, or trait: sexual passion or jealousy, the man's or the woman's, does not, as it well might, now appear. Indeed, there is only the most elementary

[20] Cf. Mr. Bonamy Dobrée's *Histriophone* (1925), to which I am here indebted.

connection between character and action, the man impelled by ambition, to be sure, but more apparently and effectively by fatal and conjugal influence, the woman herself having done violence to her nature by her appeal to the spirits that tend on mortal thoughts and by drinking to stiffen her nerves. Even so, she has not killed the King with her own hand because he resembled her father as he slept; and the scene is not so much the expression of character as, contrasted with that, the utmost imaginative and emotional realization of the 'deed of horror.' Here are all the essential circumstances of murder, and such thoughts and notions, feelings and reactions, as these circumstances would arouse — the misgivings and trepidations, the starting at sounds and the imagining of sounds that are not, the questions asked but left unanswered, the fears of what is present and is to come. In this rounded intensity of realization itself there is unity; but there is more. Why does she cry, 'My husband!' when the man staggers in with blood on his hands, as if she were not sure he still was, or as if he were now more than ever? Why does he himself cry, 'What hands are these,' as if they were not his own? And again, 'Will all great Neptune's ocean wash this blood clean from my hand?' And yet again, 'Wake *Duncan* with thy knocking! I would thou couldst.' In these wide-ranging visions and soul-searching outcries the situation is seized and comprehended rather than convincingly delineated and solidly projected; but the central ironical dramatic contrast is caught up and signalized; what has gone before and what is yet to come, what murderer and murderess once were and what they at present are, all flash out before them — and us as well. And this focusing comprehension is to be found in *Macbeth* elsewhere: as, among other places, where Macduff on hearing of the killing of his wife and children groans, 'He has no children'; and where Lady Macbeth sighs, 'The thane of Fife had a wife; where is she now?' and, again, 'All the perfumes of Arabia will not sweeten this little hand.'

It is to be found almost as frequently in *Othello*; as when, having just killed the lady, the hero, after muttering — by force of habit, by force of the still unbroken bond of Nature — at the knock of Emilia, 'She'll sure speak to my wife,' recoils and exclaims:

My wife! my wife! what wife? I have no wife;

or when, defending himself to Emilia after she enters, he declares, too truly,

> O, I were damn'd beneath all depth in hell
> But that I did proceed upon just grounds
> To this extremity . . .

or when — all the more clearly because his jealous doubts or suspicions were not naturally bred within him — he finally realizes, 'beneath all depth of hell,' his monstrous error,

> Cold, cold, my girl!
> Even like thy chastity.

It is to be found in *King Lear*, as when the hero cries out, on seeing both daughters set against him,

> O heavens,
> If you do love old men, if your sweet sway
> Allow obedience, if you yourselves are old,
> Make it your cause;

thus linking his age and sorrow to the age and sorrow of the universe,[21] or, on blindly conceiving that the daughter whom he had cast off still breathes:

> This feather stirs; she lives! If it be so,
> It is a chance which does redeem all sorrows
> That ever I have felt;

or when Kent, before that, takes account of the tragedy proceeding round about him:

> It is the stars,
> The stars above us, govern our conditions;
> Else one self mate and make could not beget
> Such different issues.

Often, as in the murder scene of *Macbeth* and the sleep-walking scene, these great spotlight glimpses are taken from a height; and sometimes, as there, from above the spiritual elevation of the

---

[21] I am here combining the ideas of Lamb and Stopford Brooke as they admire the 'splendid imagination.' But it is Hazlitt that best appreciates the flight of the imagination: 'making him grasp at once at the Heavens for support.' Cf. below, Chap. V, pp. 207 and 331n.

speaker. The murderer's and murderess's sensitiveness of conscience is, except as their crime is the contriving of fate, incompatible with the murder. The conscience is (save as fate coerces) external, is a nemesis, not the faithful expression of the redhanded one's inner nature. Without real or apparent excuse or motive, murderer and murderess suffer all the more, whereas by the laws of nature it would be the less; when we stop to think of it (as we are not expected to do), what right or reason has Macbeth at such a moment to 'say Amen' or expect a 'blessing'? This as well as later poetic utterances, like that about 'the sere, the yellow leaf,' has by some few candid but psychologically rather than aesthetically gifted critics been taken for 'mere poetical whining over his most merited situation.' Instead, like his apostrophes to his bloody hands, to the sleep that he has murdered, and to the one (whoever it may be!) that is knocking, these outcries serve luridly to reveal the gulf now fixed between him and the man he was. As mere matter of fact, in the world as we know it, Macbeth and his Lady would now be the same beings they were an hour before, and even then the warrior dwelt on the horror of the crime to be committed, not on the motives for committing it; but, as Mr. Chapman says, 'the hyper-sensitiveness of Macbeth and Lady Macbeth is one of Shakespeare's greatest strokes of genius.'[22] Both early and late the situation is not psychological but emotional, the terror being 'due to the abyss that lies between.' It is not a murder by a man with his thoughts on the crown or on his own superior fitness to wear it, but something bigger. It is murder. It is a truly tragic 'misery,' not delayed.

From an equal height, but in themselves either not so dramatic or not so characteristic, come narrower glimpses, of a moment in the play rather than of the central situation; or wider views, of the course of human existence. Of the former sort is Othello's 'Farewell the plumèd troop' and 'It is the very error of the moon,' Iago's 'Not poppy nor mandragora,' Cleopatra's 'Have I the aspic in my lips?' and Juliet's 'O churl! drunk all, and left no friendly drop to help me after?' Of the latter sort are Edgar's

[22] John Jay Chapman, *A Glance toward Shakespeare* (1922), p. 71. Cf. my *Poets and Playwrights* (1930), pp. 124, 66–67. J. M. Murry, *Shakespeare* (1936), p. 271: 'convinces us, as nothing else could now convince us, of their essential nobility of soul,' but by 'an absolute and terrible naivety.'

> Men must endure
> Their going hence even as their coming hither;
> Ripeness is all . . .

and Gloster's

> As flies to wanton boys are we to the gods:
> They kill us for their sport. . .

as well as Macbeth's 'Out, out, brief candle,' Antony's 'The wise gods . . . seal our eyes,' and Prospero's 'And like the baseless fabric of this vision.' Gloster's speech may seem too lofty for his intelligence, though the figure is within his range and the irony fits his case; but whether that or not, these higher (or wider) views give to the tragedy itself, to the image of life in it, an effect of unity. We can look before and after; we see 'the whole of it'; the sky arches over the earth.

Not merely in tragedy but even in comedy, and not merely at the greatest moments in either, there is, if a less elevated, an equally rounded and far-reaching vision. In tragedy, we have already noticed, it may be given to a minor character, and as often to the villain, Edmund or Iago. Edmund's recognition of the justice of the gods visited on both his father and himself is little short of sublime:

> Thou hast spoken right; 'tis true.
> The wheel is come full circle; I am here.

He is tolerant enough, and his father involved enough, above all he himself has imagination enough, to see and acknowledge it. But more in his native vein is what he says after the death of the Sisters:

> I was contracted to them both. All three
> Now marry in an instant;

and when their bodies are brought in:

> Yet Edmund was belov'd!
> The one the other poison'd for my sake,
> And after slew herself.

Who among the 'legitimate' can say as much? And Iago, reviewing his day and night of solid deviltry, chuckles characteristically as he declares,

> By the mass, 'tis morning;
> Pleasure and action make the hours seem short.

So in comedy there are utterances like Sir Toby's to Malvolio:

Dost thou think, because thou art virtuous, there shall be no more cakes and ale?

Trinculo's to Stephano and Caliban as their very faculties begin to stagger:

They say there's but five upon this isle: we are three of them; if the other two be brain'd like us, the state totters . . .

and Helen's to Pandarus:

Let thy song be love. This love will undo us all. O Cupid, Cupid, Cupid.

Any of these, but particularly the last, might serve as epigraph for part of the play — if Shakespeare had plays with central ideas, *drames à thèse*. And on separate occasions how the poet embodies and inspirits the scene! In *Much Ado*, when Don Pedro asks, 'Come, shall we hear this music?' the romantic Claudio replies:

> Yea, my good lord. How still the evening is,
> As hush'd on purpose to grace harmony!

So in *The Tempest*, when Miranda, seeing for the first time other men than her father and (of late) Ferdinand, bursts out, 'O brave new world, that has such people in it!' Prospero, who better knows them, answers, indulgently but comprehendingly:

> 'Tis new to thee.

5

These imaginative and emotional comprehensions and interrelations, rather independent of the strictly narrative or narrowly dramatic, the probable or logical, the purposive or causal, are transverse or radial instead of longitudinal, are neither sequential nor inferential, are poetic but not definitely suggestive. There is little of such analysis (explicit or implicit) as there is in Jonson or in Ibsen. Of the latter sort there can be but little because the action is not the close-fitting embodiment of the character; and what there is of the former — in the mouth of the character himself or of another — is mostly limited, as we have seen, to an account of his immediate purposes or present feelings, neglecting motives and characteristic ideas or points of view. Shakespeare's plays are not 'studies' either in psychology, as they have long been considered, or in Elizabethan 'humors,' as by some scholars they have been thought of late. The audience are expected not to detect and discover but to perceive and emotionally respond; and therefore, according to their natures, people do this in the play, the character in question doing it even to himself. Otherwise the emotional development might halt or waver, the harmony be broken. Indeed, so far as the heroes and heroines of most of the principal tragedies are concerned, such as *Romeo and Juliet*, *Julius Caesar*, *Hamlet*, *Othello*, and *King Lear*, there is no 'tragic fault' to be perceived or detected; and the numerous comments upon their personalities and the exclamations in the presence of their sufferings serve only to heighten the emotional effect. In real life, of which drama is supposed to be the image, how opinions of the character would differ, while here, except those of enemies and the wicked, they differ mostly in the way they are expressed! If ever there was a chance for the dramatist to dissect Lear's character and lay bare his 'fault' — 'vanity,' 'irascibility,' or whatever it be — it was at the end of the second act, after he rushes out into the storm. All who remain, except Gloster, are unfriendly; but as Goneril and Regan blame him, it is for his present 'folly,' in order to make their excuses, and as they now speak more humanly, raise their eyebrows, shrug their shoulders, and shrink from the tempest themselves, they merely make us pity the King the more. Here is no psychologizing either of him or of them, and what they say is but in emotional preparation for the scenes on the heath.

Only in comedy (and in that tragedy which, with a grain of truth, Mr. Shaw has called Shakespeare's greatest comedy, *Coriolanus*), where, in Aristotle's phrase, the characters are not, as in tragedy, 'better' but 'in some respects worse than men as they are,'[23] is there much greater freedom of analysis, controlling the action; but that is

---

[23] *Poetics*, Cap. 2, 5. The Aristotelian statement applies, of course, rather to classical and Jonsonian comedy than to the Shakespearean, where the heroes are generally romantic figures.

why Mr. Eliot, on the other hand, calls *Coriolanus* Shakespeare's most perfect tragedy, though for the hero there is, to keep our emotions active, far more of praise and blame than analysis, and, to engage our sympathies for him, far more of praise than blame. Shakespeare's comedy, however, unlike the classical, is, for the most part, sympathetic, not analytic, is emotional, not critical; differing from his exalted and terrible tragedy not so much in being comic as in being simple and cheerful, lively and hilarious. His comic figures, generally, are not 'worse' — are not, like those of the ancients or Jonson and Molière, the objects of derision or satire, but are witty or ridiculous; or, as Mr. Courtney has it, fantastically or else grotesquely humorous. In the presentation of them there is somewhat the same method as that already considered in tragedy — that of lyricism, as when the wit of Mercutio, Beatrice, and Falstaff effervesces in fantasy; and that of self-exposure, as when the corpulent coward descants upon honor and discretion, or Dogberry and Aguecheek show themselves to be asses even in saying and repeating that they are.[24] The laughter, like the terror, is often for its own sake, even at the cost of character. There is the lyricism also of witlessness and nonsense, as not only in Dogberry and Aguecheek but in Shallow and Silence, Launce, the Athenian mechanicals, Cloten, Trinculo — 'But art thou not drowned, Stephano?' — and in Falstaff when at his story of the knaves in buckram and Kendal green. Folly is not lashed but given the rein; the laughter is not 'thoughtful' or scornful but indulgent and whole-hearted. There is fun both before the stage and on it. In Jonson and Molière the vicious or eccentric as well as the normal persons who have to do with them are generally too much preoccupied for fun. In Shakespeare the comic effect, not arising out of the elaborate exhibition of a vice or a foible, as the tragic not out of that of a devouring passion, must be explicitly indicated and fully appreciated on the stage; and it is by contagion that laughter, like the weeping, breaks out in the house. In Ibsen, with whom the effect, comic or tragic either, is more as in Jonson and Molière, the very action is a process of analysis; or, rather, it prompts and provokes the spectator, by its varied method of precise suggestion, to analyze for himself.

---

[24] See my *Shakespeare Studies* (1927), Chap. VIII.

But a bird in the hand, even in art; and imaginative realization is better than ingenious suggestion. In comedy and tragedy alike the Norwegian, it would seem, has, like most other modern dramatists, no such resources as the Elizabethan for the presentation of the impression the characters produce upon one another, and no such resources, either, for justifying it. I know Ibsen only in English; but he ordinarily uses prose, not verse, the language of conversation, not of poetry, and his characters are rather humdrum and, as James once said, ill-mannered. To us, at least, they are seldom likable, fascinating, or ingratiating, as even Shakespeare's simpletons or villains are. For his more realistic purposes he had, of course, less need to make them so, particularly the leading tragic characters. They are not noble in rank or in nature as Shakespeare's are, whether in conformity to the tradition of the Elizabethan stage or, though with little direct knowledge of these, to the practice of the Renaissance and the ancients and the judgment of the contemporary criticism. This criticism insisted on 'admiration,' often, to be sure, in the interests of morality; but both Racine and Corneille lived up to the latter's principle 'de faire aimer les principaux acteurs.' Now upon the direct presentation in speech and demeanor, and upon the reaction to it on the stage itself, rather than upon narrative implication or psychological suggestion, the effect of nobility or meanness, of virtue or villainy, of attractiveness or hatefulness, predominantly depends. So it is with Corneille and Racine as well, but as we shall see in Chapter III, their poetical resources are more meager, less various. And how numerous and various are the admirers of Hamlet and Ophelia, Othello and Desdemona, Lear and Cordelia, Antony and Cleopatra, Viola, Rosalind, Juliet, Beatrice, each likewise in character as he expresses himself! How manifestly too these heroes and heroines deserve or warrant the admiration or devotion, as Rosmer and Rebecca, Allmers and Rita, Peer Gynt, Borkman, Helmer and Solness do not! Shakespeare, raising the question, can answer it; incurring the debt, can pay it.

Indeed, interrelations apart, it is a question whether the direct and ample, the poetical method of presentation is not superior generally to the realistic and suggestive. By the latter more is meant than meets the ear, but too often it misses the audience. They are required to think, rather than prompted to feel. It is the great privilege and prerogative of art to be simple, sensuous, and passionate; and that by the modern method is in part surrendered. By the Shakespearean the external reality and individuality, though not the internal, is made more immediately manifest; that circumstance of itself lends credibility to the action. And there is a farther, finer reality, whether external or internal, the overtone of it, so to speak, which cannot be made manifest except by phrasing, image, and rhythm. Here too, of course, there is suggestion, but not of facts or ideas, causes or motives. When Macbeth murmurs, or mutters,

> Duncan is in his grave;
> After life's fitful fever he sleeps well . . .

it is only from the way he says it that we feel how he envies his victim. The metaphor of life as a fever, sinking into a sleep! The fitfulness, the 'restless ecstasy,' of the first measures of the verse, and the fathomless repose of the three final monosyllables! What more is meant thus meets the ear.

Poetry! — as Cicero says of it and oratory together, whose passionate purpose is the same, it will have its rights: 'nullis ut terminis circumscribat aut definiat ius suum.' It is by poetry that Shakespeare, like the other Elizabethans and the great ancients, overrides the restrictions of realism in circumstance, logic, and psychology (as we have seen above) and in speech. Think of Cleopatra, as Mr. Granville-Barker has said, 'in newspaper English'! Think of her, of Hamlet, Macbeth, or Othello, of Clytaemnestra, Prometheus, or Oedipus, in even the most excellent prose! And while poetry enlarges the confines of the art, it is not something added. As Mr. Abercrombie, the poet, has said, it 'does not give us a copy or picture or projection of its reality: it represents reality by actually and truly calling reality into existence: it creates reality over again.' That is, it creates greater, finer things than there were, or are. And as another poet and critic, the late John Drinkwater, has said:

Let us consider one of the simplest passages of poetry in the plays, Brutus's:

> O that a man might know
> The end of this day's business ere it come!
> But it sufficeth that the day will end,
> And then the end is known.

It might be said that this roughly means, 'I wish we knew what is going to happen; but it doesn't matter, we shall soon.' But the whole point is that it doesn't roughly mean that at all. . . . It means something quite different, and what it means can be expressed only in one way . . .[25]

— that is, as above. And this enlargement and 'transmutation' Mr. Drinkwater would no doubt have acknowledged in other great poets as well.

In Shakespeare, however, it goes farther than in any other dramatist, beyond mere style. In such passages as those beginning 'Canst thou not minister to a mind diseased?' and 'Tomorrow, and tomorrow, and tomorrow,' there is so little analysis that the character thinks in figures, his spiritual experience is, so far, externalized, incorporated; and that is true of the tragedy fairly as a whole. The Weird Sisters prophesy; the spirits are invoked that tend on mortal thoughts; a visionary, bloody dagger tempts the hero's hand; a voice cries to him, 'Sleep no more'; the assassinated guest vindictively attends the banquet as a ghost; Nature is convulsed in ominous and portentous sympathy or antipathy and Night is called upon by hero and heroine both to cover their crimes. These things, like the very metaphors in the passages above, are in a sense real and actual, not, or course, hallucinations or symbols. Though related to the minds of the murderous pair they have the solidity of superstition. Of the metaphors in *Macbeth* Maeterlinck says that 'the men themselves form the atmosphere which they breathe and, at the same time, become the tragic creatures of the atmosphere which they create'; and here the latter phrase particularly applies. This is not psychology but poetry — is fatality — is temptation and almost at the same time retribution. As in *Julius Caesar* and *King Lear*, Nature undergoes an upheaval, both portending and accompanying, in virtue of a superstition not then extinct, the fall of the monarch; and his sleeping grooms (or sons, it may be), his steeds, 'the elements themselves,' as Professor Herford says, 'are shaken by one sympathy with the murdered king.' Night, an unholy thing, thrice invoked, connives at the murders, but hangs like a pall over the murderers; the Lady has light by her continually, and in her sleep she carries it. Sleep, whose sanctuary they have violated, forsakes or tantalizes the one and brings down hideous memories upon the other. In no play is there

[25] *Shakespeare* (1933), p. 94 (by permission of the Macmillan Company).

more of irony. The Sisters both prompt the thane and plague him; what was a temptation forthwith becomes a torment, as in Dante's Hell. Indeed, by the unpsychological but dramatic fiction of supernatural and conjugal influence (instead, as in *Othello*, of the villainous) the temptation really is none — is no attraction — and the crime, once committed, is no satisfaction but a horror. By the logic of circumstances as well as of superstition, 'blood will have blood,' and thus other horrors come in the trail of this. Blood, which, by the violence done to the hero's nature and, through her invocation of the spirits that tend on mortal thoughts, to the heroine's own, they are seeking and craving, sticks to them, throughout their course, with its color and its smell. 'A little water clears us of this deed,' she whispers, at the beginning; 'Out, damned spot,' she mutters when near her end. The symbolism is only that of superstition or folklore, as with the blood of Abel; the recoil of nemesis is even more marked when Banquo responds to the insincere invitation as a ghost, and reënters when his health is drunk. In these and other ways fate still more continually and relentlessly presides over the Caledonian tragedy than over the Venetian.

6

It is a function of the poetic imagination, according to Wordsworth, to 'consolidate numbers into unity.' And this Shakespeare brings about not only by his focusing vision but also by bold simplifying conventions and (as it were) a musical repetition.

To these we turn. If in Shakespeare the causal and sequential relation is neglected, a collateral one is provided. Tragedy must, we have seen, be terrible; and where, as in Elizabethan tragedy, there is much material, it must to that end converge and coalesce. In *King Lear* the underplot, which also deals with filial ingratitude, supports and reinforces the main plot; the mental derangement of the Fool and that of Edgar support and reinforce the King's. So in various ways character matches or contrasts with character. Gloster does Lear and in another way, by his fidelity, Kent; Edgar does Edmund, in another way Cordelia, in another the Fool, in still another Kent himself; Cordelia does Goneril and Regan, in another, Edgar and the Fool. Lear, Gloster, Kent, Cordelia, and the Fool dwell on the

theme of ingratitude; all of them, including Edgar, on that of houseless poverty; and the King and Gloster, Edgar and Kent, on the mystery of injustice in the governance of the world. The King himself
indicates eight times, in crescendo, that he is about to go mad. 'The
power of iteration on the stage,' says Mr. Chapman,[26] 'was never
better illustrated. . . . Perhaps the true resemblance between Shakespeare's tragedies and Greek tragedy is to be found in this passion of
Shakespeare for converging repetitions of thought.'

Othello is the perfect example of interrelation and interplay. Upon
these the very plot and the whole illusion depend. By the skillful
handling of the convention or fiction of the calumniator credited
Iago can make the hero jealous, without making him a dupe in the
process, because he himself is inscrutably honest and sagacious, not
only in the hero's eyes but in those of everybody else about him, including his own wife. And playing his part, he justifies his reputation. So (but not too mechanically or obviously) Othello is noble,
imperturbable, untainted with suspiciousness or jealousy even in the
eyes of the villain as well as everybody else about him, including his
own wife. Without playing a part he justifies his reputation. Everybody respects and trusts Iago; everybody admires Othello and
wonders and grieves at his change. Thus, as (less effectively) with
Posthumus, Imogen, and Iachimo, the characters, somewhat unreal
in relation to life as we know it, are (what is more important in a play)
'real in relation to each other.'[27] Moreover, the initial premise, that
a free and open nature 'thinks men honest that but seem to be so,'
releases great emotional energy as it permits the Moor, without a
base suspiciousness, and still loving his wife, to become frightfully
jealous; and the unanimity of the wonder and grief at the change
(like the unanimity of impression produced by Iago's 'honesty')
both reduces the improbability of it and heightens its effect.

Now there is a musical method, that is, a poetical — in music are
not the emotions but played upon more directly? — both in such
bold manipulation and accentuation and also in the hero's becoming
at the last, though of course not altogether, himself again. Even in

---

[26] A Glance toward Shakespeare, p. 65 (by permission of Little, Brown & Co.).

[27] T. S. Eliot, Selected Essays (1932), p. 162. Cf. below, Chap. VI, p. 223, for the
supposed stupidity of the characters in Othello and Cymbeline, and my Shakespeare's
Young Lovers (1937), pp. 94–96.

his rage his love is ever before us and of his old self we are continually reminded; and here in the *finale*, when the black and fateful
cloud has passed over, this effect of rhythm and recurrence is appropriately heightened and intensified as, without psychological impropriety but with a dramatic suspense and mystery, thoughts of the
sword and suicide, of the past and the future, come and go, or rise
and fall in his consciousness. It is a harmonious cadence, like the
final movement in Sophocles.

And the musical method serves not only for structure but for
emphasis. The climax of the tragedy, the temptation scene, is thus
dwelt upon, thus signalized, like the recognition scene in Sophocles'
Electra. This is advantageous to the emotional scheme and to the
whole. What is important must thus or otherwise seem important;
and that, again, is a matter of relations. Elsewhere, at great moments,
the dramatist has, for such a purpose, recourse to repetition; as when,
before this, Othello appeals to his pitiless counselor — 'But yet the
pity of it, Iago! O Iago, the pity of it, Iago'; as when Antony
moans, 'I am dying, Egypt, dying'; as when Volumnia supplicates
her son,

> for how can we,
> Alas, how can we for our country pray,
> Whereto we are bound, together with thy victory,
> Whereto we are bound?

and as when her son then turns to the Volscian for approval:

> Aufidius, though I cannot make true wars,
> I'll frame convenient peace. Now, good Aufidius,
> Were you in my stead, would you have heard
> A mother less, or granted less, Aufidius?

Antony's 'honourable men' and Iago's 'put money in thy purse' are
examples of a different sort; but in all alike the device serves a purpose similar to that of variation in the force and volume of the
language — another musical resource upon which, with both verse
and prose, high style and low, at his disposal, the Elizabethan draws
far more heavily than the modern. At the important moments he
may be quiet and simple too, like Ibsen or J. J. Bernard; but so as a
harmonist may be, not the dramatist who, with one breath-sus-
pending word, sets the seal upon his disclosure.

7

So far, mostly, I have traced the musical development elsewhere. But there is more. Three epithets, on the lips of various people, frequently recur as applied to Othello, Desdemona, and Iago — *noble*, *gentle*, and *honest*. And three matters are fundamental to the fable — that Othello should be noble (lofty and magnanimous), Desdemona be gentle (sweet and amiable), as they are, and Iago seem honest (sincere and upright), as he does. Again the question raised is answered: the epithet entirely fits. *Honest* in another Elizabethan sense, moreover, that of chastity, is, after hers is doubted, frequently applied also to the heroine, whether positively or negatively, by the hero and the villain, by Emilia and Desdemona herself. That is the problem (if we may so call it) of the play — though one not in the mind of anybody, really, but the hero when in the toils. To Iago, on the other hand, the three established epithets mean, dramatically enough, something different. *Noble* — 'the better shall my purpose work on him'; *gentle* — 'Ay, too gentle'; *honest* — 'but I'll set down the pegs that make this music, as honest as I am.'

This various and appropriate repetition is both a simplifying and a unifying device,[28] that is — for is not music the art in which structure and substance are inseparable? — a musical one. It both serves a purpose like that of Jonsonian or Restoration ticket names such as *Morose* or *Pliant*, indicating and emphasizing one quality, though without the disillusioning taint of allegory or personified abstraction; and also furnishes, as uttered anew by a different person or in different circumstances, an additional instance of a relation between character and character and reminds us of the others. Iago's rejoinder, 'Ay, too gentle,' not only is quite in his own humorous-devilish vein but (echoing Othello's 'And then, of so gentle a condition')[29] again epitomizes the situation. There lies the whole tragic contrast: her sweetness is her undoing; her virtue is turned to pitch. Likewise the hero's desperate, doubt-stifling assertion,

> No, not much mov'd.
> I do not think but Desdemona's honest . . . (III, iii, 225)

[28] As the stock epithet is in Homer and Virgil; see Lessing and Mr. Lascelles Abercrombie's fine lecture *Progress in Literature* (1929), pp. 39ff.
[29] IV, 1, 204. 'Condition' means, of course, 'disposition,' 'nature.'

is countered by the still more insidious and unsettling reply,

> Long live she so! and long live you to think so!

And the same epithet serving for both Desdemona and Iago is really an advantage. Every time the title is denied to her, or reclaimed for her, we remember him who bears it so equably and indisputably, who alone has raised the doubt.

This verbal repetition may be a device not only centering and unifying but intensifying. The sameness of the wording reinforces the emotional effect: Iago's 'honesty,' eleven times touched upon by various persons including himself, brings the irony home. And at the same time it only preserves the illusion, does not make the other characters seem silly as by a method of implications it would. The emotional effect demands, moreover, variety in the vocal expression, and the sameness of the wording affords the actor a stimulating opportunity. 'Honest,' 'gentle,' and 'noble' may thrill and must not vex or bore us as they are repeated — no more than Cyrano's 'Oui, Roxane' as again and again he tenderly, heroically lies in answer to her anxious questions about her husband just dead.

The device — a structural, musical one, I mean, as above, not that rather for purposes of characterization, as in Hamlet, Lear, and Gloster, Shylock, Falstaff, Rosalind, and Cleopatra — is employed by Shakespeare mainly in tragedy; by Italian, French, Spanish, and also Jonsonian dramatic art, mainly in comedy. For the difference there are several reasons: that Shakespeare's genius is prevailingly imaginative rather than analytic, is sympathetic and tolerant rather than critical, tragic rather than comic. None of his comedies is comic all through — that even Molière's are not — but they are fantastic, sentimental or romantic, serious, even pathetic or tragic, as well; and often several of these qualities may reside in a scene, situation, or character at once and together. One trait or 'humor' is not singled out, by repetition drolly thrown into relief and followed up in the development. In the comedies repetition is employed chiefly in the serious or (still in the good sense of the word) sentimental portions, as in the *Merchant of Venice* at the beginning and the end, where Antonio and the others dwell on his sadness and where Lorenzo and Jessica warble (as it were) to each other in the moonlight; and in *Twelfth Night*, where, as Professor Mackail has beautifully shown, the 'dying fall,' delighted in at the beginning, is realized in the action itself at the close. In the tragedies the comic element is momentary and (in a sense) episodic, yet, as noticed above, is blended and subordinated. In the scene of the Gravediggers in *Hamlet*, of the Porter in *Macbeth*, and of the Country-Fellow in *Antony and Cleopatra* there are repetitions, but not for laughter un-alloyed, if for any; they recall and impress upon us the fate of Ophelia, the circumstances of the murder, the present despairing pur-pose of the Queen. Through the very ignorance and isolation of these comic figures, knowing little and unknown, the comic element is made acceptable; lacking in psychological motive or propriety — as if it were the disembodied voice of Nature — it is all the more poetical, again linking things together; it heightens or broadens, even as it relieves, the emotional, the prevailingly tragic effect. And by the repetitions also this effect of horror, pathos, or heroism is both relieved and heightened.[30] The death *motif*, which has several times been heard in the tragedy, now reappears and is fully developed as Hamlet or Cleopatra bandies dread words with the humorous boors.

Not merely in substance and structure are these 'opposite or dis-cordant' elements merged and harmonized, but in the expression as well. It is a striking fact that Continental tragedy before the Roman-tic Movement, though poetical in both diction and rhythm, did not admit the comic, while tragic opera, like *Don Giovanni*, did. The poetry of Continental tragedy had no such range and compass, did not, like Shakespeare's, comprehend high style and low, verse and prose. Music, like Shakespeare's poetry, performs in the hybrid two essential services — both indicates the change in tone and tenor so that the audience shall not be mistaken in its response and also facili-tates the transition. Who in the audience of a time when verse was rightly spoken and sympathetically heard could fail to follow the Queen in her moods as she changes from 'Well, get thee gone; farewell' to

> Give me my robe, put on my crown: I have
> Immortal longings in me. . .?

[30] Cf. the discussion in my *Shakespeare Studies*, pp. 162–63.

And at the opera of our time how much bigger the volume of emotion generated, whether tragic or comic, than at any spoken drama; how much more pronounced the response! The theater is a sea under the winds of passion. But a response somewhat similar there must have been when Shakespeare — when Aeschylus or Aristophanes — was sung, to ears accustomed and attuned.

8

The only[31] play that can vie with *Othello* in approaching the condition of music is the only other where the dramatist had fairly a free hand, with no preceding play or well-known history to hamper him—*Macbeth*. Here, as in the Venetian tragedy, there is repetition on both large scale and small. The appearances of the Weird Sisters are of the former sort, like Othello emerging from his delusion; the details of the prophecies as they are fulfilled and the reminders of the initial murder on the lips of the ignorant Porter at the gate, and of all three murders on the lips of the Lady while sleepwalking, are of the latter sort, like the epithets in *Othello* and *gracious* applied to Duncan.

It is not the same method, but still it is musical, structural: in another dramatist the two methods would have been more nearly the same. Three times the Weird Sisters come upon the stage, for the appearance before the last, Act III, scene 5, is certainly an interpolation;[32] and when the fourth act begins,

Thrice the brinded cat hath mew'd . . . ,

the lines of incantation profit by all those which have been uttered before. Fate still has her eyes on him, the Thane of Glamis; and here her voice breaks in upon us again (with no preparation but 'I will to the Weird Sisters,' two scenes earlier) like a faraway yet not forgotten theme or *leitmotiv*, now recurring, in an opera or symphony.

Also the repetition involved in the piecemeal, alarming, but continually reassuring fulfillment of the prophecies, produces a sort of suspense; but again that of anticipation, and, if from anywhere, it would seem to derive from the Greeks. The *Oedipus*, where the

[31] Except, perhaps, *King Lear*. Cf. my *Art and Artifice*, pp. 141–43, but especially Mr. Granville-Barker's 'preface' and Mr. Chapman as above, pp. 62–65.

[32] As well as IV, i, 125–32, which is in the same pretty rather than grandly grotesque style, fussy rather than ritualistic rhythm.

method involves not only oracles but prophecies and curses, is perhaps the finest example. In both this tragedy and *Macbeth* some,
indeed, of the repetitions are essential to the story as they come true,
and to mere dramatic effect as the hero takes alarm at a partial fulfillment of the prophecy and comfort from that which remains.
But some of them are not, as in Teiresias' rumbling reiterations at
the beginning and the hero's apostrophe to Cithaeron, place of the
exposure, and the crossroads, place of the parricide, near the end.
The cumulative effect of these and the other fateful words is greater
than in *Macbeth*; but it is part of the same emotional method as there
and in the *Agamemnon*, with its bath, its *net* or *robe* of ruin.[33]

There is, however, in *Macbeth* a repetition less verbal and noticeable but perhaps still more structural, which resembles another sort
that there is in *Othello*. I mean that whereby the fatal influence, of
which the Weird Sisters are the voices, asserts itself and permeates
the action. As on his first appearance the hero echoes their last words,

So foul and fair a day I have not seen,

the relation is established even before (in keeping with their previously indicated purpose) they have met him. Their rendezvous is
to be after 'the battle,' 'ere the set of sun,' 'upon the heath.' As now
he approaches one cries,

A drum, a drum
Macbeth doth come,

and the spell that has been weaving is 'wound up.' Face to face, he
responds to their suggestion as instantaneously as the Moor to Iago's,
and afterwards recalls it. The dagger is a 'fatal vision,' not (as has
been thought)[34] the figment of a diseased imagination, but sent to
tempt him, like the voice crying 'Sleep no more' and the ghost ap-

[33] For repeated *motifs* in this and the other Aeschylean tragedies, cf. J. T. Sheppard,
Greek Tragedy, pp. 44, 45, 46–47, 51, 56, 80. Also T. B. L. Webster, *An Introduction
to Sophocles* (1936), pp. 19, 108–109. I am indebted to it above, pp. 30, 44.

[34] Coleridge (Raysor's *Coleridge's Shakespearean Criticism*, 1930, II, 193), speaking
also of the appearance of the Ghost to Hamlet: 'the preternatural appearance has all
the effect of abruptness, and the reader is totally divested of the notion that the
figure is a vision of a highly wrought imagination.' The hero's doubt of its reality
is, like Macbeth's of Banquo's ghost, part of the dramatist's technique with the
supernatural. Cf. my *Shakespeare Studies*, pp. 205–206.

pearing at the banquet, sent to plague him. Nature is here no mere background, but, as if in league with evil, she plays a double role, like that of the devil in the Christian system, 'the tempter ere the accuser of mankind'; and all that poetical externalization of fatality — of temptation and retribution — which we traced at the close of the fifth section involves repetition, still of a structural rather than verbal sort.

Besides, there is the recurrence of themes or ideas without much the same phrasing. In *King Lear*, as Mr. Chapman notices, there are the topics of gratitude or ingratitude and houseless poverty, which arise out of the action and give it point. This art is, without Shakespeare's knowing it, Hellenic, though neither he nor the Greeks wrote *drames à thèse*. And certain concrete objects reappear, whether literally or figuratively: like blood, night, and sleep in *Macbeth*; wind and tempest, predatory animals and notions of strain and strife, bodily tension and torture in *King Lear*; earth, ocean, and world, stars, moon, and firmament, in *Antony and Cleopatra*.[35] These, as we say, contribute to the atmosphere, and they make of course for unity. In the tragedies mentioned, particularly *Macbeth* and *King Lear*, this train or current, ground-tone or burden, reinforces the poetic and emotional effect of the whole; in *Othello* it does so by way of contrast — between the Olympian imagery of the hero and the Tartarian of Iago. Not quite the same can be said of the cosmical imagery applied to Antony and Cleopatra by their admirers or by them to themselves or each other. Here the dramatic appropriateness is more external and merely poetical, as thus the two voluptuaries (who, unlike the other heroes and heroines, are *not* superior to their conduct, whose crimes of love were *not* 'occasioned by any necessity or fatal ignorance, but were wholly voluntary') are nevertheless somewhat lifted above them. It can be said, however, of clusters of imagery (like Mr. Murry's 'death-Cleopatra-nurse-babe-sleep,' which becomes, as it were, the Queen's death-*motif*), recurring on the lips of a single character.[36]

---

[35] See Bradley, Rylands, the Misses Elizabeth Holmes and Caroline Spurgeon for discussion of the subject. This sort of study is, however, a delicate and questionable undertaking. Cf. my 'Recent Shakespeare Criticism,' *Shakespeare-Jahrbuch* (1938), pp. 63ff.

[36] Murry, *Shakespeare*, pp. 243–44.

9

Sometimes the verbal repetition in Shakespeare is rather like that in Ibsen, who, with all his suspense, has this resource as well; and Ibsen is probably indebted to him. At any rate seriocomic, ironical incidents before the catastrophe, such as Dr. Rank's last appearance in the *Doll's House* and Ulric Brendel's in *Rosmersholm*, owe something to the Gravediggers scene in *Hamlet* and the Country-Fellow scene in *Antony and Cleopatra*. In Ibsen the device, being less episodic, is, so far, more structural and rhythmical, the repetition involved having more to do with the central interest or thesis of the play. But there is less of a contrast, the comic character being less of an outsider; he is aware, and is also serious, while in Shakespeare he is (in himself) wholly comic but unconscious; there is, as in general, less breadth of emotion to comprehend. And the remote repetition of pregnant and pivotal phrases, like 'coming to the rescue,' 'claims of the ideal,' 'one cock in the basket,' 'castles in the air,' in such plays as *Ghosts, The Wild Duck, Hedda Gabler*, and the *Master-Builder*, has something in common with *Othello*. But it is more pronounced and elaborate, has less to do with story and incident and more with matters internal — less with the mood of the individual and more with that of the play, yet less with moods than with motives, or with central ideas. It is longitudinal in effect rather than transverse or radial; it firmly links rather than embraces; it is more definitely and substantially suggestive, but less lyrical, making the spectator think rather than feel; yet it performs the same simplifying and unifying, serious or ironic, not comic, function. Also it sometimes serves the ulterior purpose of symbolism. But in Ibsen, Shakespeare, and Sophocles alike it is the use, at succeeding important and significant moments, of an expression charged already with associations, and now by further use charged anew. And thus are secured concentration and rhythm in the play, both 'economy of attention' and 'heightening of consciousness' in the spectator.

Whether in the use of repetition or otherwise, Shakespeare provides less than Ibsen for economy and rigor of attention, more for heightening of consciousness, of emotion; but the merits of either dramatist, or of the method employed, are not now in question. What is in question is whether in adopting the inherited and estab-

lished method of anticipation — a popular Elizabethan dramatist
had, of course, little choice — Shakespeare made amends for its
shortcomings; and this, as I hope to have shown, he did by manifold
interrelating and vivid comprehension of the widespread material,
and by the fatal influence flowing through it. He made the most of
whatever suspense is by the method attainable. He took advantage
of the convention of clairvoyance and self-description as a means of
impressing the issues of the play upon us, and of harmoniously developing and varying the appropriate emotions of the characters, to
arouse our own. Emotions, indeed, in their fluctuations and relations, their contrast and harmony, make up the finer substance of the
play; and the structure, as well as the effect, is that of poetry — like
that of music. The characters (and their fortunes) arouse emotions
in other characters, and they are so presented that they justify the
emotions they arouse. And this finer web and texture is made
firmer and more perceptible by a simplifying, rhythmical repetition
of important themes and phrases.

10

What now are the bearings of the above interpretation?
In tragedy the emotions have the stature of passions, and in the
development of them and opposition of them lies the centralizing
and unifying force rather than in the characters. This is truer of
Elizabethan and ancient tragedy than of the Cornelian and Racinian,
yet truer of the classical French than of the modern. Since writing
the above I have happened upon Henley's essay on *Othello*, first
printed in 1903, in which, though like a poet, the critic presents a
conception of the tragedy similar, even in phrasing and figure, to
mine as expressed here and elsewhere.

. . . the staple of drama is Emotion . . . Dumas *père* . . . all *he* wanted
was 'four trestles, four boards, two actors, and a passion.' 'Tis the briefest,
the most comprehensive, the most luminous statement of the essentials
of drama that ever, I believe, was made; and it fits the *Othello* of Shakespeare, as it fits the Aeschylean Oresteia, like a glove. . . . Iago apart,
the interest of *Othello* is entirely and unalterably emotional. You might
play it in a barn, and it would still fulfil itself. . . . The actors change;
are now Othello and Iago, now Desdemona and Emilia, now Othello

and Desdemona, now Emilia and Othello, now Othello and Fate, the tremendous, the inevitable: even Death. But the passion persists; it shifts its quality as the Master wills, takes on the hues, speaks with the voice, dares with the furiousness of love and hate and jealousy and misery and murder and despair. But, once evoked, it never lets go of your throat; and this is what makes Othello the play of plays it is. . . . 'Tis as it were a soul in earthquake and eclipse. . . .

And since coming upon Henley I find that Mr. Yeats, in an essay on 'The Tragic Theatre,' of 1910, has said much the same:

Yet when we go back a few centuries and enter the great periods of drama, character grows less and sometimes disappears, and there is much lyric feeling, . . . Suddenly it strikes us that character is continuously present in comedy alone, and that there is much tragedy, that of Corneille, that of Racine, that of Greece and Rome, where its place is taken by passions and motives, one person being jealous, another full of love or remorse or pride or anger. In writers of tragi-comedy (and Shakespeare is always a writer of tragi-comedy) there is indeed character, but we notice that it is in the moments of comedy that character is defined, in Hamlet's gaiety let us say; while amid the great moments, when Timon orders his tomb, when Hamlet cries to Horatio 'absent thee from felicity awhile,' when Antony names 'Of many thousand kisses the poor last,' all is lyricism, unmixed passion.[37]

And in *Dramatis Personae* (1936) he goes farther:

Did not even Balzac . . . find it necessary to deny character to his great ladies and young lovers that he might give them passion?[38]

This conception is, of course, in harmony with that of Aristotle as, to the embarrassment of modern critics, he holds plot — structure and situation — not character, to be 'the first essential, and the life and soul, as it were, of tragedy'; is preoccupied with its emotional effect, that of pity and fear, considering tragedy to be 'essentially an imitation not of persons but of action and life' and (as Longinus too would have said) 'of happiness and misery,'[39] and taking for granted that it has to do with a deed of horror, preferably one done in

[37] W. B. Yeats, *Essays* (1924), p. 297 (quoted by permission of the Macmillan Company). Cf. Stevenson, "Humble Remonstrance," on the dramatic novel.
[38] Page 128 (by permission of the Macmillan Company).
[39] *Poetics*, cap. 6.

ignorance. It is still more in harmony with the conception of Horace when of the tragic poet he says that he gives my heart anguish about nothing, awakes its passions, soothes it again, and, like a magician, fills it with imagined terrors:

> meum qui pectus inaniter angit,
> Irritat, mulcet, falsis terroribus implet,
> Ut magus, et modo me Thebis, modo ponit Athenis.

Also it is in harmony (which is more important) with the practice of the ancient tragic poets, and of Homer (whom Aristotle rightly takes to be one of them), as well as of the Elizabethan, and when at their best even of the classical French and the modern. Henley is speaking of tragic art in general; and what he says is true of the con-temporary — of O'Neill, as in *Mourning Becomes Electra*, of Ibsen, as in *Ghosts*. In the final act of the latter, for instance, though there is no such wrenching or ignoring of a psychology as in earlier drama there sometimes is, still on the psychology the interest or effect does not depend, nor on ideas or 'problems,' but on the emotional force of a great situation. Only so, indeed, does the art lend itself to the pur-poses of the actor. Today, as in the times of Cleander and of Burbage, the prime prerequisite of the great actor's success is not the gift of psy-chological insight, nor even of histrionic mimicry, but of emotional expression. Today, as in the times of Sophocles and Shakespeare, the dramatist creates and differentiates emotional roles in conduct and speech, which then the actor realizes or re-creates in deport-ment and utterance. 'I doubt,' says Yeats the poet, 'if any play had ever a great popularity that did not use, or seem to use, the bodily energies of its principal actor to the full.'[40] Hamlet, for example — Othello — Lear — Macbeth! The modern dramatist, keeping mostly within the limits of plausible conversation, has necessarily kept also within the corresponding limits of deportment. As on his stage the actors no longer chant or cry, wail or roar, so they no longer wave their arms or beat their breasts, stalk, stamp, or kneel; all that is now left to opera. But though Ibsen once declared that he himself made not roles but characters, it is only in so far as he did not wholly neglect the essential matter that he reached or still holds the stage.

---

[40] *Essays*, p. 329 (by permission of the Macmillan Company).

He has other ways of doing it than Shakespeare — sympathy plays a smaller part, suggestion a larger, and the individuality is less in the form of the speech or in the poetry and more in the substance and in the context. Still, he is — a dramatist.

This point of view is, it seems, already penetrating classical criticism, which was in the late nineteenth century contaminated by the Shakespearean. A recent discerning and also appreciative reviewer of Mr. T. B. L. Webster's *Introduction to Sophocles*, dealing with the question how far that poet is a delineator of character, says as follows:

So far as character implies a capacity for emotions of a certain variety and force, his view of Sophocles is eminently true. . . . Oedipus is a good king and Creon is a bad king, and that is about all. Sophocles firmly depicts the basic situation, firmly marks his chief person's attitude to it, and then, debarred from developing the pragmatic side of character by complicated external incident [as the modern novelist and (in much less measure) the modern dramatist are not] takes the course still open to him, that of setting the passions aflame. . . .[41]

Set the passions aflame — that before aught else, above all others, Shakespeare does; and, in the words of Mr. Eliot, though while speaking of Jonson, who is more of an analyst and a psychologist, 'the characters of Jonson, of Shakespeare, perhaps of all the greatest drama, are drawn in positive and simple outlines.' If it were not so, the emotional — the electric — current would for both poet and actor be impeded. If Othello were by nature 'credulous' or 'suspicious,' 'jealous' or 'sentimental' — if Hamlet were by nature (as he has recently been thought to be) 'weak,' 'irresolute,' or 'bungling,' 'morbid' or 'hysterical,' 'sentimental' or 'stagy,' 'self-conscious' or 'inclined to attitudinizing,' and mad not only in craft but in fact — how little, then, would be their emotional power upon us! 'The theatre,' as Archer says (however it be with drama!), 'has never been, and never will be, a dissecting-room.' Merited suffering moves us far less than the unmerited; psychology is for the intellect, and anything of a riddle — even of a study — on the stage interferes with the direct response both demanded and provided for by the greatest dramatists still more largely than by the merely successful ones. Even today psychology is expected more by the critics than by

[41] *Times Literary Supplement,* July 4, 1936, p. 560.

audiences; but by most readers too much is expected of Shakespeare and the ancients in the way of mere character. They are likely to prefer Creon to Oedipus, Ismene to Antigone, Chrysothemis to Electra, as they are to prefer Horatio, Kent, and Cassio to the heroes. It is not merely a matter of the virtues, as in Professor Phelps's preference of Hector to Achilles. The extremes of conduct, thought, and feeling — of feeling above all — bewilder or repel them.

Jonson, of course, is mainly and preëminently a comic dramatist; and like the ancient, and unlike Shakespeare, he keeps the two genres apart and distinct. Yet to him no more than to the other does the received opinion, though shared by Mr. Yeats, apply — that 'Comedy is passionless.' It applies rather to artificial comedy such as Congreve's and Wilde's, to 'comedy of manners' such as Molière's and Regnard's, which deals with foibles or affectations. Jonson's deals rather with the vices. In the greater works of both him and the others, however, who are alike in the classical tradition, *Volpone* and *Tartuffe* for example, the passions are still more prominent and important than in the romantic comedies of Shakespeare. And they produce emotional response, no question. Only, it is not the same. In Shakespeare and most of his contemporaries the passions of the leading characters (such as the young lovers), being kept moderate and happy, elicit sympathy, though not of tragic dimensions. In Jonson and kindred spirits love is kept subordinate or frivolous; and the passions — avarice, jealousy, or hypocritical ambition — provoke antipathy, derision, a laughter prompted by condescension or contempt. For that, as in tragedy, the characters involved must be drawn in positive and simple outlines; for that, indeed, the 'ruling passion' is plainly marked or labeled, even in the character's name. It is so with Tartuffe and Harpagon, Face and Subtle. For the direct and complete comic response of antipathy, which is hilarity, there must be still less psychology than in tragedy; the passion must be continually apparent, and, as it reasserts itself, instantaneously effective. It is in such comedy, especially, that the minor figures are the more plausibly shaped and individualized; in Shakespeare's, on the other hand, it is for those who 'dwell in the suburbs of sense' that the exaggeration or distortion, though in a kindly spirit, is generally reserved. In classical comedy, so far as the leading figures are concerned, character may be said to be 'continuously present' only with the meaning that the passion is always apparent as dominating, and deforming, the individual; it does not, as in tragedy, pass over into the universal — 'the persons on the stage,' as Mr. Yeats says later, 'do not greaten till they are humanity itself.'

It is in earlier times, indeed, when drama more richly flourished, but the dramatists (ancient and Renaissance alike) were primarily poets, that the emotional effect was both most apparent and most clearly acknowledged. Of character — even the word they do not use as we are here using it — how little the ancient or Renaissance critics have to say! Ancient criticism and practice both are represented rightly and entirely in Milton's 'Delphic lines' concerning the Attic tragic poets, who treat

> Of fate and chance and change in human life,
> High actions and high passions best describing.

Ethos is Aristotle's word for character, or 'manners' in English seventeenth-century critical parlance; and by *ethos* the Stagirite means 'that in virtue of which we ascribe certain qualities to the agents.'[42] 'Traits,' then, 'temper,' or 'disposition,' seems to be the modern equivalent, the qualities being, in tragedy, especially emotional and moral. Both Corneille and Racine, though as dramatists now loosely taken for psychologists, are, as dramatists and critics both, concerned for the intensity, the 'violence of the passions.' Like Aristotle and Longinus, they speak of 'imitation,' but, like them, subordinate it to the higher requirement; in practice, like Aristotle in his theory, they ignore men 'as they are.'[43] And it is of tragedy that Horace is speaking (though that does not matter, for lyrical poetry is emotional still more exclusively) as he declares it to be not enough that poems have beauty of form; charm they must have, and draw the hearers' feelings which way they will. *Dulcia sunto* — he does not say they must be true to life, be psychological; nor is he thinking merely of the sympathetic charm of the characters, to be found, as we have seen, above all in Shakespeare's. As he proceeds, 'you must first feel pain yourself' means, I think, the *dramatis persona* — the author

---

[42] *Poetics*, cap. 6.
[43] See above, p. 37, and note; and Lascelles Abercrombie, *Principles of Literary Criticism* (1932), p. 84.

feeling it only in imagination — and the ancient poet himself here
seems but to be expressing the principle of emotional contagion:

> Non satis est pulchra esse poemata; dulcia sunto
> Et quocunque volent animum auditoris agunto.
> Ut ridentibus arrident, ita flentibus adsunt
> Humani vultus; si vis me flere dolendum est
> Primum ipsi tibi; tunc tua me infortunia laedent,
> Telephe vel Peleu.[44]

[44] *Ars Poetica*, ll. 99–104. Cf. to the same effect, I think, Aristotle's *Poetics*, cap.
17 (2).

CHAPTER II

'Reconciliation' in Tragedy

Shakespeare and Sophocles

I

MANY of the later critics of Shakespeare have sought in the *finale* of his tragedies for signs of a reconciliation with life, or a justification of the ways of God to men so far as they are in question in the story. Some have received vague impressions to the effect that what befalls the good and unoffending does not matter in comparison to what they are, and that the evil in the tragedy is only negative and barren; others, less numerous, who have not received such impressions, have contrasted, in their disappointment, Shakespeare with the Greeks. The Greeks, they say, both present a problem and provide a solution.

Making no pretensions to philosophy, moral or aesthetic, I will not again[1] consider the position first named. As some few have noted before me, the great critics Dowden and Bradley, who take it, have, though with taste and tact, offended against the principles of both criticism and history. It is a sort of Hegelianism that discovers this 'feeling of reconciliation' which tragedy provides 'in virtue of its vision of Eternal Justice'; it is a sort of monism or pantheism that determines this doctrine of good and evil. In Shakespeare good and evil, says Croce, are 'as light opposed to darkness' (this darkness being no negative entity). The fundamental error, however, is not so much in attributing to the dramatist ideas modern and alien as in attributing ideas of any sort. Every work of art stands alone and is self-contained. 'A play is significant in itself,' Professor Frye declares, like Schiller and Bulthaupt before him, 'or not at all'; and of any artistic writing both Johnson and Wordsworth say the

---

[1] See my *Art and Artifice in Shakespeare*, pp. 163–66.

same. That is (anticipating the next chapter), in its own time, and for the public expected. No fine work can be fully appreciated apart from the tradition to which it belongs — apart from its language (in the literal sense or the figurative), its medium and technique. Afterwards come the prolegomena and the glosses, provided by others than the author, yet only to make amends for the tradition lost.

For great popular tragedy they are even then not much needed, so far as ideas or sentiments are concerned. 'To the knowledge which all men carry about with them and to the sympathies in which, without any other discipline than that of our daily life, we are fitted to take delight,' if I may adapt the phrasing of Wordsworth, 'these poets, above all others, direct their attention.' And those far apart in time may be near to each other in spirit. Shakespeare and Sophocles, I imagine, though the Englishman in all probability knew nothing of the Athenian, are in this matter of a reconciliation, a solution, fairly at one. It is only Aeschylus (though likewise no Hegelian!) that puts the problem and endeavors piously to solve it. It is only Aeschylus that makes the hero, such as Orestes, both right and wrong, and carries the human conflict up before the celestial tribunal, or (like Euripides, though in a different spirit) brings the gods down before the terrestrial. The undertaking is necessary. For it is only Aeschylus that fearlessly and relentlessly traces the causes of human calamity back to the sufferer's own or his ancestors' trangressions (whether voluntary or not), following the long and devious course of a curse, and, in the process, representing the slayer also as an avenger, punishing or purifying him in turn. Thus the foremost of tragic poets produces great situations, like those of Agamemnon, his wife, and his son: the king entering his palace with the guilt of Iphigenia's blood and the nemesis of the Thyestean banquet upon his head as well as the envy of the gods for presuming to tread upon the purple tapestry; and Orestes pursued by the Furies for avenging his father upon his mother. But Aeschylus has need of a reconciliation or adjustment: he must bring some moral order into the primeval mythical confusion upon which he has entered.

2

Not so Sophocles, who resembles Shakespeare. He keeps the scene on earth, and the deities in the background. What interests him is action and character rather than an idea behind them; and emotions rather than the moral or immoral forces that provoke or punish them. Life for him is not a problem but a mystery, not so much a discipline or retribution as a calamitous but heroic experience, the tragedy that presents it being a tale of a great misfortune (rather than of a misdeed) cast in a compact and stimulating mold; and his heroes and heroines mostly suffer and perish without any curse upon them or even a 'tragic fault' within. Morals for him are the accepted morals of his day, insufficient and inadequate to explain God's ways with men. Therefore as he approaches the mythical material he picks and chooses. In the four tragedies where it is touched upon, the fatality which attaches to the houses of Labdacus and of Atreus is treated sympathetically and poetically, without, as in Aeschylus, reverting to the heinous cause or provocation. Oedipus and Antigone, Orestes and Philoctetes, Heracles and Dejaneira, like Romeo and Juliet, Hamlet and Ophelia, Othello and Desdemona, Lear and Cordelia, all have done little to justify the misfortune that befalls them; and, as in Shakespeare, what chiefly reconciles us to their suffering, in the spectacle of pity and fear, is the elevated, harmonious, and (within the tragic limits) veracious effect. In Sophocles, as in Aeschylus, there is Destiny; yet it is so far disentangled from superstitious, ceremonial, or really moral implications and prejudices as no longer to heighten the hero's responsibility but indeed to relieve it.

Factually, morally the fulfillment in Oedipus, long before the tragedy begins, of the oracle that he should kill his father and marry his mother, coming upon him through no fault of his own, is practically almost equivalent, as Mr. Sheppard says, to what we now call 'circumstances.' But dramatically, imaginatively, it is of far greater value; and as the hero comes to realize the horror of his plight, it furnishes a situation equal to that of Agamemnon, with a more unmingled sympathy on his side. In both situations the hero is not his own destiny: he is in the grip of it. In both there is a contrast between character and conduct. But in Sophocles the contrast is sharper and clearer-cut — between the decrees of Fate and the 'fallibility of human endeavour' — and not so much moral as merely natural and emotional. As such it is steeply ironical; and in Aeschylus, as has been said, there is none of the unconscious irony rightly called Sophoclean:

. . . [Sophocles] neither attempts, like Aeschylus, to justify the evil nor presumes, like Euripides, to deny its divine origin. That is because his gods — whether he believed in them, or exactly in what sense, does not matter — stand for the universe of circumstance as it is. Aeschylus and Euripides both demand for their worship a god who is good and just. Both therefore must attempt to solve the 'problem of evil.' The pagan gods of Homer and Sophocles require no such reconciliation. They are great and good, and great and bad, like things, and men, and nature. . . . Had Sophocles chosen he might have treated Oedipus as a willing sinner justly punished. But that method would have made the tragedy less tragic. . . . He neither justifies the gods by making Oedipus a criminal nor condemns the gods because the agony of Oedipus is undeserved. He bids the audience face the facts.[2]

And is not that, on the whole, though with no deities even in the background, but with a villain in the foreground, what Shakespeare does, in a still wider, less regular and orderly world than that of Sophocles? Evil plays in his work a much larger part; the contrast between the good characters and the bad is more complete and intense; yet in both poets there is, in practice if not in theory, an approach, so far as hero or heroine is concerned, to the present-day 'conception of tragedy as inhering in the nature of things.'

Not only does Shakespeare leave upon us such a final impression; he also secures it by similar means. Elsewhere I have shown that at his greatest he, too, has not made the hero seal his own doom — this he more nearly does in *Titus Andronicus* and the English histories — and, so far, is (though unconsciously) in keeping with not only the principle of Aristotle[3] but the practice of Sophocles, and for

[2] J. T. Sheppard, *Oedipus Tyrannus* (1920), pp. xxxv–xxxvi, xl. Cf. R. C. Jebb. *Oedipus Tyrannus* (1887), p. xxxviii. For the 'conception of tragedy as inhering in the nature of things,' cf. Ludwig Lewisohn, *Modern Drama* (1915), p. 6; F. L. Lucas, *Tragedy in Relation to Aristotle's Poetics* (1927), pp. 99–105.

[3] *Poetics*, cap. 6 — that plot comes first, character second. Cf. my *Art and Artifice*, Chap. I; the reference to Santayana, below, Chap. XI, n. 4; and Lascelles Abercrombie's *Principles of Literary Criticism* (1932), p. 102. William Archer (*Play-making*,

that matter, of Aeschylus and Euripides. He, too, has put character in sharp contrast with conduct. Othello, for instance, is, like Oedipus, in a plight; Othello's destiny is Iago; and psychology can no more explain or justify this complication than the other. It is only the convention of a villain's influence replacing that of Fate. Thus in either tragedy, as in the *Agamemnon* and the *Hippolytus*, the great advantage of a surcharged, highly explosive situation is expeditiously, though arbitrarily, secured. The situation of Othello, however, is more like that of Oedipus, Antigone, and Dejaneira, because of the greater innocence of the hero or heroine and the consequently more poignantly emotional effect. Both poets so manage as to eliminate disquieting considerations or explanations. In the *Oedipus* the fulfillment of the oracle is previous to the action; in the English tragedy the notion that hearing is believing is so deftly introduced, the Moor's noble generosity and the villain's sagacious honesty are so unanimously acknowledged, that both premises are accepted by the audience without psychological questioning or any damage to the prestige of the hero. Then, the premises having been posited and granted, comes the terrible consequence or conclusion. Having been thus precipitated, the action in Shakespearean tragedy runs its course as inevitably and almost as irresponsibly as a cataclysm in nature, subsiding, as in all Greek drama, gradually to a close. The tension relaxes; the passions die away; in the mere subsidence there is relief. And there are pity and sorrow for the deserving, reprobation or punishment for the undeserving, restoration for the distracted state, and, perhaps, some clearer recognition of the laws of human conduct. But there is no glaring moral confusion or contradiction to clear up, or pressing problem to solve, or deep difference to reconcile. Everything is set right that can be — the more easily because, as not so clearly in Aeschylus and Euripides, it is evident what is right, what wrong; and everything is explained that need be, except what cannot be. The relation of good and evil, if not in the individual, out in the world, remains a mystery; and the prevailing mood, if not of the sufferers, of the onlookers, is that of awe and wonder, of patience or acceptance. We 'feel the greatness,' says Mr.

1913, pp. 17–20) admits the priority of situation in point of time but insists that character must enter into the organizing process at an early stage. That is truer of drama today, in which fate seldom plays a part.

Sheppard, 'not the goodness or badness, of the world in which such events may happen.'[4]

3

Shakespeare, however, in securing this effect, finds it necessary, in the dramatic process, to give his noble or pure-minded hero some part at least in shaping his destiny: otherwise the probability and the justice of it as well as the hero's own liberty and dignity would be too much impaired. 'For the purposes of this art a superficial motivation is adequate'; the only condition which it has to satisfy is that it should be immediately plausible to the audience; and the hero or heroine commits an error, or is given a weakness or shortcoming, though nowise commensurate with the calamity which ensues. Othello's impetuosity, like that of Romeo and Lear, Desdemona's imprudent friendliness with Cassio and her timorous evasiveness with her husband, like the uncompromising sincerity of Cordelia, contribute to, but do not determine or at all justify, their ruin or disaster. For not everything in art is functional, 'inevitable': the ribs of Gothic vaulting do not really support it, but without them, as has been said, it would be on the point of crushing us. So Hamlet, though really he does not culpably hesitate or procrastinate, must reproach himself for doing so, and Macbeth, though by no means so innocent, must be no mere tool in the hands of his lady or of Destiny. This superficial causal connection, however slender or illusory, holds the story together. Brabantio's warning in the council-chamber is like the Friar's in his cell; it reassures us of the hero's reality and serves to make his ruin more probable and acceptable — to make this, as Mr. Lucas would say, logical or convincing, not necessarily just; it rights the balance of a tragedy in which the hero is otherwise nearly perfect, and in the retrospect is part of the final impression. Is there something of the sort, we wonder, in Sophocles?

It is not thus, at this latter point or in general, that he or Shakespeare is ordinarily judged. Those Grecians, indeed, best gifted with literary taste and dramatic instinct, such as Jebb and Butcher, Haigh, Sheppard, Bywater, and Wilamowitz-Möllendorff,[5] repudi-

[4] *Greek Tragedy*, p. 117.

[5] 'Excurse zum Oedipus,' *Hermes*, 1899, p. 55. 'Sie haben so viel von Schuld

ate the serious charges made against Oedipus and Antigone. Unlike many, they perceive that there can be little justice, either apparent or intended, in pouring down such woes upon the hero for killing the man who struck him where the three ways meet or for not being warier and more circumspect in marriage; still less, for his anger against Teiresias (and against Creon, who has had him summoned) when the prophet throws out his dire and (to such innocence) wanton and outrageous insinuations;[6] and least of all, for pressing irresistibly on to discover the identity of the offender who has brought the plague upon his city. They acknowledge that such conduct is not criminal nor ever was.[7] Also they cannot but bow in reverence before Antigone as she unhesitatingly sets aside the decree of man in favor of the 'unwritten,' 'eternal' laws of Heaven and her heart. They do not, however, make the retort to these Rhada-manthine antiquaries that seems to be most to the point. Apart, of course, from *hybris* the 'tragic sin' oftenest detected in Sophocles is — not only in Oedipus and Antigone but also in Electra, Telamon, and Telephus — no more than that of a 'harsh,' 'headstrong,' or 'hasty' temper, 'quickness to wrath,' in short, 'impetuosity' again.[8] And that of Dejaneira in the *Trachiniae* is much the same, for she allows her 'passion to precipitate her in unreflecting action.' Who doesn't, outside of convent or prison? These lighter charges, cer-tainly, unlike the serious, are warranted by the text. But if made serious and weighty, how cruel and puritanical, and also tame and unresourceful, becomes the dramatist! The mere uniformity of the

---

und Strafe im Oedipus geredet. Das ist Unverstand. Oedipus hat sich nichts vorzu-werfen,' etc. And he has the same to say of Antigone. Cf. Ingram Bywater, *Aristotle on the Art of Poetry* (1909), p. 215: 'Oedipus is a man of hasty temper, but his hamar-tia was not in that but in the "great mistake" he made when he became unwittingly the slayer of his own father.' On this subject of 'poetic justice,' cf. Lucas as cited above, n. 2, and William Archer, *Play-making*, p. 271, where he says that we do not insist on deciding in what degree a man has deserved death, if only we feel that he has necessarily or probably incurred it.

[6] Wilamowitz, *op. cit.*, p. 61.

[7] Not only would an Athenian audience instinctively allow for the impulsive recklessness of a mythical hero, like Hercules (or Samson), when, as here, no point of blood guilt is raised; but, as Sheppard observes (*Oedipus*, pp. xxviii–xxix), an Athenian jury, in such a case, would exonerate him.

[8] Cf. the two articles by Professor C. R. Post, in *Harvard Studies in Classical Philology*, 1912, 1922, on the 'Dramatic Art of Sophocles.' Telamon and Telephus, of course, are in tragedies now lost.

hamartia discovered should of itself disconcert us, and lead us to consider whether a perfectly discreet and tactful hero or heroine, if quite innocent, could, either in these tragedies or in the world outside as we know it, well come to disaster; and whether this is not, instead, a case of the superficial motivation, narrative or epical rather than dramatic, mentioned above.

It is in the same Draconian spirit that Romeo has been accused of 'impetuosity' or rashness, and Lear and Cordelia of harshness of temper; just as, on the other hand (when the tragic deed must be not expedited but impeded), the Orestes of Aeschylus and of Euripides, or the Alcmaeon of the lost Sophoclean *Epigoni*, has been made out to be a 'romantic' Hamlet before his time.[9] What of the sulking Achilles, then, and the circuitous Ulysses? By the same critical standards the conduct of both is unethical and pathological, and, like that of the nineteenth-century pusillanimous Dane, a fit subject for psychoanalysis. Does the son of Peleus really want to fight, or that of Laertes to return? And as for Romeo, this 'fault' of his is shared by the others — as Archer says, the catastrophe results from the hot-headed impetuosity of *all* the characters. Much the same might be said of *King Lear*;[10] and in some sort impetuosity is a requirement of drama, especially of tragedy. Action, movement, there must be; and in nearly all tragedy — ancient, Elizabethan, and Bourbon — the prevailing imagery is drawn from the phenomenon of motion. To interpret this matter of structure in terms of character and morals is like Alfred Berger's and Mr. Shaw's taking the various forms of deception in Shakespeare, though found as abundantly in the other drama of the Renaissance — French, Italian, Spanish, as well as English — and also in the ancient, to be an indication that to him the world was but a great stage of fools; or like Mr. Masefield's taking play after play as a whole to be 'a study in treachery.'

The outbursts of passion are to be justified differently, as well. Oedipus' moments of anger, not only in the *Tyrannus* but in the *Coloneus*, and the curse on himself in the one tragedy and on his

---

[9] Post, *op. cit.*, 1922, pp. 21–22.

[10] A recent critic has found the King and all his family wanting in tact. This is like Lowell's study of heredity in *Hamlet* — Polonius' children both inclined to giving advice.

sons in the other, are, like the outcries of pain on the part of Sophocles' Philoctetes and also of Virgil's Laocoön, necessary, as Lessing observes of the latter two, for the right and adequate effect. How else is audience or reader to feel the full measure of the hero's suffering or to appreciate the cause? And Oedipus' wrath against Creon and Teiresias is, in these extraordinary circumstances, a measure of his innocence, as well as an obstacle to his understanding. The stage, as the great critic and dramatist declares, is not the arena; the tragic hero not a gladiator, who 'conquers agony.' Nowadays, to be sure, the stage is less unlike the arena; for the action is more a matter of pantomime and setting, and of only such sober, discreet, and reticent speech as there is in conversation. But in the Periclean age and the Elizabethan it was a matter, so far as the *dramatist's* medium was concerned, of speech alone, though free of realistic restrictions, and running the whole gamut from the colloquial to the lyrical, from simple statement to apostrophe or exclamation. Hellenic tragedy, particularly the Sophoclean, as I have shown in Chapter I, is, like the Shakespearean, a system and rhythm, both a contrast and a harmony, of emotions. These break out upon the surface, do not as in our colloquial drama run underground, and are frankly displayed and amply developed: without explicit comment to give it effect there is no place in their midst for stoicism. What would become of the *Prometheus Vinctus* if the protagonist were a Zeno, or lived up to the standard of decorum set forth by Adam Smith?[11] The hero must respond and make outcry, not, like a Spartan, hold his peace — his heroism appears in his defiance, despite his pain; and the greater moments must be signalized by a more emphatic response or their importance will be lost, the emotional rhythm broken. Only under such a system of reasonings as in Corneille and Racine, or of definite suggestions as in Ibsen, and of careful and gradual internal preparations and approaches as in all three (but less frequently in Shakespeare and the ancients), can the hero, at the great moment, be confined to a phrase or a syllable, in a house where you could hear the drop of a pin. In Shakespeare and the ancients, too, there may then be, though seldom such taciturnity, the quiet simplicity at least; but mostly it is as a climax upon climax, the

[11] Lessing's *Laokoon*, IV, 3.

pianissimo after the fortissimo, Lear's 'Cordelia, Cordelia, stay a little' following his 'Howl, howl, howl.' Realism, moreover, nationality, are secondary, dubious considerations. The Periclean, like the Homeric Greeks, were, indeed, not a stoical or a taciturn people, given, whether in seriousness or in pleasantry, to understatement; the Elizabethans, like the Anglo-Saxons before them and the John Bulls of today, were both the one and the other; but because of the very nature of the dramatic method the understatement, serious or humorous, common in our Cockney vernacular as in *Beowulf* and Chaucer, is little reflected in Elizabethan drama, and the wrath of Lear or Othello is no more to be accounted a tragic sin than that of Oedipus.

4

Whether the fault be serious or such only because the critic is minded so to make it, it is owing partly to the conception that a fault there must be to bring about the hero's ruin. And this is, as we have seen, somewhat justified by the nature both of drama and also of life, which, however remotely, it imitates. In some measure the character must be his own destiny — or seem to be such. But the critic's conception is owing mainly to an inherited doctrine. It is Shakespeare criticism, perhaps, that misleads Wilamowitz into making the Aeschylean Orestes something of a Coleridgean Hamlet, doubting and hesitating, or nerving himself up, though to him, as not to Hamlet, the deed is both a duty and a crime. It is in some part an insufficient reading of Aristotle, but in greater part the influence of ethical and philosophical theory again, that misleads some German and English-speaking critics into changing the Aristotelian pity and fear to 'pity and horror,' and holding Antigone, as well as Oedipus, to be a fit object or concern only for the latter two. 'In the view of the Eternal Justice,' declares the political philosopher, 'both Creon and Antigone were wrong, because they were one-sided; but at the same time both were right.' To Hegel and Boeckh Jebb rightly replies that 'Sophocles has been content to make Antigone merely a nobly heroic woman, not a being exempt from human passion and human weakness; but none the less does he mean us to feel that, in this controversy (with Creon), the right is wholly with

her, the wrong wholly with her judge.'[12] So even and impartial
an apportionment of praise and blame would, in the bosoms of a
normal audience, considerably impede the play of the emotions, and
flatten out the tragedy. In Fletcher and Massinger's *Barnavelt*, according to Swinburne, 'We should not have been left in doubt'
with whom we were expected to sympathize. And the two Germans ignore what the Stagirite says of the subordination of character
to plot, of the preferableness of a crime committed in ignorance
(or an error in judgment, not a depravity, leading to some horrible
deed), and of a hero better than the ordinary man, or one such as
men 'ought to be'; and they firmly remember, instead, what he says
of its being intolerable to see a good man passing from happiness to
misery, and of the right hero's being not preëminently virtuous and
just. Almost immediately after this last dictum, however, he modi-
fies it, 'the man himself, being either such as we have described, or
better, not worse than that.' The various utterances on the subject,
his ablest commentator[13] remarks, are difficult to reconcile; and here
the master appears to swerve a little because of religious or moral
considerations. The theory of Catharsis, whether purgation or purification, is more moral or philosophical than critical; and leads him,
in defending the tragic art against the disapproval of Plato, at moments to disallow of innocence in the hero and to ignore emotions
other than his celebrated pair (but recognized by Corneille and later
critics) such as admiration and love. Even in his own time he has
against him Antigone and Oedipus, and also, as Mr. Abercrombie
says, Prometheus; but in the interests of his theory 'he ignored the
unmistakably tragic effect of innocence suffering undeservedly, of
Right punished by Wrong — and punished for *being* Right.'[14]

In any event the Aristotelian 'fear' is not 'horror'; the sage himself
says that it is sympathetic, 'for one like ourselves';[15] and the connection of it with pity, continually reasserted whether in the *Poetics* or
elsewhere, is not casual or idle but complementary and indissoluble.
On the sage's part it is an intuition. Without fear tragedy would be

[12] Jebb, *Antigone* (1900), p. xxii. Cf. Goethe, in Eckermann.
[13] Bywater, *Aristotle on the Art of Poetry*, pp. 213, 216.
[14] *Principles of Literary Criticism*, p. 114.
[15] 'Pity is occasioned by undeserved misfortune, and fear by that of one like ourselves' (cap. 13). 'This disinterested fear, which rests, just like pity, on a basis of
sympathy' (Bywater, p. 215). 'The primary error in . . . interpretations of Παθημά-

sentimental; without pity, melodramatic. These emotions are central and pivotal — love or admiration serves but to heighten their
effect. Horror also may enter into the tragedy, as it does into that of
the Oresteia and of Macbeth, but not of the Antigone as we have it.

The maiden's offense against the king — that is, the state —
would, to be sure, go farther in justification of her suffering and
death than willfulness or harshness of temper; but that is even less
warranted by the text or Sophocles' general dramatic attitude and
method. As Haigh and others with him have observed, 'it is difficult to see how the view could ever have been maintained; the whole
tone of the play is against it.' At first the chorus is inclined to blame
her for her disobedience; but this, as Jebb says, only isolates her and
heightens the effect of her heroism; and in the early (not the later)
part of a Sophoclean tragedy the chorus, like the modern *raisonneur*,
is frequently thus mistaken, or expresses apprehensions rather than
judgments, as in the *Oedipus Tyrannus* and the *Ajax*, the *Philoctetes*
and the *Electra*.[16] 'The chorus too,' says Aristotle, 'should be regarded as one of the actors,' which in both Sophocles and Aeschylus
it is; and near the end of the tragedy (ll. 1257–60, 1349–50), it
'informs Creon that he is the cause of his own misfortunes, and that
"reverence for the gods must be preserved inviolate."' Sophocles
clearly distinguishes between disobedience to the decree of a tyrant
and disloyalty to the state, one's fatherland; as also Aeschylus does
(though in other regards he makes Agamemnon, Orestes, and
Eteocles both right and wrong) when, at the end of the *Seven against
Thebes*, Antigone, and half the chorus with her, resolve to bury
Polynices. Her brother had been disloyal; but, declares the princess,
the gods have already punished him (l. 1053); and as the Theban
chorus, more discriminating than some modern scholars take it to
be or than they themselves are, aptly remembers (l. 1077), 'what a
state deems right changes with change of time.' *Her* laws, though

---

των Κάθαρσις is [a reading of] a directly moral interpretation into the term. . . .
The great function of the tragic poet, [Aristotle] thinks, is to excite certain emotions,
and procure us the pleasure that must accompany such excitement. This pleasurable
excitement of emotion, in fact, is with him the end and aim of Tragedy, so far as the
poet himself is concerned' (p. 161).

16 Cf., also, A. E. Haigh, *The Tragic Drama of the Greeks* (1896), pp. 153–54, 184.
And Wilamowitz, *Hermes*, 1899, pp. 59–61; Sheppard, *Greek Tragedy*, introduction,
Chap. III.

written, are not, like those of Olympus, eternal; and though patriots
and soldiers, Aeschylus and Sophocles were no such worshippers of
the state as Hegel and Fichte, along with many other Germans in
their day, not to mention ours.

5

Why, then, must Antigone die? Why must Desdemona, Ophelia,
or Cordelia? The last question, propounded by the greatest Shakespeareans, is parallel, for the British princess betrays a similar 'pro-
vocative' or refractory spirit, and has likewise been indicted — to
be sure, by Gervinus — for an offense against the state, that of raising an army to invade it. The simple answer — fundamental
answers to questions of art are generally simple — is that the play is
a tragedy, and in the greatest tragedy as well as the worst, character
is, as Aristotle would have it, subordinate. An answer less obvious is
that tragedy, which arouses pity and fear, is, other things being equal,
the better when it arouses them at their greatest intensity — in their
violence, says even Racine[17] — life itself being most piteous and
terrible when the undeserving, not the deserving, perish. To the
highest tragic effect 'poetic justice,' with its nice and neat awards
for good and bad, is decidedly inadequate; though rightly in both the
Greek and the Elizabethan tragedy the venial fault of the hero, as
well as the heinous one of the villain, has discernible consequences,
and there is some recognition of these on the part of the chorus or of
minor characters like Emilia and Ludovico in *Othello*. Mr. Bradley
goes so far as to say that 'the ideas of justice and desert are . . . in all
cases — even those of Richard III and of Macbeth and Lady Macbeth
— untrue to our imaginative experience. When we are immersed
in a tragedy, we feel towards dispositions, actions, and persons such
emotions as attraction and repulsion, pity, wonder, fear, horror,
perhaps hatred; but we do not *judge*.' A fine and proper but rather
remarkable thing for Mr. Bradley to say, for in all the heroes he finds
a flaw and an imperfection even in Cordelia; but he is now on his
way to transcendental conclusions, to the effect that what happens
to her does not matter, 'all that matters is what she is.' And there
too he is judging (though Heaven or Providence rather than the

[17] Preface to *Bérénice*.

lady), as indeed we in some measure must do. At least we must receive the impression that justice of some sort has been done, that, though the good and deserving have been made to suffer, the undeserving also have been, or else our aroused emotions will at the last be not calmed but outraged. In fact, the emotions will not have been fully aroused unless the matter of desert has been somewhat kept before us, and evil has been made more of a positive thing than Hegel and Mr. Bradley find it, as with the Elizabethans and the Greeks.

So far, however, as Cordelia or Antigone is concerned, the question, primarily, is not whether she would come to such an end without being herself more to blame for it, but whether, without offense to our sensibilities and our experience, she does so here. The dispositions of Goneril, Regan, and Edmund in the one play, and of Creon in the other, as well as the high spirit of the heroines themselves, make Cordelia and Antigone come to such an end convincingly. And death staring them in the face, Cordelia, as she undertakes to save her father or, without repining, goes with him to prison, and Antigone, as she yields to no persuasions of sister or chorus, to no menaces of her uncle, only shine forth the brighter. Cordelia, moreover, must die to break the heart of her father, who had cast her off but has now found happiness, even when going to prison, in reunion with her. And Antigone must die to break the heart of Haemon, and so of Eurydice, and to bring Creon low. If Edgar with the countermand, or Creon driven by Teiresias to the rescue, had arrived in time, there would, of course, have been an anticlimax, and, after all these high preparations and fateful approaches, an aesthetic fiasco. The main consideration is that this is not life, nor a comedy, nor a drama merely; and the upshot, as Professor Elton says, 'is largely dictated, not by ethical theory at all, but by the amount of imaginary pain that the average spectator will tolerate.' He 'must be indemnified, if only a little,' for the death of Desdemona by that of Iago, for that of Cordelia by that of Edmund and the sisters, which latter 'might in the real world escape and prosper.'[18] And so might Cordelia and Desdemona there.

[18] Oliver Elton, *Modern Studies* (1907), pp. 98–99.

6

Oedipus is the center of a still more imposing though more improbable situation, like Othello and Lear, Hamlet and Macbeth. It is more imposing even because it is more improbable — because it comprehends a wider range of experience, offers a bolder and more arresting contrast. 'Les grands sujets,' says Corneille in the *Discours du poème tragique*, transcending Aristotle, 'qui remuent fortement les passions, et en opposent l'impétuosité aux lois du devoir ou aux tendresses du sang, doivent toujours aller au delà du vraisemblable.' Mr. Yeats, another poetical dramatist, puts it negatively, glancing at the very different drama of the present day — 'with its meagre language and its action crushed into the narrow limits of possibility.'[19] These five heroes are alike precipitated into great misfortune, all of them undeservedly except Macbeth — though at the outset he, too, is an honorable man; and still more than Cordelia and Antigone they are made subordinate to the plot, in order that they may be superior to their conduct. By the very premise or postulate of the traditional fable they are in the situation already, like Oedipus, or (in keeping with Elizabethan art, which tells the whole story) thrust into it at the beginning, like the Shakespearean heroes. All of them are 'impetuous,' 'precipitate,' even violent, and most of them, when occasion arises, as 'quick to wrath' as a moralizing classical scholar would require, including (where the story permits) even Hamlet himself: were they not so (again) there would be no tragedy. But that their tragic fate is in any considerable measure their due, or satisfies our sense of justice at the end, is not much truer of them than of Juliet, Ophelia, or Desdemona, or than of Duncan, who has been blamed for his trustfulness and imprudence as the three young ladies have been for lying. The hero is not his own nemesis. He is not like the Scottish poet, who 'died of being Robert Burns' — not like a character of James, George Eliot, or Balzac. And Oedipus bears no responsibility, as, according to both Wilamowitz and Sheppard, he might easily have been made to do, for the nemesis laid upon him. He might have been the aggressor 'where the three ways meet'; for both the slaying and the marriage he might have had enough responsibility (which is quite contrary

---

[19] *Essays* (1924), p. 341 (by permission of the Macmillan Company).

to the hypothesis) immediately to suspect the truth. And instead of being reproached, and held guilty of *hybris*, for relentlessly pressing on in his discovery, he is, as Mr. Sheppard says, to be sympathized with and admired for his courage. So is Hamlet, like the Orestes of Sophocles, neither of them really blamable, though one is blamed for remissness by himself, the other by his sister; and so in lesser and varying measure, and with varying admixture of pity and fear, are Romeo, Othello, Lear, and even Macbeth. But this of Oedipus is probably the most thrilling single situation ever produced upon the stage, this 'passionate search for the truth [in the words of Mr. Sergeaunt] and devotion to it though it kill him'; and how the poignant contrast of 'Man proposes, God disposes' would be dulled if the man were touched with guilt! Also, the Theban king is thus doing his duty; deeply concerned for his stricken people and bidden by the oracle to drive the murderer from their midst, he has vowed that to this end he will leave naught untried, laying upon the man a curse. How incurious and craven, not to say impious, if now at Teiresias' warning or Jocasta's supplication he had refrained! How circumspect and discreet!

Hybris is another ready-made, overworked 'tragic sin'; and to be sure, unlike Antigone, Oedipus is a little tainted with it as now, on hearing the news of his putative father's death, he, like Jocasta, doubts the earlier oracle and defies augury. But that is in a natural wild reaction which the most pious of audiences will here comprehend and not condemn. Indeed, it is necessary as an indication of passion, which is, we have seen, quite desirable in tragedy, and (again) as a measure of his innocence; but this trace of human frailty, sufficient, I think, to satisfy Aristotle, is a different thing from a tragic fault or a psychological defect. It is different altogether from a temperamental irascibility, or (what is worse) an 'insensate conceit of his own sufficiency . . . gross moral impropriety in the bias whereby he seeks for himself the solution of his own problematic existence.' Oedipus, who dreads and trembles at the thought of the thing he may discover — 'Forbid, forbid, ye pure and awful gods, that I should see that day!' — Oedipus, one of the noblest and (though, on great provocation, irascible) tenderest figures in poetry! 'My children, latest-born to Cadmus who was of old' —

ὦ τέκνα, Κάδμου τοῦ πάλαι νέα τροφή.

In dignity of phrase and rhythm there is no one equal to him except Browning's Pope —

Líke to Ahasuérus, thát shrèwd Prínce —

and (always) except Othello. But so the Moor has, in various fashion, by carping critics, been made 'a goose,' and 'conceit' or 'vanity' has repeatedly been attributed to Lear! For such petty ignoble traits in hero or heroine have, strangely enough, not been considered incompatible with tragedy.

And what would any one, on the stage or in the theater, have Dejaneira do but send the love-charm to win back her erring husband? It is in the old story — for that situation did Sophocles undertake the tragedy — and the poet makes it sufficiently clear that love, not jealousy or revenge, is impelling her.[20] The sweet lady's failure to perceive the wounded Centaur's purpose is as freely to be granted as Othello's failure to perceive Iago's, or as Oedipus' failure, before the play begins, to detect the pitfall in a marriage of any sort. It is one of the ironies that the Theban has read riddles; but it is no crime or folly not to read one's own. How few of us, even, students of tragedy, in our wisdom, do! And these heroic beings all are the playthings of Fate, the objects only of pity and (sympathetically) of fear, and not of 'horror' or censure.

7

Aeschylus, to be sure, is in some ways a better mate or match for Shakespeare. Aeschylus has a bolder, more engrossing imagination, commingling sense with spirit, the natural with the supernatural, even (as in the nurse scene of the *Choephori*) the comic with the tragic. But he is less clear-sighted and equable than Sophocles, and ventures in where Shakespeare, whether because of Elizabethan popular stage tradition or Renaissance paganism or his own temperament, dares or cares not to tread. It is not, of course, because he teaches a philosophy that the Eleusinian initiate produces much effect upon us. It is because he dramatizes it: it is because he conceives of Orestes as both performing a duty towards his father and committing a

[20] J. T. Sheppard, *Aeschylus and Sophocles* (1927), pp. 74–75. She speaks only the language of affection, and is not resentful against Iole. Cf. Haigh, *The Tragic Drama*, p. 160.

crime upon his mother. And the justification (also dramatized), in virtue of ceremonial, political, and even sophistical considerations, by the vote of the Areopagus, though under the presidence of Athena, leaves, poetically, something to be desired. So far I must prefer the reticence, or wistful reverence, of Sophocles or Shakespeare. Both, as Swinburne in another connection has said, are 'imbued with the old faith at once in the necessity of things and in the endurance of man.' The poet of Prometheus is more akin to that of Faustus.

Both Athenians, indeed, have considerably more of a religious element in their dramatic work than Shakespeare. The chorus, which, in the end, is a fairly impartial or disinterested observer, furnishes the opportunity; but the chief reason is that with the Greeks there was no separation between the secular and the spiritual such as there is today and was in Shakespeare's time, particularly in poetry and the drama. From the Renaissance down, English poetry, like the French and the Italian, has been prevailingly pagan, and tragedy almost wholly so. Even when penned by unimpeachable Christians like Corneille and Racine, it has been unreligious, with no definite hopes beyond; and in the background or outlook of Elizabethan tragedy if there is anything religious it is for the most part classical, mundane — the gods, fate, fortune, or the stars. Yet this is owing not mainly to the influence of Seneca nor (as is often said) to governmental regulation, which had to do only with heresy and profanity, but to the requirement of tragedy itself. It must be tragic, and rouse the passions in their intensity. Christianity, like some philosophy, is an alien system of values, which deprecates the passions, inculcates renunciation, and holds death to be the gate of life. It is too comforting, too dogmatic and unpoetical. God and Heaven in the *finale* would break or dull the tragic point as Zeus and Hades do not. They would be an intrusion also, and not merely as an anachronism. Except rhetorically or colloquially, they could not play a part in the tragedy before the end: in the Greek, Zeus and Hades have played a part already. There religion is natural and human, not supernatural and superhuman, is poetical and of the tragic warp and woof: at the end of the *Trachiniae*, Hyllus may say, 'And in all this there is naught but Zeus.' That is no conventional piety — to the grief-stricken son of Hercules 'all this' is not convincingly to the Olympian's credit. It is He that hath made us, and not we ourselves. And when Oedipus knows not with what eyes he could have looked on his father and mother when he came to the place of the dead, that sentiment, too, remains sufficiently deep in the tragic vein. It is not facile and shallow, official or perfunctory, edifying or regenerating, like that of the pulpit or hymn-book. To be sure, Sophocles penned the *Coloneus*, a more religious play than any of Shakespeare's, and there the woes of the much-enduring hero attain to a peaceful and lofty consummation; yet comfort for his daughters, who must needs live on, does not rise above 'Come, cease lamentation, lift it up no more; for verily these things stand fast.' And no higher is the strain at the end of the *Tyrannus*, the *Antigone*, and the *Ajax*.

There is still less, however, not only of dogma or of faith but even of any religious spirit or outlook in Shakespeare's maturest work in tragedy and drama. 'In no play,' as Churton Collins has observed, 'is the hamartia a sin against God as distinguished from a sin against man'; and in no play are there any questions raised and kept before us, as there are in Greek tragedy, concerning the mystery of evil, the sufferings of the just and the prosperity of the wicked, or the doubtful ways of God with men. What is more, heroes and heroines alike are not supported in their hour of trial by the thought of the life beyond or even by trust in God and his righteous but unsearchable counsels. Nor is there any religion of humanity, either, or new ideals to replace the old, such as liberty, social reform, or advancement. In fact, Shakespeare has even been accused of indifference or blindness to moral issues as well, especially in the sex relation. But this is chargeable only in comedy, as in *Much Ado*, *Measure for Measure*, and *All's Well*, in which the dramatist, more intent on entertainment and less careful of secondary effect, makes use of an old story or a *novella* not truly comic — often tragic[21] — in quality, and, particularly in the denouement, forces it, by facile forgivenesses and perfunctory marriages, into the comic mold. He is not *im*moral, not unconventional. In comedy and tragedy both, Shakespeare is, as we have seen in the previous chapter, not interested in problems or prin-

[21] As W. L. Courtney says (*Old Saws and Modern Instances*, 1918, pp. 132, 135), such a tragic background is required in Shakespeare's romantic comedy in order to stiffen the plot; and that is because love there is not dramatized (my *Shakespeare's Young Lovers*, 1937, pp. 1–3, etc.).

ciples, religious, moral, or social, but accepts the reputable customs and opinions of his day. He calls none of them in question — to please his audience but also himself. He is not sceptical, is cynical still less — it is a mistake to consider him so even in his 'darker' comedies — and his last word, as Professor Elton says, is not 'critical and ironical.'[22] The conventional moral opinions, indeed, as we have seen in the previous chapter, he must, in tragedy and comedy alike, take for granted in order to arouse in the audience the emotions which are his aim. The religious opinions, on the other hand, as we have seen in the present chapter, he must restrict or evade in order to keep the emotions from failing of their full effect. 'In *Macbeth*, *Othello*, even *Lear*,' says Professor Grierson,[23] there 'is an acceptance of the ideas of God, Sin, Retribution. . . . But it is implicit, even obscure, never made explicit and clear.'

8

Aeschylus, then, is religious, and provides a solution, justifying the ways of God to men. Sophocles is religious; without attempting to do that. Shakespeare, as dramatist, keeping more in the background, is reverent but reticent and hardly religious at all. What sort of 'reconciliation,' then, does he provide?

The answer is not easy, and is neither single nor simple.

There is high imaginative vision and comprehension. These sentiments, since there is no chorus, are molded and colored to fit the lips of the particular character, like Macbeth's

> Out, out, brief candle,

or Edmund's

> The wheel is come full circle; I am here.

Yet we have Edgar's words,

> Men must endure
> Their going hence even as their coming hither;
> Ripeness is all;

[22] *Modern Studies*, p. 116.

[23] *Cross Currents*, p. 122. In this paragraph I am somewhat indebted to the discussion in Chap. IV. But cf. also Chap. III of my *Shakespeare Studies* (1927); and J. Churton Collins, *Studies in Shakespeare* (1904), pp. 147ff.

Gloster's

> As flies to wanton boys are we to the gods;

and his of Lear,

> O ruin'd piece of nature! This great world
> Shall so wear out to naught;

as well as Hamlet's in defiance of augury or in farewell to Horatio, Antony's about mortals mutable as clouds and water, Prospero's about life as a dream, ending in a sleep. And these higher views relieve us, if they do not console us; these wider horizons calm us. If the immortals, however remotely, do not look down upon the scene to ennoble it, mortals, at least, look up and round.

There is sanity, and, as we have already noticed, harmony in the presentation. In art sanity and harmony are almost one and the same. In neither Shakespeare nor Sophocles is there a reconciliation in any definitely moral or philosophical sense. But drama is art, not philosophy or theology. In poetry what is terrible, as in painting what is mean or ugly, takes on proportions and a beauty when touched by a master-hand; and though, of course, in painting the ugly is not essential, in tragedy the terrible is so, as the cause of the profoundest emotions, upon which the beauty of this, the highest sort of poetry, depends. The tragedy of these poets (or of any) is not the perfect image of life — for that it is necessarily too one-sided and too concentrated, and yet also too poetical and harmonious — but normal life is in the background, and at the end presses forward, closes in upon us, to resume its sway. As the tension relaxes and the passions subside, pity displaces fear. And there is the satisfaction of crime adequately punished, the consolation of misfortune boldly confronted and nobly borne. In Sophocles still more than in Shakespeare, who has also his Coriolanus and his two Richards, is the hero's or heroine's character superior to his conduct — to the plight wherein he is placed and the fate under which he succumbs. But this consolation, when really offered, must needs be partial and meager, or the tragic point (again) would be dulled, its effect obscured. Moreover, the hero himself, as we have noticed, has not been discreet or prudent, nor entirely free of blame. In Sophocles there is more of moralizing on this subject, with counsels of moderation and wisdom; yet since the calamity comes from above, there is also more of humility and troubled piety. In Shakespeare there is more of the sense of the brevity and illusoriness of our pilgrimage — an actor's hour on the stage, a walking shadow, a dream that ends and not by waking. In both, our pain is thus somewhat assuaged. But less so than by the spirit in which hero and heroine meet their fate; still less — witness Oedipus, Lear, Othello, Hamlet, and even Macbeth — than by the recognition of their errors or the regeneration of their natures. They are the wiser if not the finer for their sufferings, though that does not reconcile us to these. And if in neither poet moralizing or justifying plays a conspicuous part, there is no tampering with morality. As I have elsewhere said,[24] the verities are in the end unshaken, the moral values and even the social sanctions are unbroken. On the one hand, there is not the transcendental consolation of evil as but negative, barren, and self-destructive, nor, on the other, the desolation of good and evil merged and confused. There is no scepticism or cynicism, no enveloping irony, as in Ibsen and O'Neill; no bitter despair or mockery on the lips of the survivors or (except the villains) of the dying. There is no hollow echo at the close. Order, something solid, is behind or above: there are the laws of Heaven, which, though unwritten, we can read, or the book of Fate, which we cannot. For both poets (though the Englishman only implies it) the ways of the supreme will are past finding out.[25] These, however comfortless, are steadying — more so at any rate than chaos and the all-engulfing abyss. As mere art they are better. Tragedy within tragedy, chaos within chaos, as nowadays we have it, somewhat fails of effect. There is no relief as the sun rises and glares upon the glacier at the end of *Ghosts*, as the shutters and the door slam at the end of *Mourning Becomes Electra*. And in tragedy relief — if not reconciliation — there should be.

A mere matter of proportions and balance may seem too negative. But the necessary positive element is not morality, not philosophy or theodicy, but vision and emotion. It is not truth, but an imagina-

---

[24] *Art and Artifice*, p. 165.

[25] Of the Oedipus tragedies, though so different, Wilamowitz remarks (*Hermes*, 1899), 'Beides ist gleichermassen ein Beleg für die unerforschlichen Wege des göttlichen Willens.'

tive experience; not fact, but the poet's 'sense of fact.' For great
tragedy is poetry; poetry, as Mr. Housman, after Milton, has lately
said, does not transmit thought but transfuses emotion — thought
and moral quality are there, so to speak, in solution; and tragedy, as
Aristotle averred, transfuses or produces pity and fear, the nobly
'pleasurable excitement of the emotions being the end and aim of
tragedy.'[26] Those in the audience are the reflux of those upon the
stage; and those on the stage, in Shakespeare and Sophocles alike,
constitute, in their frank and overt expression and varied tone and
tension, in their fluctuation and interaction, a rhythm and harmony
in preëminent measure. The emotions aroused are allayed. So they
are in Aeschylus, as well. What, however, in tragedy is for reconciliation indispensable is that the dissonance should proceed to a consonance, and that the tragedy should descend, as in Sophocles and
Shakespeare it does, and in Ibsen and O'Neill it often does not, to a
tonic chord, a rest tone. Or (in terms of another harmony) after the
spasm and convulsion, rest and quiet breathing. And for other
reconciliation than that we must turn, if to tragedy at all, to
Aeschylus.

9

Not that this is the whole of it. It is not enough that the emotions
should be aroused, developed, and conducted to a close. They should
be intense and beautiful, in both spirit and expression, far beyond
any we can experience of ourselves, as they are also in Aeschylus,
an outspoken poet like Dante and (though a greater one) like
Spenser and Milton. The philosophy of these is not a discredit to
their poetry; in fact it is a warrant and, so to speak, by-product of
their sincerity; only, it is not for their philosophy, which in itself,
reduced (as it can be!) to prose, is but a poor thing, or at present
even a dead thing, that we should turn to them. Nor is it chiefly
for 'criticism of life,' or 'a consolation and a stay,' as to a sort of
scripture, that we should turn to them, any more than to the remote
and elusive, the reticent and diffident Sophocles and Shakespeare.
Poetry is not a gospel, tragedy not a play with a 'message,' no answer

[26] If this interpretation of Bywater's (cf. n. 15 above) be, as Mr. Lucas may say,
untrue to Aristotle, still, as he would certainly say, it is true to tragedy (*Tragedy*,
p. 52).

to the riddle of existence in either ever satisfied; and Matthew Arnold has happier words than those above quoted, for a higher, if less neatly edifying, experience — words which are appropriate, if the writing be sufficient, to both verse and prose, not only to tragedy but also to the epic, the lyric, and the novel:

The grand power of poetry is its interpretative power; by which I mean, not a power of drawing out in black and white an explanation of the mystery of the universe, but the power of so dealing with things as to awaken in us a wonderfully full, new and intimate sense of them and of our relations with them. When this sense is awakened in us, as to objects without us, we feel ourselves to be in contact with the essential nature of those objects, to be no longer bewildered and oppressed by them but to have their secret, and to be in harmony with them; and this feeling calms and satisfies us as no other can.

Or we may, more austerely, keep within the limits of the work of art itself, with another poet, Mr. Abercrombie. To what end, he asks, is this communicating of pure experience — and by that he means not actual experience of course but an imaginative one — in plays, poems, and novels? It is not that thus we readers or spectators gain experience — this would put literature in competition with actual life — and to add to our experience is not our deepest desire but to discover its significance. That we cannot do in the thought or philosophy; thought is not expressed in literature for its own sake but for the sake of the organization it gives to experience (or, as Mr. Murry has it, tragic poets are not pessimistic philosophers; if they were, they would have written pessimistic philosophies):

In literature we do not need to make, or to discover, significance in our experience there; experience there is significant, simply by virtue of being literature. And that by reason of the form which literature gives to experience. . . . Experience is perfectly significant when everything in it is a focus of relationships with everything else in it . . . everything there exists not only for its own sake but also for the sake of the whole . . . the only significance which is absolutely necessary to our minds — the revelation of law and order in things.[27]

And of this state of affairs there is in the greatest tragedy, such as that of Aeschylus, Sophocles, and Shakespeare, the highest example.

[27] Abercrombie, *Principles of Literary Criticism*, pp. 52–56.

Nowhere else is imaginative experience communicated in so intense and condensed a form, nowhere else is everything so closely related to every other thing. The nearest approach in narrative art nowadays perhaps is in the tragic short stories of Mérimée, Maupassant, and Chekhov, which inherit something of the earlier technique of the theater; and there, says Chekhov himself, problems may be stated, not solved. As we have seen in the present chapter and the preceding, there are improbabilities, in Aeschylus and Sophocles more especially before the tragedy begins, in Shakespeare even afterwards; and the causal and purposive connections are more often neglected and overridden than in Ibsen and the other moderns. But, as we have there also seen, the imaginative and emotional, the poetical and (so to speak) musical relations are far finer, stronger, and more abundant. And it is there above all that 'by reason of the unity of tragic drama even the misfortune of life becomes an instance of the world we most profoundly desire. Things which in real life would be merely distressing become in tragedy nobly exhilarating. They do not cease to be distressing; but something is added to this; whereby their evil becomes our good.'[28] In large part this comes about by way of the expression. As Arnold says again, in the spirit of the other poets whom we have quoted — Racine, Corneille, Yeats, and Abercrombie — though in the more careless style of a letter: '. . . the problem for the poet is, or should be, to unite the highest degree of agitatingness on the part of his subject-matter, with the highest degree of control and assuagement on the part of his own exhibition of it — Shakespeare, under immense difficulties, goes further in this respect than the Greeks, and so far he is an advance upon them.'[29]

10

'Every true tragedy,' says Lady Gregory, 'is a joy to him who dies.'[30] Why, this is Aristotle's 'imitation,' and (though on the grand scale) here we are! But the exhilarating effect comes about in various ways, in varying degrees, for really undiscoverable reasons. Aeschylus, Mr. Sheppard says, 'always makes the story stand for

[28] Abercrombie, *Principles of Literary Criticism*, p. 112.
[29] *Unpublished Letters* (1923), p. 38.
[30] Quoted by L. A. G. Strong, *Common Sense about Drama* (1937).

something greater than itself, and it is that greater thing which is the subject of his poem':

To Sophocles the story is the thing. His aim is not to use the story as the basis of a religious poem, but to present the story itself: he accepts its morality, and uses its religious ideas: but as Mr. Mackail has well remarked, it is neither ethics nor theology that he gives us: it is the endless wonderfulness of life. In that respect he is like Homer.[31]

In that respect he is still more like Shakespeare, who, more than either, upon the everlasting 'wonderfulness of life' depends.

[31] *Greek Tragedy*, p. 89.

CHAPTER III

Shakespeare and Jonson

Characterization and Tradition

I

MANY nineteenth-century critics treated Shakespeare more as a psychologist than as a dramatist and poet; they analyzed his characters and furnished them with recondite motives as nineteenth-century novelists did their own. The novelists were within their rights. But upon psychology in any scientific sense no dramatist relies, and perhaps, even in our day, no effective novelist; 'the psychology of which our literature is full,' says Lanson, 'has nothing in common with science.'[1] Certainly Mr. O'Neill, whether or not he was justified in thus disavowing Freud for himself, has, in so far as he has aroused tragic emotions, been, as he says, 'simply guided by an *intuitive* psychological insight into human beings and their life impulses that is as old as the Greek drama.' With the psychology of the dramatist's or novelist's time it is as with the philosophy: modern and Elizabethan alike may incidentally employ some of the more familiar phrases and notions but, except as they are matters still more familiar, will not venture to embody the conceptions or principles in a work of art. What, then, shall we say of the twentieth-century critics who follow those of the last generation in discovering Freud and Jung (as the last generation did Hegel, Fichte, and Hartmann), the unconscious and the subconscious, complexes and fixations, not, to be sure, in the theory but in the practice of the great Elizabethan? That sort of thing is, contrary to the general impression, even today beyond a dramatist's ambition or at any rate his reach. In this contention I now

[1] Gustave Lanson, *Hommes et livres* (1895), p. 355.

have here to warrant me the welcome authority of an actor, stage-manager, and producer, Mr. Samuel Barron:

There was a time when the dramatist was concerned wholly with the objective reactions of a character to a given situation. . . . The *Merchant of Venice* is built on objective behavior, and yet each succeeding century could find, because of the accurate picture Shakespeare gives us of this behavior, its own values in the play. . . . [But modern playwrights have] found that in spite of all the marvelous new equipment the theater, which could deal in dramatic form with the who, the how, and the where of human behavior, could not present the why. . . . They could talk about the subjective causes, they could discuss them, but they could not project them in purely theatrical terms.[2]

And Mr. Barron points to the subconscious soliloquies in *Strange Interlude* and to the masks concealing the real man or woman in *The Great God Brown* (which are attempts to secure for this sort of material the simplification and objectivation required by the theater) as failures.

Why failures? In his brief discussion Mr. Barron does not touch on that, but it must be because they do not serve to produce the strong imaginative and emotional effect indispensable to drama in earlier times, indispensable (really) in our own. For one thing, the actor's talking now loud, now low, or putting off or on his mask, too frequently interrupts the dramatic current; for another, the disclosure thus made is too studied, too merely intellectual or mechanical. 'You know my theory (founded on personal experience),' Galsworthy wrote to Garnett, 'that the physical emotional thrill is all that really counts in a play.' Mr. Auden, who as a poet-dramatist shares with Mr. Yeats the opinion that the drama is an art of the passions and the body, declares that 'the drama is not suited to the analysis of character, which is the province of the novel.' Even nineteenth-century novelists, like Hardy, as I endeavor to show in Chapter XII, are less concerned with subjective behavior than has often been thought. 'After all, in fiction,' wrote Galsworthy again, who was a novelist too, 'there is no such thing as psychology; there is only the impression on the reader's mind.' Still less concerned are the writers of short stories. Maupassant, according to Mr. Somerset Maugham, does not analyze his characters, takes little interest 'in

[2] 'The Dying Theater,' *Harper's Magazine*, December 1935.

the reason why.' Chekhov himself says, according to Mr. Edward
J. O'Brien, that 'the writer should never explain a character's state
of mind. The character's state of mind should be perfectly clear
from his actions' — how much more so in a play! Both writers
were prompted, as Mr. O'Brien has it, by considerations of com-
pactness; but above all they were by those of simplicity and sen-
suousness — how much more by either sort the write: of a play!
And Maupassant, in such improbable stories as *Le Port* and *Le Champ
d'oliviers*, falling back for the great situation's sake upon the time-
honored conventions of ignorance and mistaken identity, takes, like
Shakespeare and the ancients, no interest in the reason why perforce.

Objective behavior itself, moreover, was not, and still is not,
presented by a great dramatist so faithfully as by a contemporary
novelist. Even the external motivation is often omitted or overridden: the necessities of a highly emotional action — simplification
and compression, pity coupled or mingled with terror — demand it.
In Ibsen, who resists the demand, there are simplification and compression, indeed, and more of study and insight, but less of either
emotion. 'The great subjects of tragedy,' says Corneille, as we
noticed in the preceding chapter, 'pass beyond the bounds of the
probable': and by Lanson the novel is not excepted. Speaking of
masterpieces, he declares that it is especially these which pass beyond
reality. 'Les plus grands, les plus beaux échappent le plus au con-
trôle, à la vérification, dépassent le plus l'expérience, et celle de
l'auteur comme celle du lecteur.'[3] How comes it, he continues, a
little like Voltaire before him, that to some our classics seem a little
cramped and petty? From their determination to be true to life.
'Et si Shakespeare les dépasse, c'est par ce qu'il a mis de plus dans
son œuvre que le simple vrai, le vrai certain et connaissable.' Othello
must in temperament be unsuspicious, and yet in a single (though
interrupted) conversation become jealous in the extreme; Macbeth
must be brave and honorable, and yet kill an old man, his bene-
factor, his king and his guest; and we need not recall the good men
doing dreadful deeds in ancient tragedy. The psychology here
causes difficulties, that is, for those who are seeking it, and it always
will; the tragedy itself is an undoubted triumph. The motives can

---

[3] *Op. cit.*, p. 360. For Voltaire, see below, Chap. IX, p. 326.

never be discovered, or reconciled; indeed, only a superficial motivation is provided — for the illusion, for the conduct of the story.
Not in the motivation does the character lie, and still less, of course,
in any psychological structure. The character is not easily separable
from the action; yet he is not, as the psychological critic would have
him, the sole source of it. Consequently he is, here or there, not
wholly recognizable as a human being: he has been shortened or
elongated, so to speak, to fit into the pattern. Or to speak more
plainly, his conduct is, here or there, inconsistent, inexplicable. It
has been diverted, though with precautions to make this plausible,
from the course which it would normally have taken; as when the
clever and clairvoyant Hamlet accepts the invitation of the King,
his enemy, whose plot upon his own life he had lately thwarted and
whom he had by letter defied, to a fencing-match with Laertes,
whose father he had killed, and with whom he has just quarreled.
The same is true, as in subsequent discussions we shall see, of the
hero's acceptance of the maiden's sacrifice in the *Arme Heinrich* and
of Hector's flight from the onset of Achilles before the walls of Troy;
and even in the novel at its greatest, such as *Clarissa* and *Tess*, as
well as the short story, such as Maupassant's *Le Port*, the author,
though with no audience to consider, sometimes breaks in upon the
objective behavior of hero or heroine, likewise incurring an improbability for a higher emotional effect.[4]

At such moments, manifestly, it is not in his conduct or motives
that the identity of the character is preserved: 'A "living" character,'
says Mr. Eliot,

is not necessarily 'true to life.' It is a person whom we can see and hear,
whether he be true or false to human nature as we know it. What the
creator of character needs is not so much knowledge of motives as keen
sensibility; the dramatist need not understand people; but he must be
exceptionally aware of them.[5]

[4] See below for Hauptmann, p. 229; for Homer, p. 380; for Hardy, pp. 404–5; and
for Richardson, my *Art and Artifice in Shakespeare*, pp. 68–71. As for *Le Port*, which
reads, says Taine, as if it were written by Aeschylus, nothing could be more improbable than the brother and sister's not at once recognizing each other in the
house of ill fame after four years' separation; but failure to do so is a prerequisite to
the effect of horror in the successive stages of disclosure. Enough years added to
make their blindness probable would have detracted from the poignancy.

[5] T. S. Eliot, *Selected Essays*, p. 188 (by permission of Harcourt, Brace and Company).

Mr. Eliot must here be right; for in the great dispute over Hamlet more than seventeen years ago,[6] Mr. Clutton Brock, not without some reason, as Mr. Eliot will no doubt magnanimously acknowledge, bade him remember these searching words of his own. In point of mere principle most great critics agree — and in their failure to observe it. For thereupon Mr. Clutton Brock, on his own account, proceeded to forget them, as well as a distinction, equally truthful and apposite, that he had just established — 'the business of drama is character and action, not psychology, which is science, not art' — and eagerly and sedulously psychologized the Dane for himself. Now the dramatist's awareness, his own sensibility — where does it most directly and continuously manifest itself, most authoritatively assert itself, if not — where it is by most critics neglected, but where alone the *dramatis persona* is seen and heard — in the mere traits and the speech, the wording and the rhythm? In these the character's temper and attitude are given a being, his thoughts, sentiments, and emotions, an imaginative and poetic, if not a logical or psychological, unity. And if in these, not behind them, it were sought for, the critic's sensibility would more aptly respond, as it should, to the creator's. Especially at those points where the character, for the higher purposes of the action, is 'false to human nature as we know it'; where, for instance, Othello, the noble and generous, comes under Iago's spell, steps into his snare. By the characteristic utterance and rhythm the identity, though not the perfect integrity, of the role is preserved when thus for a time the attitude is changed, the original temper or disposition obscured.

2

It is by such means that all great dramatists and, to a lesser degree, all narrative artists, have presented character; and Tolstoy — who but Dostoyevsky knew so well? — declared 'individuality of speech the most important, if not the only, means of portraying character.'[7] Aristotle would have assented; the epic poet, he says,

---

[6] *Times Literary Supplement*, May 18, 25, June 1, 8, 1922; and with echoes elsewhere.

[7] L. P. Smith, *On Reading Shakespeare* (1933), p. 129. See also p. 135: 'for this shimmering texture of human speech, significant as it is both with the states of soul

'should say very little in *propria persona*, as he is no imitator when doing that'; for speech is his special province or resource. That is, speech is the right narrative medium, as line and color, not volume, is the pictorial; only there does the full mimetic power have play. A boy reading a novel knows this, for he skips the solid printed stretches between conversations. Analysis is exposition; and opinions and principles, 'point of view' and mechanism of motives, even when presented or suggested in the character's own words, are rather intellectual, less simple and sensuous, than speech itself when reflecting only traits, temper or disposition, and the relations of character to character. Still more is speech the dramatic medium. On the force and quality of it drama is more directly dependent than the novel — in it, not behind it, lies the character; and Mr. Auden rightly holds that 'dramatic speech should have the same self-confessed, significant and undocumentary character as dramatic movement.'

It is by such means that all great dramatists have presented character from Aeschylus to Ibsen; and the difference is only a matter of emphasis and proportion, of changing taste and of greater or lesser imaginative and emotional, concrete or sensuous quality. In Shakespeare and the moderns, particularly the northern writers, the characters are more salient, as individuals more audible and visible if not more distinct and interesting than in Hellenic drama and the Mediterranean; and in Shakespeare as well as the other Elizabethans speech and rhythm are for the purposes of characterization more highly and variously developed, more boldly and finely differentiated, and therefore more depended upon by author and spectator, than ever before or since. In Ibsen the character and his conduct are more nearly at one; in the ancients, who present only the final stage of the action, the improbabilities are more often relegated to the background. In Ibsen and the moderns there is less of poetic liberty, and relatively greater attention is paid to analysis or suggestion — to motives, whether superficial or recondite, to ideas and 'point of view,' and speech is kept mainly within the limits of plausible conversation; in Shakespeare and the ancients greater attention is paid to the mere traits, and to an imaginative and emotional

---

and with the meanings and tensions and clashes of human beings in their relations with each other, is, for the writers of drama and fiction, the very stuff of life.'

(rather than intellectual temper or attitude) embodied in poetry. For by poetry, as we saw in the first chapter, reality is enlarged and refined, transmuted or re-created. But in the ancients speech is less individualized than in Shakespeare and the moderns. In Shakespeare there is generally the flavor of conversation, though without the realistic restriction. Agamemnon and Cassandra, Clytaemnestra and Orestes, speak with their own accents; and so do Homer's Achilles and Ajax, Nestor and Diomed, Paris and Helen, Hector and Andromache, and Sophocles' Oedipus and Antigone; yet they do this somewhat remotely, as, until recent times, characters in French and Italian literature have done. By their voices, by the mere fashion of their talk, or its fitness for time, place, or occasion, they are not so easily to be told apart. The traits and doings, the thoughts and feelings, the attitude and temper are the chief thing, not the individual verbal realization; the utterance, though poetically appropriate and discriminated, is not so vivid and various, so daring and intimate; while from *Love's Labour's Lost* to *The Tempest* the lofty and the lowly, the lovable and the hateful, the fine and ethereal as well as the coarse and earthy speak up distinctly and unmistakably, however incoherently they may at times think and however inexplicably they may at times conduct themselves. As never before or since, from any stage or in any book, they make us hear and see them.

Why is this?

In part it is due to the fact that with Shakespeare, as with Chaucer according to Professor Manly, technique — vocabulary, rhetoric, versification — developed first, and content — thought or characterization — afterwards. So it has probably been with most great poets as with other great artists — at first a musician's or a painter's imagination inspires him only to master his medium — but with Shakespeare it was so to an extraordinary degree. At the age of thirty, as Mr. Pearsall Smith observes, 'he was still a euphuist.'[8] *Love's Labour's Lost* exhibits an amazing variety of verbal and rhetorical expression — the speech of each person completely differentiated, the character incompletely. The clever characters revel in words; the affected twist and distort them; the stupid are at their mercy. So it is when these voluble puppets take on life. Dull,

[8] *Op. cit.*, p. 67.

metamorphosed into Dogberry, is no sharper or brighter — he flounders still but now so as to show his good-humored condescension, his vanity and virtue.

In part it is due to the age. Here as elsewhere Shakespeare reflects it; with the other Elizabethans, the poets and (which is as important) their public too, technique likewise came first and content afterwards. The idiom and the vocabulary were expanding and were interesting everybody, both in and out of the theater. This was the day of Lyly and Sidney, of *Euphues* and *Arcadia*, of the pun, the conceit, of endless and riotous experiment in language and style. Before Lyly and Sidney there was continual discussion of rhetoric and versification, and now all the tricks were played. Literature had been the national art as music has for centuries been in Germany, and now it was more than reviving. Literary technique, and not only in verbal expression but in composition, had been developing before Shakespeare came upon the scene, and as an inheritance he took it for his own.

In part it is due to English traditional preoccupation with character, even at the expense of plot. In all narrative, from *Beowulf* and Chaucer to Meredith and Hardy, there has been a more ample, a more naturally, variously, and richly colored, thought not more exactly delineated, presentation of character than on the Continent. What English dramatist, when asked when his play would be finished, ever answered: 'It is already — I have only to write the lines'? For him, too often, the lines are the beginning. Not that when drama was at its best, as in Shakespeare, the whole was not greater than its parts, nor that then any more than in France or Italy character unduly dominated the action — as we have already seen character was at times thereby dominated — but always in English literature there has been a greater relish than in others for the flavor of human nature, for the actualities of human intercourse, particularly as it appears in the speech itself. Even in the novel, from Richardson to Hardy and Meredith, preëminently in Richardson and (as both Professor Elton and Mr. Pearsall Smith have noticed) in Dickens, the characters have been made 'to talk themselves alive.'[9] Shakespeare, more or less, was the teacher, but the method he

[9] Cf. L. P. Smith, pp. 129-36.

could not have 'invented.' It was that of Lyly and Kyd, Greene and Marlowe, before him, as of Chaucer. In the English mysteries mortals are much more tangible and recognizable than in the French; that is, their speech is simpler and more concrete, more colloquial, more highly differentiated and plausibly presented. And from the rise of English secular drama under Elizabeth to its decay under Charles, its most conspicuous achievement is not plot or fable but (after the poetic whole) the persons involved in it; this being so, not because of their motivation, but because of the happy combination of traits, the individuality residing primarily in the utterance.

In part it is due to the traits themselves. In Elizabethan and Shakespearean drama they are many, not, as in the ancient and Gallic, few; are private and personal as well as public, social, or professional; are emotional and concrete rather than intellectual and abstract; are often surprising or contradictory. Romeo, Hamlet, Brutus, Othello, Lear, Antony, Coriolanus, even Richard and Iago, are friends and companions as well as heroes or villains, with homely or intimate as well as lofty or terrible ways of talking or doing. With Horatio, with Rosencrantz and Guildenstern at the outset, and with the players, the Prince for the moment forgets himself; King Lear, waiting for the horses to fly from his ungrateful daughter, guesses a riddle for his jester, who tells him he 'would make a good fool'; and with his mother, his wife, and the ladies who attend them the rough and irascible Roman is as gracious and courtly as a squire. The characters in tragedy have comic traits — have wit and humor — and those in comedy have tragic or lofty ones. All these qualities make for realism: vital fulness and amplitude replace a definite outline, a clear and logical structure. But still more, especially the contradictory qualities, they make for a dramatic situation and for sympathy. Noble and tender souls like Hamlet, intending atrocity, or like Coriolanus, hampered by serious shortcomings, have need of accumulated evidences of nobility and tenderness to keep us on their side. For, like most Elizabethans, Shakespeare does not so much undertake thoroughly to motive their conduct — that is, explain or justify it by way of circumstances, heredity, or environment — as (in Hamlet, for example) to make us accept it as imposed upon them, or (in Coriolanus, for example) to redeem them in our eyes. None of them is *confronted* by the situation — a conflict between inclination and duty, love and honor — like a hero of Corneille's or Racine's: the contrast is between the character and his conduct or within the character himself. In his traits, consequently, the character does not always hold convincingly together; but in his speech he does.

3

In Elizabethan times the breadth of the technique at the dramatist's disposal for this purpose is amazing. Apart from the variety of phrase and locution, and of rhetorical arrangement, the mere vocabulary in Lyly and Greene, Kyd and Marlowe, is enormously larger than in the contemporary or later French drama; and out of Stratford comes the deluge. This fact may be owing to the admission of all orders of society to both the comic and the tragic stage, to the lack of a rigorous, settled distinction between poetic diction and the familiar and (indeed) between the tragic and the comic, but quite as much to the lack of a Latin or Hellenic taste for a character that speaks only to the dramatic question in hand. The character's attitude is not so strictly or exclusively an attitude to the particular situation. The structure of the greatest Shakespearean tragedies is more imposing than that of any ancient one; but the unity is looser, more poetic and imaginative and less intellectual and logical, than that of the Greek or the Latin, the French or the Italian. It is far less the product of criticism. The Continental dramatists after the Renaissance kept, both in tragedy and in comedy, to a narrower range of discussion for the action's sake, and to a narrower vocabulary and phraseology for propriety's sake or decency's, out of regard for tragic dignity or the rank or status of the persons. The English rather neglected such limitations, whether of criticism or of a traditional taboo. Their tradition, to be sure, was one of liberty. Not only is their language broad and abundant; it is also fresh and untarnished, racy and actually or potentially poetical. Synge, in his evil day, complains, like Yeats, of the divorce between poetry and the novel and drama, Mallarmé and Huysmans producing the poetry, and Ibsen and Zola dealing with the reality of life in joyless and pallid words: 'In a good play every speech should be as fully flavoured as a nut or apple, and such speeches cannot be written by any one who works among people who have shut their lips on poetry.' This the Elizabethan people had not done, still less the dramatists. Lyly's comedies and *Love's Labour's Lost* are striking evidence. All the characters are copious and voluble; nearly all have wit or humor, or else are remarked because they haven't. Each has his own personal, idiosyncratic, but poetical way of talking, and the action not infrequently subsides whilst he follows his bent. It is noteworthy, even in the later plays, as seldom in the Continental, how characters of an eccentric cast, with a highly colored and picturesque store of talk, themselves often rather external to the action, like the fools and clowns, or even Shakespeare's Jaques and Marston's Malevole, are openly delighted in and commented upon by the other characters, are questioned and drawn out. Falstaff himself is such a character — everybody on the stage has his eyes on him, agog to hear what he will say.

So had everybody in the audience. Their taste and the dramatist's and company's were fairly at one; and that, as I have elsewhere observed, is the secret of the enormous, headlong development of Elizabethan drama. It is in large part the secret of the development of Shakespeare's own. Dramatist, company, and audience, in such plays as *Damon and Pythias* and *Cambyses*, began on the same simple and humble level; and together — because together — they steadily and swiftly climbed the heights. Tragicomic medleys or romantic-clownish farces were rapidly transforming into the tragedies or comedies of mingled web that we now consider immortal. After a single decade popular plays like the old *Hamlet* and the old *Taming of a Shrew* had, when revived, to be recast and rewritten. The dramatist, of course, led, but never so fast or far that the company and audience failed to follow.

It is not a matter of speech alone. Nowhere do the sympathy and solidarity of the congenial three appear so conspicuously as in that matter which lends itself to statistics — the development of metrical rhythm. From *Love's Labour's Lost* to *The Winter's Tale* and *The Tempest* Shakespeare's progresses from about six per cent of run-on lines to nearly fifty, from about four per cent of feminine endings to thirty-three, from twenty-three light and weak endings in *Macbeth* to a hundred in *The Winter's Tale*; and within the line itself the innovations were as remarkable. Shakespeare was not improbably the leader, was certainly the master; but as with the Greeks at any single period, there was on the whole one style, one taste. The style of an author, in so far as it differed, did not challenge or attempt to override the taste of the time; but wooed it, in some measure accommodated itself to it. 'A dramatic author, if he write for the stage,' says Wordsworth, 'must adapt himself to the taste of the audience, or they will not endure him; accordingly the mighty genius of Shakespeare was listened to.' It was not a matter of his catering or truckling, but of submitting to the conditions of his art. Both at the time of *Macbeth* and also at the end of his career the other dramatists were penning verse technically similar to his, though less various and beautiful. And in versification, as also in diction, plotting, and characterization, the greatest of poets did not venture 'to please himself' — did not undertake to write in *Macbeth* as he was to do in *The Tempest* or *The Winter's Tale*. Indeed, the progress was so gradual, mutual, and instinctive that only when an old play was to be revived did he or his company become aware of it; earlier he had not thought of writing as at present, at present he did not think of writing as he was to do in the end, and to please himself and to please his public were, as for every true artist, one and the same.

There was action, and reaction. Achievement awakened and was stimulated by appreciation; art both formed and was formed by taste. One fortified and fructified the other; and at last in the same play, even in the same character and the same single utterance, the language could be delightfully (what it had long been recklessly and crudely) both comic and tragic (or comic and sentimental), both colloquial and poetical, both lofty and familiar, in a fashion to Hellenic and Latin art unknown. Character and situation developed similarly. At every point there was a continually mounting and accumulating tradition: and as Shakespeare refined upon the expression, in wording and rhythm, of the hero or villain in Marlowe, or of the humorous, tender, and dreamy heroine in Greene, or of the gay and witty one in Lyly, or of homely and earthy, rich and racy human nature, male or female either, in most of his predecessors, he could count on the audience immediately and delightedly responding. Of speech, even in poetry, they were, like the Greeks, connoisseurs, particularly in its individuality. Nowadays, for lack of a living tradition, the audience, especially when Shakespeare's characters dilate and expatiate, are, even when the language presents no difficulty, often a little bored. Mercutio on Queen Mab, Touchstone on the degrees of a quarrel, Jaques on 'All the World's a Stage,' fail to interest a public not brought up to delight in personality thus disclosing and asserting itself, thus displaying its qualities or developing its flavor and in phrase and fantasy disporting itself — a public, for one thing, not in a position to perceive what improvement there is here upon what in this kind there has been before. But it is partly because in those days the audience responded that the dramatist was able to advance farther — from Jaques to Hamlet, from Touchstone or Feste to the Fool in *Lear*. The tradition, in art and taste alike, to which he himself contributed, carried and swept him on.

4

By it Shakespeare immensely profited: against it the redoubtable Jonson at some points rebelled. The ordinary reader may think it strange — and so it is — to speak of the classicist as an innovator and secessionist, but in respect of the living English tradition he was. Knowing the Greek and Roman plays, and very likely the Italian, he resented the looseness and improbability of Elizabethan structure,[10] and insisted on not only the unities of time and place but those of action and of tone. His comedies are comedies, his tragedies tragedies, fairly through and through; and he both subordinated the presentation of character to the requirements of the play as a whole and also, when these permitted, made the action more intimately and exclusively dependent on character. So far Jonson is classical rather than English and Elizabethan. And yet, for all the greater veracity and exactitude of his motivation, he too at his best relies upon poetry and the quality of the speech. The scenario finished, his play, as well as Shakespeare's, was only begun. Shakespeare relies upon the quality of the speech in general to produce the effect of a richer reality, and in particular, to float the character over the reefs of improbability in its course. Of the latter function Jonson has little need; but he is not so classical as to disdain the former, nor so uncompromising as to contemn success. He was not a rebel altogether.

[10] Cf. the discussion above, Chap. I, pp. 16, 38, 56.

5

First and foremost comes the 'immortal and inimitable Bobadill,' in *Every Man in His Humour*. It is a current superstition or popular fallacy, descended from the days of romanticism, that Jonson does not present characters but caricatures, not real people but single traits or abstractions. We need not be troubled by it, if only as we revert to the authority of Dryden and Congreve or bow to that of Mr. Eliot today. In Jonson's better work the figure is no such mannequin or robot; the 'humor' itself is little more than what was later to be called the 'ruling passion'; and in personages like Volpone and Mosca there is, as Mr. Eliot[11] notices, no discernible 'humor' at all. The dramatist's purpose was not an analysis and schematization of human nature, but a rationalization and (as Mr. Eliot observes again) a 'simplification' of it, for the behoof not of science but of art; and while sometimes the framework, or clockwork, is a little too apparent, the proportions too eccentric and lopsided, the character is generally both intelligible and dramatic. The motivation (and this, even on the Elizabethan stage, has its importance) is perfect; he has, so far, a psychology. But this is objective, is rather superficial, no other being needed. It has been said that in Jonson's characterization 'there are no mysterious depths': there are at any rate no muddled ones.

Not only is there truer and more consistent 'psychology' than in most Elizabethans, it is also, in our sense of the word, more dramatically presented. The method is rather modern. On the one hand, we know more nearly and continuously *why* the character says or does what he is saying or doing, and on the other hand, we are not 'told.'[12] We gather it from the dramatic context; we are by previous events and developments so prepared that when the time comes we see it, perhaps feel it, at any rate accept it. Still less are we told, as in Shakespeare we often are, *what* he will do. Bobadill is a *miles gloriosus*, but is not treated in the fashion of the other specimens of that time-honored extravagant type. His cowardice does not expose but betray itself. There is here no scene of anticipation like that

[11] *Selected Essays*, p. 136.
[12] I am here following Mr. Percy Lubbock, in his *Craft of Fiction*.

between Prince Hal and Poins, where the latter arranges for the trick on Gadshill and foretells Falstaff's cowardly demeanor there, his boasting and lying afterwards. Nor is there a giveaway soliloquy and up to his ignominious beating by Downright there is of his cowardliness no explicit indication. The captain before his appearance is commented upon favorably by Cob and Mathew; he is the object of admiration and emulation, in both speech and conduct, by Mathew and Stephen; and his boasting and braggadocios, which might lead us to expect conduct that should belie them, are veiled in self-depreciation, and lend him, as Ward says, something of the 'dignity of calm courage.' (Had he been Shakespeare's, his cowardice, like Falstaff's, and so far as technique is concerned, more justifiably, would by the critics have been denied.)

It is by the delicate gradations of a dramatic rather than descriptive preparation, by the focusing of our attention and rousing of our curiosity through the discrepancy between admiration and its object — between the soldier's renown and his unsoldierly weakness of stomach, between his exalted reminiscences of combat together with his insistence upon the noble art of the rapier which he inculcates and practises, on the one hand, and the beating of Cob the water-bearer together with his threat of the bastinado for Downright, on the other — it is by these preparations, rather than anticipations, that the full comic effect of his pretenses is brought home to us when he is soundly trounced himself. And in the scene after his disgrace he is twitted, not by those who have seemed a little unsympathetic or sceptical, but more subtly, in their stupidity, by his admirers:

Mathew: I wonder, Captain, what they will say of my going away, ha? . . . Why so! but what can they say of your beating? . . . Ay, but would any man have offered it in Venice, as you say?

To the last anxious query Bobadill responds in some pique, but still under the spell of his infatuation,

Tut! I assure you, no: you shall have there your *nobilis*, your *gentilezza*, come in bravely upon your reverse, stand you close, stand you firm, stand you fair, save your retricato with his left leg, come to the *assalto* with the right, thrust with brave steel, defy your base wood!

The last word, however — there is your right dramatic psychology!
— brings with it a pang, and he relapses into his habitual melancholy
mood and rhythm:

> But wherefore do I awake this remembrance? I was fascinated, by
> Jupiter, fascinated; but I will be unwitched and revenged by law.

(Before the last two words there should be a dash, to indicate the
actor's pause, our Captain's 'discretion'!) So, before this, immediately after the trouncing he cried:

> Sure I was struck with a planet thence, for I had no power to touch
> my weapon.

And the brave illusion he preserves to the end. He has no sense of
humor, no gift of gaiety; and his own evasions, unlike Falstaff's
'By the Lord, I knew ye as well as he that made ye . . . the lion will
not touch the true prince,' and the rest, do not avail to turn bodily
disgrace into a verbal triumph. Like most of Jonson's characters,
and Molière's as well, he is a comic figure, not a humorous one:
there is laughter in the house, but little on the stage, and none at all
from out of Bobadill's lungs.

His solemnity still envelops him as, in being 'revenged by law,'
he exposes himself to the ridicule of Justice Clement with his plea,
for not defending himself, that he has been bound over by Cob to
keep the peace. A more consistent and identical character could
scarcely be found. Falstaff is much less so,[13] and therefore, though
(in a sense) not so suggestively depicted, has, unlike Bobadill, been
in our psychologizing day misunderstood. A coward, he is much
more than that. He, for his part, carries his drink with ease. 'A
liar,' as Dryden says, 'a glutton, and a buffoon,' he is a rich and ample
personality besides, most of this being rather aloof and apart from the
action. He reaches far beyond his role. A butt as well as a wit, he
has irreconcilable contradictions in his make-up. His identity preserves or asserts itself, not in the fabric or texture of his motives, or
any intellectual structure or mechanism, but in the fashion of his
thought and utterance, his Epicurean outlook and humorous point

---

[13] See my *Shakespeare Studies*, Chap. VIII, especially pp. 431–56; and below, Chap.
X; also the article, 'Recent Shakespeare Criticism,' *Shakespeare-Jahrbuch* (1938),
pp. 55–63.

of view. His every sentence or phrase was coined only in the mint of his lips. Whatever he does, he continually talks like himself, a prodigious human being, natural but like no other in the world. His inner make-up we do not, when we stop to consider, quite understand, but of his effective reality we cannot but be 'aware.'

6

Yet Bobadill, so much smaller in compass (and therefore the more easily presented), so consistent and identical in motive and conduct, so firmly articulated with the action, depends for effectiveness on speech nearly as much as Falstaff himself. Psychological consistency does not suffice. The psychology is, as it well may be, only the mechanism: in the speech, since features and facial expression are necessarily missing, is the life and soul of the man. By the psychology we may better understand; only by the form and pressure of the speech are we convinced and captivated. And it is in this, not his psychology, that lies the captain's superiority over all other cowards but the Eastcheap knight.

Cob, at the outset, has been lauding his warrior lodger, and swearing after the latter's lofty and esoteric fashion; and now, in the immediately following scene, the paladin is discovered flat on his back.

> Hostess, hostess!
> (Enter Tib)
> Tib. What say you, sir?
> Bob. A cup of thy small beer, sweet hostess.

There, even in that unheroic posture and plight, as he would work off the effects of generous potations with the meager, are the tone and the accent heard in his later utterances (as above) and kept throughout. He is speaking (as well as drinking) small and humbly at present, but the voice is the same as when he rises to the heights. It has the same languid lilt and melancholy grace. That this is not wholly native to him presently appears. 'There's a gentleman below,' says Tib, and at that he is quick and direct enough:

> A gentleman! 'odso, I am not within.
> Tib. My husband told him you were, sir.
> Bob. What a plague — what meant he?

He is startled, for a moment, out of his heroical illusion. But even amid his protestations and evasions he soon regains his composure, and relapses into his circuitous phrasing and ample rhythm:

Master Mathew, in any case possess no gentlemen of our acquaintance with notice of my lodging. . . . Not that I need to care who know it, for the cabin is convenient; but in regard I would not be too popular, and generally visited, as some are. . . . For do you see, sir, by the heart of valor in me, except it be to some peculiar and choice spirits, to whom I am extraordinarily engag'd, as yourself, or so, I could not extend thus far. . . . I confess I love a cleanly and quiet privacy, above all the tumult and roar of fortune.

Here again is psychology of the right, perceptible sort. In his circumlocutions and undulations we not only see but hear the flustered Captain, despite his solicitude, gradually resuming his lofty indifference, his solemn condescension. 'Cette chose quasi indicible,' says M. Lefèvre, 'qui fait que nous sommes nous-mêmes et non pas un autre, par quoi la rendons-nous sensible à autrui? Par le rhythme.' This is said of the author's own individuality — it equally applies to that of his characters.

Always good, Bobadill is best melancholy and reminiscent, passing lightly, allusively over his unparalleled, incomparable achievements. He is a *miles gloriosus* with a difference. No cheap alehouse liar or vulgar blusterer like Pistol or Parolles, or buoyant and exuberant one like Falstaff, he is a day-dreamer and romancer. He has fed, apparently, on the same tales of chivalry as the Knight of the Rueful Countenance, and before him.

Wel. Captain Bobadill, why muse you so?

.   .   .   .

Bob. Faith, sir, I was thinking of a most honourable piece of service, was perform'd tomorrow, being St. Mark's day, shall be some ten years now.

E. Know. In what place, Captain?

Bob. Why, at the beleag'ring of Strigonium, where, in less than two hours, seven hundred resolute gentlemen, as any were in Europe, lost their lives upon the breach. I'll tell you, gentlemen, it was the first, but the best leaguer that ever I beheld with these eyes, except the taking in of — what do you call it? last year, by the Genoways; but that, of all other, was the most fatal and dangerous exploit that ever I was rang'd in, since

I first bore arms before the face of the enemy, as I am a gentleman and a soldier.

.   .   .   .

Bob. Observe me judicially, sweet sir; they had planted me three demi-culverins just in the mouth of the breach; now, sir, as we were to give on, their master-gunner (a man of no mean skill and mark, you must think), confronts me with his linstock, ready to give fire; I, spying his intendment, discharg'd my petronel in his bosom, and with these single arms, my poor rapier, ran violently upon the Moors that guarded the ordnance, and put 'em pell-mell to the sword.

Wel. To the sword! To the rapier, captain.

E. Know. Oh, it was a good figure observ'd, sir. But did you all this, captain, without hurting your blade?

Bob. Without any impeach o' the earth; you shall perceive, sir. (*Shews his rapier.*) It is the most fortunate weapon that ever rid on poor gentleman's thigh. Shall I tell you, sir? You talk of Morglay, Excalibur, Durindana, or so; tut, I lend no credit to that is fabled of 'em. I know the virtue of mine own, and therefore I dare the boldlier maintain it.

Act III, scene i

This tall talk is not in the outlandish and bombastic vein of Pistol or Pyrgopolinices; this fiction does not beggar belief; this bragging is scarcely bragging at all. He does it in a way not wholly beneath the dignity of that 'gentleman' by whom he swears. For even his oaths are in a high style, ingenious, chivalric, fitted to the tenor and meter of his discourse. And his cadences, despite the Dorian rather than Lydian mode that, because of his exalted theme, he must now be intoning, are, though sometimes picturesquely in keeping with the theme —

lóst their líves upon the bréech . . . pút them pèll-méll to the swórd —

they are, I say, for the most part, hovering or trailing, in keeping with his temper:

as I am a géntleman and a sóldier . . . the most fórtunate weápon that ever ríd on poor géntleman's thígh . . . and thérefore I dare the bóldlier maintaín it.

His illusion, as I said, he keeps unbroken, or — it's a matter of subjective behavior — nearly so. For the discomfiture that befalls him, nothing less than some planetary interference, or the diabolical, will do. But though not much enlightened, he is chastened. He rises in whole-hearted admiration (and more than that perhaps) for the humble City Serjeant who, serving a warrant upon Downright, 'procur'd by these two gentlemen,' that is, Bobadill himself and Mathew, prevents that worthy from beating the same. 'The Varlet's a tall man, afore heaven!' he generously — consistently — confesses as he makes good his own retreat. But before Justice Clement, who has jeered at him, he has no more of a reply to the inquiry whether he has had Clement's own warrant for Downright's apprehension than the crest-fallen

Ay, an't please your worship.

He is crushed, as the justice notices; he is a sadder, meeker, not, apparently, a wiser man.

7

The captain is the best thing in the play; but Kitely, the jealous husband, is not much inferior; and most of the characters are skillfully distinguished in accent as well as type. In *Volpone, The Silent Woman*, and *The Alchemist* the *dramatis personae* are less fully and directly depicted, are presented more by contrast and in conduct. Still more than Bobadill they are part and parcel of the action. The three legacy-hunters in the first play — Voltore the lawyer, Corvino the merchant, Corbaccio the half-blind, half-deaf miser — are alike intent on being Volpone's heir, each to that end going the length of sacrificing either his professional reputation, or the honor of his beautiful wife, or the inheritance of his dutiful son. Yet, like as they are in interests, purposes, and doings, they only throw each other into relief.

With less of tragic grimness in the portraiture, there are as much distinctness and variety in *The Alchemist*. Both Puritans in the latter play are done grimly enough. But how Ananias and Tribulation, similarly sanctimonious and Hebraic in sentiment and speech, zealous and covetous for the cause, not only contrast but supplement each other: the former, downright, rigid, and literal, the latter, cautious, slippery, and jesuitical; the former, averse to any compromising intercourse with the children of this world, the latter, eager to make friends of the Mammon of unrighteousness! Yet once Tribulation discloses how the end justifies, not to say sanctifies, the means, Ananias is heart and soul with him, more headlong and unscrupulous than his teacher. And into temptation Subtle leads them, and on:

> If the holy purse
> Should with this draught fall low, and that the saints
> Do need a present sum, I have a trick
> To melt the pewter, you shall buy now instantly,
> And with a tincture make you as good Dutch dollars
> As any are in Holland.

Tri.   Can you so?

Sub.   Ay, and shall bide the third examination.

Ana.   It will be joyful tidings to the brethren.

Sub.   But you must carry it secret.

Tri.   *Ay; but stay,*
This act of coining, is it lawful?

Ana.   *Lawful!*
We know no magistrate; or if we did,
This's foreign coin.

Sub.   It is no coining, sir.
It is but casting.

Tri.   Ha! you distinguish well;
Casting of money may be lawful.

Ana.   'Tis, sir.

Tri.   Truly, I take it so.

Traits here are so distinct, they so vividly set one another off, that even through a less fitting expression the character would in some fashion still appear. But it would not be alive. In the passages italicized how either saint, after his own fashion, snaps at the bait demurely dangled before him! And in rhythm how dogged is Ananias, how devious Tribulation, and Subtle how worthy of his name!

No one else has such insight into the involutions and contortions of the 'nonconformist conscience,' so far as they may be made sensible on the comic stage. In the later play, *Bartholomew Fair*, Rabbi Zeal-of-the-Land, put in the stocks for breaking the peace, looks upon himself as a martyr, and cries out upon Waspe for taking his chance to escape, yet instantly seizes the first chance, as a 'miracle' and a 'mercy,' to escape himself. Waspe's case was different, he thinks, as he would; yet it is not on Busy's consistency in his inconsistency, whether moral or mental, that the dramatist depends, but, as with the other persons in that gross but 'colossal' comedy, on a voice and idiom (none too agreeable) all his own.

8

It is the victimizers, however, rather than the victims, that, as the center and source of the action, are both more complex and more amply delineated — Face and Subtle in *The Alchemist*, Volpone and his parasite Mosca in the other play. Like Iago, they have wit and humor, a dramatist's delight in situations and a different strategy and style for each, with words (the medium of their art as well as the dramatist's own) in abundance to suit. These are not only the expression but (necessarily) somewhat the concealment of their natures. Only at a point where speech has by a tradition been highly developed and differentiated can it well serve such a purpose, and of that tradition Jonson is, if despite himself, an heir. It is truly, as Swinburne says, 'a glorious impudence' when Face, as the Alchemist's 'Lungs,' dismisses Surly with a promise to bring him word to his lodging if he can hear of "that Face" whom Surly has sworn to mark for his if ever he meets him.' Volpone, the magnifico, likewise plays two parts, both the arch-plotter (or stage-manager) and a leading role in his own performance, that of the rich invalid whose approaching death calls forth both homage and tribute. And it is a great moment as he peers through the curtains at the Vulture, the Crow, and the Raven swooping down at last upon his property, while Mosca checks off the items of the inventory in the interest, as each aspirant takes it, of the heir. 'They never think of me!' he whispers with a sigh not utterly forlorn, while Mosca, so busy, lightly hands them the will where no name is inscribed but his own. Indeed they do not, after all their solicitude by word and gift.

Mosca himself, however, the 'rare,' the 'exquisite,' surpasses, even as he outwits, them all. He is nimble as a lizard, changeable as a chameleon, slippery as an eel, and with his tongue as much as with his brains. Acting for his patron, seeming to act for the legacy-

hunters, he is really playing these off against one another and working wholly for himself; but how at the same time he relishes the
comic contrasts of his poses and employments! On a stage within
the stage, he would not be elsewhere for thousands. When Corvino,
Volpone being now very low, brings in the pearl and (if need be!)
a diamond, Mosca, to make sure, bids him 'show't, sir,'

> Put it into his hand; 'tis only there
> He apprehends: he has his feeling yet,
> See how he grasps it!

What he says means one thing to Corvino, another to Volpone,
still another to Mosca and the audience; and how innocently he rejoices at this pitiful vestige of spirit in his patron! Tears and laughter
here meet and conspire. Then he tells the merchant, as he has done
the others, how he has been furthering his cause, in this case by slip-
ping his name into the will whilst Volpone, in his witless fondness,
had Corvino's continually on his lips. 'O my dear Mosca!' and they
embrace. 'But does not he perceive us?' — 'No more than a blind
harper,' and here is another situation with more sides or aspects
than one! But the embracing is mostly of Corvino's doing; the parasite is not fulsome in his endearments like the villains Barabas or
Ithamore, Richard III or Buckingham. He provokes instead of bestowing them: he shows a nicety in his knavery, a continence and
delicacy in his guile.

He is happier however (who is not?) when more truly himself —
at the above-mentioned inventory, where, though after a function-
ary's fashion, he dangles the treasures before the legacy-hunters'
eyes; handing the will 'carelessly over his shoulder,' and interrupting
his malicious, delicious singsong (as they pester him amid their
agitated perusal of it) with preoccupied deprecations and with
'business in his face.' By what other device could he have so tanta-
lized the legacy-hunters all together, without seeming to do so?
And here speech, as in both the highest comedy and the highest
tragedy of the ancients and the Renaissance it not infrequently does,
approaches 'the condition of music.'[14]

Mos.   'Two cabinets.'
Corv.   Is this in earnest?

[14] Cf. my *Shakespeare Studies*, pp. 157–66.

Mos.   'One
    Of ebony' —
Corv.   Or do you but delude me?
Mos.   'The other, mother of pearl' — I'm very busy;
    Good faith, it is a fortune thrown upon me —
    '*Item*, one salt of agate' — not my seeking.
Lady P. Do you hear, sir?
Mos.   'A perfum'd box' — Pray you forbear,
    You see I'm troubl'd — 'made of an onyx.'

The torture itself is 'rare' and 'exquisite,' exotic or Oriental; the
last description, coming after the parenthesis, is a sprightly, wicked
thrust. And finally, when the heirs presumptive insist on a 'fairer
answer,' they get it, as the parasite bids them 'quit my house,'
'thanks' them for the pearl and the diamond, or promises not to
betray them. Voltore, the lawyer, tarries, certain that 'he doth
delude all these for me':

                Now, my faithful Mosca,
    I find thy constancy —
Mos.   Sir!
Volt.   Sincere.
Mos.   'A table
Of porphyry' — I marle you'll be thus troublesome.

And thereupon the perturbing, imperturbable music, thus resumed,
is again interrupted, with Mosca's masterpiece of provocation, less
disguised:

Volt. Nay, leave off now, they are gone.
Mos.   Why, who are you?
    What! who did send for you? O, cry you mercy,
    Reverend sir! Good faith, I am griev'd for you,
    That any chance of mine should thus defeat
    Your (I must needs say) most deserving travails:
    But I protest, sir, it was cast upon me,
    And I could almost wish to be without it,
    But that the will o' the dead must be observ'd.
    Marry, my joy is that you need it not;
    You have a gift, sir (thank your education),
    Will never let you want, while there are men,

And malice, to breed causes. Would I had
But half the like, for all my fortune, sir!
If I have any suits, as I do hope,
Things being so easy and direct, I shall not,
I will make bold with your obstreperous aid,
Conceive me — for your fee, sir. In mean time,
You that have so much law, I know ha' the conscience
Not to be covetous of what is mine.
Good sir, I thank you for my plate; 'twill help
To set up a young man. Good faith, you look
As you were costive; best go home and purge, sir.

Act V, scene iii

'How his villainy becomes him!' whispers Volpone from behind his curtain, not perceiving, in his *hybris*, that there is more of that in store. The magnifico legally dead, and too much entangled to revive unaided, Mosca plays on, this time in earnest. In court, Voltore having been driven, in retaliation, to contradict his own testimony, and declare that Volpone is still living, the heir in state arrives. And now between master and man, Greek meeting Greek in roguery, comes the tug of war. Volpone, in disguise, whispers, 'Say I am living,' but the parasite, consummate impersonator, is every inch the magnifico he pretends to be:

> *What busy knave is this?* Most reverend fathers,
> I sooner had attended your grave pleasures,
> But that my order for the funeral
> Of my dear patron did require me —
> *Volp.* (aside)   Mosca!
> *Mos.* Whom I intend to bury like a gentleman.

Also he is every inch himself: his wit follows him into high places, and to the brink. And even there the struggle goes on between them — 'Will you gi' me half' — 'Thou shalt have half' — 'I cannot now afford it you so cheap' — till Volpone, as game as his supplanter, throws both him and himself over the precipice by disclosing his own identity.

The play and glitter of Mosca's wit, the chameleon changes of his impersonation, are in his speeches directly apparent. But his inner character is revealed as dramatically as Bobadill's, and is still more a part of the drama. So is his wit or humor in comparison to the Captain's fantasy. It has little or nothing of the incidental or episodic, to be found in that not only of Falstaff but of Mercutio and Benedick, Beatrice and Rosalind, and, more especially, of Shakespeare's Fools and Clowns. The parasite does not give it the rein and let it gallop away with him. He is not like Touchstone and Feste, Mercutio and Jaques reveling in their arias or fantasias, while the action pauses. His speeches are less highly colored even than Bobadill's; and so far his individuality is less marked and distinct. It is to be gathered from his conduct, from the way he manages the inventory, as much as from the spirit of his words. Still there it is, and in the rhythm, as if he were Shakespeare's own:

> he has his feéling yét,
> Sée how he grásps it!

This is the same malicious innocence or tender cruelty that is to be found in the later speeches, quoted above:

> But I protést, sir, it was cást upón me
> And I could álmost wísh to be withóut it,
> But that the wíll o' the deád must be obsérv'd.
>
> . . . .
>
>   'twill hélp
> To sét úp a yoùng mán.

And it is the same sly vein again, amid his pride as magnifico, in the high-stepping iambics:

> What búsy knáve is thís?

9

The individuality is, however, not greatly appealing. Jonson's characters are interesting and entertaining, but do not awaken our affection or sympathy; and what fails to awaken either one or the other, so far fails to give us the impression of life. In this as in the psychological and structural qualities that we have noticed he is less like Shakespeare than is any other of the leading writers for the Elizabethan stage. He has force, point, subtlety, not charm. He resembles Shakespeare — in his greatness. They are like the other eminent couples and corrivals in art — Aeschylus and Sophocles, Sophocles and Euripides, Corneille and Racine, Ibsen and Björnson, Wordsworth and Coleridge, Byron and Shelley, Browning and Tennyson, Dickens and Thackeray, Meredith and Hardy, Michelangelo and Leonardo or Raphael, Reynolds and Gainsborough, Turner and Constable, who in the process of becoming artists, of developing or preserving their individuality and securing a public of their own, were necessarily thrown into opposition or asunder. One (or each) reacted against the other. Each fell back on what he could do better than the rest, especially than his foremost competitor, or could do differently; or else took to what had not been done before or not of late. The lesser spirits of the time, on the other hand, while they naturally cultivated and fostered any particular talent or attraction that they discovered themselves to possess, yielded more, even from the same instinct of self-preservation, to the main current and tendency, which in this period was that of Shakespeare. Of the two in question, it was Jonson that reacted, as the weaker, though such in his own day and to the casual eye he did not seem. But it was in part the main current, the accumulated energy and momentum, the tradition in practice and in taste, that, as Shakespeare accepted it, reinforced it, and controlled it, made him the stronger, and that swayed writers and public both even after he was gone.

And that tradition, from Lyly, Greene, and Peele, Kyd and Marlowe, traced above, leant to sympathy and romance rather than to realism and satire. In this spirit it prevailed in Dekker and Heywood, Beaumont and Fletcher, Webster and Ford, even in Middleton, Massinger, and Shirley. The critics say that Jonson, not Shakespeare, Marlowe, not Shakespeare, founded a school — and that is so. But Lyly and Kyd founded schools as well. Shakespeare established no tradition; he received it, absorbed and blended it, developed and ennobled it. He was the most Elizabethan of the Elizabethans; and therefore he could leave no such perceptible impression on the others. His influence is — that of the Age. He himself was influenced by Kyd and Marlowe, Lyly and Greene before him, and even by Beaumont and Fletcher and Jonson beside him, in the dramatic romances, on the one hand, and in *The Merry Wives* and *Coriolanus*, on the other, as these later dramatists were not by him in turn.

Of those above mentioned as belonging to the tradition, it is in most cases clear that their characters are to be found chiefly, sometimes almost wholly, in their speech. Psychology and even motivation are often confused or wanting: the speech is rich and varied, ample and vital, accented and individualized, and only less so than with Shakespeare himself. So it is with Dekker's Bellafront, Matheo, and Orlando; Beaumont's Evadne and the Citizen's Wife in *The Knight of the Burning Pestle*; Webster's Flamineo and Bosola, Vittoria and the Duchess of Malfi; Middleton's Beatrice and De Flores; Ford's Ithocles and Calantha. Even from the way they are made these characters were made in England — that is, Shakespeare's England — as Jonson's were. What is more, though we have not undertaken to show it, the dramatic movement is in the dialogue, as it is not in the chitchat of today. The dialogue has been composed and orchestrated. It rises and falls in pitch and volume, is accelerated and retarded, is widely varied in quality and tone, to suit and fit the changes in incident and passion. So it is preëminently in tragedies like *Lear* and *Othello*, but also in comedies like *Volpone* and the *Alchemist*. 'The spate, whirlwind, and thunder of words' is the phrase of a reviewer for a recent London revival of the Venetian comedy — for *Volpone*, for hardheaded, laconic Jonson! And it is to show Shakespeare in his art, as I have conceived this, to be of the main tradition, not original or eccentric, yet not in a backwater either, but in the middle and the full force of the stream, that I have written these words.

10

To many nowadays that is not so satisfactory or reassuring. 'Originality' is what is demanded; the word 'traditional' or 'conventional' is generally a reproach. Of tradition and convention, therefore, art must (though it has more than we acknowledge)[15] have proportionately less. But thereby it loses. A really great, truly popular art there cannot be — and today we have none — without a convention within it, a tradition behind it. The art really trite is that in which the convention is outworn, the tradition spent.

[15] See J. A. K. Thomson, *Irony* (1926), p. 173: 'We speak of a "new note" in literature. . . . Not, of course, an absolutely new note, for literature can only develop out of itself . . . an absolutely new note, if possible at all, could say nothing in literature to anybody.'

Shakespeare's *Hamlet*, cast in the Senecan and Kydian mold, is, of course, not objectionably conventional; the revenge tragedies of the later seventeenth century are. Shakespeare's art has moved men in after times — and in its own day it moved them still more — because it employed familiar means and material and profited by established associations. It has moved men, not because of the imitation or inertia in it, but because of the re-creation and energy, which thus met with less resistance and awakened a more eager response. A *path* is the easiest and speediest, if not the directest, approach to a place, even in the heart of man. Artistic genius is to be measured not by its force but its skill, not by the effort exerted but the effect produced; and Shakespeare's is like that in the *Iliad* and the *Nibelungen*, on the one hand, and that of Burns and even Heine, on the other. As the best critics have noted, Burns — though the same person as when he writes English — is really great only in the vernacular, in the popular lyric tradition. Scarcely one of his good songs but bears some recognizable or probable relation to an earlier one. Like Shakespeare he had a retentive memory — with him Mnemosyne was still a muse. His songs, like Shakespeare's own, reach our hearts so immediately because similar, humbler songs had reached ours, or others like ours, before. The greatest lyrists, like Burns and Shakespeare, Heine and Goethe, are such when the spirit of folksong or of their humble but popular predecessors comes upon them. Receiving most, they have most to give. It is not, of course, mainly substance that they inherit, though this they may inherit too, but the form, the mood, the approach or method, the situation, the movement, the diction or idiom. 'Ubi sunt?' — 'Where are they then?' — 'Who is Sylvia, what is she?' — 'Sigh no more.' — 'Ask me no more.' — 'Hark, hark.' — 'Hear ye.' — 'Tell me.' — 'Come away, come away.' How happily, engagingly, these *motifs* recur; and after two thousand years the noblest and most poignant elegies penned are, against all reason, still the pastoral! But the relation of the lyric or elegiac poet to his tradition is nowise so immediate or so unconscious and inevitable as that of the Elizabethan actor-dramatist to his own, which continued daily or weekly for years, and which, growing, but remaining identical, had through generations descended to him.

This, to be sure, is only scratching the surface. The substance, the content, need not be inherited, along with the form, but it must be not too strange. 'The writer frames the patterns with which, like every other artist, he encloses, subdues, and satisfies the soul,' observes Vernon Lee, meaning the imaginative writer, the poet, 'out of material given entirely and solely by the memory.' (That is, not any mysterious racial or atavistic memory, as some recent poets and psychologists have imagined, but the experience or hearsays common to author and public.) The remark applies to not only the patterns but the texture — the words and imagery, even if new to poetry — and, in some measure, to the sentiments; for a work of art, in so far as it really is such, is, as we have in some measure noticed already, a work not only of communication but of coöperation. As Mr. Abercrombie says, 'the experience (and he means, of course, imaginative experience) which lived in the author's mind must live again in the reader's mind . . . must be transplanted from one mind to another.'[16] 'The fool,' says Lord Verulam, 'receives not the words of the wise, unless thou speakest the things in his heart.' 'And not only the fool,' adds Francis Thompson. 'By the law of Nature, no man can admire, for no man can understand, that of which he has no echo in himself.'

In the other arts memory coöperates too, but to a less degree. In music this is evident: Italians and Argentineans can appreciate the compositions of the Finns and the Muscovites. And in painting we can appreciate the art, though of a novel sort, expended upon scenery, animals, and people such as we have never had a glimpse of; but less completely than that expended on what is familiar, as Vernon Lee finely perceives. And

if . . . the preference for a picture, a building or a song, indeed, the feeling and realizing of its presence, depends upon stored-up and organized experience of our own activities, how far more exclusively does the phantom-reality called literature exist only in the realm of our recollections! It is not composed of objective, separately perceptible lines, masses, colours, note-sequences and note-consonances; it has no existence, no real equivalent, outside the mind; and the spoken sound, the written characters, have no power unless translated into images and feelings which are already within us. . . . We are not much impressed by writings which deal with people and circumstances outside our own experi-

16 *Principles of Literary Criticism*, p. 34.

ence; and not impressed at all by writings, however eloquent, in a language which we do not understand.[17]

That is, by writings in an English which is difficult, embodying imagery or allusions, sentiments or ideas, which are essentially unfamiliar. The novelty of good poetry is mainly not in the ideas or the expression but in the application and adaptation of them to poetry; and not so much in the ideas as in the subjects, the attitude or the point of view. In Wordsworth or Browning, as they appeared, the novelty was the deeper interest in the simple and lowly or the complicated and questionable, in the cottage girl and the leech-gatherer or the prelate and the impostor; it was the conception of nature and of life; it was the imposing individuality of spirit and style. And more than the beginnings and rudiments of these, of course, was there in the life roundabout or in the literature that preceded them. New, difficult ideas are for prose; and even in that, if it is to be of any quality, the notions and language employed must have been part of our lives, not something technical or esoteric.[18] (Hence the folly of much of our source-hunting — sources, if they are such, need little hunting and still less proving — and some recent ingenious interpretations of Wordsworth's and Shelley's phrasing and imagery by way of seventeenth-century English philosophy, eighteenth-century physics, and the even remoter, fantastic Paracelsus, seem to me, if really relevant, to undermine the poetry. There, then, for once, the poet would be but 'pleasing himself' — and scholars yet unborn!)

Still truer is this of drama, the spoken rather than the written word, the effect of which must be instantaneous, and unanimous. If, as Bacon[19] avers, drama 'has been regarded by learned men and great philosophers as a kind of musician's bow by which men's minds may be played upon,' it is a failure unless the various tones

[17] *The Handling of Words* (1923), pp. 74–75 (this and the above passage by permission of Dodd, Mead and Company). On this matter of the writer's playing upon the memory compare the fine passage in Raleigh's *Style* (1918), pp. 10f.: 'an underworld of dead impressions . . . a sleeping company of reminiscences . . . to be awakened into fierce activity at the touch of words.'

[18] 'No novel "concept," ' says Mr. Belgion, replying to Mr. Ezra Pound, 'can be communicated to a spectator or auditor except in terms with which that spectator or auditor is already familiar' (*Criterion*, October 1930, p. 122).

[19] *De Augmentis*, II, xiii.

are, as expected, produced; and if, as he further says, 'it is most true, and one of the great secrets of nature, that the minds of men are more open to impressions and affections when many are gathered together than when they are alone,' this can be only when the strings played upon are common to them all. There should, of course, be some novelty, that of poetry, of beauty: out of the stuff of memory the dramatist makes 'new wholes' — situations and characters, images and phrases — which are moving, perhaps striking or startling; but not out of discoveries, his own or other men's. For his art is not only the poet's but the orator's, as described by Hazlitt:

[Chatham] electrifies his hearers, not by the novelty of his ideas, but by their force and intensity. He has the same ideas as other men, but he has them in a thousand times greater clearness and strength and vividness. . . . He is not raised above others by being superior to the common interests, prejudices, and passions of mankind, but by feeling them in a more intense degree than they do.

A popular dramatist cannot, in the ordinary sense, be original. Death in Shakespeare, as one scholar[20] has recently shown, whether as a mental image, or an idea, or a situation, is treated in thoroughly traditional fashion. As an image, for instance, it is the 'lean, abhorrèd monster,' the 'paramour' that it is for Romeo in the tomb, as for Juliet when she first sets eyes on him, a notion as old as the Greek anthology;[21] or else there is the equally familiar notion of blackness or darkness, of sleep, of a sergeant's arrest, of delivery from prison, of beginning a journey, of putting the candle out. The poetry, and still more the drama, lies in the old image given life anew. A novel, original image, like Rossetti's

> The wind of death's imperishable wing,

or Rupert Brooke's

> Rose-crowned into the darkness,

or Browning's

> Freed by the throbbing impulse we call death,

---

[20] Theodore Spencer, *Death and Elizabethan Tragedy* (1936).

[21] I, v, 136, 'my grave . . . my wedding-bed'; cf. Mackail, *Select Epigrams from the Greek Anthology* (1911), p. 280, Meleager.

would have troubled an Elizabethan audience (if not a modern) or left them cold; and Donne's 'death,' which, instead of putting the 'brief candle' out,

is but a groom,
Which brings a taper to the outward room,

would, though from the pen of a contemporary, have quite bewildered them. So sunset is, as Miss Spurgeon[22] has noted, a depressing sight to Shakespeare (or to the dramatist, I had rather say, for the purposes of expression); and that is because since the beginning of the world it had been, and was immemorially associated with notions of downfall or the end.

Even in larger matters a popular dramatist is not so original as he appears. Elizabethan art is notable for its freshness and freedom, but those qualities are owing to its being a native and natural development, like Gothic architecture. Like that it accords liberty to the artist, variety to the public, embracing both the beautiful and the grotesque, the sublime and the simple. Influenced by the classical models, it is, for the most part, either comedy or tragedy, both being, however (though with different proportions and emphasis), really tragicomedy, commingling also high life and low, the natural and the supernatural, verse and prose. The liberty has limits, is partial and more apparent than real. In both *genres* the motives recur, and the situations. In comedy it is intrigue or deception of various sorts, in the interest of a love affair or simply for its own sake; in tragedy it is intrigue or deception out of revenge, jealousy, or ambition. In both, without giving offense, artificial devices recur again and again, such as disguise and overhearing, feigning or slander. So do the characters, recognizably familiar despite the richness and variety of detail and originality in the treatment. In comedy it is two pairs of young lovers; in tragedy it is a nearly faultless hero and a double-dyed villain; in both, these roles as well as the others — character parts (male and female), ingénue, juvenile, fool or clown — are such as are provided for by repertory companies of that time and even of ours. 'Artificial,' 'trite,' or 'stereotyped' — the words apply only to the work of the second-rate Elizabethan dramatist. 'Traditional' and 'conventional,' on the other hand, not unfittingly apply even to

[22] Caroline Spurgeon, *Shakespeare's Imagery* (1935), p. 63.

that of the first-rate, who moved men more by thus keeping within the bounds of ordinary comprehension and sympathy.

What oft was thought, but ne'er so well express'd, —

although the arch romantic of our day says much the same as the pseudo-classicist, like him not speaking of the drama alone:

The old images, the old emotions, awakened again to overwhelming life, like the gods Heine tells of, by the belief and passion of some new soul, are the only masterpieces.[23]

Between masterpiece and consummate commonplace — witness Sophocles and Addison, witness even Yeats and Pope — there is often a hairsbreadth (a precious one) and no more.

Only within limits can the successful dramatist be original or ingenious, and he cannot be scientific. Hamlet, the hero of a play not only traditional and conventional — a popular Senecan tragedy of revenge — but also rewritten, is not to be explained by psychology, modern or Elizabethan. Even if Timothy Bright's *Treatise of Melancholie* (1586) had been perused by every pair of eyes in the audience, still it could not conceivably contain the key to Hamlet.[24] Of no character or play or poem worthy of the name can it be said that the key is in any book, or that a key is required. Art is expression, not secretion. In early drama or poetry statements or allusions, historical background or technical materials, may now require research to be understood; but a touch of nature, a stroke of art, does not. So with the ethics in *Othello*, *King Lear* and *Henry IV* — the study of Elizabethan treatises or chronicles does not warrant scholars in making out Iago and Falstaff, as professional soldiers, to be more justified in their conduct, and Lear, as king and father, to be less so, than they plainly are in the play. If, as Wordsworth declares, a poet does not write for poets alone but for men as such, a dramatist does not for psychologists or for antiquaries. If he does not write 'to please himself,' neither does he to please the intelligentsia, and still less, 'posterity' — that is a chimera of criticism! A dramatist ahead of his time would be a fish out of water, a speaker

<hr />

[23] W. B. Yeats, *Essays* (1924), p. 437 (by permission of the Macmillan Company).
[24] See 'Hamlet the Man,' below, p. 124, n. 3. This particular extraneous consideration has recently been again put forward, by Mr. J. D. Wilson.

without a hearer. For his traffic is in his hearers' emotions, or in the inverted emotion which is laughter, and it is only by way of their recollections, their experience, that either sort of response is secured. He should be more intelligent than his audience but intelligible to them; be blest with morals, manners, ideas, and an imagination finer than theirs but of a similar sort. And if his *Hamlet* has to wait till the nineteenth century to be comprehended or his *Prometheus Unbound* till the twentieth, that, then, is a different play or poem, not his own. So far as art is concerned, aftertimes can only explain more clearly and justify more adequately what was felt, rightly enough, at the time itself.

His story may be new, but then the treatment should not wholly be, and the sort of life presented, the customs and conduct, the very names of persons and places, still less so: 'unknown names,' says Coleridge,[25] 'are non-conductors, they stop all sympathy'; and it is to his advantage in rousing the emotions that instead of producing new stories he should refashion or refine the old. As Mrs. Woolf[26] says of the Greek dramatist, he 'naturally would choose one of those legends, like our Tristram and Iseult, which are known to every one in outline, so that a great fund of emotion is ready prepared, but can be stressed in a new place by each new poet.' Goethe, in his old age, repeatedly made an actual recommendation to this effect for poets yet to come, and his own practice had been in keeping. The greatest tragedies the world has seen have embodied familiar stories, and some of them, like *Hamlet* and *King Lear, Phèdre,* and the *Electra* of Sophocles or Euripides, were only new versions of what had been on the stage not long before. To the Greeks familiarity of fable was more necessary because, owing to the unities and the presentation of only the latter stage of the action, there would otherwise have been laid too great a burden of explanation and narrative upon a dialogue already much restricted by the singing and dancing chorus. So it was to the classical French, who also observed the unities and kept something of the chorus. And yet though the Elizabethans went in for more novelty than Aeschylus, Sophocles,

[25] J. W. Mackail, *Coleridge's Literary Criticism* (1931), p. 140. Even in his epic Milton observed the principle, and invented no names for his devils, like Shakespeare in *King Lear.*
[26] *The Common Reader* (1925), p. 42.

and Euripides, Corneille and Racine, they too used old stories in both tragedy and comedy; and if they did not in so many instances recast or rewrite plays early or recent, they are known to have done it in many and probably in more than is known. In this process, according to the precept of both Horace and Corneille and the practice of the dramatists themselves, they must be conservative, not audacious. The audience will be not moved but perplexed and vexed if, in its main features, situation or character be much changed. And that mistake Shakespeare was not the one to make in Lear or Hamlet by troubling either with a psychology, with vanity or irascibility for the motive in the one, a morbid turn or irresolute nature in the other.

Nowadays, to be sure, the audience coöperates less, however much it may be expected to do so. Dramatists seldom treat old stories or rewrite old plays, though when, like Alfieri, like Hauptmann or D'Annunzio, they do, they are more successful than when they don't. Determined to be original, they now invent their plots and frame their characters more independently; but, as I have elsewhere suggested, they must, as a result, content themselves to forgo some of the sympathy (or, in comedy, the antipathy) of the audience and fall back upon their curiosity. What will happen? is the question, or, still more momentous, what will the inner nature of the character turn out to be? Even then some coöperation is required; plot and character must not be too foreign or strange: but it is a coöperation more intellectual than emotional and often insufficient for dramatic effect. Shakespeare seldom or never depends upon curiosity, however excited, as Ibsen does in *Hedda Gabler*; Jonson, in his comedy, does not either, but keeps to simple and elemental interests like avarice and hypocrisy, which bring an immediate response. It is in characters like Sir Politick Would-be, creatures of ingenuity rather than of the imagination, that he fails: and though a rebel and an innovator, Jonson also is, in the larger sense as in the narrower, a traditionalist. In rationalizing and simplifying plot and character he is a classicist, a traditionalist by one remove. And for the effect of vividness and reality he depends on the imaginative method of trait and speech as much as his immediate predecessors and contemporaries.

CHAPTER IV

Hamlet the Man

Literature exists not only in expressing a thing; it equally
exists in the receiving of the thing expressed.

LASCELLES ABERCROMBIE, *Principles of Literary Criticism*

His purpose was to tell tales that any lackey could understand, in terms of poetry that would storm Olympus.

JOHN DRINKWATER, *Shakespeare*

Now with all the courage of humility, I say that this [our
Hamlet criticism] is, nine-tenths of it, rubbish. . . . Can
we suppose that it would have been a popular play had
it been a mystery, a problem, or anything like the psychological enigma that, etc.? . . . It is never a test of the
highest art that it is unintelligible. Do we, knowing
Shakespeare, suppose that he wrote the longest of his
plays to hide what he meant?

SIR ARTHUR QUILLER-COUCH, *Shakespeare's Workmanship*

I

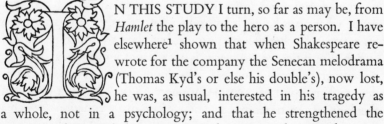N THIS STUDY I turn, so far as may be, from
Hamlet the play to the hero as a person. I have
elsewhere[1] shown that when Shakespeare re-
wrote for the company the Senecan melodrama
(Thomas Kyd's or else his double's), now lost,
he was, as usual, interested in his tragedy as
a whole, not in a psychology; and that he strengthened the
structure, sharpened the suspense, and in particular pitted against
the hero a King that was more nearly and worthily a match
for him. The difficulty was the hero's delay, which was unavoidable. The dramatist could not (if he would) much change the
popular old story: the capital deed must, as there and in all other

---

[1] *Art and Artifice in Shakespeare*; *Hamlet* (1919). In briefer form the present study
was delivered as a lecture at Wellesley.

great revenge plays, ancient or modern, come at the end. Therefore, like Kyd and Seneca, though more skillfully, Shakespeare motived this 'postponement of the catastrophe' by the hero's self-reproaches, not in the sense of grounding it in character, but of explaining it and bridging it over; by these reminders he makes the audience feel that the main business in hand is, though retarded, not lost to view. What indeed he (and the Ghost after him) charges himself with is 'forgetting' — that which at the outset he was bid 'remember' — a shortcoming which has no ethical or psychical significance, for that Hamlet does forget or is by nature so inclined does not appear. It is a superficial, a narrative explanation, not satisfactory even to the hero. Reproaching himself, he exhorts and, in effect exculpates himself — he cannot lay his finger on the fault, but he mends his ways; and pretty much everything in the old story is suppressed or subdued that would reflect upon him or put squarely before us the duty undone. No one else reproaches him or finds any fault with him; on the contrary everyone loves, honors, or fears him; and as Swinburne declared two generations ago, his words being still truer of drama than of life itself, 'a man whose natural temptation was to swerve, whose inborn inclination was to shrink and skulk aside from duty and action, would hardly be the first and last person to suspect his own weakness. . . .' Or if a recent development in him, all the more that would have had to be indicated clearly and by means of another observer. In his role of revenger he is kept aloof and reticent; he has no confederates, and (except Horatio, late in the story) no confidants; what plans he discloses or discusses are only to thwart those of his enemies; he cherishes his purpose, but plays a waiting game. This aloofness or reticence, however, is not meant for evasion, and he does not waver or deceive himself. His doubt that the Ghost may be a demon is, in point of doctrine, at one with the orthodox Protestant theology of the time, and in point of dramatic situation (which is more important) with the practice of Shakespeare elsewhere and of the ancients; his reason for sparing the King at prayer, that he may not send his soul to Heaven (or Elysium) is that of other revengers, psychologically above suspicion, in tragedy and epic, Greek, Senecan, or Renaissance; and if he were meant to be deceiving himself this must necessarily have been made clear, since there is no comment, by letting him again flinch or falter at such a juncture, as when he does find the King (he thinks) about an act that hath no relish of salvation in it, spying upon him. In short, as often elsewhere, the dramatist hedges and finesses. Or rather, for the big situation, like that in *Othello*, *King Lear*, and *Macbeth*, he boldly 'risks or even sacrifices,' in the words of Mr. Robert Bridges, 'the logical and consistent; and as such a flaw, if it were perceived, must ruin the interest, he is ready with abundant means to obscure the inconsistency.' That he does and more.

The difficulty is not only in the hero's delay but in his cruelty and his feigned madness. Accepting the Elizabethan, Senecan, and for that matter Homeric and Biblical principle of the vendetta as a duty, an eye for an eye and a tooth for a tooth, Shakespeare takes up with Hamlet's desire to send his uncle's soul to hell as the measure of his love for his father; and he makes the love apparent not only in his conduct but in his utterance. If it is cruel, it is like the love of Achilles (who mutilates Hector's body and refuses it burial) for his friend. And accepting the familiar and most popular feature of the old story, he takes up with the feigned madness as the theatrically effective (though psychologically improbable) cover for the hero's intrigue. But as the 'antic disposition' for three acts or more would, to his own finer taste and that of his audience, be in danger of growing tedious, he supplemented it, perhaps after the example of Marston, with a stage version of the Elizabethan 'humor' of melancholy. Himself deeply indebted to Kyd's *Hamlet* and *Spanish Tragedy*, Marston preceded Shakespeare's version with his *Antonio and Mellida*, *Antonio's Revenge* (1599), and *Malcontent* (probably 1600). Both his revengers are disguised; but in the last-named, a revenge-play with a cheerful ending, the madness and idiocy of Antonio are by such a 'humor' replaced. Malevole, the hero, impersonating like Hamlet and Antonio, is incisive, barbarous, and boisterous — 'extraordinary merry, yet extreme lumpish again in an instant'[2] — meditating on the abasing processes of Nature, dwelling on the corruption or affectation of humanity, and scorning or mimicking the specimens of it about him. Here, in the two roles — the designated revenger and the madman or Malcontent — merged in one, there was, for the cruder Elizabethan theater, a sufficient, though

---

[2] Robert Burton, *Anatomy of Melancholy* (1896), I, 447.

external, motivation — not only craft to match craft, blood to pay for blood, but also madness (or else 'melancholy') to warrant satirical audacity or impudence; and for a Shakespeare, letting his hero play madman and Malcontent both, there was, through his finer treatment, a dramatic value in the wider scope and freer vent thus given the hero when in company. It is a good thing on the stage to keep a secret and yet in a manner tell it; but it is a better, for a stricken and indignant soul, also to have his say concerning the world about him.

Yet in thus amplifying and enriching Kyd's lunacy Shakespeare was, I think, providing nothing that can be called a psychology[3] — no cause either for Hamlet's delay or for his 'almost savage irritability, on the one hand, and on the other, his self-absorption, his callousness, his insensibility to the fates of those whom he despises, and to the feelings even of those whom he loves.' In himself the hero is not melancholy in the technical, the medical Elizabethan sense, whether by nature or, before the second act, now in the play. There we see him take the 'humor' on as he tells Rosencrantz and Guildenstern his symptoms —

I have of late — but wherefore I know not — lost all my mirth . . .;

and the failure to distinguish the feigned role (though as we shall see, one not wholly alien) from the real, has been one of the chief sources of critical confusion. In the theater it caused and still causes no trouble. When playing a part, whether in disguise or not, a character on the Elizabethan stage undergoes, as Miss Bradbrook calls it,[4] a 'dissociation' of personality; and thus Marston's Antonio and Malevole, Tourneur's Vendice, like Shakespeare's Duke in *Measure for Measure*, do not altogether preserve their identity. Even

---

[3] Cf. Bradley, *Shakespearean Tragedy*, p. 124, who says that he was. — In T. Bright's Treatise (1586), as not in Burton's, indisposition to action is recognized as a symptom in a certain extreme form of the disease. Even if Hamlet suffered from it, and the audience of themselves knew it to be of this variety, and duly recalled the symptom, how strange a dramatic method, that he should wonder whether his seeing a ghost were not due to the devil's taking advantage of his weakness and his melancholy, but, when it comes to his procrastination, should say he 'does not know'! (See my *Shakespeare Studies*, p. 146, and above, p. 118.)

[4] *Elizabethan Tragedy* (1935), pp. 62, 67. 'In disguise,' Miss Bradbrook says, but she would surely admit that the feigning is the point.

in his feigning, however, except in his gloominess and freakishness, the Prince is no mere incarnation of the 'humor.' But — and this is the point — he is a recognizable specimen of the established stage-version of the 'humor' as the mask of a waiting revenger — like Marston's version, whether owing to his influence or not, the pessimistic mocking critic that he calls a 'Malcontent.'[5] His meditations on the processes and transformations of life and death, as in the graveyard, his indecency with women, his doggerel and snatches of old ballads allusively and derisively used, his jeering, mimicry, and gibberish, his abrupt enigmas, his agile and macabre misinterpretations of the words of others — these have, of course, nothing necessarily to do with the 'humor' of the physiologists.

2

How, then, has the dramatist dispensed with a psychology, yet, out of all this highly colored abundance, or indeed in spite of it, made a character? Mainly as other great dramatists, and even epic poets and the novelists, have done. Like the Greeks, like himself at his greatest, he has drawn 'the character in positive and simple outlines,' and despite the detail and many shifting aspects 'a clear and sharp and simple form remains' — Hamlet is noble and fearless, loving and generous, mettlesome and spirited, and, like a true romantic or epic hero, continually more than a match for his enemies with both weapon and wit. And like the Greeks and the great Frenchmen, though with more abundant means for the purpose at his disposal, the dramatist makes this effective, convincingly individual, by the arrangement and expression, by stroke or touch, not by science but by art. Motives grounded in character, logical or even psychological consistency, are not prerequisites to character-

---

[5] The above explanation does not depend on the date of 1600 for *The Malcontent*, as given above, which has lately been impugned, though (see my rejoinder, *Review of English Studies*, January 1935) I think it probable. Feliche, in *Antonio and Mellida* (1599), exhibits all the traits of the Malcontent but that of brooding on the transformations of corruption. Besides, the heroes of the *Spanish Tragedy*, the German *Hamlet* or the *Brudermord*, as well as of Quarto I, are all called melancholy; in the last two they mock and jeer at Corambis (Polonius) and Phantasmo (Osric); and it is only as a convenience that I use the word 'Malcontent.' By Shakespeare himself, as by other dramatists and in common parlance, it is used loosely, in the sense of a melancholy, discontented person; and in *Hamlet* it does not appear at all.

ization; and here, if ever, they must be dispensed with. 'Had Hamlet gone naturally and promptly to work,' says the first critic who noticed the want of them, the author of *Some Remarks on the Tragedy of Hamlet*, in 1736, 'there would have been an end of our play.' And Mr. Santayana (without knowing it) rescues me from ridicule for quoting that by (also without knowing it) saying the same — 'there would have been no occasion for four more acts and for so much heart-searching soliloquy.'[6] 'The simple truth is,' he says more particularly of the 'antic disposition,' 'that the play preëxists and imposes itself here on the poet. The given plot . . . must be accepted as a fundamental datum on which incidents and characters are alike built up.'[7] Of Garrick's alterations and omissions in Shakespeare's own version Tom Davies remembers that 'the audience did not approve what they barely endured'; and one cannot but share the opinion of Mr. Murry that in general 'the degree of Shakespeare's liberty to adjust his dramatic action to his imaginative need must have varied greatly according to the definiteness of popular expectation.'[8] Pretty definite that must here have been, and the dramatist's business was only to raise melodrama to the level of tragedy. He did so by making it, though without knowledge of them, after the fashion of Aeschylus, Sophocles, or Euripides, not less sensational but more imaginative and emotional, not less illogical but more plausible and harmonious; he took the situations for granted, but developed, intensified, even rearranged them; not explaining them, even making them, for intensity's sake, as by the shifting of the nunnery scene from the second act to the third, at some points into a less coherent story.[9] On the familiarity the dramatist, in his hasty opportunist way of working, at times depends. By the shift he leaves the hero without provocation for his disrespectful treatment of Polonius in Act II; and in the process of making the ambassadors the sort that the Prince would have had for comrades he neglects to show them up as accomplices (which in Belle-

---

[6] *Life and Letters*, June 1928, p. 25. Cf. my *Hamlet*, p. 5.

[7] This Mr. J. D. Wilson (*What Happens in Hamlet*, 1935, pp. 89–90) seems not to understand. It is, of course, not a matter of the audience being 'students of sources' nor of their 'recollecting details.' See Appendix, Note A, p. 417, and my articles there referred to.

[8] *Shakespeare*, p. 173.

[9] See Appendix, Note A, p. 418; and my *Hamlet*, pp. 32–34.

forest's story, Kyd's source, they are), deserving of death. (This last is probably altogether the result of haste and carelessness — the old play was scarcely so familiar as all that!) The motive for the antic disposition given in the seventeenth-century German *Hamlet*, the *Bestrafte Brudermord*, and probably in Kyd — to find an opportunity for revenge — and that for the delay — the King's being surrounded by guards — he did well to omit, on the sound principle that poor reasons are worse than none. But leaving out the lunacy itself — that he no more thought of doing or, indeed, wanted to do, than Aeschylus, Sophocles, or Euripides in the Orestes story. Hamlet without his madness — Cleopatra without her asp — Tell without his arrow and apple? But it is not merely that this would be an old story mangled, which the audience as well as the company would not have put up with, and Aristotle, Horace, and Corneille alike would have warranted him in judging they wouldn't; it would also be a play despoiled of what, as we have seen, and are still to see, is its chief opportunity for both dramatist and actor. The most, no doubt, Shakespeare was expected to do was to rewrite the lines. He did more than that — gave shape to the structure, sweep and rhythm to the movement — and by the changes in the arrangement of Quarto II (1604) as compared to Quarto I (1603), which, like the *Brudermord*, has more of Kyd's story and structure as well as his style and spirit in it, heightened the effect of climax and suspense; but thus he did not make it more consistent or, on second thoughts at least, more intelligible, and the greatest thing he did was to ennoble and rightly accentuate the situation, to breathe life into the speech of the agile, yet wooden puppets — into that of the hero, unpsychologically enough, a spirit alien to the undertaking.[10]

Despite its primitiveness and unreasonableness, the play thus lent itself to Shakespeare's favorite procedure. Like the later Lear, and like Othello and Macbeth, of whom there was no previous dramatic treatment, Hamlet is made superior to his conduct; as with them, 'the situation is fixed, and the character is, as it were, rushed into it,' the emotional contrast that arises being the central effect in the

---

[10] See my *Art and Artifice in Shakespeare*, Chap. V; *Hamlet*, Chap. III. On the matter of the comparative intelligibility and originality of Quartos I and II, and the original position of the nunnery scene, in II, ii, as in Quarto I, see Appendix below, Note A, p. 418, and articles there cited.

tragedy. So he is, through the ghostly behest or by way of his feigning, both vindictive and high-minded, active and reflective, ironical and pathetic, merry and melancholy, indecent and decorous, insolent and courteous, cruel and tender, both suspicious and crafty and also (as Claudius himself has noted) 'most generous and free from all contriving.' Here certainly are the makings of drama, however it be with the psychology. Not that the effects in the tragedies referred to are quite the same. But Ghost, villain, and Weird Sisters (in alliance with the Lady) perform analogous incentive functions, which, along with the feigning of the hero (or the slander and hypocrisy of the villain) both widen the hero's emotional range and lighten his responsibility; and thus his character, not the chief source of the action, appears mainly in his temper and attitude, his moods and sentiments, which require no analysis or fundamental motivation, but perfect, immediately perceptible expression. The role is double, or triple; when feigning, as we have seen, the Prince is almost a different person; and his vindictiveness is owing to the Senecan *atrocitas* as well as to the Ghost's command and the part he must play in the well-known and popular stage story.

This is both an advantage and (for us at least) a disadvantage. The dramatist must keep the game of ruthless intrigue and counter-intrigue, with the harsh treatment of Ophelia and the pitiless turning of the tables on Polonius, Rosencrantz, and Guildenstern, as familiar effective situations; to engage our sympathy for the hero he refines and ennobles his inner nature, but he does not and cannot nor in his own day even needed do much to justify these deeds. For in Belle-forest (however it was in Kyd) not only the ambassadors but also the counsellor and even (in a measure) the 'belle dame' were the King's tools. With Othello the dramatist is freer. The story being much less familiar, and not previously on the stage, his jealous cruelty can be credited to Iago's impenetrable arts and 'the unwritten law.' Hamlet, relatively, has had to be made much better than his conduct: though by his intellectual acuteness and alertness he is fitted for intrigue or the checkmating of it, he is not bloodthirsty or consumed with hatred or rancor. Both heroes, to be sure, are in an improbable plight, are, internally — for those who must peer and pry — not all of a piece. Yet (far more than the Hellenic or Gallic heroes) they are integral and unmistakable, vivid and enthralling, in their bearing and accents, in their words and ways. Each has an individuality if not a psychology (which is less a matter for the imagination), a shape or figure if not an anatomy, a voice if not a visage; and with this external but intimate, poetic and dramatic, rather than rational or scientific consistency we here particularly concern ourselves, as, for the most part, it is revealed directly in the lines. By means of these we 'hear and see' them, become 'aware' of them, are moved by them; and then if (as Mr. Eliot says we may not) we do not understand them, still, as Grillparzer, another poet and dramatist, has it, for the purposes of poetry and drama we do.

So far as mere plot is concerned the hero has doubtless been little changed. Hamlet the revenger is, as in Kyd, high-born and high-minded, crafty, ironical, and self-reproachful, blameless, in this world of the vendetta, except for the matter of tardiness in carrying out its mandate. He still meditates on justice and his own remissness, and (often in general terms) on suicide and the life after death. And Hamlet the Malcontent (amid his enemies, in Act II and after) is, as in Marston, vivacious and abrupt, witty and uncouth, sportively familiar and rude, somber and gruesomely merry. He still meditates, often again in general terms, on vanity and decay, hypocrisy and affectation. Even in Marston's hands[11] the two roles have elements in common, such as a brooding melancholy, and in particular a penetrating turn, itself perhaps developed from Kyd, which has no necessary connection with the Elizabethan 'humor'; but in Shakespeare's hands, as we shall see, the feigned role is made more congenial and plausible.

And what of the hero apart from the plot? He has, of course, been changed considerably. None of Shakespeare's protagonists is both so high-strung and so many-sided, so various in thought and nimble of tongue; by his feigned madness he later enlarges his scope, but even apart from that none is both so finely poetical and so mutably human. What makes him more popular than the others is somewhat his mere story — that of both pathos and heroism, of the world against him and him against the world — but mostly his personal charm — his flexibility and intimacy, the ardor of his affection and the fierceness of his hatred, the complexity of his

[11] For a fuller comparison see my article in *Modern Philology*, January 1906, pp. 289–302.

nature and the simplicity of his manner, the sincerity of his feeling in the complexity of his situation, his idealism and his pessimism, the rare quality of his melancholy, of his humor and wit. (The 'vaster and more vehement' passion and utterance of Lear and Othello, Macbeth and Antony, are farther from the sympathies of the ordinary public.) And what gives unity to this multiplicity is the penetrating quality mentioned. Here is a fine example, not of life imitated, but of a hint taken, a tradition consummated, the character not only residing in the speech but developing from that of another. As with Goethe the 'starting-point is the mental image,' and what was the germ in Kyd and Marston comes to full flower in Shakespeare; somewhat as the malicious chuckle of the Vice rings clearer in Richard III and Iago.[12] The penetrating quality, which in Kyd and Marston appeared mainly as cynical irony, is now nearly all-pervading. Below there are examples of the Marstonian incisive and gruesome misinterpretations, and in the graveyard Hamlet is Malevole ennobled and refined. But Hamlet's affections as well as his hatreds, his thoughts as well as his imagery, have a poignancy and vibrancy, an intimacy and vivacity, not elsewhere to be found together, that often attain the happiest expression in high seriousness mingled with grim mirth, in poetry seasoned with homely figure and racy colloquialism:

> To die; to sleep; —
> To sleep? Perchance to dream! *Ay, there's the rub!*
> The potent poison quite *o'er-crows* my spirit.

There may be no direct connection, but that sounds remarkably like Kyd, as in *The Spanish Tragedy* the hero mutters to himself:

> Hieronimo, 'tis time for thee to *trudge* [into the other world].
>
> III, xii, 6

3

And it is time for us to take our seats at the play, in the second scene.

> A little more than kin and less than kind,

---

[12] Émile Legouis and Louis Cazamian, *History of English Literature* (1927), I, 156.

the Prince's first speech, aside, as he stands in black at the King's formal audience; the next following, aloud,

> Not so, my lord; I am too much i' the sun,

— how exciting and arresting both are after what we have already heard of disturbances in the state and of the certainty that 'this spirit, dumb to us, will speak to him'! Elizabethans well knew that ghosts had their reasons for appearing, and what these were. Horatio, in his address to the specter, had spoken of two, the country's fate and a buried treasure, but — naturally enough as well as dramatically — *not* of another. For the spectators' interest, the hero himself must not now speak or appear to think of it. But he must be thinking, as he is; and he must speak already, as he is doing, with the unmistakable, unforgettable voice of Hamlet.

This has many notes and inflections; but it keeps ironical now, with a growing bitterness:

> Ay, madam, it is common . . .
> Seems, madam, nay, it is . . .
> 'Tis not alone my inky cloak, good mother. . . .

Perfunctorily, nonchalantly, comes his consent not to return to Wittenberg; but impetuously, spontaneously, after he is alone, his outburst of grief, disillusionment, and disgust:

> O that this too too solid flesh would melt. . . .

And whether in manner or matter, the whole speech is characteristic. His melancholy, which really is of no technical, 'humorous' sort, reaches beyond the death of his father and the frailty of his mother, and embraces life itself. But there is no languor or paralysis, no weakness or indifference, such as has been, not perceived, I take it, but inferred or presumed. There are, instead, exclamations and execrations, impatient interruptions and parentheses; and the reiteration is energetic and insistent:

> Fie on't! oh fie, fie! 'Tis an unweeded garden . . .

the hero showing no disposition to add, as the critics do for him, 'Why pull one weed?' With a like bitter emphasis is repeated the word *month*, and also the feminine pronoun, the parentheses coming in pell-mell:

> and yet, within a month —
> Let me not think on't — Frailty, thy name is woman! —
> A little month, or e'er those shoes were old
> With which she followed my poor father's body,
> Like Niobe, all tears — why she, even she —
> O God, a beast, that wants discourse of reason,
> Would have mourn'd longer — married with mine uncle.

And in his soliloquies this pointed or jagged, though deep and quivering, energy of style and rhythm prevails.

It is of *this* that Hamlet has been thinking; from Horatio and his friends now comes news of the Ghost, and it touches him off. Was ever utterance more energetic, eager, and alert, as well as affectionate and intimate? But it is Hamlet still, though now no longer aloof and despairing. The exclamations and interjections are somewhat replaced by questions, but these and the repetitions alike are signs of the same bitter, restless mental activity. The rhetorical devices are, to be sure, found in other and very different roles in Shakespeare, as well as in other dramatists, the repetitions particularly: there are those of personages so diverse as Rosalind and Cleopatra, Falstaff and Shallow, Othello and Brabantio, Shylock, Lear, Kent, and Gloster. For the devices of art are few; the combinations and applications of them, endless. Hamlet's questions, in general, are prompted by curiosity, irony, emotional excitement, or, as often with his friends alone, are, like his exclamations then, prompted also by his intimate, confiding, affectionate spirit, craving sympathy —

> Would I had met my dearest foe in heaven
> Ere I had ever seen that day, Horatio!

Here the questions are rather of the first sort, though breathless with wonder and filial love. And his repetitions? Bitter at first, like those quoted above or that to Horatio before the news is given —

> Thrift, thrift, Horatio! The funeral baked-meats
> Did coldly furnish forth the marriage tables —

they are now those of wonder and excitement too:

> Indeed, indeed, sirs. But this troubles me.
>
> .   .   .   .
>
> Very like, very like. Stay'd it long?

As often in Shakespeare, the rhythm itself half tells the tale.

Now this excitability has been explained as due to the hero's unbalanced character, his deranged nervous system, or else his Elizabethan 'melancholy' — now 'merry,' now 'lumpish'; but the only comment to guide the audience in that direction, the Queen's after Hamlet's outbreak at the funeral,[13] is too belated for the purpose, and at any rate has to do with the apparent madness which as yet the Prince has not assumed. That he should be unbalanced, neurotic, 'frustrated,' or already in himself a specimen of the Elizabethan 'humor' of melancholy taken on in Act II, is (quite apart from the contradiction) impossible. Shakespeare's romantic tragedy, like other great popular tragedy, presents human nature, not a doctrine of human nature; heroes, not weaklings, or psychopathic cases; and, above all, men as we know them, not curiosities of our contemporary or even the Elizabethan psychology or physiology. In himself Hamlet is no more a prey to 'melancholy' than he is (as thought by other recent scholars) to the 'deadly sin' of sloth; or than Lear, to that of wrath; or than Othello, to jealousy. How unexhilarating, unprofitable the conception! Better the psychology of the literary critics as applied to these poetic, tragic figures — better 'frustration'! — than the physiology of some recent American and German antiquaries![14] Psychologists themselves are to be found who think we should not expect in our dramas the technical psychology of the day,[15] and what would they think of the critics who discover the like in Hamlet and Oedipus? The author of *Mourning Becomes Electra*, we noticed in Chapter III, requires no knowledge of Freud, and claims to have been 'simply guided by an intuitive insight into human beings . . . that is as old as the Greek drama.' It is not a question whether the dramatist, or even whether the audience, had the requisite learning,

---

[13] V, i, 307–11.
[14] See Appendix, Note B, p. 419.
[15] A. R. Chandler, *Beauty and Human Nature* (1934), p. 328.

but whether learning of this bookish, pseudo-scientific sort lends itself to the purposes of the imagination. 'Shakespeare,' says one of these scholars (and, so far, with reason enough) 'possessed more than an uninformed layman's knowledge of the subject': a good play-wright knows plenty of things, we may be sure, that he does not put into his play. And what of the many uninformed laymen in the audience? But even if not uninformed, they would be as untouched by such a presentation as we are now. 'The Poet,' says Wordsworth (and it is still truer of the dramatist), 'writes under one restriction only, namely, the necessity of giving immediate pleasure to a human Being possessed of that information which may be expected from him, not as a lawyer, a physician, a mariner, an astronomer, or a natural philosopher, but as a Man.' 'The *poet*' — a score of years ago the deadly seven were similarly visited on Chaucer — and how much truer the words are of the playwright! At all events, in an Elizabethan tragedy or in any, it would be puzzling and baffling to present, without plainly making a point of the matter, a character, averse from action, as alert and energetic in speech; and rather un-dramatic and unenlivening to present a hero's excitement at the news of his beloved father's return from the grave as owing to a psychical or physical malady.[16] Of course he is excited — who that is half a man wouldn't be? Audiences at a tragedy even now are not — certainly then were not — expecting to sit in at a clinic; and 'humors' — not the merely technical ones, either — belong, as the actual motives, in comedy.

4

There are, however, three occasions when Hamlet's excitement expresses itself in so extravagant a fashion that it might, in the closet, seem to lend itself to such a pathological interpretation; that is, after the Ghost's appearance and disclosures, after the King's self-betrayal at the play, and (as we have noticed already) at the funeral. The first two outbursts are natural enough. The last, afterwards explained by the hero himself, to Horatio, as provoked by the 'bravery' of Laertes' grief, and to Laertes, not untruly, as arising out of his madness, is, very probably, owing to the melo-

---

[16] See above, Chap. III, pp. 118, 120.

dramatic situation in Kyd's version;[17] and, in any case, is so indecorous and bombastic, so incongruous with the finer traits of character which Shakespeare has given him, that psychologically it merits
no serious consideration. It is a striking stage-effect, this sudden
reappearance, before the King, of the banished Prince, jumping into
the grave, mimicking and mocking the chief mourner, who, though
he knows it not, is (after the King) his chief enemy, and threatening
him when he (naturally enough) retaliates. But it would be unseemly at anybody's funeral, and, with the blood of Ophelia's and
Laertes' father on his head, can on no psychological or merely
aesthetical grounds be defended. There is, to be sure, enough of
Hamlet there — his love for Ophelia, his scorn of affectation, his
now accumulated indignation against his uncle, his dauntlessness in
face of the danger that he anticipates and the audience does still more
— there is enough, I say, to make this outbreak, after the quiet
brooding in the churchyard, an irresistible theatrical sensation and
attraction. Furthermore, the sympathy of the audience, which for
Shakespeare is the main thing, is even here retained for Hamlet,
inasmuch as Laertes had been perfidiously plotting against him, and
has just now called curses down upon him, and there is reason for
still playing mad. Theatrically there has been no mistake. Indeed,
the rhythm of the dramatic movement requires at this moment such
a demonstration on the part of the hero — after that when the
Ghost first appears to him, that at the 'Murder of Gonzago,' and

---

[17] Compare the outbreak of Marston's Antonio when Pandulfo mourns over
Feliche's body:

> 'Slid, sir, ye lie! by the heart of grief, thou liest!
> I scorn'd that any wretched should survive,
> Outmounting me in that superlative, etc.

IV, ii, 77

In the play Marston is so generally under the influence of Kyd's *Hamlet* and of
The Spanish Tragedy, its pendant, that this seems indubitably an echo. See also
Shakespeare Allusion-Book, I, 272:

> Oft have I seene him leape into a Grave
> Suiting the person (which he us'd to have)
> Of a mad Lover, etc. —

On the Death of the famous Actor R. Burbadge (1618-19)

By Mr. Santayana the encounter is called a 'grotesque bout, . . . bit of old rodomontade left unexpunged'; by Professor Elton 'that barbarous business'; by Mr.
Dobrée (*Criterion*, January 1934, p. 327), the 'most sublime and moving moment in
the play.'

that in the Queen's bed-chamber; and a clash with Laertes, under the eyes of the King, is particularly exciting and acceptable in view of the treachery already planned. But some of the writing is rant, and the motive is not only external but specious.

That, however, one so high-strung as Hamlet from the outset appears to be, as well as so grief-stricken for his father's death and his mother's infidelity, who has heard of his father's spirit walking abroad, but who, amid his hopes and his misgivings, has had to wait all day and up to twelve at night to set eyes upon it — that such a one, after the shock of the vision and of the terrible disclosure and deadly behest, should, in meeting his friends and coping with their curiosity, experience something of a nervous, a (momentarily) 'hysterical' reaction, is only natural enough. There is nothing 'morbid' about it — especially since no one on the stage is disposed to think so. There is nothing morbid, is there? about Byron's and Hunt's shouting and laughing after the uncovering and cremation of Shelley's corpse at Viareggio,[18] an experience considerably less harrowing than this.

Nor is there about the revenger's jubilation upon the public betrayal of the King's guilt. All day, again, he has been waiting for the outcome of the experiment, nay, in a sense from the time of the Ghost's grim charge. For Hamlet's doubt that he may have seen the devil, natural and proper, as we have noticed, appears first, not, as has been asserted, at the end of Act II, but even when he hears the tale from Horatio — 'though *hell* itself should gape' — and when he himself adjures the specter,

> Angels and ministers of grace defend us!
> Be thou a spirit of health or *goblin damn'd*,
> Bring with thee airs from heaven or *blasts from hell*,
> Be thy intents *wicked* or charitable . . .

as well as in the immediately subsequent warnings of his friends.[19] And 'it is an *honest* ghost' he tells them after it is gone. In fact, so

---

[18] Cf. Professor Elton's *A Sheaf of Papers*, p. 23.
[19]   What if it tempt you toward the flood, my lord,
        Or to the dreadful summit of the cliff
        That beetles o'er his base into the sea,
        And there assume some other horrible form. . . . I, iv, 69f.
So James I, *Daemonologie* (1616, but first published 1579), III, ii (of the Devil's pur-

proper and natural is the doubt that for acceptance it is not dependent upon the current Protestant opinion that ghosts were devils, being the same that occurs to Odysseus or Orestes when he sees or hears a god.[20] Shared by his friends, it has not psychological or theological but merely human and dramatic import and value, deepening the mystery, heightening the excitement, as, despite their solicitous interference, the hero dauntlessly presses on; and only such value it has (since manifestly the devil may feign not only a shape but also a voice to 'damn me') now that the Ghost has spoken. It is not a pretext, invented and lugged in, but a dramatic *motif*, already in hand, not yet exhausted.

After the *Murder of Gonzago*, accordingly, with Horatio, the hero is, though similarly, still more demonstrative than after the sight of the Ghost, simply because of the long-continued accumulation of expectation and anxiety that must find 'release.' For days (or hours)[21] he has been brooding and doubting; and now it is a triumph (to compare it with lesser things) like that of a chemist with his experiment, or a mathematician with his problem, or rather a detective with his clue, hitting upon the solution. Eureka, he cries; and though the gentle reader may be aghast at his glee upon proving his uncle and stepfather a murderer, and himself the appointed avenger, the reader must again allow for the natural reaction as well as the *atrocitas* and the delight in intrigue of Senecan-Kydian tragedy.[22] The Prince is *not* in tail-coat and pantaloons, as both on the stage and off it he of late has been. When, moreover, Rosencrantz and Guildenstern and then Polonius enter, Hamlet's deportment is only part of the madness he is feigning — in fact, some of his extravagance with Horatio just before may be owing to that role, which he has been playing at the theatrical performance and cannot immediately lay altogether aside.

---

poses): 'The one is the tinsell of their life, by inducing them to such perrilous places,' etc. (Spalding). Compare also Brutus' question, 'Art thou some god, some angel, or some devil?' — *Julius Caesar*, IV, iii, 274.

[20] See Appendix, Note C.

[21] The time system, as usual, is flexible, 'for purposes of effect.' See below, p. 148.

[22] See above, p. 128, and below, p. 154, note. And for vindictive glee, *Antonio's Revenge*, V, ii, 47–49; 'Then will I dance and whirl about the air,' etc. Malevole is frisky often; and in anticipation of vengeance, see *Malcontent*, V, ii, 275–end.

5

In this second scene, then, where Hamlet first appears and where he receives the startling news, his deportment is only a fitting preparation for what follows. There is nothing to indicate that it is unnatural — it would be unnatural and unappealing if collected and cool; and if so excited at the mere word of the Ghost's appearance, it is bound to be more so after his disclosures. First impressions on the stage are momentous, and now, as afterwards, like Romeo and Othello, he is meant to call forth all our admiration and sympathy; which he would fail to do if his melancholy at the outset were not merely owing to what had befallen him. Neither now nor afterwards, by him or any one else, except in the way of madness, by those who know not that it is feigned, is a hint given of his being defective or diseased: if he were, how could he have become, as for three centuries he has been, the object of popular devotion? And if he were the embodiment of Elizabethan melancholy or of any other 'humor,' the fact must needs have been announced, with some of the symptoms, beforehand, as in introducing Shakespeare's Jaques, Marston's Malevole, or any of the 'humorous' figures of Jonson. That function, once there is need of it, is performed by the hero himself — as he alludes to the antic disposition he may put on, and as, later, he gives an account of his 'humor' to Rosencrantz and Guildenstern.

Later still, in the soliloquy at the end of the second act (ii, 630), that is, in his own person, he does mention his weakness and melancholy as a possible cause of his seeing the Ghost, the devil being 'potent with such spirits.' That conjecture, again, is natural, and it serves to justify his misgivings; the misgivings are natural, and they serve to motive the test of the King's guilt; a test of some sort is natural (if Hamlet is not really insane), this one being adopted because it was in the original tragedy: and even if the word 'melancholy' must be taken in a technical sense, such an incidental remark is not enough to make the 'humor' the center and motive of his character. The conjecture, not uncommon in such a situation on the Elizabethan stage,[23] is fairly inevitable after the exhibition of Ham-

---

[23] That is, when a ghost has appeared, as in *The White Devil*, III, iii; V, i ('beyond melancholy'); *The Duchess of Malfi*, V, ii; and is according to the doctrine in Burton, whether the ghost be the devil's work or not.

let's spiritual melancholy in the first act and his taking on the physiological in the second. As things turn out, moreover, neither that nor the devil either has anything 'to do with the case'; and certainly if the hero thinks of melancholy as the cause of the Ghost's appearance when it isn't, he himself should think of it as the cause of his procrastination if it is. Interpretation of the sort is like the critics' making out of Hamlet's 'from whose bourn no traveller returns' a proof of his ineptitude and irrelevance, or out of his remark that his uncle is no more like his father than he himself 'to Hercules' a proof that he is physically feeble. Who expects 'young Hamlet' to be a Hercules? or would like it if he pretended to be? or what traveler from that country ever really returned?[24]

By this circuitous or retroactive, this psychological method, foreign to the Elizabethan stage and not native even to ours, a method, indeed, of literary criticism rather than of dramatic practice, Hamlet's simplest and most casual remarks are turned against him and he cannot open his mouth without incriminating himself, whether he is lamenting Danish drunkenness in the 'dram of e'il' speech as he and Horatio await the Ghost, or praising his comrade's justice and independence of spirit — 'not passion's slave' — as they await the players. Even what the wild or the wicked say or do is made 'a reflection' upon the high-souled youth, and the moral is supposed to be pointed against him by means of an expert in perfidy and poison egging on a novice — 'that we would do,' quoth the adulterous regicide and fratricide, 'we should do when we would.'[25] If *there* is to be found the moral, why! is it not then in favor of procrastination? Not so say Tieck and Börne, all for psychology and efficiency, and boldly extolling the villain at the hero's expense. (It is the same pair that thought Hamlet had seduced Ophelia.) Coleridge, however, despite his sensitiveness on this particular subject and despite his psychological bias, was still too much of a moralist, yes, and of a dramatist and poet as well, to

[24] See Appendix, Note A, p. 418; my *Hamlet*, p. 35, for the phrase as a natural, and ancient, commonplace; also Catullus, iii, 11–12 (Douce); Seneca, *Herc. Fur.* 545, 715. And the reader will remember that six books before the end the hero of the *Aeneid* (vi, 425) crosses the '*inremeabilis* unda.'

[25] Contrast Wilson, *What Happens in Hamlet*, pp. 206–208, 263–65. — As if to forestall the comparison with Laertes the dramatist in Q 2, IV, iii, 140, lets him share in the project of poisoning, as not in Q 1.

interpret any of these speeches after such a fashion; and with that on 'the vicious mole — dram of e'il,' he sets a fine example by going no farther than to note Hamlet's tendency, certainly not discreditable, to reflectiveness and generalization.[26] In itself the speech has to do, not with a 'touch of evil that brings a noble character to ruin,' but with one little defect that spoils the Danish people's reputation. And in its connections it is not a doubly, but a simply, self-revealing speech, a natural and dramatic one. It fills in the interval that serves to keep the entrance of the Ghost from being too punctual — in this play, too *un*-procrastinating! — as if he had an appointment; it is suggested by the sounds off-stage — by the drinking to which Hamlet has already sarcastically alluded (I, iii, 175), and the carousing of the King whom he hates and mistrusts; it lends itself, by its irrelevance when the Ghost enters, to the effect of surprise. Indeed, the speech is more truly, though more directly, psychological than it is thought to be. At such a moment a person does not allude to defects in his own personal character any more than he does to the harrowing business in hand (which Hamlet, quite naturally, is, as Coleridge says, avoiding); but talks on about trivial or indifferent matters — of the customs hereabouts, and what is said of them elsewhere, or, as just before, of the weather or the hour, like the sentinels in scene i, or like Decius, Casca, and Cinna, outwardly engrossed in the question where the sun now rises, while Cassius and Brutus whisper conspiracy. And the 'not passion's slave' speech before the theatrical test of the King's guilt is an expression of the Prince's confidence in his friend's trustworthiness, of admiration for his equanimity, and of affectionate reliance upon him at this crisis, an expression which, though it may be an avowal of inferiority, is still less than the earlier self-reproaches intended to lower the speaker in our esteem. In fact, like many other features of the character and of the play, it seems to have been suggested by the reading of Euripides on the part of the classical Kyd, this one by Orestes' first speech, in a similar situation, in the *Electra*;[27] and like that, of course, it is not psychological but dramatic. What in the world would the critics have the hero say instead, to preserve with them his reputation?

[26] T. M. Raysor, *Coleridge's Shakespearean Criticism* (1936), I, 25, 39; II, 274–75.
[27] See my *Hamlet* (1919), appendix; and Davies, *Miscellanies* (1785), III, 92.

At bottom, however, the trouble with the method is simply this: the critics are not witnessing the play but reading it. Nay, they are rereading it, are poring and puzzling over it; and in the light of what they find or think they find in the soliloquy at the end of Act II they turn against the Prince what he incidentally says about the Danish national fault in Act I, scene iv, when as yet there has been no trace of a hint of any fault in him. That is not the way to read a play, still less see it. 'Dramatic speech should have,' says Mr. Auden in our day — and had not Shakespeare's that in his? — 'the same self-confessed, significant and undocumentary character as dramatic movement.' Even in Ibsen something would have to be said or done, by the speaker or one of his listeners, either at this time, to make us prick up our ears, or later to remind us.

6

In his next scene, on the platform, the youth's eagerness of interest and ardor of filial affection more fully appear, but in the same penetrating accents, of the same vibrant voice. He who has said,

> My father! methinks I see my father.
> (*Hor.* Oh, where, my lord?)
> *Ham.* In my mind's eye, Horatio;

who, when he learns his sire has actually been seen with the bodily eye, implores his friends,

> For God's love, let me hear,

and questions them so breathlessly: — surely he is the same that, after the first outburst, cries in the spirit's presence,

> I'll call thee Hamlet,
> King, father; royal Dane, O answer me!
> Let me not burst in ignorance. . . .
> .   .   .   .
> Say, why is this? Wherefore? What should we do?

The dauntless impetuosity of the wish —

> I would I had been there
> .   .   .   .   .
> Would the night were come —

reappears with no loss of vigor (despite his own fears and his friends' that the Ghost may be the devil) when carried out in action:

> It will not speak; then will I follow it

> . . . .

> It wafts me still.
> Go on, I'll follow thee. . . .

And at their endeavoring to hinder him there is the same familiar turn of speech and freakish inclination to far-flung jest in the midst of bitter grief or excitement as in

> A little more than kin and less than kind . . .

> Thrift, thrift, Horatio, —

now as he replies:

> I do not set my life *at a pin's* fee.

> Unhand me, gentlemen;
> By heaven, I'll make a *ghost* of him that lets me.

Othello, too, jests in the face of danger —

> Keep up your bright swords, for the dew will rust them.

> What drugs, what charms,
> What conjuration and what mighty magic —

but that is because he is *not* excited. And a hesitant weakling? — 'Unhand me . . . I say, away! . . . Go on, I'll follow thee' — such he is no more than when he kills the man behind the arras, boards the pirate, wrestles with Laertes in the grave, fights him, kills the King himself in presence of them all, and, though mortally wounded, wrests the cup from out of Horatio's hand.

After the ghost is gone, as at the only other febrile or 'morbid' and hysterical reaction worth considering — after the theatrical experiment — Hamlet's expression is perfectly consistent. Not only would one so high-strung experience after such tension such a relaxation, but his native disposition to familiarity and colloquialism, sportiveness and wild wit would now crave this freer play. 'Ay, thou poor ghost. . . . So, uncle, *there you are*! . . . *Ah, ha! boy* . . . art thou there, *truepenny*? . . . *this fellow* in the cellarage. . . . Well said, *old mole*! Canst work i' the earth so fast? . . . It is an honest ghost, *that let me tell you*.' Both the wording and the 'business' of the 'tables'[28] and of shifting ground as they swear, are, like the crafty *non sequiturs* and mystifications and the injunctions of secrecy in his report of the Ghost's disclosures, in similar familiar, demonstrative, and sprightly vein. Even his intimacy and affectionateness, as in his first conversation, reappear, despite his reticence. 'And now, good friends. . . . Once more remove, good friends. . . . So, gentlemen, with all my love I do commend me to you, and what so poor a man as Hamlet is, may do to express his love and friending to you. . . .' Also there is something of his previous reiteration when under excitement, though now more spasmodic and insistent, in

> Why, right, you are i' the right —
>
> I'm sorry they offend you, heartily;
> Yes, faith, heartily.
>
> Indeed, upon my sword, indeed . . .

and there are the same expletives, or others still more colloquial — 'faith,' 'by heaven,' 'fie,' 'Yes, by Saint Patrick, but there is,' and only bitterer execrations — 'O villain, villain, smiling, damnèd villain.' The Elizabethan audience — if not the modern reader, less attentive to speech and more so to psychical processes and

---

[28] The writing down of the horrible disclosure is, as Mr. Bradley has noted, like that by Titus Andronicus (IV, i, 102). Since this play is otherwise like the lost *Hamlet* as we know of it through not only Shakespeare but *The Spanish Tragedy* and the like, the device in both was probably derived from there. It is not a matter of psychological significance but of stage 'business,' to make the disclosure momentous, and here, in Shakespeare's version, one effectively colored by the hero's nervous excitement. The 'business' may have been suggested by 'from the table of my memory' nine lines above. To us it seems grotesquely self-conscious: really it is in keeping with the superficial motive of 'remembering'-'forgetting' and also the primitive self-descriptive technique. Even Othello similarly marks a similarly important moment:

> Look here, Iago.
> All my fond love thus I blow to heaven.
> 'Tis gone.

And later, to prove his heart is turned to stone, he strikes it 'and it hurts my hand.'

phenomena — would see him to be, for all his changes, the very same man. See it? they would hear it, as they should.

7

The lively lunacy that Hamlet now assumes is indispensable to the plot, not only because of its popularity, of which we know from the contemporary allusions, but because scarcely otherwise could the necessarily roundabout activity and free-spoken utterance be made acceptable. In Kyd, apparently, as in Belleforest before him, the hero, till near the end, had, except contrivances like his theatrical Mousetrap, nothing else to occupy him as he played his waiting, defensive game. That it is not, any more than the undertaking just mentioned, a subterfuge, a refuge in activity instead of the act itself, appears from the way it is announced to his friends at the close of the scene just discussed, in which the Ghost has broken silence. If a subterfuge it were, the procrastinator should, as Professor Lewis says, only drift into it, fall back upon it. To a spectator subterfuges must look like subterfuges, pretexts like pretexts, as hypocrites must look like hypocrites though in life they dare not:[29] they must do so more unmistakably than to a novel-reader. Unknown to us except in prison, to escape the hangman, feigned insanity nowadays is a subject for detection or diagnosis. But in Elizabethan story, concerned with motives indeed, yet not, as we have seen, with psychological causes, it demands no such treatment, if for no other reason, because of its familiarity as an artifice — witness David with the Philistines, Ulysses, Brutus the Elder — and on the Elizabethan stage, besides the old Hamlet, there had been Hieronimo, Antonio, and Titus Andronicus. Like that of all these, moreover, it is not real madness too, a heresy which, despite Quiller-Couch, has recently again raised its head. In the play nobody but Polonius and Ophelia adheres to it; after her soul-searching tête-à-tête with her son the Queen, like her husband before her, knows better. And actually there is no lunacy, real or pretended, in Hamlet with his friends or alone; if there were, without comment to right us, it would be bewildering. Company may make a man crazy, but here it doesn't; or it will not leave him sane, but here it does.

[29] Cf. 'Tartuffe, Falstaff, and the Optique du Théâtre,' below, and pp. 254ff.

The pretense, however, since the audience know it as such, does not look too much like one. In company the madman must really appear such. Yet it is well devised that the Prince's madness should be not far removed from his natural demeanor when in a state of excitement. This Marstonian Malcontent 'humor' of melancholy is only an exaggeration and distortion of his own grief and cynicism, his irony and penetrating wit. For all his cunning, 'mad Hamlet' is somewhat the sportive and familiar, scornful and bitter one we have known when in company from the outset, but with now the shutters half open, the inhibitions nearly off. One of his earliest repartees to Polonius —

> (Pol. Will you walk out of the air, my lord?)
> Ham. Into my grave?

is, in its incisiveness and subversiveness, like that, in the second scene, to the King's words about the clouds still hanging on him, —

> Not so, my lord; I am too much i' the sun;

and like those to the Queen, 'Ay, madam, it is common,' 'Seems, Madam! Nay, it is.' But it is still more like him who may be the original Malcontent:

> I once shall rise [in station].
> (Men. Thou rise?)
> Mal. Ay, at the resurrection.[30]

His repetitions now, as in 'Words, words, words,' 'Except my life, except my life, except my life,' 'Well, well, well,' are manifestations of a bent no longer restrained. And his importunate, detective-like questioning of Rosencrantz and Guildenstern about the cause of their coming and the players' reminds us, though prompted by a different spirit, of his of Horatio and the others about the Ghost.

At the first it is a pretense of madness for love. Availing himself of her repelling his advances and returning his letters, the hero appears to Ophelia in her chamber, with (as has long been recognized)

---

[30] *The Malcontent*, I, i, 320–22. This is much more characteristic of Marston than of Shakespeare, of Malevole than of Hamlet. Cf. *Malc.*, IV, i, 179: 'I'll make you both emperors' — 'Make us Christians, make us Christians'; II, iii, 170: 'God arrest thee' — 'At whose suit?' — 'At the devil's,' etc.

the conventional signs of lovesickness upon him, such as pallor, sighing, his stockings down, 'and everything about him' (quite as Rosalind would fain have it) 'demonstrating a careless desolation.'[31] And this impression is presently borne out by his conduct with Polonius as he harps upon his daughter, not to mention his talk with the lady herself in the nunnery scene and at the play-within-the-play. Manifestly that is all designed to throw both Counsellor and King off the track, and has no psychological significance. In his silent perusal of the maiden's face he does not, as has sometimes been said, search her soul and find it wanting; such a procedure, with not even an indication of the pointless purpose or meaningless result (or for that matter, with it), would make neither drama nor sense. If he had not sounded her character before, what likelihood, in such a garb and with such deportment, of doing it now? The announcement, after the ghostly mandate, of his intention to 'put an antic disposition on'; Polonius' previous injunction to keep aloof from Hamlet, which Ophelia has promised to obey; her tale of his visit, her description of his appearance, and Polonius' and Ophelia's agreement about the cause of it; Hamlet's abrupt broaching of the subject of his daughter when next he meets the wiseacre — these incidents and circumstances so hang together that the most inattentive audience could scarcely miss the point, the point intended. And the effect of the deception, obviously, is not tragic. Genuine madness, however sympathetically treated, has, on the Elizabethan stage, momentary comic effects, as when King Lear is in company with the Fool; for Elizabethan art is Gothic, commingling tragic and comic, comic and pathetic. · Madness pretended, moreover, like the *motif* of deception in general, which from of old has been supposed to be-

---

[31] *As You Like It*, III, ii, 391f. With Rosalind it is 'a lean cheek . . . a blue eye and sunken,' but 'pale' comes to the same thing in view of what Burton says of the symptoms of Love-Melancholy (*Anatomy*, III, ii, 3, 1), 'paleness, leanness . . . hollow ey'd'; and what Shakespeare himself, of lovers' paleness and sighing, 'the lover sighing like furnace,' etc. See Bartlett, as well as Ovid, *Ars Am.* i, 729–34. Mr. Wilson and Mr. Adams think Hamlet's madness is not for love, is therefore not designed for Ophelia in particular; but what they miss in Rosalind's account — unbraced, hatless, and stockings down to his ankles — is there pretty well provided: 'Your hose ungartered, your bonnet unbanded, your sleeve unbuttoned, your shoe untied.' Cf. 'without a hatband' in *The Knight of the Burning Pestle*, II, viii, as a sign of melancholy. 'Ungartered' is a common sign of melancholy in Elizabethan writing.

long to comedy, is in itself not tragic or pathetic either. One of the reasons every actor aspires to the Danish role is that it is not either tragic, pathetic, or comic but, successively or together, all of these; and in the second and third acts the Prince, when in company, is nearly as often grimly comic as tragic. About the fooling of Polonius there can be no question; but the misleading of Ophelia is not entirely different. As in her report she makes comment, she is not what can be called pathetic; nor is the impression we there get of the Prince himself. His bare bosom and legs, his knees knocking together, his look as if loosèd out of hell, his silence and backward exit — these things do not in the circumstances, and (what is as important) certainly not by phrasing or rhythm, move the sounder and sturdier among us to tears.[32] Nor were they meant to. Hamlet, we know, is not mad, as Juliet lamented by the Capulet household is not dead, and as Ferdinand's father full fathom five does not lie; and sympathy is not to be wasted on any of the persons made to think so. And yet, described by Ophelia, this demeanor must, of course, not move us contrariwise, either, as it certainly would have moved the Elizabethans, and most playgoers at any time, if visibly presented on the boards. The dramatist has shown his tact.

Moreover, this deception is undertaken with little or no delay. Mr. Bradley's idea that for two months the hero 'has done absolutely nothing . . . during this long period sunk for the most part in bestial oblivion or fruitless broodings, and falling deeper and deeper into the slough of despond,' is owing to Ophelia's much later remark, just before the dumb show, ''tis twice two months, my lord'; as well as to the circumstances that at the beginning of Act II Polonius is already sending his truly parental remittance (with advice attached) to Laertes in Paris, seeking meanwhile information about his conduct, and that the King, when Polonius reports to him, is already so alarmed as to have summoned Rosencrantz and Guildenstern, who

---

[32] 'Unbearably poignant,' Wilson (*What Happens*, p. 112). The critic also thinks the hero is not 'play-acting'; and if he isn't, though the dramatist makes it so plain that he is, why, then, for all we know, he may really be so crazy or so senseless as 'instinctively to turn' — in such a fashion and such array — 'for support to the only being who might give it him'! I do not wonder much that 'she fails'; though, since the Prince tells nothing and asks nothing, I do not well see what she could have been expected to do. Could the audience have seen that any better, or the need for it in the first place?

presently appear. This, however, is only an example of that free treatment of time, place, or details of circumstance and incident, 'in terms of effect' (as Mr. Granville-Barker has it), frequently to be found in Shakespeare and other Elizabethan drama (at the end of this same act, for instance, discussed below), a treatment which is the result of an epical breadth of character and incident crowded into the narrow dramatic mold. Otherwise (as for dramatic interest we should) we receive the impression that Hamlet has gone almost immediately to work at his deception; as a matter of fact, in the continuous performance, the business of the remittance and information-seeking serves little other purpose than to allow him time to have made the deceptive visit. And Ophelia's remark is like other casual ones in Shakespeare, such as Lady Macbeth's about her children, or as the 'traveller' to the undiscovered country not returning, or as the contradictory details concerning Horatio and Cassio, which are the result sometimes of carelessness, sometimes of concern only for the requirements of the moment. Time-references such as these, like those of the Gravedigger, from which scholars, unlike the audience, have hard-headedly reckoned up for 'young Hamlet' (and, ergo! for Fortinbras too) the age of thirty,[33] are not to be taken so seriously; indeed, in their contradictoriness, they cannot be, especially one so belated as Ophelia's, so far removed from the place in the action where it is being applied. The point, then, is, there is no evidence that the antic disposition arises out of any disappointment, either before the visit to her chanber or as a result of it; or that for such a cause, or any other, there has been such an interval of inaction and brooding as would make the hero really deserving of the reproaches he is presently to heap upon himself, or would suggest to us or actually produce in him a state of melancholy and freakishness approaching to that which he now assumes.

Such an interval before putting on the antic disposition would be

---

[33] My Hamlet (1919), p. 66. Cf. Lady Capulet, at fourteen mother of Juliet, who is fourteen, and yet speaking of her 'old age' at the end. See Granville-Barker, Prefaces to Shakespeare, Second Series, p. 41. At the theater such time-references were not — still are not — noted in their implications or in their connections with one another. Cf. Shakespeare-Jahrbuch (1921), pp. 101–102, and (1924), pp. 185–86, to the same effect, and on the conventional use of thirty, as in the 'Murder of Gonzago.' Cf. also above, Chap. I, p.16. As Professor Keller observes, both Hamlet and Fortinbras are manifestly youthful, no thirty-year-olds.

of importance to the psychological interpretation of it; but then the
announcement of his intention immediately after the Ghost's mandate must still be attributed, as by Mr. Bradley, to a 'forefeeling of
his need.' Good critics who believe in the need find some difficulty,
naturally enough, in the forefeeling. With the interval or without
it, how frail and feeble and spiritually decrepit our Prince must be
if the command to avenge his father, whom he loves, on his uncle,
whom he has suspected and detests, together with disappointment
in his mother, and in his sweetheart who has jilted him, can drive
him headlong into feigned madness — and immediate preparations
for it — in order, as has been thought, to escape the real! Whether
as subjective behavior or the objective, which the dramatist actually
deals in, does the situation correspond to anything we know of in
either? Who ever feigned madness for such a purpose, or so instantaneously anticipated the 'need'? The psychology is as specious
and sophistical as that presumed in Othello, distrusting because he
trusts.[34] Even if Hamlet in conduct, reputation, or manner of utterance made an impression upon me more in keeping with conscious
frailty, still, I must confess, the situation would be to me pretty incomprehensible; and for a hero in high tragedy, whether Elizabethan or modern, quite unimaginable. If there is to be psychology
in Shakespeare we have the right to demand that it shall in itself be
worthier of credence.

When it becomes more credible, it retreats appreciably from the
text. Mr. Clutton Brock's psychoanalytic study of Hamlet, which
was acclaimed in England twenty years ago, is a sufficient example.
Here is no feigning or 'forgetting,' and no Elizabethan melancholy
either. The shock of the Ghost's disclosures makes a wound in the
hero's mind and the more he tries to force himself into action the
more his unconscious self invents pretexts for delay. So the incentive becomes a deterrent, somewhat as Othello's trust becomes
distrust; but things are changed accordingly. He *misexpresses* himself, in action and in talk. The play itself is not a conflict of persons
but a conflict within the mind of Hamlet, the tragedy not one of
revenge but of irrelevance, 'the dramatisation of a disordered mind.'
He is busy eluding his thoughts and purposes, not the pitfalls of his
enemies. And to this and the similar but less coherent interpreta-

[34] See my *Art and Artifice*, pp. 14–16.

tions since, it is not thought sufficient to answer that no audience Elizabethan or modern could have so understood the play, or even (what is still more important) that it runs counter to the dramatist's manifest intention. *He* too was a prey to the unconscious and builded better than he knew. Yet as Sainte-Beuve said long before Clutton Brock, Bradley, and their present-day successors, though 'one may see in a work something other than what the author saw . . . what he put there unconsciously,' that is quite different from finding what he himself wouldn't have understood when brought to his notice.[35]

The ideas, the conceptions, the technique must be, if not quite that of his time, his own. As Mr. Walkley said, also before Clutton Brock but after the Frenchman, 'a dramatist's personage is a mere function of the dramatist, and can utter nothing, think nothing, be nothing outside the dramatist's own nature and mental vision.' What can be discovered (instead of invented) by the critic is not in the matter but the manner, not new truths but new or improved strokes of art, or, more particularly, the reasons for these, which to the dramatist himself were partly traditional, partly instinctive. Or if aspects of character or human experience were depicted that had not been before, they were not reserved for us alone. It is as with a good artist even today. Critics or other artists may appreciate beauties, artistic effects and their causes, that he himself may not until brought to his notice; and in Shakespeare there are more of these simply because he was as an artist much greater, richer, and more impetuous, more instinctive and traditional, less conscious and critical.

8

For the critics the feigning is the chief stumbling-block. Those who do not turn it into something subconscious make of it 'self-consciousness' or 'attitudinizing,' just as they turn Kyd and Shakespeare's rant at the funeral into a 'staginess' of the hero's own. In the technique they would see nothing but character, as in the incidents themselves. Yet whether in the Shakespearean or the earlier version, the feigning was, for both player and spectator, undoubtedly one of the chief attractions of the role; and despite changes in

[35] *Causeries*, 3rd ed., xiii, pp. 257–58.

taste and the obscurities in the witty allusions, it still is. It is involved
in an action that is really dramatic: the King and his satellites are
endeavoring to pluck out the heart of the Prince's mystery, and he
is baffling them or plucking out theirs. And it is dramatic in itself,
with its striking contrasts and its startling changes. As we have seen,
it both enlarges his scope and also lightens his responsibility in the
eyes of the people on the stage and (by the convention) even of the
audience. He can be freakish and frisky, indecent and impudent,
mocking and insulting, sarcastic and cruel, without making us forget
that he is a noble soul and a gentleman. Feigning is one of the artificial devices of ancient and Elizabethan story-telling and drama,
like disguise and mistaken identity, slander and fatal instigation; and
when, like Hamlet's but unlike Iago's, provided with a morally
justifiable motive, it in a small way does to the character engaged in
it what villainous influence in *Othello* or the supernatural in the
present tragedy and *Macbeth* does to the object of it — relieves him
of the consequences of his conduct. But it is as the feigning is the
extension and exaggeration or else the pointed contradiction of the
character's native traits that it is most effective; and it is only by
superlative mastery of speech that this dramatic effect of continuity
and therefore of contrast becomes apparent. Not that it always is
apparent. The Prince's treatment of Polonius grates upon us: he is
old, is the father of Ophelia, and, in the text as we now have it,[36]
has given little or no cause for offense. The mimicry and mockery
of him is, no doubt, like that of Laertes and (near the end) of Osric,
somewhat owing to the original play or to the requirements of the
Malcontent's professional role of critic and censor. But the antic
disposition is a great success in the Presence, and in the nunnery
scene, and particularly in the second act, when brought to bear upon
Rosencrantz and Guildenstern or the Players. There Hamlet the
gentleman and 'good fellow' is only, as it were, in disguise; and
never before or since was there so many-sided and convincing a
combination of colloquialism and (though in prose) of poetry —
of friendliness both hearty and forced, of curiosity and suspicion,
frankness and craftiness, intimacy and dignity, courteous address
and penetrating irrelevance, liveliness and melancholy, sallies of wit

[36] See below, Appendix, Note A, p. 418, for the original position of the nunnery
scene.

and flights of somber imagination. One moment it is, 'And yet to me what is this quintessence of dust?' The next, 'Welcome, good friends. O, my old friend! Thy face is valanc'd since I saw thee last; com'st thou to beard me in Denmark?' The next, it is the mirth and the melancholy, the colloquialism and the poetry, flung, in the Malcontent's incisive fashion, together. The news is, says Rosencrantz, 'the world's grown honest.'

Then is dóomsday near. But your néws is nòt trúe.

'Denmark's a prison,' says the Prince. 'Your ambition makes it one,' replies the Courtier; ' 'Tis too narrow for your mind.'

O God, I could be boúnded in a nútshell and count myself a king of infinite spáce, were it nót that I háve bàd dreáms.

And by the rhythm, the phrasing and the accents, the role holds together. 'What a piece of work is a man!' cries the Prince. What a piece of work is this one on the stage!

9

In the third soliloquy, 'O, what a rogue,' at the close of Act II, the fantastic and extravagant style of thought and expression is, of course, at once thrown aside; and this is the Hamlet of Act I. 'Now I am alone!' he cries out in relief. It is the same restless energy of rhythm and incisiveness of phrasing, the same scorn and indignation, though much of this now is, because of his dilatoriness, heaped upon himself. The energy, indeed, is heightened: accumulated under long constraint, it at last explodes. For parentheses he is at present too impatient; and to point his rage and contempt he frequently, as not before, cuts his lines short:

> For Hecuba.
> Yet I,
> Ha!
> O, vengeance!
> A scullion!

Of such sort is the psychology that is offered by Shakespeare, and was of him expected — speech fitted to mood and occasion. But to be really that, the speech must still be, as it is, characteristic — interrogations and interjections, exclamations and execrations, spiced with an unelevated vocabulary (certainly not the *style noble*), like 'muddy-mettled rascal,' 'peak like John-a-dreams,' 'breaks my pate across, tweaks me by the nose,' 'ass,' 'whore,' 'drab,' 'scullion.' The Prince even keeps his 'fie' and 'foh.'

The soliloquy has been thought to be special and particular evidence for Hamlet's frailty and self-deception: he rages impotently, he turns from self-abuse to — a play as 'the thing'! But he is only overwrought, as one who has had no vent for his feelings the whole act through; and the notion that the Ghost may be the devil is no pretext. The charges of cowardice and mouthing that he brings against himself he immediately brushes aside. Unlike the title of 'villain' coolly or humorously taken to themselves by Richard and Iago, 'rogue,' 'rascal,' and 'ass' do not — manifestly do not — fit. Unlike other Shakespearean confessions (or warranted self-reproaches) in soliloquy, none of these is confirmed but all are contradicted by the comments of the other characters or by the hero's confidences imparted to them. Unlike the charge of villainy, this of inaction is a negative matter, which on the stage, preferred by the man himself, and not complacently either, but in the spirit of self-laceration, scarcely counts. Moreover, in his clear-seeing judgment, Hamlet is, presently, himself satisfied with the immediate undertaking. In the next soliloquy, while that pends, 'To be or not to be,' there are no more self-reproaches; in the next two after it is over,

'Tis now the very witching time of night,[37]

and

Now might I do it pat, now he is praying,
And now I'll do't . . .

there are none either, but only concern for the success of the action in hand. He spares the King, indeed, but because he would kill more than the body of him who had 'taken his father grossly, full of bread, with all his crimes broad blown, as flush as May': an excellent and

[37] Certainly modeled, in its melodramatic gruesomeness, upon the original. Cf. *Antonio's Revenge*, III, i, 184:
    Now barks the wolf against the full-cheek'd moon, etc.

appropriate reason, in not only Elizabethan but other Renaissance and ancient tragedy, as it would have been in Homer.[38] And in the last soliloquy,

> How all occasions do inform against me!

after he has kept his word (though mistaken his man) in killing at the proper unholy moment, he is only troubled, and puzzled, on finding that 'this thing' is yet to do, though still certain he will do it:

> O, from this time forth,
> My thoughts be bloody, or be nothing worth.

Again he is as good as his word.

In the dramatist's own time, that is to say. The Prince, at this later moment, is under guard, on his way to England; but Rosencrantz and Guildenstern, as well as the pirates, are not to find him indecisive or tardy. And on his return, in the few hours left to him, there are both no opportunities neglected and also no expressions of regret. Only one occasion is fairly and openly offered Hamlet to kill the King; and then, for not doing so, he has not merely the valid reason of the *vendetta* to the uttermost, but also, as Mr. Bradley notices, a reason unmentioned, though potent with the audience — that the man is defenseless, at prayer. Only a critic would here cry out for Claudius's blood; and a critic, too, who forgets the dramatic requirement, in such matters, of repetition. Twice Coriolanus swallows his pride to beg the people's favor, and twice he belches it up again. But at the next chance at his man (as he thinks it) Hamlet kills him, and there again (as Mr. Bradley also notices, though taking

---

[38] See above, p. 122. Also my *Hamlet* (1919), pp. 51–54; *Art and Artifice*, p. 102, note; and, independently, Oliver Elton, *A Sheaf of Papers*, p. 20. Sending the soul of the slayer of one's beloved to hell is only the Christian equivalent to the pagan's mutilating the body and refusing it burial, as Achilles does to that of Hector and Orestes and Electra to that of Aegisthus. In all three such revenge is the measure of the hero's or heroine's love and makes for a bigger situation. For Orestes and his sister have, unlike Achilles (though Hector had intended the offense), the same provocation and duty as Hamlet: the slayer had done similar harm to the soul or shade of the beloved (Aesch. *Choeph.* 439; Soph. *El.* 444–46, 1488–90, 1504; Eur. *El.* 288–90, 323). No 'hire and salary for them'! In story and drama motives persevere after they have died out in decent society; yet so late as 1428, by the decree of the Council of Constance, duly executed by the Bishop of Lincoln, united Christendom did its best (or worst) to prevent the eventual resurrection of Wiclif.

this, as on the previous occasion, for a minor consideration) the audience would be with him.

There is delay, and the hero twice reproaches himself for it; but there is no weakness in him, no vacillation or serious procrastination, and yet that does not mean that the author himself is merely 'spinning out his plot.' Of *Hamlet* that is no more to be said than (though it has been) of the *Oedipus Tyrannus*, *Othello*, and Jonson's *Volpone*. Oedipus, as I show in the second following chapter, has, in not seeing the truth sooner, been, like Othello, taken for a fool. What else, then, is Claudius himself in the present tragedy, if not in being so slow to suspect the cause of Hamlet's madness, yet in setting on others (not in his confidence) to discover it, such as Polonius, Rosencrantz and Guildenstern, and especially the Queen? Better not discovered, at second hand! And if at the theatrical entertainment he is clever enough, but grits his teeth and braces himself, what of the whole Court there that never takes the hint? What of the Queen both there and in the closet scene? In every story there must be an obstacle, and in many of the greatest — consider the best of Richardson or of Meredith, and even the *Iliad* and the *Odyssey* —[39] it is here or there rather arbitrary or improbable. There is no more psychology, or even simple motivation, underlying the lack of effect on the Court[40] than there is, for that matter, in the expectation of any effect upon the criminal in the first place; that after this fashion murder will out is only an old story-telling *motif*; and the justification for this detective device, as for that of Claudius just mentioned, is that it was in the original play and had proved its theatrical, histrionic value. The Ghost, moreover, must, once doubted, be proved true or false, real or unreal, and how else could that be done so summarily and strikingly (as it should be) on the stage? The Mousetrap could no more be left out than the antic disposition — than the Ghost at the beginning or the fencing-match at the end — without mangling the familiar story, killing the popular play.

[39] Cf. above, 'Reconciliation,' p. 66; and on the matter of keeping the principal heroes alive, and Achilles and Hector apart, until near the end, Ovid, *Met.* xii, 76–77; *Art and Artifice in Shakespeare*, pp. 103–104.

[40] Mr. Wilson, to be sure (Appendix, below, Note A, p. 418) has motived the Court's obtuseness, by recasting the scene. See the passage from 'Sophocles the Dramatist,' below, p. 160.

Unlike these features the delay is not an attraction in itself: it is the price paid — by the original dramatist — for these and others. Two of his most telling situations were the Ghost revealing the murder and demanding revenge upon his brother and successor near the beginning, and the fulfillment of it, by ironically turning the fratricide's own weapons against him, at the end; and the delay thus involved was no doubt even then motived, or taken account of, not only by questionings concerning the authenticity of the information[41] but also by reproaches or self-reproaches, as both in the later *Spanish Tragedy* and in the revenge tragedies of Aeschylus, Sophocles, Euripides, and Seneca. In Belleforest the madness and the delay together are motived by a desire not only for such exact and ironical justice but also for a studied and cunning revenge, a *bella vendetta*, 'to be on earth for ever memorable,' as well as by considerations of caution and prudence, though prompted mainly by fear of failure in the undertaking.[42] In *The Spanish Tragedy*, the *Brudermord*, *Antonio's Revenge*, and *Titus Andronicus*, these motives reappear, but even for Kyd are too calculating or ignobly emotional to have been wholly depended upon; and (though in the later play there is something of the effect retained, as in Hamlet's hoisting the enginer with his own petard and Horatio's 'fallen on the inventors' heads') they are still more so for Shakespeare. In the *Brudermord* the difficulty lies, quite definitely, in catching the King alone.

All these motives Shakespeare slights or omits, keeping only the reason for sparing the king at prayer (that in the *Brudermord* being still more compelling because the German Hamlet's father is not in a papistical Purgatory but a Wittenberg Hell). To the sophisticated the delay seems to demand some psychological motive — seems necessarily to imply a defect or incapacity in the hero. Against this interpretation Shakespeare has guarded, but only to invite it. The hero canvasses the reasons, but in 'O what a rogue' as well as in 'How all occasions' says 'I do not know'; and that (if we do not distinguish popular Elizabethan art from the contemporary high-

---

[41] See Appendix, Note C, pp. 419–20.

[42] *Histoires* (1576), pp. 209, 210, 225, 227, 236, 257 (by the murderer's own sword). — *Spanish Tragedy*, III, xiii, 21, 'not as the vulgar wits of men,' etc. Andronicus (IV, ii) cries 'beware' like Hieronimo and makes a note of the matter like Hamlet.

brow variety) throws some of us back upon a subconscious mystery. A mystery it is, but of a simpler sort.

As with the ancient noble heroes like Orestes, and vigorous hero-villains like the Senecan Atreus, Medea, and Clytaemnestra,[43] the reproaches and self-reproaches for inaction serve not only as re-minders to the audience that the undertaking has not been forgotten but as indications of (what in a tragedy is indispensable) its momen-tous and formidable nature. They belong to the narrative, emotional method that in all the masterpieces of drama we are discussing pre-vails, and, appearing so prominently in *The Spanish Tragedy*, where there was less need of them, must have figured in its predecessor. The mere omission of the motives could not affect an audience, however familiar with the original, in the theater, where in general the negative does not count, and particularly since the self-re-proaches are no innovation. These may, as in the present tragedy, point to a fault. But so far as is indicated Hamlet is not otherwise chargeable with dilatoriness or any other shortcoming, and at his delay in the present juncture who can wonder? In itself, indeed, the fault — 'si *mora* pro culpa est,' as Ovid has it — is not a 'tragic' one. Three separate times (ll. 169–72, 305, 319, 1155) Sophocles' Electra bitterly complains of her brother's dilatoriness — promising to come and never coming — but when he appears he is reproached by neither her nor himself and is, as expected, all resolution and promp-titude. He too 'forgets' — 'all that he has suffered and heard' (ll. 167–68); but for the *hamartia*, when really provided, the an-cients and the Elizabethans alike demanded something more sizable and imposing. Something deeper-rooted too. That the trait of pro-crastination, together with the particular form of Elizabethan 'melancholy' supposed by some to have caused it, is for tragedy insufficient, is apparent, if from nothing else, from the fact that after this last soliloquy it disappears.[44] So does his melancholy in our sense of the word, his pessimism and desire for death. It all is cured, as some of the psychological critics admit, by time and change, by a trip to England! What now, for dramatic purposes, is to be made of a 'tragic fault' that is, even as Claudius pretends

[43] My *Hamlet* (1919), pp. 17–19. Cf. also *Thyestes*, 179, 'questibus vanis agis,' 'unpack my heart with words' (Miss Spens).

[44] Wilson, *What Happens*, p. 267.

to expect of the mental distemper,[45] cured by an outing, and before Act V?

'Frustration' is the up-to-date diagnosis for the psychical disease. That, by hypothesis, would be deeper-rooted and more sizable, however little imposing; only, it does not apply. Neither Hamlet nor any one else is aware of his own futility, and it would take an audience of extraordinary perspicacity (beyond the hero's own, as we shall see) to detect the failing, where at least it should come to light, in the final scene.

10

In every story there is an obstacle, the fundamental one here being (as not only in other revenge tragedies but in most notable stories of any sort, such as the *Iliad*, the *Odyssey*, and *Othello*) the necessity that the principal incident — 'decimum dilatus in annum Hector erat' — should come near the end. Now since this necessity must not be apparent, another obstacle must be provided which may be; and when that, like delay, is negative, there must be overt references to it, explanations or self-reproaches. But in drama, in tragedy, there must be more than an obstacle — a contrast, a struggle or opposition. This there is, and the self-reproaches point to it. Above we have seen that in most of Shakespeare's tragedies the hero is made superior to his conduct; Hamlet, because the bloody and atrocious plot could not be much changed, is made particularly so — and stands in contrast with it; a villain, a ghost, or the Weird Sisters together with the Lady — not the hero himself — being the chief source of the action. The contrast is emotional, the spectator's sympathy is kept more or less unimpaired; and the opposition necessary to drama is, as with the ancients, that of an external resistance, not of an inner one — by way of self-analysis and introspective debate, as, for the most part, with Corneille and Racine. In Othello it is his love for Desdemona; in Macbeth it is his sense of honor; but what resistance can there be in Hamlet? The deed, to which he is by another's influence or mandate prompted and impelled, is, not like theirs, but like that of Orestes, by him and his confidant, by the author and the audience, considered to be his bounden duty. And

[45] III, i, 179–81.

for the Greek there is some question about his mother, but for the
Dane the only question is whether the Ghost is a fake. Not only by
weakness of will or any other frailty would the audience be alien-
ated but also by any definite aversion to the deed — a scruple
against bloodshed, or the conception of justice as the prerogative of
the state or the Deity. The audience must 'not know,' however it
be with the hero. Such deterrents from vengeance for the blood of
one's kin are foreign to ancient or Elizabethan tragedy, above all
to this, in which the vendetta is taken for granted, is demanded by a
good father in another (and not a better) world. Therefore Hamlet
is eager and ready directly upon the Ghost's disclosures; and when
for the last time he wonders at his own inaction he is careful to add,
never doubting himself:

> Sith I have cause and will and strength and means
> To do't.

It is in the same spirit and to the same effect that he has already rejected every explanation which has occurred to him.

What, then, has Shakespeare here done but have recourse to a
dramatic artifice? The hero's words about himself are really like
those of Iago about Othello at the outset,

> The Moor is of a free and open nature
> That thinks men honest that but seem to be so —

which dramatically, but superficially, not psychologically, explain
how he can convince one not jealous or suspicious, but wholly pre-
possessed in favor of his newly married wife and his friend, that
they together have betrayed him. Forgetting, tardiness, oblivion —
this is the only unrejected explanation, which, however, does not
explain. 'I do not know,' mutters Hamlet; and the audience must
not know, to keep their sympathy and interest; but as if he were a
real person, not a fiction, students will know despite him. And here
is only another instance of what I have often insisted upon, and what
an accomplished Grecian has recently found it necessary to apply to
the criticism of Sophocles: 'the dramatist is to be taken at his plain
word . . . and we have no right to use the dramatic difficulties and
compromises, the necessary short cuts and stretches of probability,
for the purpose either of complicating the psychology or otherwise

deepening the meaning of a play.'[46] No right, that is, if criticism is to preserve any claims to integrity and relevance, or to be worthy of its name. Truth — 'to see the object as in itself it really is' — that should be the aim of criticism; the aim of art, on the other hand, is not primarily truth but emotional effect, and, if need be, no more than a momentary or conditional acceptance. 'Ne consultons,' says the greatest of comic poets (and in his day 'comedy' ordinarily meant comedy or tragedy either) — 'ne consultons dans une comédie que l'effet qu'elle fait sur nous.' The right criticism is a faithful and humble impressionism, which avoids 'tous ces raffinements mystérieux.' What has here been done is to break up the author's own simple and dramatic effect of mystery — 'I do not know' — as criticism discontentedly presses behind it to discover a profounder one.

For the great situation and emotional contrast, then, as in *Othello*, *Macbeth*, and (though differently) also in *King Lear* the dramatist has done what Burke says the true artist should do — 'put a generous deceit on the spectators, and effect the noblest designs by easy methods.'[47] And it is to be accepted, as generously. Hamlet has no such abyss to cross as Othello or Macbeth; still, as for them, an effect of difficulty and resistance there must be, not only to explain the delay but to preserve the impression of superiority to the vindictive and atrocious task. Therefore the first act, the scene of the Ghost's revelations, must end, despite the hero's resolve, with the outcry

O cursèd spite,
That ever I was born to set it right!

(here too he 'does not know'!); and it is partly to keep up this effect of resistance, as well as of his will to overcome it, that he lashes himself so impatiently in the soliloquy 'O, what a rogue,' which we have been discussing.

II

How little, indeed, this soliloquy serves the purpose of psychology, instead of drama, appears upon a moment's inspection. The

[46] E. T. Owen, 'Sophocles the Dramatist,' *University of Toronto Quarterly*, January 1936, p. 228.
[47] *On the Sublime and Beautiful*, Pt. ii, §10.

hero has already arranged with the players for the 'Murder of Gonzago' and a speech of his own penning and inserting. Now, at the
outset, he upbraids himself for his inactivity; but bethinking him of
what he has heard of 'guilty creatures,' he resolves to have the actors
perform something like the murder of his father, as if he had not
already resolved upon and even arranged for that. 'For the spirit
that I have seen may be the devil . . . I'll have grounds more relative
than this.' The cart has come before the horse. The truth seems to
be that, Hamlet being here at the end of the act for the first time
alone, Shakespeare has, effectively enough for an audience interested in what he has been thinking and is now intending to do, but
ineffectively for a psychologist interested not so much in results as
in causes and processes, telescoped these private and internal matters
together. And the narrative phenomenon is not unique. It is somewhat the same summary, and more dramatically convenient and
significant but less plausible, arrangement as that whereby the hero
serves notice of the 'antic disposition' immediately upon the Ghost's
disappearance; as that whereby, before this, in scene ii, the King and
Consort of the widowed Queen holds his first audience — as if he
had just become such — nearly two months after his predecessor's
death and more than a month since his marriage; as that whereby,
in scene iii, Laertes and Polonius warn Ophelia against the dangers
of Hamlet's love, of which, Ophelia confesses, he hath of late —
very oft of late, says Polonius — made many tenders, though he
has already appeared to be, since his father's death and his mother's
marriage, in the depths of grief and melancholy, longing for his
own end, crying out upon woman's frailty, and before this was at
Wittenberg; and as that whereby after the exit of the royal pair the
Prince meets Horatio for the first time since his arrival from the
same university to attend the funeral.[48] Not that it is a matter of

---

[48] It is what Lang (*Homer and the Epic* (1893), pp. 97, 123) calls 'naïve poetic perspective,' as when, in these last days of the ten years' war, there is the duel between
Paris and Menelaus, Helen points out and names to Priam the Achaian heroes, etc.
In real life these incidents would have occurred much earlier. Both poets are more
concerned for a good story than for fidelity to reality and due consideration of time
and place. Homer presenting here, as in the *Odyssey*, only the last stage of the
conflict, must nevertheless not forgo the advantage of these interesting and dramatic
incidents. Shakespeare, keeping the unities so far as the funeral and the marriage are
concerned, and presenting only the consequences, must not forgo the advantage of

convenience merely, but, again, of effect. Less interest would attach to the King and Queen's appearing if with nothing to announce
or determine; or to Hamlet's meeting with Horatio *after* the first
since the funeral and the wedding; or to Laertes' and Polonius' discussing matters already familiar or of no recent occurrence: and in
the present situation the sudden glint of Hamlet's detective purpose
produces a sensation on the stage. How arresting and startling when,
after the prolonged feigning and beating about the bush, the Prince,
dismissing the Players with 'We'll hear a play tomorrow,' but de-
taining First Player with a sign or look, whispers him, without the
slightest previous hint to the audience, 'Dost thou hear me, old
friend? Can you play "The Murder of Gonzago"?' *That* is what he
has had up his sleeve!

To this effect of explanation postponed there is another and apter
parallel in Hamlet's disclosure of the King's treachery on the voyage
only after the graveyard scene. By letter the Prince has summoned
Horatio 'with as much haste as thou wouldest fly death'; but together they come upon the gravediggers and engage them in talk
without (apparently) any previous discussion of recent momentous
events, for Hamlet has not learned of Ophelia's insanity and drowning or of Laertes' insurrection, and the story of his fingering the
packet he does not tell till after the funeral. Thus throughout the
questioning by the grave, the clown's quibbling answers, and the
priest and Laertes' dispute about the manner of burial, the audience
await in suspense Hamlet's discovery of the dead person's identity
as well as the news of his own escape. But if the dramatist had been
concerned for the psychology or even the mere probabilities of
ordinary human intercourse the two friends would not have been so
easily diverted from their all-absorbing confidences. They enter
together 'afar off'; but all they have as yet said to each other, the
inquisitive reader (though not the receptive spectator) might infer,
is 'How do you do?'

_____

the first meetings, more interesting than later ones could be. Thus the unnatural is
for the purposes of story-telling natural. All three incidents serve the purposes of
'exposition'; there is occasion as otherwise there would not be for retrospective and
explanatory remarks. — For similar free treatment of incident, see above, p. 148 and
Chap. I, p. 17.

12

'To be or not to be' has been reckoned against the hero as well.
Yet not only for the reason I have already given — that for the time
being it is disposed of — does he say nothing of the business in hand,
but for another still better, that now the walls have ears. Whether
he suspects this or not, there is nearly the same dramatic result —
anxiety in the audience lest, as he comes in ruminating, he should
step into the trap. Instead of this, we have, quite properly, a further
development of Hamlet's vein of melancholy meditation, which
appeared in his first soliloquy. There, and often afterwards, he looks
beyond his particular grief; and it is the dreamy poetry of his
pessimism that finds expression here. In the first soliloquy life was
in general not worth the living, and still he thinks so. Again he
meditates on suicide. Manifestly he cannot here bethink him of his
revenge if Hieronimo, with his rope and poniard, soliloquizing on
the same subject but without eavesdroppers, suddenly can; but by
failing to do that he does not alienate the audience. His grief
and disillusionment, so keenly but remotely expressed, though
it deepens their sympathy, momentarily relieves, without unduly
allaying, their practical apprehensions. It is less immediately personal than in his first soliloquy; the whips and scorns of time, the
proud man's contumely, the pangs of dispriz'd love, the law's delay,
the spurns that patient merit of the unworthy takes, he cannot himself have known; but that his feelings should assume this universal
form, and that for him at the moment 'no traveller returns,' is in
Quarto I made more plausible by the fact that, like Hieronimo in
his next soliloquy, he enters book in hand.[49] And though without
such a groan as in

> O God, God,
> How weary, stale, flat, and unprofitable,
> Seem to me all the uses of this world!

[49] In Quarto I (see above, p. 126 and notes 9 and 24) the soliloquy stands in Act II
immediately after his first appearance, and before the conversation with Polonius
where he takes that worthy for a fishmonger. In Shakespeare's final version he kept
the business of the book in Act II as a point of departure for the talk with Polonius —
'words, words, words,' and 'slanders' — and it could not well be repeated in Act III.
Ophelia here is reading already, and for both to be reading when they meet, as in

and without the parentheses of impatience, it breathes the same fine
sensitiveness, in a poetry again picked out with the vernacular:

<blockquote>
To die; to sleep; —
To sleep? Perchance to dream! *Ay, there's the rub;*
For in that sleep of death what dreams may come,
When we have *shuffl'd off* this mortal *coil,*
Must give us pause. There's the respect
That makes calamity of so long life. . . .
</blockquote>

The verse next to the last lacks a foot; yet not that circumstance,
but the movement of the last verse itself, is what makes calamity
so unending. Here, as in the quotation immediately preceding, is,
despite the apparent impersonality of the sentiments, the ground-
tone, so to speak, of Hamlet's utterance; which (beneath his indignation and impatience) is not jagged but flowing, and again and
again comes to the surface, as in his addresses to his father's spirit
and to Horatio, his reconciliation with his mother, his graveyard
meditations, his premonition, and

<blockquote>
If thou didst ever hold me in thy heart.
</blockquote>

Though in this soliloquy the theatrical project is, for the reasons
given, relegated to the background, and the tension is thereby somewhat slackened — that when he perceives Ophelia it may again be
tightened — here or elsewhere there is no trace of supine resignation
or frail acquiescence, and (still less) of lassitude, inertia, or 'sloth.'
Such a Hamlet it is impossible that Shakespeare should have intended
and not have put (if nowhere else!) into the rhythm. Read this or
any other of his speeches in the play and then *Andrea del Sarto,*
though penned by no such master-hand:

<blockquote>
days decréase,
And aútumn gróws, ‖ aútumn in éverything.
</blockquote>

<blockquote>
I feél he laíd the fétter; ‖ lét it líe.
</blockquote>

<blockquote>
Hów could it énd ‖ in ány óther wáy?
</blockquote>

<blockquote>
Só — ‖ still they overcóme
Because there's still Lucrézia, — as I chóose.
</blockquote>

Quarto I, no doubt seemed to him ridiculous. But the chief reason is that Hamlet
would then a second time come on the stage reading, too manifestly a scholar, no
man of action. See my *Hamlet*, pp. 30–37.

There, in the accents and the pauses, is the unstrung will. And sloth or acquiescence, that is in the cadences of Milton's Belial.

I have here turned to Browning and Milton because in Shakespeare or other poetic tragedy for the popular stage I know not where to turn: the Hamlet of criticism has, naturally enough, in heroic tragedy no parallels. Only in Richard II, an historical figure, not an heroic one, has Shakespeare given us anything like him; and that, too, when the dramatist had not yet reached a point of supreme mastery in molding rhythm to reveal the speaker's nature. The outlines of the verse, as compared with those of Shakespeare's best, are a little stiff and monotonous; the personality of Richard appears rather in his sentiments and fancies, imagery and phrases; but even so, his is more nearly the way Coleridge's or Goethe's, even Raleigh's or Bradley's, Hamlet should be speaking:

> Or that I could forget ‖ what I have been,
> Or not remember ‖ what I must be now.
>
> .   .   .   .
>
> And my làrge kíngdom ‖ for a líttle gráve,
> A líttle, líttle gráve, ‖ an obscúre gràve.

Or, as to Bolingbroke,

> Your ówn is yours, ‖ and Í am yours, ‖ and áll.

Richard's languor is unfavorably contrasted with Bolingbroke's alertness; but who in the theater would receive a corresponding impression from Laertes' swaggering wrath or the business-like accents of him who has 'sharked up a list of lawless resolutes'?

13

On the colloquy with Ophelia we cannot dwell. Hamlet, necessarily, plays mad again, but with a difference — as the disillusioned lover, though evidently anxious and concerned. 'Get thee to a nunnery. . . . Go thy ways to a nunnery. . . . Get thee to a nunnery, go. . . . To a nunnery, go, and quickly too. . . . To a nunnery, go.' He hurts her, but would save her; he lacerates himself with self-reproaches, though now to another purpose. Yet the accents, the traits both of speech and of character, the spiritual outlook are unmistakably his own. The repetitions spring out of his poignant excitement, and in

What should such *fellows* as I do, *crawling* between heaven and earth?

there is that familiar, penetrating turn which we have seen in him again and again.

14

While the players are dressing and making ready, the Prince takes Horatio into his confidence (he has already told him the Ghost's story). In the final version, as not in Quarto I, Belleforest, the German *Hamlet* (the *Bestrafte Brudermord*) or, *mutatis mutandis*, *Antonio's Revenge* and *The Spanish Tragedy*, and (very probably) the original *Hamlet*, both the secret and the project of revenge are kept from the hero's other associates and the Queen, who give or offer assistance; and this may seem to lend color to the psychological interpretation. But in both Quarto I and the *Brudermord*, as well as in Quarto II, the Ghost himself bids the Prince's friends swear the oath of secrecy concerning his appearance; hence the hero's singlehanded and wary undertaking seems in both Kyd and Shakespeare to have met with supernatural approval. Certainly Hamlet's not confiding the Ghost's information to them is not to be charged, as it has been, to his Elizabethan melancholy, which, indeed, he has not yet assumed. I myself think this, like the other changes, is designed only to heighten the effect of mystery and suspense, and in order both to avoid the ignoble situation of the conspiracy and confederacy of several against the life of one, as in the above-mentioned melodramas and even in *Julius Caesar*, Corneille's *Cinna*, Racine's *Athalie*,[50] the ancient Orestes tragedies, and also to lend the avenger pathetic and heroic isolation. The change is in keeping, too, with the elimination of lethal cunning and treachery from his character, particularly from his irony, as compared to that in Elizabethan melodramatic tragedies such as Marston's and Webster's, as well as Quarto I and *Titus Andronicus*, all in the Kydian style. (Even this is reckoned

[50] Cf. Francisque Sarcey, *Quarante Ans de théâtre* (1900), III, 277, where he speaks of the 'piège abominable' into which the high-priest, by foul play and lying, lures the wicked Athalie. Cinna in one scene, M. Mornet declares, becomes odious.

against the youth[51] — that as a revenger he is not like unto these!)
In fact the change is in keeping with Shakespeare's apparent disposition generally to leave hypocrisy or deliberate deception, for
vengeance in tragedy or for profit in comedy, to villains or rogues
and (if compared with his predecessors and the ancients) to restrict
the scope of this in either. (Even when the purpose is not profit or
vengeance but only escape, there is something antipathetic about the
hero's or heroine's imposture, as in Euripides' *Helena*.) But it has
still more to do with the delay, with Shakespeare's, not Hamlet's
evasion. Delay there must be, we have noted, or it would be a different story; hence disclosures of the secret and avowals of a purpose,
with or without a plan, as in Belleforest, Quarto I, the *Brudermord*
(which has a similar origin), *The Spanish Tragedy* (which is *Hamlet*
transposed), and *Antonio's Revenge* (which is Kyd's Hamlet carried
to Italy) would, with help either accepted or rejected, be, as even
there, embarrassing to everybody concerned, including the author.
How incompetent the conspiracy, how pitiful the hero! Hamlet's
own noble self-reproaches have a very different effect; and in keeping with that, the important disclosures to Horatio are made off-
stage, their discussion of the King's self-betrayal is interrupted by the
entrance of Rosencrantz and Guildenstern, and the only occasion
given them to speak of the revenge before us is the single one when
he and Horatio are together alone again, in the second scene of
Act V, two hundred and seventy lines before he accomplishes it.

Horatio lends assistance, and quite properly is expected to do so,
only in observing the King. But if, now, the Mousetrap be a subterfuge, why does the hero not keep his counsel, observe (if at all)
only for himself, and avoid exposing his faint-heartedness or vacillation, 'frustration' or self-deception, to one who need not know of
it? The same psychology that attributes it to Hamlet requires (as
the art of the drama does still more) that he should later excuse it
to his friend, or that the latter should take him to task for it; also,
in either case, that Horatio should say something of it, which, in

---

[51] There is something of this scheming and double-dealing left, as when Hamlet
tells the King 'I see a cherub that sees them,' and the Queen (or merely himself),
' 'Tis most sweet when in one line two crafts directly meet'; yet both times he is not
mining but countermining. He is not, like Hieronimo, playing a friendly-deadly
role.

his last two speeches, he doesn't, in carrying out the dying request to 'tell my story.'

Or if the hero be deceiving himself here and when he doubts the Ghost or later spares the King, why should he not have been given reasons less traditional and plausible? The Prince himself says he has 'heard that guilty creatures at a play,' etc., and most of the audience, probably, had heard of it too. And 'the spirit that I have seen may be the devil . . . and perhaps abuses me to damn me' — that misgiving, we noticed, is not only natural in its place and native to Elizabethan thinking but is fully prepared for. Moreover, both Banquo and Macbeth have similar doubts and similar reasons for them after a 'supernatural [a devilish] soliciting,' though by way of witches instead of a ghost:

> oftentimes, to win us to our harm,
> The instruments of darkness tell us truths;
> Win us with honest trifles, to betray's
> In deepest consequence.

And not to his credit but his own damnation does Glamis, as the critics would have Hamlet do, brush the scruple aside. Or if Hamlet be meant to be constitutionally sceptical, why not a reason more evidently betraying that turn of mind? An hallucination he might have called the spirit, like Horatio at the beginning, and left the devil out. But if either impression were that which Shakespeare had intended he could hardly have managed worse. Hamlet doubts the Ghost, but his suspicions are so simple and sincere that he can share them with Horatio unabashed, and wholeheartedly at once proceed to put them to the proof. This is eagerly awaited by the audience, for the doubts, expressed at the outset, but allayed by the awe-inspiring speech of the Ghost, recur to them as naturally as to the Prince; verification in such a matter, as in any, is a requirement of justice and common sense; and this now before them — if a subterfuge, it certainly wouldn't be! — is the *scène à faire*. He gives the play, and upon the blenching of the King the doubts are ended. 'I'll take the Ghost's word,' he cries in solid, rough-and-ready fashion, not a doubter's, dreamer's, or self-deceiver's, certainly, 'for a thousand pound.' Had the play been a subterfuge, would he not have forgotten the purpose of it — noted the King's guilt but not remembered the Ghost? Or if he had been the incorrigible sceptic or self-deceiver that since Coleridge and Schlegel's day he has been thought to be, would he not have doubted still? At least he would have doubted others; but all Hamlet's suspicions — of the King, of Rosencrantz and Guildenstern, of Polonius, of his daughter playing with her prayer-book, of the treacherous letter — are justified and sound. The Dane is no Tasso, as in Goethe's drama.

And the reason, presently, for sparing the King at prayer, why is it one appropriate and natural in revenge stories, ancient or Renaissance, and, quite probably, the very one used in the original, where certainly no such subtlety could have been intended or expected? A mere excuse or subterfuge would not be much in keeping with the time-honored narrative tradition, whether as alive in the minds of the audience or as fairly prominent here — blood demanded from the other world, and not only a life for a life but a soul for a soul. But even because Hamlet's reason is so much in keeping with that, is so fiercely and exactly just, it has been questioned — as if in his own day Shakespeare did not greatly care to be understood.

What is perhaps still more to the point, why, if in this or in any other fashion he deceives himself, does he, before that or after, blame himself, and not others, or circumstances, as such people do in life, and in dramas like *A Doll's House*, *Borkman*, *The Wild Duck*, and Becque's *Corbeaux*? If in soliloquy he must do so for the audience, he should do otherwise with Horatio. Why, on the other hand, do not his comrade and the others blame him instead of all praising him? Some might be aware of his hesitating, procrastinating, or vacillating nature, even if they didn't know of the Ghost; faults more obvious are nevertheless also duly noted by friends or enemies in Romeo, Cassius and Brutus, Lear, Othello, Macbeth, Antony and Coriolanus; and unless the tragedy were meant to be more difficult and perplexing — less effective — than Goethe's *Tasso*, Schiller's *Wallenstein*, or Ibsen's *Peer Gynt*, *The Master-Builder*, and the plays above mentioned, of this particular fault in the hero not only one but a couple of the numerous other characters would necessarily show themselves aware.[52] To Horatio, who does know of the Ghost and the Prince's duty, it might at least have been given to point the

[52] For the Ibsen plays and Becque see my *Shakespeare Studies*, pp. 133–35; for the others, *Art and Artifice in Shakespeare*, p. 112; *Hamlet* (1919), pp. 24–25.

contrast with Fortinbras (or if intended, that with Laertes) instead of — rather to his credit — the Prince himself.

Without comment, there is, so far as my knowledge reaches, no self-deception in drama.[53] In real life, especially in public life, words are often as much the concealment as the revealment of the inner thought. Through the words of presidents, prime ministers, and dictators the inner thought is discernible (though to the nation in general it may not be) both because of their conduct not only at the moment or for a couple of hours but for many years, and also because of the leisure at our command in judging of it. *That* theater never closes! But in Racine's *Andromaque*, Act II, scene v, though Pyrrhus, even as he puts his love for the heroine from him, betrays its power over him, Phoenix must needs be there to remark the fact; and how much clear previous indication of the motive and satirical comment upon it are required for the effect of self-deception in the Reverend Davidson of Colton and Randolph's *Rain* as, in converting the prostitute, he yields to his repressed and accumulated sensuality, and in the William of Milne's *Truth about Blayds* as he ingeniously explains away the imposture of his dead hero, whose life he expects to write and whose money he expects — but legitimately — to inherit! In Shakespeare what self-deception there is, is made plain as day; as when, in the midst of his passion, the Moor exclaims, 'Not a jot, not a jot!' in answer to Iago's observation 'this hath a little dash'd your spirits,' and even then the Ancient must needs be permitted his rejoinder, 'I' faith I fear it has.' Or if no other can know, as with Iago motive-hunting, the comment must be furnished, unrealistically, by the self-same character: 'but I for mere suspicion in that kind' — 'to plume up my will in double knavery' — 'but partly led to diet my revenge' — 'Divinity of hell!' . . . Not only such indications and comments are required but (as with the doubt of the Ghost) repetition as well — Hamlet should *fail* to strike at the man behind the arras whom he takes to be the King! Why, indeed, is he not, like William, like Helmer,

---

[53] Cf. my *Hamlet*, Chap. IV, especially pp. 59–60, *Shakespeare Studies*, pp. 125–27, for both Shakespeare's and Ibsen's procedure; and Racine's *Britannicus*, III, vi, where the hero makes up excuses for seeing Junie, whom, apparently, he is casting off. Also, for Iago, below, p. 232. — As for the effect of Pyrrhus, I fall back on Lanson: 'presque comique.' In French classical tragedy!

Borkman, Hialmar, even Pyrrhus for the moment, as well as those other self-deceivers, the cowards and hypocrites in both ancient and modern drama, made, particularly by the glaring repeated contrast between protestation and conduct, a comic figure, which on the Elizabethan stage such a Hamlet must necessarily have been, and in the hands of the critics at times really is?

It is possible, evidently, to read a play, especially one of Shakespeare's, as one pleases, at least with the Shakespearean's favorite formula of self-deception in hand. Hamlet, Iago, and (with Professor Nicoll's fundamental formula of the 'unrevealed as important as the revealed' in the other hand) Othello and even Desdemona can thus be adjusted to the requirements of a psychological study. So (with the fundamental one at least) comedy can, partly or wholly, be turned into tragedy, as (similarly, though without the formula) in the Romantic period *L'École des femmes* was and (even by Goethe) *L'Avare*. At the same time it happened to the *Merchant of Venice*. And *Coriolanus*, in turn, has of late, by Mr. Shaw, though how seriously I know not, been pronounced to be Shakespeare's greatest comedy. That place may yet be claimed for *Hamlet*. The *reductio ad absurdum* is perhaps all that will clear the air.

15

Just before the Prince confides in his comrade and bids him keep his eyes open at the play, he bursts out in admiration:

> Give me that man
> That is not passion's slave, and I will wear him
> In my heart's core, ay, in my heart of heart,
> As I do thee. — Something too much of this.

It is the same tone of manly sweetness as in his remark about his father:

> He was a man, take him for all in all,
> I shall not look upon his like again.

During the theatrical experiment and immediately after, the hero is his other self, playing a part (but here one that he scarcely needs to play) wittier and more satirical, more familiar and colloquial, because more excited, than ever. And the play ended, his excitement naturally (not morbidly) rises:

> For if the king like not the comedy,
> Why then, belike, he likes it not, perdy —

which, Hamlet all over, is probably only a Shakespearean improvement. Hieronimo, the paternal revenger, is given an appropriately sober variation upon the theme:

> And if the world like not this tragedy,
> Hard is the hap of old Hieronimo.

In the soliloquy ' 'Tis now the very witching time,' and in that while the King is on his knees, he is merely the Senecan-Kydian revenger, cruel and cynical, though still like himself in his colloquialism: 'Now might I do it *pat . . . trip* him that his heels may *kick* at heaven.' In phrasing and spirit both he is now again like Hieronimo,

> And heere Ile *have a fling at him, that's flat*;[54]

and neither in his sentiments nor as he draws his weapon and sheathes it is he pulling the wool over his own eyes. For that, since the reason for sheathing it is valid, the audience would have no clue; the notion of 'thinking too precisely' comes four scenes later. Hamlet's eagerness for revenge now that he is certain of the King's guilt is needed not only to make the present situation, with its excitement, but to hold the story together; and the contrast intended is not, as has been thought, one between big words and small doings but between purposes and the opportunity given by fortune.

16

The scene with his mother, which ensues, is the chief support for the opinion of a contemporary German scholar, as of many not German, that Hamlet is weak, neurotic, and a prey to hallucinations. But of Macbeth his opinion is about the same; and, as often with a Shakespearean's psychology, it does little to differentiate the characters. If the gallant and formidable youth is weak (or as Mr. Simpson and his predecessors would have him, 'hysterical') like the

---

[54] III, xii, 21. Cf. also Hamlet's 'It is an honest ghost, *that let me tell you*,' I, v, 138.

robust and redoubtable thane, why, then, let him be so! The Ghost in the Queen's bedroom is identical with the substantial one on the platform — and who at the theater could think he wasn't? And his being visible to one person present and not another, that is as much a part of ghost-lore, Renaissance or ancient, as appearing at midnight, vanishing ere cock-crow, demanding revenge, and bearing (Banquo's 'twenty'!) the death-wounds on his shadowy figure.[55] If at his second appearance to the Prince the Ghost is an hallucination, he, in this or any other drama, must have been so at the first; and then, as one contemporary Elizabethan scholar actually holds, and another seems to do, Hamlet's imaginations (to the destruction of the tragedy!) *are* 'as foul as Vulcan's stithy.'[56]

The Ghost's reproach is another and more serious matter: the critics are right in thinking that such words carry weight. And if in every tragedy the incidents must all be interpreted in terms of the hero's character, and in every hero there must be a tragic fault or psychical defect, the matter might be considered then and there to be settled. But, as we have seen, the contrary is the case; and in a tragedy, as (of course) in life itself, 'tardiness' is not a crime any more than its opposite, impetuosity or hastiness.[57] The latter, which is far more often the effect in a tragedy, is likewise charged against the hero; the former, I have endeavored to show, is fairly unavoidable here. Heads or tails — action slow or speedy — the hero loses, for of course he is not perfection. 'Sie haben so viel von Schuld und Strafe,' grumbles the great Wilamowitz, 'im *Oedipus* geredet. Das ist Unverstand.' And vastly more has been said of guilt and punishment, or psychical defects and their consequences, in *Hamlet*. But dramatic and emotional matters are more relevant (though now I can only touch upon them) than the ethical and psychological. The Ghost must appear again, and in the Queen's bed-chamber, not only because he did in the old play[58] — otherwise a situation

---

[55] See my *Shakespeare Studies*, chapter on Ghosts, especially pp. 211–17.

[56] *Modern Language Review* (1917), pp. 393ff., 'Hamlet's Hallucination.' And Mr. Wilson's *What Happens*, pp. 42, 131, 260.

[57] Cf., above, the chapter on 'Reconciliation in Tragedy,' p. 66.

[58] There, very probably, as in the *Brudermord* and *Antonio's Revenge*, he appears also to protect her against the Orestean hero, into whose firm bosom had entered more of the soul of Nero. See my article '*Hamlet* and the *Spanish Tragedy*,' *Modern Philology*, August 1937.

would be lost — but because the structure of the present one would be damaged. If he didn't, he would, though the impelling force of the tragedy, become merely protatic, and lose in importance as much as the Weird Sisters would if they did not reappear in the fourth act of *Macbeth*, or as the mob or the family feud if it did not reappear in the third act of *Julius Caesar* or of *Romeo and Juliet*. Besides, Hamlet, having doubted the Ghost, must have a chance loyally to acknowledge him; and the Ghost himself, Hamlet having just now spoken of his father, must (as elsewhere in Shakespearean and other Elizabethan drama, and in the world of superstition as a whole) rise, like Banquo's, in consequence. But the chief reasons — with the aesthetic interpretation, unlike the psychological, the reasons are many, the parts 'mutually supporting and explaining each other' — the chief reasons, I say, are still more essentially dramatic. The fabric of the whole is thus reënforced, and in particular that of the scene in question. The passion is raised in intensity and the action is given point. Though the spirit is not a symbol, yet there is dramatic significance and effect in the Queen's not seeing or hearing him, in the dead King's not desiring it. And by his appearance our attention is in a striking and startling way focused again on the main business and issue, now that the hero 'must to England.' This is the merely dramatic or narrative equivalent of the psychological requirement: the audience needs to be reminded, and more than Hamlet. *He* has not forgotten; he anticipates the rebuke. Now, if ever, was the chance for speaking out severely to the hero and clearly to the audience, could either have profited by it. But, compared to other ghosts, amid their purgatorial pains, as in *The Spanish Tragedy* and *Antonio's Revenge*, the present one is extraordinarily forbearing: 'do not forget . . . thy almost blunted purpose.' That light word is, in his judgment, enough (as in the sequel it really is); and the warrior-king, little impressed with his son's degeneracy, bids him comfort his mother.[59] The rebuke is commensurate with the slightness of the Prince's resistance to the incentive, noticed above.

[59] *Art and Artifice*, p. 99, where are other examples in drama of 'forgetting,' with no ethical or psychological import. — If Hamlet be much at fault the Ghost should have here comported himself more like that of Sir George Villiers in Clarendon's history, who, reappearing to the remiss and dubitative Towse, is 'severe' with him and gives him 'sharp reprehensions,' and, appearing once more, has 'a terrible countenance,' 'bitterly reproaching him' (1888, I, 51).

In colloquy with the Queen the Prince fairly drops the mask, and speaks in his native character, as with Horatio, though through a greater range of emotion; and his scorn for his uncle's person and his mother's marriage is expressed with force, his affection for his father and shame for his mother, with poignancy. One trait, however, which did not appear at the outset but did in the company of Polonius and Ophelia, now asserts itself as he deprecates her relation to his uncle — the Malcontent's cynicism, penetrating into matters of sex.[60] Yet that does not mean that he has, as the German scholar thinks, a morbid taste for 'erotic phantasies.' He is neither erotic nor neurotic; and his mind is not 'tainted,'[61] his imaginations not really 'foul.' There has been occasion enough in his mock-mad and cynical role, and provocation enough in his mother's adulterous relation and hasty, incestuous marriage.

Also, it is something of the Malcontent's bent for burrowing under the surface of things, and confounding the high and the low, the mean and the mighty in the laystall of death, that later appears in the graveyard. In his feigned madness he played with the notion of Polonius' body putting on corruption, and dwelt on a king's going a progress through the guts of a beggar; but now, with a difference, sanely, decently, as well as appropriately enough for one going himself down into the valley of the shadow of death, he wonders how long a man may lie in the earth ere he rot, and whether in imagination the noblest dust might not be found stopping a bunghole — in a beer-barrel. Who is it if not Hamlet as in his true character we have known him that repeatedly questions the gravedigger, and thereupon Yorick, as if present in the flesh as well as the bone, and, in particular, Horatio? After asking him much else besides —

Prithee, Horatio, tell me one thing.
(What's that, my lord?)
Dost thou think Alexander look'd o' this fashion i' the earth? —

[60] See the article in *Modern Philology*, cited above, n. 11, for the parallels in Marston, pp. 296, 300–301.
[61] As used by the Ghost, the word has, of course, a different meaning: 'do not bring the guilt of matricide — the Orestean furies — upon thee.' It has recently been taken to mean 'avoid mental disorder' — an injunction that he, strangely, disobeys. Cf. Wilson, *What Happens*, p. 46, etc.

how familiar, how pathetically intimate, his arm linked in his friend's, his eyes searching the other's, though scarcely for information! From the beginning his meditations have been preoccupied with death and what follows it; that his own now hangs over him the audience who have heard the King and Laertes plotting are aware; he, in his soul, must suspect or expect it — he has sent the menacing letter and later he utters a premonition — but of himself he says nothing; and here is only the climax and *finale* of all his 'curious' impersonal thinking, though most personally expressed.

17

An account of himself comes after the funeral, and who but Hamlet could give the alert narrative of his audacious exploit, with the parentheses of scorn and irony, the questions and exclamations for sympathy or approval, the glintings of merriment?

> With, ho! such bugs and goblins in my life . . .
> And many such-like *as*-es of great charge . . .
> *Popp'd* in between the election and my hopes. . . .

In phrasing and imagery it is the normal Hamlet, without the exaggerations of feigning, who speaks lightly and familiarly, fantastically but poignantly and poetically, of serious and desperate things, — the very same as in 'there's the rub,' 'shuffled off,' 'now might I do it pat,' and as in the lines of his last soliloquy:

> Whose spirit, with divine ambition *puff'd*,
> *Makes mouths* at the invisible event,
> Exposing what is mortal and unsure
> To all that fortune, death, and danger dare,
> Even *for an egg-shell*.

In all Shakespeare, in all drama, no voice could be mistaken for that. And the solid, direct, comrade-like manner of

> Why, man, they did make love to this employment,

is quite in keeping with the tone of cool confidence as he refers to his revenge —

> is't not perfect conscience,
> To quit him with this arm?

> It will be short; the interim is mine.

If ever resolution spoke, it was in such accents as these. If he be conscious of dereliction of duty, why in his last soliloquy or afterwards has no specific instance of it, like sparing the King at prayer, occurred to him; or if (as has been supposed) it was part and parcel of his malady not to be able to kill a man deliberately but only on the spur of the moment (and yet for all that kill two men by a stroke of the pen), why does not or did not so remarkable an internal psychological discovery perplex or fascinate, startle or distress him? Reflecting without acting, and acting without reflecting, violent in words but not in deeds, or violent in deeds only but (so to speak) with his eyes shut — all that, so interesting to the critics, should be still more so to him, or if nothing new to him, would be new and baffling enough to the audience! Not what he hasn't done but has done should perplex or appal him, but actually neither now does the one thing or the other or for more than a moment did so before. A strange dramatic method, according to which the purposes and processes of intrigue, tragic or comic, in this play or in any, should be made perfectly, sometimes obtrusively clear, and the simple wickedness of a villain like Richard, Claudius, or Iago should (against nature) be made so by the villain himself, but this complicated state of affairs within the hero should be left, not a mystery, not a question even, but a blank! And how can he now look Horatio in the eye, who, though he has not learned of the project in our presence, takes it for granted? If subterfuges on the stage must look like subterfuges, vacillation must look like vacillation, a pretense of action like a pretense. If Hamlet's delay and his self-reproaches for it are to be reckoned against him, how can he, so clear-seeing, so hungry for sympathy, fail now to say — or the greater dramatist fail to make him say — like John Gabriel Borkman to Foldal, as, day-dreaming in the gallery, he prophesies his own rehabilitation:

You're looking so doubtfully at me. Perhaps you don't believe that they will come? That they must, must, must come to me some day? Do you not believe it?

Or like Hialmar Ekdal, who never bestirs himself to that end, as he declares to his wife that he means to fulfill his life mission: 'Do you not believe it?' his own faith much needing reinforcement.

Hamlet's does not need it; these firm accents are not new, the man himself is not changed, and only circumstances (along with the requirements of the drama) have thwarted him. In the same tone he said in the third soliloquy:

> If he but blench,
> I know my course.

And after the play:

> O good Horatio, I'll take the ghost's word for a thousand pound. Did'st perceive?

And at the end of the closet-scene:

> and 't shall go hard
> But I will delve one yard below their mines,
> And blow them at the moon.

And on his way to embark:

> O, from this time forth,
> My thoughts be bloody, or be nothing worth!

18

He is cooler, quieter now, just before the struggle: a weakling or frustrate would not be. With inaction he need no longer reproach himself; if with inaction in the particular matter of revenge, why, 'considerations which are not suggested to the audience,' as Mr. Courtney observes of drama generally, 'are considerations which do not exist for them'; and, if ever, that must be remembered in reading the popular tragedy before us, rewritten, not recast. How else for generations (if we may turn to another matter) have not only spectators but readers and critics as well received the impression that Hamlet is 'a great gentleman'? How else can the hero's Senecan and Kydian vindictiveness and cunning, though by Shakespeare much reduced, be tolerable, or his treatment of his mother and Ophelia at the play, or, above all, his ruthlessness with her in the nunnery scene and his indifference to the consequences of the killing of Polonius? In the original undoubtedly, as in Belleforest before it, she was only a pawn in the desperate game between Hamlet and the King, and here it is but for moments that she is anything more. Cruelty and cunning are indispensable to the revenge undertaking;

but here the cunning is, as we have seen, to thwart his enemy's and keep up the game of madness, the slurs upon his mother at the play are to throw dust in the eyes of Claudius and the Court, and his apparent brutality towards the maiden there and in the nunnery scene is partly to mislead and mystify the listeners, partly to warn her of her danger, partly to wreak himself on one who has jilted him, is deceiving him, and is of the same sex as his mother. Yet Shakespeare's emotional, strictly dramatic method prevails: if Hamlet hasn't her on his mind, we haven't her on ours. She is kept subordinate and is not permitted to touch us too nearly. She is delicate, but in the distance. Her grief is not presented to us immediately and directly but only by way of her poetically treated distraction, and that seems to be mainly for her unheroic father. The Prince's unconcern for the maiden's filial feelings is a negative matter to which our attention is not called. Above, in Chapter I, we have noticed that in Shakespearean and other Elizabethan drama the character does not much reside in the implications of the action; and this is especially true of what, without comment, is *not* done — Macduff's and Polixenes' taking no thought for the safety of wife and child or of the lady, Emilia's and Banquo's silence and acquiescence, the young lovers' showing no concern (as Romeo and Juliet, Desdemona and Imogen show none) for the unhappiness of their parents. Indeed, it is also true of much that *is* done, particularly the *atrocitas*. Even before Seneca there is plenty of that, but still more of it at the Renaissance; and what is to become of Hamlet (as of Romeo) before an audience if he is really cruel and 'callous,' and 'scatters death like a universal plague'? What of Othello, 'if nothing that is in Iago is absent from Othello,' as 'both the best and the worst of men'? If high tragedy is not a faithful image of life, and the conduct of the hero there not the unbroken reflection of his nature, still less is it a matter of cool estheticism, of mere pattern or paradox.

If no word about inaction, however, and the past, why none about action and the present? Since Coleridge's time the avenger has had no credit for his vengeance, 'impelled, at last, by mere accident.' But even here, near the end, a deliberate and definite, crafty and insidious, homicidal plan, like those of Orestes in the ancient tragedies, or though for himself unaided, like Luigi's in *Pippa Passes*, would appreciably diminish the sympathy, and what is more, slacken the suspense. That sorry part has been the King's once already, and is his now again as well as Laertes', with perfidy and poisoning thrown in; yet there the effect is — emotional too. Claudius' respectability and dignity, his bravery in the face of danger and his affectionateness towards the Queen, which have tended somewhat to justify in our eyes the doubt and delay, are at present overshadowed and nearly forgotten, but with no result except to heighten our concern for the fate of the hero; and if Laertes' headlong activity in revenge for his father and sister has for a moment cast a reflection upon the hero's inactivity, that is totally eclipsed. Hamlet plots only to discover the truth of the Ghost's disclosures and to checkmate the cunning of the King; if we may judge by *The Spanish Tragedy*, *Antonio's Revenge*, and the *Brudermord*, Kyd's Hamlet also, in comparison with Belleforest's, played something of a waiting game, as a result of the Senecan villain-hero's being resolved into that character's two component elements; but this notable innovation of a high-minded revenger performing a sacred duty, delaying and reproaching himself for the delay like the Hellenic, yet leaving not only conspiracy but the contriving to the villain, such as Claudius, Kyd's Lorenzo, and Marston's Piero, has, in modern critical opinion, but reacted against the hero himself. It is intended not to diminish our sympathy but enlarge it. After his mockery of Osric, somewhat in the Malcontent vein, after the lord's message that all is ready, he has still only his confidence — 'I shall win at the odds' — and a premonition; to the critics, who here of suspense will have none, he seems to be going into the fencing-match, 'with a man whose hands but a few short hours ago were at his throat,' wholly a prey to a sentiment. It is as if he were committing suicide and — there's frustration for you! — by another's hand. So they shake their heads at him meditating in the graveyard, and not on revenge! In the same spirit they take his quibbling with the Gravedigger, his jeering at Osric. 'Has this fellow no feeling of his business?' (to turn the words of the hero against himself). There is irrelevancy in the character — and in the criticism! This is drama, is poetry, not psychology, is a matter not of motives but of the emotions; and in either scene, if he were presented as the critics would have him, would he be so interesting, or the audience so anxious and intent?

Marked for death, entering without a word of recent experiences or present undertakings, to brood over the grave into which Ophelia is presently to be lowered, Hamlet alarms us indeed like drama, but uplifts us like a sudden yet subtle change in poetry or music.[62] There is no motive but a *motif*, the death-*motif*,[63] which in his solitary meditations has appeared twice already and now dominates the play. The last time, too, in the 'To be or not to be' soliloquy, he might have been considering the business in hand — if the play were only a psychological record, and the audience were to be studious and analytical, not emotionally responsive and concerned. In both that scene and this the hero talks — thinks and feels — unmistakably like himself; and so far as character is concerned, that is the dramatist's chief interest, not why he is talking on this subject rather than another or is not acting instead. In the graveyard scene the motivation is deeper, but still superficial. What we have at this juncture is not the complete expression of Hamlet's psychology any more than that of Macbeth's and his Lady's after the deed is done. This is Death, not the avenger: that is Murder, not the ambitious pair. Still, we have an adequate and effective expression of Hamlet's personality; and superficially taken, as they should be, his liberty of spirit and play of wit and fancy are here, near his end, a sign of strength (not of weakness, of irrelevancy or frustration) as Romeo's and Cleopatra's are, and, in real life, on the scaffold, Sir Thomas More's and Sir Walter Raleigh's were.

So, just before the fencing-match, when, in the light of the premonition, he more immediately confronts the situation, the question for the dramatist is, though delicate enough, not one of character alone. As I have elsewhere said, it is how the tragedy shall remain a tragedy, and at the same time the hero act like the gallant gentleman he is and yet be not a fool. If he really suspected, he would not keep the engagement; or else he would then be followed with less sympathy and anxiety, since he must needs come out ahead again, as the better man. Hamlet must perish, but neither falter nor fail. And in going to his death he preserves his reputation for astuteness

---

[62] Cf. the discussion of the scene, *Art and Artifice in Shakespeare*, pp. 130–36.

[63] Neither the phrase nor the idea in this connection, which appear in my *Hamlet the Man*, English Association pamphlet no. 91, March 1935, p. 26, is taken from a book on *Hamlet* which appeared the same year.

as well as reckless valor by hearkening to a premonition and with a smile defying it. How manly is his misgiving, how fearless!

The readiness is all. Since no man has aught of what he leaves, what is't to leave betimes? Let be.

Magnanimous daring is what in a hero the audience desire, not homicidal cunning and scheming, particularly when, as in the present juncture, it is on the whole a match for them. Even a hint — of craft meeting craft, as before he sets out for England — manifestly here will not do, at the end. 'Most generous and free from all contriving,' said the King; and it is so, with the cards all against him, that the generous audience would have him now lose and win.

19

'Shakespeare seems to have determined,' says Mr. Bradley, now happily abandoning psychology, 'that his hero should exhibit in his latest hour all the glorious power and all the nobility and sweetness of his nature.' And not only that but the rest of him — his filial love and grief, his generosity and his gallantry, his fierce energy and self-assertiveness, his scorn for evil-doers and his affectionateness for his friend, his wide and melancholy outlook, his poetical and familiar, penetrating, parenthetical, and ironical utterance. What changes in him — the mutable, unmistakable one! — as, mortally wounded, he turns from the King to Laertes, to Horatio, to the Queen, to the pale and trembling Danes, and to his friend again! He curses the King to his face with still greater vehemence than behind his back, and as he bids him drink, jests about the pearl of poison like an embodied nemesis:

> Here, thou incestuous, murderous, damnèd Dane,
> Drink off this potion! Is thy *union* here?
> Follow my mother.

He appeals to the others, his people who love him, in parentheses, and with a waving aside of personal matters as after his premonition:

> Had I but time — as this fell sergeant, Death,
> Is strict in his arrest — O, I could tell you,
> But let it be.

He wrests the cup from Horatio's hand, though with a still nobler ardor, as he flung him and the others off when they would stop him on the platform:

> As thou'rt a man,
> Give me the cup. Let go! By heaven, I'll have't.

And then, with a characteristic recoil, counting upon the friend's love to the point of his living on alone, he implores him,

> If thou didst ever hold me in thy heart,
> Absent thee from felicity a while
> And in this harsh world draw thy breath in pain
> To tell my story.

All of life as Hamlet has found it seems to be caught up in the last two lines; yet he is no sentimentalist, no Werther or Aprile. He is not now lost in a haze of reverie, still less is he choked by the damps of apathy. His time is short and (the frustrate!) he has business to attend to: his 'wounded name' — 'things standing thus unknown,' his King's and father's brother's blood upon his hands — and the succession. In this last what interest could the Hamlet of criticism conjure up, the dreamer all adrift? His final words are 'The rest is silence'; but as if to keep the detective critic, still afar, from making overmuch of them, he has already declared:

> O, I die, Horatio;
> The potent poison quite *o'er-crows* my spirit.

The most copious and various talker in all Shakespeare's prodigiously talkative theater, 'silence' is certainly not, as has been thought, his refuge and 'haven.' Yet this, like his other personal matters, he takes lightly and passes it over. O'er-crowed? Let be.

And death itself? No longer is it 'a consummation devoutly to be wished': of that then and there we heard the last. In the graveyard death does not seem sweet and easeful: in the premonition he is 'defied.' Now, as he in visible shape appears, he is a fell sergeant, strict in his arrest. Only in 'absent thee from felicity a while' does life seem not worth the living; but those dubious and elusive, probably ironical, words are addressed to his friend, and are followed by the outcry:

> O, I die, Horatio!

The venom overpowers him: 'felicity' draws only too near.

If Hamlet were the sick, world-weary spirit he has in after days been reported to be, would he not embrace it; or if death comes to him in the guise of a sergeant, gladly make his surrender? The effect, then, would hardly be tragic. His desire to die was for a space the refuge, and the measure, of his grief, doubt, and despair; and by certainty, activity, achievement, it has been dispelled. Though from his fate he does not shrink, he now would live, being fit to do so; that, at the end, is the irony. He dies young, at the moment of his triumph, dies, as to others it must seem, with all this blood on his head. But to render that tragic catastrophe its full effect readers must be willing to yield to the hero, as ordinary, unlettered audiences have for three centuries done, and as the presentation of his character warrants, their admiration and sympathy without misgiving and almost without reserve.

20

For is not Shakespeare a dramatist, a poet, an artist, one of the greatest in the world, and *Hamlet*, from the very beginning till now, his most popular play? And is it not a fundamental principle of drama and poetry — of all art — that, appealing to the senses and imagination as it does, not primarily to the intellect, it should be readily intelligible, and what is important in the work should there appear so? If, then, this be a play of inaction, not action, the hero being unfitted or really unwilling to perform the duty which is laid upon him, the fact, very remarkable in tragedy of that time as indeed of ours, should come rather clearly and emphatically to light, if nowhere else, at the most important and prominent place, the end. There, if not elsewhere, the truth must out; and if Horatio, as has been declared, 'certainly cannot explain Hamlet,' why, then, if Shakespeare was not a very peculiar, not to say futile dramatist, some other should have been commissioned who could. The secret may be kept in a stage play, but not to the very end and after; there we may find a sense of mystery as in life but not the mystery of life itself, which is insoluble. In Shakespeare, on the other hand, as we saw in Chapter I, there are few secrets kept and those not for long; the chief business of the play and the course of the action, the purposes of the characters, if not their motives — but their motives also, when to the dramatist's purpose — are made extraordinarily clear and explicit; there is not only no riddle but not even a problem, and the excitement is not that of curiosity but of anticipation. Even Iago, though at the last he in Satanic arrogance locks his lips, must needs, not for the sake of the audience, who already know it, and yet not for his own satisfaction merely, but for that of the other characters, for dramatic effect, in short, spit out the dread secret of his cloven hoof, 'I bleed, Sir, but not kill'd'! The spectator, declares Corneille (whose plays were for a far more cultivated and attentive sort) must at the end be satisfied and in a state of repose: 'si bien instruit des sentiments de tous ceux qui y ont eu quelque part, qu'il sorte l'esprit en repos, et ne soit plus en doute de rien.'

Or if among Shakespeare's plays this should really be an exception, should have turned out to be the most popular through three centuries by an inexplicable mistake, and should after all be something of a highbrow, futuristic, undramatic drama, long before its time (a time indeed after our own), in which the truth is not to be expected to come óut and the subconscious element in the character is to be such for the audience too, why, then, should not the character at the close act somewhat more clearly in keeping with his inhibited but unexhibited nature? Should he not at least give a cry of triumph, breathe a sigh of relief, or break into a wan ironical smile of amazement, even though he too 'cannot explain himself,' now that he has stabbed the King and made him drink of the cup? What hands are these! he should exclaim, though not like the thane of Glamis. Instead, he takes this quite as a matter of course, as, except at moments, he has done throughout; and now would have Horatio live to tell, not why he has not done the deed of blood before, but why he has done it at all —

> Report me and my *cause* aright
> To the unsatisfied —

an appeal which, says Sir John Squire, 'though Horatio doubtless responded to it, has fallen on deaf ears elsewhere.'[64] And that the hero should be like *that* but act and speak like *this*, in a well-wrought

---

[64] 'A New View of Hamlet,' *Living Age*, December 13, 1919, p. 676, reproduced from *Land and Water*. 'Unfortunate in his death as in his life.' Cf. Swinburne, *A Study of Shakespeare* (1879), pp. 168–69 (ed. of 1895).

drama, with nothing to justify or make a point of the discrepancy, is to my mind impossible.

It is so impossible in fact that it did not occur to any one until near the end of the eighteenth century — not, before that, to Addison, Rowe, Shaftesbury, or Fielding, to Johnson or Voltaire; but, far from the theater and beyond the Border, to William Richardson, the university professor, and Henry Mackenzie, the Man of Feeling — to minds that turned in upon themselves as those of writers were now beginning to do, thus unfitting them, if not for drama, certainly for dramatic criticism. The much pondered and expounded Dane has been sentimental with Mackenzie and Goethe, reflective and vacillating with Coleridge, pessimistic with Schopenhauer, heroic and warrior-like for the day of Sedan, subconscious and psychopathic for our day, and whatever else he has of late become in the hands of the historical-minded who would take him back to Shakespeare's own. But why should a drama, intended not to be read but to be heard and seen, designed for the effect of the moment, depending on its intelligibility for its success, present such insuperable difficulties, be so variously and contrariously understood? Partly, indeed, because it was heard and seen no longer, the Hamlet of the actors not pleasing the critics, nor that of the critics the actors; and Wordsworth, Coleridge, Lamb, Hunt, Hazlitt, Goethe himself now began declaring that Shakespeare in general, Hamlet in particular, was, because of his 'excellence,' not fitted for the stage.[65] Lamb even deems it necessary to explain the fact that the hero's 'silent meditations with which his bosom is bursting are reduced to *words* — for the sake of the reader, who must otherwise remain ignorant of what is passing there'! His Hamlet existed, mysteriously, apart from or (indeed) *above* the expression, and therefore apart from the Hamlet of two centuries, less remote from Shakespeare's own. A preface 'should please all,' wrote Anthony Scoloker, in 1604, 'like Prince Hamlet'; in 1711 Shaftesbury referred to the tragedy as 'that piece . . . which appears to have most affected English hearts and has perhaps been oftenest acted of any which have come upon our stage'; and a hero so popular then or since was not, we may be sure, either a puzzling or a pusillanimous one. As Steele

[65] I am in this sentence indebted to a yet unpublished 'History of *Hamlet* Criticism,' by Paul S. Conklin.

saw Betterton play him he was 'a young man of great expectation, vivacity, and enterprise'; and for actors and audiences, and down to the Romantic age for everybody, he measured up, like Shakespeare's other heroes, to the requirements of Boileau, who, despite his neo-classicism, was more healthily romantic than the nineteenth-century Romantics themselves. To hold the stage for long and never be tedious, choose, he bids the poet, one heroic even in his faults (as in procrastination, vacillation, self-deception, and the rest of them he certainly could not be) —

> En valeur éclatant, en vertus magnifique;
> Qu'en lui, jusqu'aux défauts, tout se montre héroïque.

Lamb himself presently says the same as he refers to 'a great or heroic nature' as the proper hero of tragedy. Even the Stagirite was, so far, romantic, with the foremost Greek tragic poets to bear him out, as he insisted on the hero's being noble or illustrious, 'better than men are' — 'greater than they are,' said Longinus — and on the impor-tance in tragedy of the 'marvelous.' A hero defective or frustrate, 'stagy' or 'hysterical' — what would Aristotle or Longinus, Aeschy-lus or Sophocles, have said to that, not to mention the sound and solid Athenian or Elizabethan spectators?

Now this or any other playwright's plays have, as Mr. Lawrence says, 'not two meanings, one for the pit and the other for the gal-lery,' one for the lowbrow, another for the high, still less one for the stage, another for the closet, and least of all, as in sparing the King at prayer, meanings 'exactly opposite.'[66] If both are capable specta-tors, the highbrow enjoys the play as the lowbrow does, only more keenly and deeply. Shakespeare's art is not unlike other art. Speng-ler's notion that classical art is popular, the Gothic esoteric, does not hold for Shakespeare at any rate, who in his own day both was popu-lar and intended to be, above all in this particular play. For that matter, Titian's 'Assumption of the Virgin' and Michelangelo's frescoes in the Sistine, a symphony of Mozart or of Beethoven, nay, a tragedy of Marlowe, Beaumont, or Webster, the *Divine Comedy* and *Faust* itself when at their best, require little if any elucidation; and *Hamlet*, if it hadn't had this (and were not a familiar play re-

---

[66] Cf. Prof. Elton's *Modern Studies*, p. 106.

written, here and there a little carelessly too) would require no more.
As in all the greatest poetry, the ideas, reduced to prose, are simple
and obvious; their subtlety and originality are but those of beauty,
of poetry, that is, of a fitness for place and occasion. And what
Wordsworth said of poets is obviously still truer of playwrights —
'that if their works be good, they contain within themselves all that
is necessary to their being comprehended and relished.'[67]   Hamlet
(together with the old *Hamlet*) certainly contains it; and scholarship
or criticism is to little purpose except to remove the obstacles in the
way — chiefly those of scholarship and criticism.

21

'So tantalising and ineffective a play!' exclaims Matthew Arnold,
now a sexagenarian, in a Letter of an old Playgoer, in 1884, which
I first read some weeks after writing the above:

To the spectator who loves true and powerful drama and can judge
whether he gets it or not, 'Hamlet' is a piece which opens, indeed, simply
and admirably, and then: 'The rest is puzzle.'

And that, rightly and for the proper reasons, the great critic and poet
declares drama should not be —

'Hamlet' thus comes at last to be not a drama followed with perfect comprehension and profoundest emotion, which is the ideal of tragedy.

The only question is whether with perfect comprehension and profoundest emotion *Hamlet* cannot be followed. By actors and audiences it has been, the world over. Arnold found it a puzzle — did
not make it so — but did not, honestly and properly did not, like
those who had made it so for him and for too many others, take keen
pleasure in it. Strange that he did not rebel, invoking Molière,
who saw his own plays being turned into puzzles, though of a different sort: 'Laissons-nous aller de bonne foi aux choses qui nous
prennent par les entrailles, et ne cherchons point de raisonnements
pour nous empêcher d'avoir du plaisir.'

[67] Cf. Appendix, Note D.

22

Criticism repeats itself, and who knows but Shakespeare's fate will be shared by Ibsen? *Little Eyolf* is becoming another *Hamlet*, only it is now the dramatist himself that, perversely, is 'keeping us from our pleasure'! By actors and audiences and even the critics he had been 'taken at his plain word,' and the hero, Allmers, had been received sympathetically; but by an intelligent and, in many ways, really discriminating critic he has been made out to be fundamentally insincere.[68] Hitherto he had been an earnest though self-centered seeker, who finally gets out of himself and reaches the light: now he has become a thoroughgoing charlatan. In Ibsen there is self-deception, as we have seen above; and moments of it, likewise plainly indicated, there are in Allmers, as might be expected in the presentation of an egoistic idealist: this newly discovered, larger element is not presented, but inferred. The self-revelation in the last act, which, the critic himself acknowledges, is (like Shakespeare's soliloquies) ordinarily to be taken at face value, as in *The Master-Builder* and *Rosmersholm*; the lofty reconciliation with human life; the solemnity of manner and 'organ tones' of the close — all these he considers, so far as the hero is concerned, to be misleading. To judge by the technique or means of expression — and what else is there to judge by? — Ibsen intended a worthy, not unsympathetic character. But here expression no longer counts. The dramatist set 'a trap' — 'with an almost satanic smile of satisfaction he decided to keep to himself his esoteric knowledge of the man's real nature.' That is the present-day equivalent, the logical development, of Shakespeare's writing 'to please himself,' 'for posterity,' and of his making a character a puzzle because the living and breathing are. Only, the modern goes the Elizabethan one better. The latter is not understood; the former — who knows but his fate will be shared by Shakespeare? — prefers not to be understood. And that is dramatic art!

[68] H. J. Weigand, *The Modern Ibsen* (1925), Chap. X (by permission of Henry Holt and Company).

CHAPTER V

Othello the Man

I

THELLO THE MAN is my subject, not Othello as the central and inseparable element of a great dramatic structure and as a figure on the stage. With the latter I have dealt elsewhere,[1] and have shown that he is led to hearken to Iago, not with a psychological justification, but by means of a time-honored convention, in order to precipitate a more effective situation, that of a hero, by nature not jealous but noble and lovable, becoming jealous nevertheless. To this end he is made neither stupid, on the one hand, nor pliable, on the other; and neither suspicious, nor (what comes to the same thing) improperly trustful; for if he were any of these, he would fall short of our full sympathy and weaken the situation. By the convention Iago's hypocrisy is presumed to be impenetrable: by Shakespeare's handling of the convention it is so indeed. Cassio and even Desdemona, as well as the hero, turn to the villain for counsel; the villain, truly sagacious, plays the part of honesty convincingly: and therefore the hero himself is not a dupe or gull. He is, on the contrary, one of the most tragic figures ever put upon the stage —

> An honourable murderer, if you will;
> For nought I did in hate, but all in honour.

How, then, can he convince or content us today, thus lacking in a predisposition, a psychology? Still, as of old, by his character, by trait and speech; and not only by the individuality of the one and the identity of the other but by the poignant charm of both. Like the ancient dramatists, the other Elizabethans, and more of the moderns

---

[1] Most fully in my *Art and Artifice in Shakespeare*, Chap. II.

than we care to acknowledge, indeed like artists generally, Shakespeare appealed not primarily to the intellect and reason of the audience but to their eyes and ears, their imaginations and emotions;
and like them he drew immediately perceptible characters, did not
work up psychological studies. Poetry, with its infinite differentiating power, was his chief resource, as line and color, not anatomy
(nor geology or botany, for that matter), are the chief resource of
the painter. Art, as both Burke and Wordsworth say, has to do not
with facts but with appearances. Drama, as in the two preceding
chapters we have noticed, has to do not with subjective but objective behavior, and, if need be, takes liberties even with that. The
dramatist provided motives, and considered mental processes, often
but in so far as was necessary for a stage presentation, even as a sculptor carves only the front of a figure designed for a niche. And for
the purposes of the play as a whole, for the intensity of the central
situation, he, unlike the sculptor, sometimes found it necessary, as
here, not to provide or consider further. He is in the theater, his
primary material is action, and, not to impede it, he must reduce
and simplify the other material that his situation involves. He must
project it, model in high relief. We, then, must not look behind the
figure but at it, attending to the dramatic performance, marking the
traits as they appear in the moving picture, drinking in the speech,
with its tones and overtones. There, unmistakably, is the character —
in a work of art.

2

It is in scene ii that the Moor first comes before us. Iago has been
telling him how out of loyalty he had felt like yerking Othello's
enemy, Brabantio (or, possibly, Roderigo), 'here under the ribs.'
''Tis better as it is' is the reply. Nothing could be simpler or, in
itself, more commonplace; such a speech who of us could not have
written, and why attach to it any importance here? Many of the
finest strokes of art are nothing in themselves, but, like this, significant only in their place or at the moment; and now at once is
heard Othello's voice, and in his vein — his tolerant calm and dignity, which, except when eclipsed by an alien passion, appears
throughout. Even when thus obscured his native temper is discernible; and though not in original brightness, it fully emerges

before the end. By no coincidence Othello's last words to Iago, as he vows himself in Titanic pride to eternal silence, are an echo of the first:

> Well, thou dost best.

That is not merely a repeated *motif*, or a rest tone at the close of the harmony, but also what Othello, as we have known him, must certainly have said. Even then he can give the devil his due; even then he would have no futile discussion or disturbance.

All that follows the hero's first speech lends it the effect of harmony and propriety: what precedes lends it that of relief or force. Iago has been telling of the animosity and abusiveness of his enemy, but with our own eyes we had seen the General's informant contriving against him. The Moor and his love are in danger, and it is thus that he takes the news! The effect is accentuated as this limb of Satan endeavors to work upon him. 'Nay, but he prated,' and Iago hints at divorce or imprisonment. 'Let him do his spite,' says the Moor. If anybody could have written the hero's first words, not everybody could have made them so momentous; and those which presently ensue nobody else could even have written, still less have put in their place. Hitherto Othello's character has been appearing, as if in Ibsen, by way of fairly realistic everyday conversation; but presently it appears heightened by poetry, and then his voice takes on tone and resonance. It rises, as it were, from speech to song. But he is speaking still, in character and to the point. Unlike Hamlet, he has few idiosyncrasies or pet expressions, is not addicted to questions or parentheses, repetitions or colloquialisms. He is no such moody and impatient, mutable and startling spirit; and his dignity, serenity, and amplitude of nature become manifest in a fuller, rounder, weightier utterance (the parentheses, if any, flowing, not zigzagging like Hamlet's), and in a more gracious deference or condescension of address, than is to be found in Shakespeare's other heroes:

> for know, Iago . . . .

> Good Signior, you shall more command with years
> Than with your weapons.

> Most potent, grave, and reverend signiors,
> My very noble and approv'd good masters . . . .

The crown of dignity is courtesy. The Moor has the leisure and the inclination to speak the name (often with title or attribute) of the person before him — 'Desdemona,' 'Cassio,' 'Iago,' 'sweet Desdemona,' 'O my fair warrior,' 'good Michael,' 'honest Iago,' 'Nay, stare not, masters'; and before the Senate, the Doge, and Brabantio his ceremoniousness is heightened. In general he has an easy approach:

> Yet, *by your gracious patience,*
> I will a round unvarnish'd tale deliver. . . .
>
> *I do beseech you,*
> Send for the lady to the Sagittary.
>
> *Why, why is this?*
> Think'st thou I'd make a life of jealousy?
>
> . . . Had it pleas'd Heaven
> To try me with affliction; had they rain'd
> All kinds of sores and shames on my bare head,
> Steep'd me in poverty to the very lips,
> Given to captivity me and my utmost hopes,
> I should have found. . . .
>
> *Why, anything.*
> An honourable murderer, *if you will.* . . .
>
> *Well,* thou dost best.
>
> *Soft you*; a word or two before you go.

But though easy, his tread is stately:

> She lov'd me for the dangers I had pass'd,
> And I lov'd her that she did pity them.
>
> Then must you speak
> Of one that lov'd not wisely but too well;
> Of one not easily jealous, but, being wrought,
> Perplex'd in the extreme.

Seldom, and never sharply, does he turn aside:

> Wherein of antres vast and deserts idle,
> Rough quarries, rocks, and hills whose heads touch heaven,
> It was my hint to speak — *such was the process,* —
> And of the Cannibals. . . .

And it is much in keeping that he should be given to inversions —
'rude am I in my speech. . . . And little of this great world do I
know' — and should frequently quit the more direct and dramatic
metaphor for simile or comparison. In short (until after he is
wrought upon) he is not high-strung and mutable like Hamlet,
abrupt and impetuous like Macbeth, violent like Lear, bluff and
arrogant like Coriolanus; at no time could he be mistaken for any of
these; and if Hamlet's voice is vibrant and penetrating, Othello's is
resonant and full.

All this, however, has to do only with the manner or deportment,
the gait or vesture, of the spirit that we know and love; and this
spirit is now at once disclosed, possessing traits and qualities in
abundance.

> . . . for know, Iago,
> But that I love the gentle Desdemona,
> I would not my unhousèd free condition
> Put into circumscription and confine
> For the sea's worth.

Here already are the richness and the volume of his voice; here is
the largeness as well as the tenderness of his spirit; and the measure
of both the magnitude and the sanity of his affection is the adven-
turous freedom which he has, half reluctantly, surrendered. He is
no Oriental voluptuary, as has been imagined, 'brought up in a
harem,' and no black unnaturally infatuated with a white. Indeed,
except in complexion and feature, there is no more of the Moor, or
negro, in him than of the Italian in Desdemona. And he has neither
the obsequiousness nor the resentment, and still less the sense of
inferiority, of a subject race. On the contrary, though devoted to
Venice, he is proud of his royal lineage and untouched by shame for
the stigma of his color. (Stigma there is none except in the eyes of
Iago, Roderigo, and Brabantio.) Of a racial psychology or a pa-
thology,[2] either, there are no traces in him; such notions, in fact, are

[2] This notion of *Kulturgeschichte* and *Völkerpsychologie* in Shakespeare, which, so
far as Othello is concerned, seems to have been started by Schlegel, but was long
since knocked on the head by Bradley, still comes to life now and then. Nor is there
racial antipathy in the play. Iago makes capital out of Othello's color, as he does
out of his age; but it is only under his spell that the Moor considers either matter, and
then only for a moment. 'Haply for I am black . . . and for I am declin'd into the
vale of years — yet that's not much'; and he never refers to the matter again. The

foreign to Elizabethan dramatic art — to great popular drama of any time; what is African or Oriental about him is merely a matter of sentiment and poetry, of adventures in faraway places and of imagery drawn from nature and from battle; and for all the stalwart vigor of his manhood he is as romantically conceived and inclined as his young and gentle wife.

3

A party with torches appears, and Iago, declaring it to be Brabantio and his friends, artfully begs him to retire. 'Not I; I must be found' — for him no retiring or retreating! — but it turns out to be Cassio and the messengers of the Duke, whom Othello then receives with his natural and ample courtesy. Presently comes Brabantio indeed, with officers and weapons; on both sides they draw; and thereupon we perceive the source of the Moor's calm and dignity, a courage so great as to be cool, a self-possession too lofty to be troubled:

Keep up your bright swords, for the dew will rust them.

He evidently was born to command; but this is much the same sort of pleasantry that later appears in the Senate Chamber, as he undertakes to tell with

what drugs, what charms,
What conjuration and what mighty magic,
(For such proceeding I am charg'd withal)
I won his daughter;

and as he ends:

This only is the witchcraft I have us'd.
Here comes the lady; let her witness it.

Elizabethans, who had no negroes amongst them, were not prejudiced; mating with a black was repugnant to them, as in *Titus Andronicus*, or romantic, as in *Othello*, according to the way it was presented; and here there is no suggestion of miscegenation as an 'ugly business' or 'horror.' The only charge before the Senate is witchcraft.

It is in comedy, and comically, that Shakespeare deals with foreigners as such; and it is only with those familiar to the Elizabethans — Welshmen, Irishmen, Frenchmen — and in accordance with the Elizabethan popular conception. His realism is mainly a matter of mispronunciation, of manners or temper. In Shylock a larger fund of both prejudice and knowledge was at his command through the public's acquaintance with both tradition and the Scriptures.

It is not wit, with point or edge — that is to be found in Hamlet, in Iago; it is the ease and liberty of a mind equal to whatever befalls. In the happy fullness of his being his utterance breaks into a ripple in the face of danger; but the voice is the same as when he is really touched. How naturally, how unhesitatingly and graciously he bows in deference to the Magnifico, his father-in-law:

> Good Signior, you shall more command with years
> Than with your weapons.

And, on the later occasion, who but he would so begin his defense before the Senate — the tale of his whole course of love — after Brabantio's abusive interruption and the question (about poisoning the young maid's mind) put by the Senator squarely at him:

> Her father lov'd me; oft invited me. . . .

If with that he does not smile again a little, though sadly, it is only because courtesy forbids.

4

But we are anticipating. The Moor's deference at the first encounter calls forth only reproaches, which end in the old man's order to lay hold upon him. Again Othello bids them stay:

> Both you of my inclining and the rest.
> Were it my cue to fight, I should have known it
> Without a prompter.

He is every inch a general; and his tone of authority, as it should do, now rises; yet quietly and conciliatingly he informs the Magnifico of the Duke's summons to the Council, which they answer then together.

There Othello is towards Brabantio deferential and reticent still, noticing none of his personalities, replying only to the charge before the Court. 'What, in your own part,' asks the Duke, 'can you say to this?' 'Nothing,' puts in Brabantio, 'but this is so'; and thus the Moor's first words before them,

> Most potent, grave, and reverend signiors . . .

ring out with only a higher and clearer dignity. This native inclination is now stimulated by the oratorical opportunity, and its effect
is enhanced by his own depreciation of his powers.

Again there is a contrast with Brabantio's indecorum as, at
Othello's words, 'I won his daughter,' he breaks out, amid his
griefs, like one talking to himself:

> A maiden never bold;
> Of spirit so still and quiet that her motion
> Blush'd at herself; and she, in spite of nature. . . .

And that not only is such psychology as both the dramatist employs
and audiences can appreciate but also is dramatic art.

The daughter is a subject still tenderer to the lover, and as he takes
up the tale, the verse — his voice — is respondent to it:

> And, till she come, as truly as to heaven
> I do confess the vices of my blood,
> So justly to your grave ears I'll present
> How I did thrive in this fair lady's love,
> And she in mine.

How much of the tender pride of the final phrase would be lost to
us under another metrical arrangement, without the pause before
and after! How much would be lost in prose! And how delicately
and indirectly he puts the matter as he intimates, in their common
defense, that she, in her simplicity, had met him half way! When
she was wooing he was thriving.

Then comes the famous passage of the reciprocal courting, too
long and too familiar to quote. Some critics have taken it not so
much seriously as grimly, and found Othello rather too romantic
to be a responsible and steady-going husband — a prey to fancy and
sentiment, a gull (or 'goose,' as Rymer called him) already. Like
Desdemona, like Romeo and Juliet, he has not learned 'the facts of
life,' as everybody now does or should do; like them he knows not,
as every welfare-worker or heart-to-heart columnist does, that inter-
racial or runaway marriages, prompted by pity or love at first sight,
are liable to disaster. Shakespeare himself does not know it, in his
plays. As for this one, the 'love of Othello and Desdemona,' observes Mr. Middleton Murry, 'is in itself unclouded,' and had there

been no Iago it 'would have endured to death.'[3] The critics do not
go so far as the Ancient, who charges the Moor with bragging and
telling fantastical lies; and yet they knit their brows. The men
'whose heads do grow beneath their shoulders,' however, came
straight out of Raleigh's *Discovery of Guiana* (1596), and were in
those days accepted; and if there be any flaw in Othello's metal the
dramatist himself takes all possible pains to conceal it. 'I think this
tale would win my daughter too,' says the Duke. Except Iago (and
Brabantio at this moment) everyone in the Senate — everyone in
the play, whether in Venice or in Cyprus afterwards — is filled with
admiration for the Moor and, including Iago, impressed by his
professional ability. Here again the dramatist is dealing in stuff of
the imagination and the emotions; and to hint at such defects in the
hero would be, like giving him a jealous predisposition from the
outset, to throw the advantage of the convention, or initial premise,
away.

With Doge and Senate at any rate the Moor has won his case; and
now, when the cause of the summons is put before him, he begs,
though newly wedded, no exemption or indulgence. 'You must
away tonight.'

Des. Tonight, my lord?
Duke   This night.
Othello   With all my heart.

His wedding-night! In Cinthio's *novella*, the source, his general is
loath to accept the honor because of the separation, and does not till
Desdemona assures him there shall be none. If anything were wanting to prove Shakespeare's sound and solid to the core, without
taint of Oriental voluptuousness, erotic infatuation or infirmity,
that, after what he has already said to Iago about his unhousèd free
condition, is provided here; and the dramatist's work upon him in
this act has been swiftly and surely done. He clearly is not what the
later Raleigh calls him, 'a man carried off his feet, wave-drenched
and blinded by the passion of love':[4] he has, he himself says, 'a natural

---

[3] *Countries of the Mind* (1922), pp. 25–26.

[4] That, like the unsuspiciousness that suspects, is, in the upshot, jealousy; though
this Sir Walter has just denied him (cf. *Shakespeare*, 1907, p. 197, by permission of the
Macmillan Company, New York). These psychological paradoxes displace Shake-

and prompt alacrity in hardness,' and not only our sympathy but
our admiration is now wholly engaged.

5

One of the many causes for Shakespeare's success in his artistic
endeavor, both in this drama and in others, both in his own time and
afterwards, is the way his two chief means of characterization — the
direct and the indirect — confirm and support each other. Here
folk are of one accord in thinking the Moor noble and lovable,
valiant and capable. Of one accord are the Senate in calling him to
meet the Turk. 'Another of his fathom they have none,' Iago admits
at the outset; 'whom our full Senate call all-in-all sufficient,' says
Ludovico in Act IV; 'for he was great of heart,' says Cassio at the
close. And the effect is not incommensurate with the cause. We
in the audience are of the same mind, as we hear him speak, see him
move. It is not merely because the other characters agree — that
they do also concerning Iago's honesty — but because we have ears
and eyes of our own. We find no reason to demur as we often do at
a play by Ibsen or O'Neill, who cannot bestow upon the characters
the qualities he attributes to them. The 'noble Moor' does not disappoint us, nor 'the gentle Desdemona,' nor 'honest Iago,' either —
have we not heard him betimes with Roderigo and in soliloquy? —
as we turn from the reflection to the figure. Now and then in drama
there are effects to be secured by a contrast between these, but,
except through confession to the audience, not in Shakespeare.

Not between figure and reflection is the contrast, but between
these together before and after the tragic change; and to get, and
give, the full shock of that, Ludovico must needs in Act IV come all
the way from Venice. Or between figure and figure — the General
and his Ancient — the contrast being not merely in morals but in
habit of thought and speech. Iago shares some traits with Hamlet,
though different, of course, in the impression they make upon us.
Like him he is penetrating, not ample and embracing, and inclined

---

speare's dramatic contrasts. I wonder that Othello's martial readiness to postpone
his wedding-night has not been turned into 'a fear of his own love,' like Macbeth's
'fear of his own courage.' What a morbid tribe, these Elizabethans — for the characters are taken to be 'documents'!

to colloquialism and repetition, to metaphor rather than the more roundabout simile and comparison. It is when Hamlet is playing the cynical or gloomy madman that there is most resemblance. But to the Ancient the ugly and indecent notions and imagery are a sheer delight, as they are not to the melancholy Dane; and his repetitions are not the explosions of excitement or impatience but the deliberate devices of mesmerizing and tantalizing, as he weaves his spells round Roderigo and then Othello himself. When he is not maneuvering or jesting, his expression, like his thought, is straight as the flight of an arrow or the electric spark. Othello, on the other hand, is like the lion until he is roused, all magnificent repose. Both until then and after, his imagination, instead of piercing, expatiates, and over the phenomena and wonders of the visible universe — antres vast and deserts idle, hills whose heads touch heaven, moon and stars, eclipse and earthquake, the plumèd troop and the Pontic sea. Until then, he shows no inclination to repetition at all; afterwards, only in the momentary ejaculations of his rage or anguish, as in 'blood, blood, blood.' And when the storm is over there is, in the undulations of the ground-swell, almost no verbal repetition but, as we shall see, the recurrence of notions and emotions.

6

In a brief essay it is impossible to follow the character throughout the play; and elsewhere I have shown how skillfully Shakespeare has contrived to approach and lead up to the in itself improbable complication of a generous hero causelessly in a jealous rage. In every way he is the 'noble Moor,' 'whom passion could not shake,' but who by Iago's arts is shaken: that, by the poet's genius for making the improbable probable, is his tragedy, more moving than any psychology on the stage could be. When Mr. Shaw declares that *Othello* is 'pure melodrama,' without 'a touch of character in it that goes below the skin,' and that 'the fitful attempts to make Iago something better than a melodramatic villain only make a hopeless mess of him and his motives,'[5] the critic's unerring perceptions, as so often with him, are overridden by his principles, he makes short work of the dragon of error but without setting the captive free. He sees

---

[5] *Dramatic Opinions and Essays*, II, 279. See above, Chap. I, p. 29.

that there is no psychology but not that there is no need of any. 'There is melodrama that rises into the empyrean,' says George Moore, 'and melodrama unredeemed by poetry. . . . Shakespeare appeals to all the senses, it is true, but he never fails to appeal to the mind.'[6] This melodrama is not '*pure*,' and the absence of fundamental motivation does not make it so. Here there is preparation enough, though external rather than internal. There are superficial, narrative motives (instead of the psychological), such as Hamlet's doubting the Ghost, his unwillingness to kill the King when at prayer, and his simple announcement at the outset that he may 'think meet' to pretend madness, without reason of any sort. Even in Act I Iago's honesty and sagacity are insisted upon; and it is he and his wife that are given charge of Desdemona. Brabantio warns the General against her deception: Iago counts upon it. On his arrival at Cyprus Othello enjoys such happiness that he fears Fate can have no more of it in store for him; and he who by reputation cannot get angry comes pretty near to it when there is an uproar on the watch, and in his inquiry thereupon (though Cassio, to be sure, makes no defense, and Iago is impenetrably 'honest') shows scarcely a judicial spirit. Desdemona, importunate in Cassio's favor, *is* deceitful in denying the loss of the handkerchief. Cassio himself at the beginning of the Temptation scene, upon Othello's approach, 'steals away.' But her conduct, which is owing only to her heedless innocence or to her fright, and Cassio's, which is owing only to his sense of disgrace, are matters which, like Desdemona's 'deceiving' her father by her elopement, the perilousness of such a union — with a white woman, Othello's ignorance of the Venetian women's ways, and the sight of his love-token in Cassio's hand, have unfavorable effect on the hero, not through any uneasy or suspicious nature of his own, but wholly as Iago's fastens like a leech upon him. The 'improbable' is thus made as 'probable,' the unnatural as natural, as may be; but it is only as we keep the attitude of a Renaissance audience (accustomed to story, not psychology, on the stage, and to the convention of the calumniator credited) that we do not take the hero to be really a little gullible when succumbing in the Temptation scene. The convention, the dramatist rightly thinks, must not too plainly appear.

[6] *Conversations in Ebury Street* (1930), pp. 83–84 (by permission of the Liveright Publishing Corporation).

The improbable is, of course, not desired for its own sake, but for the startling situation and extraordinary passions thereby attainable. To most critics the Temptation scene, the *scene à faire*, where they are raised and let loose, has been a stumbling-block. Either they fall back upon 'subjective behavior,' some of them making him out to be jealous by nature from the outset, others making him out to be not really jealous in the upshot; or else, admitting that Othello becomes jealous too easily and quickly, they take that, like Desdemona's having as yet had no opportunity to be unfaithful, for a flaw, indeed, but one not noticeable in Shakespeare's swift-moving and all-engrossing action; or else they throw the blame for this and the other improbabilities on the predetermined plot, though that, unlike Hamlet's or Lear's, was not a familiar old story, already on the stage, with which few liberties could be taken, but one rather novel, and, so far as we are aware, the dramatist's own, not the company's choice. Neither the psychological nor the theatrical nor the scholarly critics look upon the improbabilities as the price of a great and positive artistic advantage. The mere fact that time and occasion for the infidelity might easily have been provided, as Mr. Archer says, 'by a few strokes of the pen,' and that Othello might easily have been ensnared, not in one scene but less precipitately in two or three, proves that in neither matter there is an 'inadvertence' and that the poet and his audience had aesthetic interests and conceptions rather different from those current in highbrow circles today. For Shakespeare, as for the Greek poets and Aristotle too, the price of the highest tragic effect was — melodrama.[7] The critics, however, do not take kindly to the startling situation, the extraordinary passions; do not take to the sharp and striking contrast between the Moor generous and noble and the Moor jealous and furious, and would fain have something of a case for him against Desdemona — have her 'enough of the "supersubtle Venetian" of Iago's description,' as Mr. Shaw himself would, 'to strengthen the case for Othello's jealousy.' They would have the improbable not made probable, as by the external preparations above mentioned, but done away with; would have only reasonable considerations brought to bear, only plausible suspicions excited, and the purity of our sympathy with

[7] Cf. L. A. G. Strong, *Common Sense about Drama*, p. 47. And cf. the next two chapters, pp. 219, 230, 243, 248.

Desdemona and Othello somewhat alloyed, its intensity allayed. For their purposes Desdemona should have made the voyage with Cassio, not with Iago, or Othello should have been tempted after some interval in Cyprus, not at the height of his happiness, the day following his arrival, his wedding-night. Just so, they do not take to the sharp and striking contrast between Romeo in love with Rosaline and Romeo instantaneously in love with Juliet; and for their purposes, as in the source, he should have come to the ball to forget Rosaline, not, as in Shakespeare, to prove her fairer than any other.[8] They would, in short, have adequate motives and no convention, not realizing that the 'most moving works of art,' as Mr. Aldous Huxley puts it, 'are always those in which passion is confined within a severe formal scheme.'[9] But for his own purposes Shakespeare, as was his custom, here did well enough. For the supreme emotional effect there must be no quite reasonable considerations or plausible suspicions; not only because there must be no good case against Desdemona, but because those are matters for the intellect rather than for the imagination and emotions, to which Iago appeals, which must have sway; and there must be no such lapse of time before or during the temptation because that would dull the contrast and retard the momentum. For the dramatist's purposes a spell must be cast upon the hero; and that openly and manifestly, in a single (though once interrupted) climacteric scene. If to save his reputation with us Othello had been permitted a respite in order to think for himself, on his own, he would have sadly and irretrievably impaired it.

7

Even under the spell, in the state of jealous and sensual rage, he is kept, though of course not consistent, continually recognizable. By his manner and bearing we are constantly reminded of his old self — 'And she in mine.'

> For she had eyes, and chose me.

> No, not much mov'd,
> I do not think but Desdemona's honest.

[8] Cf. my *Shakespeare's Young Lovers*, lecture I.
[9] *Essays New and Old* (1927), p. 150.

And poetically — imaginatively and rhythmically — we are made to see that if such a man, so changed, could still be himself, this one certainly is. The 'Pontic Sea,' 'the error of the moon, which comes more nearer earth than she was wont and makes men mad,' 'aspics' tongues,' the Sibyl 'in her prophetic fury,' 'one entire and perfect chrysolite' — these are not out of keeping with 'some nine moons wasted,' 'antres vast and deserts idle,' and 'hills whose heads touch heaven.' And what more fitting as a climax to his full-throated utterance and ample movement than the almost epical simile of the Pontic, or the farewell to 'content,' which antiphonally answers the forebodings concerning his 'content so absolute' upon arrival at Cyprus? In poetry, indeed, in rhythm, the Moor, like all the nobler characters of Shakespeare and those of the ancients before them, has his authentic being. Like Macbeth, and Lear, and Hamlet, but unlike the characters of Pinero or Galsworthy, he will *not* 'abide our question'; these last are nothing if they won't.

What is more directly dramatic is that, under the spell, in speeches almost as convincingly Othello's own, his love is ever before him, is not, as in the naturally jealous, converted and distorted into hate; and this of itself produces glorious effects upon the stage.

> If she be false, O, then heaven mocks itself!
> I'll not believe 't;

> Villain, be sure thou prove my love a whore,
> Be sure of it!

Nay, that's certain. But yet the pity of it, Iago! O Iago, the pity of it, Iago!

> Come, swear it, damn thyself,
> Lest, being like one of heaven, the devils themselves
> Should fear to seize thee!

> O thou weed,
> Who art so lovely fair and smell'st so sweet
> That the sense aches at thee, would thou hadst ne'er been born!

> One more, one more!
> Be thus when thou art dead, and I will kill thee
> And love thee after.

And what is as important to our sympathy, not only has he mani-festly not bred the gross and bestial, selfish and egoistic passion within his own black bosom, but he does not nurse and cherish it, as the jealous do, before our eyes. The sensual images and promptings are Iago's; and for the most part Othello only responds to these. By this unpsychological contrivance of the convention he has not the soul of a sensualist amid his tragic agony, and he can be really 'an honourable murderer' (if the *critics* will) before the end. In his own right he is impelled, not by carnal and vindictive desire, but by a notion of duty; and he is swayed by love. At this point there are both the convention of credulity and a now extinct notion of conjugal rights to accept: in Shakespeare's hands, he kills her, still her lover, as her judge. Thus at the climax, as in the role ever since he falls into the Ancient's toils, there is that 'balance or reconcilement of opposite or discordant qualities' essential to drama. But this is as in poetry, not as in drama nowadays, nor as it sometimes is in the tragedy of Corneille and Racine. The contrast is not at the center, in a soul naturally divided against itself, whence the action must ensue. The two lines of feeling — love and jealousy — run parallel, do not proceed from a burning-point or focus. The contrast is one of juxtaposition, like that in other artificial ancient and Elizabethan situations — disguise such as Kent's or Edgar's, feigning such as Hamlet's or Iago's, or evil-doers such as Macbeth and his lady confronted by a conscience not really their own.[10] And it is mainly by the power of poetry that this contrast is made acceptable, by the unmistakable ring of Othello's voice, the throb or quiver of his passion.

> It is the caúse, it is the caúse, my sóul —
> Let me nòt náme it to you, yóu chàste stárs! —
> It is the cause. Yet I'll not shed her blood,
> Nor scar that whiter skin of hers than snow
> And smooth as monumental alabaster.
> Yét she must díe, élse she'll betráy móre mèn.

What a tone and a gesture for the apostrophe to the stars; what changes at 'Yet I'll not shed her blood,' where we are buoyed up as in consolation, and at 'Yet she must die,' where the meter snaps!

Why must she die? Why not 'kill the woman with kindness' like Heywood's hero, or kill himself? One or the other is certainly what he would do if the action proceeded wholly from the char-

[10] See above, Chap. I, p. 34.

acter. But this is high tragedy. He loves her still; he imagines himself the minister of justice; but a virus has been shot into him —
jealous, sensual, brutal, murderous. Thus moved, Othello is not the
man to think, as Mr. Shaw would have him, that if there is poison
to be taken, he is the one to take it — if there is choking to be done,
he is not the one to do it. In Shakespeare generally, as in the other
Elizabethans down to the time of Fletcher and Massinger, and as in
the ancients before him, altruism, self-effacement in the main matter
in hand, was, if for any one, rather for the heroine, like Sophocles'
Antigone (to whom, however, as to the other Greeks, a funeral duty
to a brother is a greater thing than life and love). It is not, as has been
thought, that altruism then seemed unmanly, but that it is generally
less dramatic. In the hero it would slacken the tragic intensity,
would blunt or soften the passionate impact. Even in the heroine
it often does that, as in the Dame aux Camélias. Of Othello's treatment of his wife it has been said that 'gentlemen don't do such
things': Heywood's and Mr. Shaw's gentlemen, though, would be
rather unmanageable — unimposing — as tragic heroes. Browning's Moor, Luria, who, rising to the heights of self-renunciation,
kills himself, moves us to admiration, but little to pity and less to
fear. He does not suffer deeply enough to commit a deed of horror;
and therefore we know not, feel not, how he suffers. He rises above
his suffering, and therefore we do; he has consolations within him,
therefore can dispense with ours. Not so with Shakespeare's Moor.

8

The scene begins solemnly, religiously; but when the lady wakes,
it becomes, though more terrible, rather more appealing to the
realistic taste. Justice comes nearer to breaking her sword: the innocent tears of the lady only steel it. 'Have you pray'd tonight,
Desdemona?' and we are reminded of what he had said of her, not
many hours (or minutes) before, in the scene where he enacts the
part of a visitor at a brothel:

And yet she'll kneel and pray: I have seen her do't —

a memory still more natural and more poignant at its reappearance.
And the pangs and throes of affection are more perceptible in what
follows:

> Well, do it and be brief; I will walk by;
> I would not kill thy unprepparèd spirit;
> No, heaven forfend! I would not kill thy soul.

(The final syllables are heavy with all the weight of his purpose on his heart.) Still more perceptible are the pangs and throes after the deed:

> What noíse is this? nòt déad? not yét quìte déad?

(If the Moor were jealous by nature, and not merely laboring under a strong delusion, there would be less of a clash of feeling, or it would touch us less.) And again:

> Ha, no more moving?
> Still as the grave. Shall she [Emilia] come in? Were't good?
> I think she stirs again: — no. What's best to do?
> If she come in, she'll sure speak to my wife.
> My wife! my wife! what wife? I have no wife.

There, in the last line, is one of the full and sudden flashes of the Shakespearean tragic lantern, which illumine and project the scene, which make the stage wide as the earth and narrow the action to an instant. In the latter part of the play they abound:

> What committed!
> Heaven stops the nose at it, and the moon winks . . .

> Methinks it should be now a huge eclipse
> Of sun and moon, and that th' affrighted globe
> Did yawn at alteration. . . .

> ask thy husband else.
> O, I were damn'd beneath all depth in hell
> But that I did proceed upon just grounds
> To this extremity;

> Be thus when thou art dead, and I will kill thee
> And love thee after.

> Cold, cold, my girl!
> Even like thy chastity.

The last two outcries are like Lear's:

> No, no, no life!
> Why should a dog, a horse, a rat, have life,
> And *thou* no breath at all?

and Macbeth's:

> Wake *Duncan* with thy knocking! I would thou couldst!

In Ibsen's dialogue there is more of penetration and suspense; in Shakespeare's more of seizure and comprehension.

Again Emilia, whom he has already answered, cries out within, and he goes:

> I had forgot thee. O, come in, Emilia.
> Soft; by and by. — Let me the curtains draw. —
> Where art thou?

Here is more psychology of the right dramatic sort, in this stage business; and at the word 'wife' he *had* forgotten. There has been, in his own words, an 'eclipse,' and he is now groping and stumbling in its shadow.

9

The *finale* of *Othello* is, I think, the most poignant in any tragedy except *King Lear*; but the great stroke is where the hero so manifestly, so spectacularly comes from under the spell of his delusion, and is almost, but by no means wholly, himself again. All along he has been Othello, though under the baleful shadow of Iago; now he shines forth, in wonted though troubled splendor. And the spectacle moves to music. There are actual echoes, such as 'Well, thou dost best,' spoken to the demi-devil when he refuses speech, and such as, a few moments before that, the rejoinder when he hisses, 'I bleed, sir, but not killed':

> I am not sorry, neither; I'd have thee live;
> For, in my sense, 'tis happiness to die . . .

which is antiphonally related to the *other* half of the foreboding on the quay,

> If it were now to die,
> 'Twere now to be most happy.

I have elsewhere[11] traced an effect of rhythm and recurrence, not at this point only, but also as, with dramatic suspense and mystery, thoughts of the sword, of the past and the future, come and go,

---

[11] See my *Art and Artifice in Shakespeare*, pp. 43–47.

or rise and fall, by a sort of undulation. All I can touch on here is the effect as his full voice, which has been, as it were, disguised, or dramatized, peals out again at intervals, amid the varied tragic action, but carrying now another, a covert burden of woe. It is music not only to the mind but to the ear, and we listen for it:

> Nay, stare not, masters; it is true indeed.
>   Are there no stones in heaven
> But what serve for the thunder?
>   I am not valiant, neither,
> But every puny whipster gets my sword.
> But why should honour outlive honesty?
> Let it go all.

> I have another weapon in this chamber;
> It is a sword of Spain, the ice-brook's temper, —
> O, here it is. Uncle, I must come forth.

> Look in upon me, then, and speak with me,
> Or naked [unarmed] as I am, I will assault thee.

>   Behold, I have a weapon;
> A better never did itself sustain
> Upon a soldier's thigh. I have seen the day
> That, with this little arm and this good sword,
> I have made my way through more impediments
> Than twenty times your stop. But, O vain boast!
> Who can control his fate? 'tis not so now.
> Be not afraid, though you do see me weapon'd. . . .

> Soft you; a word or two before you go. . . .

In the final speech, which with these last words begins, he looks forward, through the past. He remembers his services to the signiory, as in reassuring Iago at the outset; remembers his deeds of prowess, as in the tale of his wooing: and as when one is near the end it will do, the past possesses him. His utterance is more deeply tinged with Oriental memories and imagery; but it is like Othello directly, in mood, tone, and rhythm. He speaks pregnantly, weightily, masterfully, though not serenely as of old. Even now, a prisoner, he comports himself, as in the presence of the Senate, like one clothed in authority: 'Speak of me as I am — Then must you speak — Set you down this — And say besides, that in Aleppo once.' So, before that, 'I must come forth — Look in upon me . . . or . . . I will assault thee.' He is Othello still.

He says nothing now of Desdemona, of his love or his despair; all that sufficiently, and terribly, appears again at the end. Mr. Eliot is of the opinion that the Moor has, for the moment, forgotten her, and is turning himself into a pathetic figure: he remains a tragic one. 'Speak of me as I am; nothing extenuate.' Could that be manlier? Mr. G. W. Knight thinks the speech, particularly at

> one whose subdu'd eyes,
> Albeit unusèd to the melting mood,
> Drop tears as fast as the Arabian trees
> Their medicinal gum,

studied and artificial, 'nerveless and without force.' Presently he adds, 'there is something sentimental in Othello's language, in Othello'; and then, 'he loves emotion for its own sake, luxuriates in it, like Richard II.' Before that he says, 'that Iago should scheme . . . to undermine Othello's faith in himself, his wife, and his "occupation," is inevitable'; and then, 'Othello is indeed "a gull, a dolt." '12 Thus the 'tragic fault' — morality and psychology — is provided for at the expense of admiration and sympathy as well as of the whole tragic structure. Contrasting the above verses with Macduff's

> O, I could play the woman with mine eyes,

Mr. Knight ignores the situation. All the passages have in common is the tears which one man is shedding and the other refusing to shed. Drama ebbs, of course, as well as flows. The high point of Othello's passion, at the discovery, is past, as Macduff's is not; another high point is coming, at the stabbing; and it is a proud and mournful, retrospective and prospective mood that possesses the hero now. Like the paladin Roland, whom there is really more reason to call sentimental,

> De plusurs choses à remembrer li prist.

But here, as in those earlier spacious musings on the verge of the beyond, there is only the finest possible use of the ancient and

---

12 *The Wheel of Fire* (1930), pp. 111, 129, 130 (by permission of the Oxford University Press).

Elizabethan convention of self-description, far more appropriate than with Macbeth, who, when fearing the sound of his footsteps may diminish 'the present horror,' has himself been called 'almost an epicure in crime.' Othello, Macbeth, Hamlet — in the hands of the critics what a morbid, degenerate, *fin de siècle* set these popular romantic heroes become! The convention here serves to keep the situation — the character's qualities rather than the character — fully and immediately before us. There is variation but no relaxation, no sentimentalizing or luxuriating. The Paladin does not reproach himself for his great error as the Moor indirectly does. The Moor thinks of one thing and speaks of another, speaks of himself and thinks of the lady; and what can be more dramatic? Moreover, he must now at the last think a little well of himself, even because he has thought so ill; and what can be more tragic? Tragedy deals with the extremities of human feeling; but we are surer the character has passed through them when he arrives at the limits. Several times already, in the musical but dramatic movement in his mind, touched upon above, and in the passages cited, this endeavor to think better of himself has appeared. He is not only a lover but a soldier, a governor —

> But why should honour outlive honesty?
> Let it go all.

What a groan of surrender! Honor is as the breath of his nostrils:

> For nought I did in hate, but all in honour.

That high and tragic but improbable situation has in the play been comprehended and realized in both speech and action. What is more remarkable, the hero also has been realized as a man. By consonance of traits, not consistency of motives, by poetry, not analysis or inner disclosure, by word and figure, by accent and rhythm, this great thing has been brought about. The dramatist keeps to the medium he has chosen, as a painter does to line and color, the sculptor to masses and surfaces; he keeps away from science — from psychology — and to his art. And it is by virtue of the imagination at its highest potency, not of the intellect, that the improbable becomes probable, even at the intellect's expense.

What is almost equally important to the illusion, the hero belongs to the world in which he is presented, a romantic, poetic world. That is far away, at Venice or Cyprus, and not really there. Certain hard-headed sociological considerations do not apply. He does not see through Iago, for others do not; he is thereby not a gull, for the others are not. And no more than Desdemona does he come to grief in his love-making through want of a solid and extensive knowledge of the other's character; for nobody in this play or in any other of Shakespeare's takes such a point of view. In fact, this pair of lovers have known each other better and longer than most of them. But the Moor's travels and exploits have been marvels, and it is his tale of them that has won Desdemona's love. Brabantio thinks he has won it not by 'undue influence' but by spells and medicines. This is a court where such charges may be entertained, for the Senator inquires of the Moor if the Magnifico's report be true,

> Or came it by request and such fair question
> As soul to soul affordeth?

The language itself is not of the tribunal! And the handkerchief that she loses is not such as women are daily with impunity losing, but has magic in the web of it, as Desdemona believes. The motives are those of romance, the atmosphere that of poetry. Othello and his lady are enveloped in auras, as also Iago is, though in one somewhat electrical and murky. They and the other figures are not wholly real except in relation to one another: 'they are alive,' as Mr. Eliot would put it, 'with the life of the play.' Their thoughts are images, their passions make harmonies, their words are notes of music; and like Hamlet and Ophelia, Macbeth and his Lady, Lear and Cordelia, Antony and Cleopatra, as well as the characters of all great drama, epic, and novel, they belong to their own world, not unlike ours, yet remote, transformed. 'On admet en art,' says Lanson, 'un art qui dépasse la nature en la respectant.'

CHAPTER VI

Oedipus and Othello

Corneille, Rymer, and Voltaire

I

THERE is significance, I think, in the fact that the *Oedipus Tyrannus* and *Othello* produced upon some of the earlier critics, in France and in England, an identical impression. Both heroes were, very remarkably, considered stupid. And the reasons for the opinion seem to me similar, residing in the artistic method of the two tragedies and in the aesthetic prepossessions of the critics.

That the tragedies are comparable may sound strange. One observes the unities, the other begins at Venice and ends at Cyprus. One is a play of fate, the other of intrigue. One is of retrospect and disclosure, the other of action. One contains few characters, the other many. One deals with religious, political, and domestic interests; the other with romantic love. But both are masterpieces, masterpieces not only of poetic but of dramatic art; and both alike produce great effect on the stage today. And this effect is owing to similar causes. Of great intensity, it arises out of a peremptory compression and a violent contrast. In *Othello* the action conforms to the unities once it is started; fate presides over it in the person of Iago, the hero (not jealous or suspicious by nature) being, like Oedipus, not the cause of the tragic situation in which he is placed; and the denouement, as in the Greek tragedy, is that most esteemed by Aristotle, one of peripeteia (or reversal) and anagnorisis (or recognition) combined, the deed, done in ignorance, recoiling, as the doer in horror acknowledges, on his own head. In both tragedies this fatal ignorance is procured at the cost of a great improbability. In one it is that the hero should fail to see through the villain and his purposes; in the other it is far greater — that he should, in fleeing from the fulfillment of the oracle, have killed his father and married his mother without even later suspecting it, and then, the plague having come upon the city, and Delphi, in another oracle, having demanded atonement for bloodshed, should not perceive the import or credit the truthfulness of Teiresias' disclosures.

2

It is no less personages than Corneille and Voltaire,[1] both of them dramatists, and classical ones too, who thus mistook the art of Sophocles. Venturing by versions of their own to improve upon it, they also openly found fault with it. The improbability of what has happened before the tragedy begins they, for the most part, passed over: either their own dramatic sense or the authority of Aristotle bade them forbear, and in the initial situation they recognized the postulate or premise. Some of the improbability, as it should be, is in the background; but what of that which is not?

As Lemaître, whose report[2] I now follow, observes: To Corneille, who was at the time in his old age, the tragedy seemed a little childish; and to Voltaire, who was twenty-five or younger, formless and barbarous. Two objections they had against it, — that the denouement is apparent from the beginning and that the hero himself cannot perceive it till the end. In the second scene Teiresias declares that Oedipus is the slayer of Laius. 'This man whom you seek, this murderer whom you curse, is here. He passes for a stranger, but he shall learn that Thebes is his fatherland, and thereat he will have no cause to rejoice . . . he will be the brother of his children, the son of his wife, the murderer of his sire. . . .'

Nous n'avons donc plus rien à apprendre, dit Voltaire, et voilà la pièce entièrement finie.

But, rejoins Lemaître, not for Oedipus. So great and terrible a truth cannot at a blow force an entrance into his consciousness. The pronouncement troubles and provokes without enlightening

---

[1] His Œdipe was published in 1719; Corneille's in 1659; to each the criticism is prefixed.

[2] Impressions de théâtre (1889), 3ᵉ série, pp. 1–14.

him. . . . He rears up under the vague accusations of the prophet: he thinks him suborned by Creon, his brother-in-law, and quarrels with both. Then he questions Jocasta, who, to reassure him and prove to him the vanity of soothsaying, tells him how it had long ago been predicted that her son should be the murderer of Laius, and to thwart the oracle she had exposed him on Cithaeron. Oedipus then bethinks him how once at Corinth a drunken man had called him a foundling; how an oracle had foretold that he should kill his father and defile the bed of his mother; how to escape this abomination he had quitted the city, and on the way to Thebes he had slain a man who might have been Laius.

Et voilà, reprend Voltaire, la pièce finie une seconde fois! Il faut que cet Œdipe soit idiot pour ne pas comprendre.

A messenger arrives who announces to Oedipus the death of Polybus (and his accession to the throne of Corinth). Presently, to console him in his loss, the messenger informs him that Polybus was not his father: he himself had received Oedipus on Cithaeron as a baby from the hands of Laius' shepherd. The latter, having been summoned, declares that he in turn had received the infant from Jocasta.

Troisième dénouement, dit Voltaire, troisième conclusion, identique aux deux premières. Quelle pièce mal faite!

Rather, exclaims Lemaître, what a remarkable idea this of Voltaire's! When we read the tragedy of Sophocles, is it to know who killed Laius and who Oedipus' parents were? That we knew long ago. What makes the dramatic power of the *Oedipus Tyrannus* is precisely the fact that we do know what the hero is ignorant of, or wishes to be, and that the last word of this gradual revelation is a thunderclap for him alone, not for us. What from point to point excites our curiosity and arouses our compassion is to see this unfortunate, driven to ruin by a superior power, passionately invite, and in turn avoid, the verdict of destiny; to see the veil slowly rent, by him and despite him, before his eyes . . . to see by what progression of inquietudes — glimpses doubtful for him alone — and by what stages of amazement, horror, and rage, he will arrive at the solution of this problem that both fascinates and affrights him. . . .

So far, in brief, Lemaître on Voltaire; his presentation of the stripling critic's pronouncements, in the four paragraphs above, being, though not verbally exact, essentially so.

Sarcey,[3] without taking account of Corneille and Voltaire, said much the same about the supreme qualities of the tragedy upon its performance seven years earlier. Those were the great days of the theater (in Paris happily not yet ended) when Sophocles revisited the stage, and critics of such caliber had scope in the daily press! The play, he says, is made precisely for the playhouse; the spectator is swept along towards a goal set up beforehand, towards a denouement that he divines in the distance without knowing how it is to be reached. . . . It is the first and greatest detective story. . . . Here it is the assassin himself that, not knowing the murder he has committed, seeks to discover the doer, upon whom he has poured frightful imprecations; he is carried on from disclosure to disclosure, and it is he himself that elicits them, till face to face with his crime, which he must recognize and expiate. . . . And, thing unheard of, skill without parallel, while he rushes on to the discovery of the secret, those most interested partly perceive it and beg him to desist. . . . He brushes them aside and proceeds. He yields to the fascination and the audience follows breathless. . . . And with audacity inconceivable, the audacity of a true man of the theater, Sophocles opens the tragedy on a scene in which the assassin is apprized that he is himself the perpetrator of the murder whom he seeks. . . . And matters are so arranged that all the audience believe the words of Teiresias, that Oedipus alone does not believe them, that he must not believe them; and this same audience, who do believe them, nevertheless discern full well that Oedipus cannot. It is the pinnacle of art.

3

So far Sarcey. Both he and Lemaître, then, recognize the improbability within the play, but celebrate the art whereby, in both plot and character, it has been turned to advantage. Whether as the result of deliberate choice or not, Sophocles has, according to Lemaître, surrendered the momentary shock of surprise for the prolonged tension of 'inquietude.' He has somewhat sacrificed the

[3] *Quarante Ans de théâtre*, III, 307–22.

psychology of the hero to gain a higher and wider range of passion. And by this bold management of plot and character together he has put himself in a position to develop the ironical contrasts, and the overwhelming boomerang effect of the peripety, latent in the improbable situation from the beginning. The discovery would be tragic enough to one who had killed his own father and married his own mother: it is doubly and trebly tragic to a king concerned for the welfare of his people, in duty bound to avenge his predecessor — a discovery through his own doing, despite the warnings of his friends, 'désespérément et comme malgré lui.' Both Sarcey and Lemaître recognize that the dramatist has retrieved the damage done to the psychology by making the King proud and, in the circumstances, irascible and impetuous. But the suggestion of infatuation and *hybris*, which Sarcey seems to entertain, and which many Greek scholars insist upon, must be accepted sparingly and with caution.[4] Sophocles has not the moral prepossessions of Aeschylus; Oedipus, like Antigone, is meant to call forth our sympathy and approval; and Lemaître is nearer the spirit of the dramatist as he says, 'Une si grande et terrible vérité ne saurait entrer du premier coup dans son esprit.' In his innocence and conscious rectitude the hero naturally repudiates so appalling and preposterous an accusation; and Teiresias having made it in anger, it is so that the King receives it. It is too much to believe, or conceive. Indeed, the improbability of the action in the past supports and warrants the improbability at present.

In judging the critics, however, neither Sarcey nor Lemaître quite takes an historical point of view. Corneille and Voltaire as critics and dramatists alike belonged to their era; and they judged according to their lights. Though classical in allegiance, they shared the neoclassical taste for keeping the secret, and for centering the action in the hero's character. The Greeks, and in a different way and measure Shakespeare, subordinate the claims of character to those of the tragedy as a whole; and of this principle the *Oedipus* is only the most notable example. Yet in failing to appreciate this principle, both Corneille and Voltaire had too much of the dramatist in them to think the impression of stupidity in Sophocles' hero was intentional. Voltaire, especially, saw clearly enough one thing that Sophocles

---

[4] See above in 'Reconciliation in Tragedy,' p. 74.

was doing. 'Such obtuseness on the part of Oedipus and Jocasta,' he declares, 'is nothing but a coarse artifice of the poet, who, to give his play proper dimensions, spins out to the fifth act a "recognition" already made manifest in the second, and who violates the rules of common sense that in appearance he may not be out of conformity with those of the theater.'[5]

That is, the great Athenian was 'holding the situation' — was, as Racine puts it, 'making something out of nothing,'[6] or 'building a palace on the point of a needle,' which achievement, as preëminently in the work of Racine and Molière, Flaubert and Maupassant, is the glory of French art, foremost successor to the Greek. And what a situation it is, a single one furnishing forth the tragedy; what a recognition, filling not the last scene but the whole! As Voltaire himself would surely have admitted, it is a great dramatic development, perhaps the greatest — gradual, intense, climacteric, with moments of illusory relief. It is a magnificent *tour de force*, no question; but is it no more? If Voltaire had not only read but also seen it (and like Shakespeare's plays those of Sophocles of course were meant to be seen), he would no longer have doubted, any more than Sarcey — than Lemaître — than the audiences at the Comédie Française of their time or the packed and fascinated theater when I saw it there ten years ago. Despite all the changes in life and drama of over two thousand years the effect today is overwhelming. It is not that of a *tour de force*, but of art at its highest.

4

What makes it so? In part, the fact that this 'artifice' of obtuseness — for such it may be called — turns from a coarse to a fine one in Sophocles' hands. The artifice is motived, as we have found — the truth is too terrible to be accepted; but it is also obscured. The audience is permitted to see more than Oedipus sees, even apart from what by his natural prepossessions and present excitement he is blinded to. Teiresias is not so explicit as Voltaire (or Lemaître in reporting) makes him out to be; Creon only keeps to the oracle about the plague which he has just transmitted, and defends him-

[5] *Œuvres* (1877), II, 24.
[6] Racine, preface to *Bérénice*.

self; and Jocasta at the beginning does not tell the King all she knows or has heard, and at the end is fearful of betraying her fears. The King then draws wrong conclusions, but often naturally. Moreover, the chorus, which, as Voltaire reproachfully notices, is made up of 'enlightened folk,' sees no more clearly than the King; after Teiresias' imputations it no more credits them than he does; and at the moment of last suspense, before the arrival of the Herdsman, when the King has turned out to be no Corinthian, it openly rejoices at the prospect of his proving to be a Theban. Now in a tragedy which is also a poem, in which the parts 'mutually support and explain each other' — that is, a stage play, not a psychological study, not an image of life but a new creation — such an artifice as the above is not the blemish which Voltaire takes it to be, but a beauty. For comparisons we are not expected to look beyond the confines of the work of art itself; and the King is as discerning as, in their wisdom, the Theban Elders.

This, however, is negative, palliative; and the positive and fundamental justification of the improbability, not only in the prolongation of the situation but also at its inception, lies in the greatness and the loftiness of the passions thus provoked and developed. Undertaking to present a situation the most tremendous conceivable, the poet rises equal to it. The commotion within the hero is commensurate with his discoveries, and thus raises horror to the level of tragic terror. Where else indeed lies the essential difference between tragedy of the highest sort and melodrama? There is physical horror in both, but in melodrama the passions are not intense enough or not sufficiently noble. And the prerequisite to this nobility is here secured as never before or since by the innocence of the hero in committing the crimes, which, in turn, as we have seen, justifies, more than anything else does, his tardiness in recognizing them. But that would be of little avail if the poet's imagination, thus set free, did not assert itself. As in Shakespeare, it is the passions, noble and appropriate, but extreme enough to match the extreme situation, sometimes, like the actions forced by fate upon the hero, overstepping the bounds of nature — like the very utterance at these great moments, which, in exclamation or apostrophe, exultation or lamentation, prayer or malediction, oversteps the bounds of human intercourse — it is these passions that keep the tragedy, as it were, in equilibrium. They hold 'the structure brave' high in the air.

A thaumaturgy which, though their dialogue was passionate and rhetorical too, Corneille and Voltaire did not sufficiently acknowledge or admire! Though poets also, they as critics did not steadily bear in mind that supreme art creates another world, not a copy of this. They were intent on motivation, on probability and verisimilitude. Their insistence on the unities, like that of nearly all the neo-classicists, was mainly due, not to a respect for economy of attention, but to a hard-headed regard for realism, in remembrance of the fact that the place of the performance did not change and the duration was — for twice Voltaire says so — only two hours. Indeed, so far with these sticklers for the unities did realism go that in their own versions they even infringed upon them. Knowing a great tragic situation when they see it, they themselves keep the contrast of innocence and crime, but still, by explanation and motivation, trouble and blur its effect. The question is no longer only, Am I the slayer? but, Is it Philoctetes? or, What really does the oracle mean? The action is not only widened but lengthened; to this end, ironically enough, the unities are violated; and what was a mere 'recognition,' that is, a series of thrilling and tantalizing disclosures, a unity on the stage (whether in time, place, or action) such as never was before or since, becomes a mystery and puzzle, and a structure of two or three acts instead of Sophocles' one. They make the hero more reasonable, or at least more addicted to reasoning, but (particularly Corneille) unsympathetic, and rob him of his impulsive charm. They diminish and obscure the supernatural intimations, instead of putting the truth before the hero and then blinding him to it. And thus they reduce the emotional force and impair its quality. The attention of both hero and audience is distracted and dissipated. There is more machinery and friction, more of thought — that is, contriving and detecting — but less of feeling. And thereby not much is added, as Voltaire himself here and there confesses, to the hero's reputation for perspicacity, and much is lost in the matter of keeping the issue vividly before him. Curiously enough, near the end, Sophocles' Oedipus is far cleverer than either Corneille's or Voltaire's. The young critic, more logical than psychological, complains that Oedipus questions the Herdsman only concerning the identity of the child which he had received to expose, and not also concerning that of the slayer of Laius. And in his own version and

Corneille's there are two stages to the inquiry: first it is established that Oedipus is the slayer, then that he is his victim's son. In Sophocles the first stage is made unnecessary; though the Herdsman was summoned as only surviving witness of Laius' death, that matter has in the meantime become of less absorbing and poignant importance. Even on the subject of his own identity and paternity Oedipus gathers as much from the manner of the Herdsman's disclosure as from the matter. And certainty on this point involves and implies certainty on the other: the accumulation of evidence now at last breaks down his resistance. One word from the Herdsman about the slaying suffices, as he gives the motive for the exposure:

> The tale ran that he must slay his sire.

Thus the thunderclap is at the same time a lightning-flash; but this great effect there could not be if it were not for the clear and repeated indications, and the undeviating attention, before.

5

Voltaire, indeed, as he advanced in years and wisdom, made amends to the *manes* of Sophocles. In his commentary upon Corneille's version of 1764 he continually finds fault with the author when he departs from the original; and declaring this the masterpiece of antiquity, notes that in the modern plays on the subject what is imitated, however feebly, is always successful and what is mingled with it fails.[7] In this censure he magnanimously includes himself,[8] though his own version, which was a success on the stage as Corneille's wasn't, is far closer to Sophocles. In the *Dissertation sur l'Électre* (which bears the name of Dumolard), in 1750, he praises Sophocles still more highly, and returns to him the laurels of superiority that in his preface to *Œdipe* he had bestowed on Euripides.

---

[7] *Œuvres* (1880), XXXII, 170. Cf. on Corneille's tragedy, again, *Dissertation sur l'Oreste* (1750), V, 181, where he explicitly says that in striking out for himself Corneille made 'un mauvais ouvrage.'

[8] He several times found fault with the motivation of his own version, even in the *Lèttre sur Œdipe* prefixed to the text, as at the point where Oedipus' ignorance of the cause and circumstances of his predecessor's death is ascribed to his disinclination to discuss the matter with his wife. 'Trop de discrétion et trop peu de curiosité.' Who but a Frenchman or a Greek ever mocked at his own verses or plays?

And it is in keeping with this higher estimate of ancient art that in these later days he fully appreciated the two tragedies of Racine, *Phèdre* and *Iphigénie*, where, inspired by Euripides, he subordinates character and makes tragic use of fate. The 'role' of the Cretan princess and Athenian queen Voltaire judges to be the finest ever put upon the stage in any tongue, 'the masterpiece of the human intellect.' In his own day Boileau speaks of Phèdre's 'douleur vertueuse,' and thinks her perfidious and incestuous only despite herself — 'malgré soi.' Her horror of what she is impelled to do is like the Theban King's of what he has done, and even his discovery of that is, as Lemaître says, 'malgré lui.' And of a role Voltaire is speaking properly if not advisedly. The unity of her character is impaired in the interest of the total effect. Like Othello, Lear, and Hamlet, and in part like Macbeth, she is not betrayed by what is false within; and plot comes first, according to the principle of Aristotle.[9]

6

In *Othello* the situation is as extreme and the passions are as respondent to it. In mere terms of fact the burden upon the hero's soul is not so great, but as realized by the poet it is. The situation has not, indeed, so great dimensions, so many sides. That of Oedipus, who slew his father and espoused his mother in ignorance, in ignorance laid a curse on his own head and himself brought about the disclosure, is comparable only to that of Orestes, who rightly avenged his father's death upon the murderess, yet, since she was his mother, could bring himself to do it only at the command of the god. But it is Shakespeare that now wields the pen. Moreover, since the guilt has been incurred more recently — Othello's hands have just been at Desdemona's throat — the recognition is, proportionately, more poignant. It is a revulsion, a convulsion; and the sharpness and magnitude of it in him, and in the spectator sympathetically after him, are owing to his innocence.

7

If in taking this same quality in Oedipus for stupidity the French critics recognized that it was not so intended, they at this point

[9] See below, the chapter on *Phèdre*.

differ from the English-speaking critics of Othello. Their interpretations have been, roughly, of three classes: that the hero has the
germ of jealousy in him from the beginning; that he is not jealous
even in the sequel; and that in the faculty of reading human character or discerning human motives he is positively wanting. The
first two opinions alike are in direct contradiction both to repeated
authoritative utterances in the text and to the tenor of the presentation; and the third, with which alone we have here to do, is
incompatible not only with the admiration for the Moor which is
expressed by everybody in the play except Iago but with that which
is manifestly expected of us in turn. It is incompatible also not only
with the glory of poetry shed upon him but with the highest tragic
effect. A fool for a hero may be more or less tolerable in certain
esoteric, highbrow theaters, preoccupied with psychology or pathol-
ogy, in our day — there are some novels at any rate which admit of
him, though Dostoyevsky's Idiot is not a fool — but in the popular
theater of Elizabethan times he would be out of the question. Few
now think Othello a fool in general, but even a dupe or gull would
kill the play. That role, in Elizabethan times, as really in ours, is for
comedy; and even there it could not be the leading one in the
romantic sort that Shakespeare nearly always wrote.

The notion of Othello's stupidity began apparently with Rymer,
in 1678, but unlike the similar misapprehension of Oedipus, at least
in France, it has not yet ended. Only a few years ago it was revived
under the euphemism of 'lack of intellect'; and there has also been
more or less of the notion mingled with the other interpretations.
Jealous or not jealous, Othello has seemed 'simple,' 'naïve,' 'trustful,'
'childlike'; and something of this effect, to be sure, is almost inevitable as he stands in the presence of Iago. That is the price the English
dramatist must pay for his hero's innocence and our sympathy, a
greater one than what was demanded of the Greek. Sophocles' hero
contends with a fate which is invisible, that which no man can know,
under which all men bow. But like the Greek, Shakespeare pays as
little as he can. In one respect the situation here is the reverse of the
other. It is the Moor's belief, not his unbelief, that is improbable
and may seem stupid, and therefore the other characters in the play
are not permitted to hear of the charge against Desdemona and
Cassio. The anxious but necessarily reticent warnings and supplica-

tions addressed to the Theban King greatly heighten the suspense, and, rightly understood, do not impair the effect of his intelligence; for, whatever the outcome, he cannot stay. Such is the complication that the more he learns the more he must seek to learn, or be unworthy of himself and the occasion. And such intervention might have been striking in *Othello*. But in this tragedy, where it is the honor of wife and friend primarily, not himself, that is at stake, for the hero then to persevere (as he must) in his belief, like the other in his inquiry, might be fatal to the impression we receive of a noble and generous nature, as it is not, in the other tragedy, to that of a courageous one. The precaution therefore to be taken in order to safeguard the leading character's reputation for intelligence, against the imputation of credulity, is that he should have no reason to suspect — should have every reason to credit — his informant. The dramatist as a matter of course avails himself of the immemorial convention that, whether in drama or other story, one should, when a situation is at stake, accept, however unwillingly, what one is artfully told; but to make the device effective and plausible as never before, the Elizabethan sees to it that the slanderer both is extraordinarily cunning in the telling and also seems 'honest' and 'wise' to everyone else as well as to the hero, even, despite her loyalty to her mistress and her good reason for suspecting himself, to his own wife. And (what is as important) the dramatist sees to it also that the hero both is and seems noble and imperturbable and, to *his* wife, quite free of a jealous spirit. Again the parts mutually support and explain each other. Eminent critics, even Bridges and Courtney, think not Othello but Emilia and Desdemona stupid; though they see how the women's blindness increases the tension, they do not see how it holds the play together. If the wives are so stupid, everybody else is, as well as Othello, just as, if Oedipus is stupid, the chorus is; and then nobody, and particularly not Othello, is stupid at all.

'Violates the rules of common sense that in appearance he may not be out of conformity with those of the theater,' quoth Voltaire — but is not that, if we omit the derogatory phrase 'in appearance,' really what Sophocles and Shakespeare alike have done? Particularly if one of the chief rules of the theater be that which Voltaire himself acknowledges, not in the criticism of Sophocles' version but

of his own, 'toujours songer à être intéressant plutôt qu'exact'!
'For,' he continues (and, at all points but one, how great a critic he
was, seeing through every pore!), 'the spectator pardons everything but boredom, and once he is moved, rarely considers whether
he have reason to be so.' Or, as his contemporary Dryden, likewise
both an apostle of common sense and himself a model of it, declared
before him, though after Aristotle and Longinus, 'reason suffers
itself to be so hoodwinked that it may better enjoy the pleasures of
the fiction.' The only question is whether the effect be worth the
cost, whether the spectator *be* moved, and, at that, more profoundly,
than with the rules of common sense observed. If so — and of
Othello and the *Oedipus* there can be no question — the trickery
rises to the dignity of a stratagem, the artifice to that of art. The
words of Samuel Johnson, that weighty incarnation of common
sense, who, however, like Voltaire and Dryden, was a poet, are here
in place. As in his later years he reconsiders the dread rules of the
unities on the grounds upon which they then rested, he diffidently —
for common sense respects tradition — he diffidently but convincingly denies their universal authority. 'Delusion, if delusion be
admitted, has no certain limitation; if the spectator can be once persuaded that his old acquaintance are Alexander and Caesar, that a
room illuminated with candles is the plain of Pharsalia or the bank
of Granicus, he is in a state of elevation above the reach of reason
or of truth, and, from the heights of Empyrean poetry [can this be
the lexicographer and law-giver?] may despise the circumscriptions
of terrestrial nature. There is no reason why a mind thus wandering
in ecstasy should count the clock, or why an hour should not be a
century in that calenture of the brains that can make the stage a
field.' It is a prime quality of common sense thus to recognize the
difference between itself and poetry; indeed this, on its own ground,
is common sense, the logic of illusion. And surely a mind thus
wandering in ecstasy can override as easily the restrictions of psychology as the stubborn and tangible ones of time and place. Of
art M. de Miomandre has lately declared:

La beauté c'est sa vérité à lui, il ne saurait avoir d'autre règle. C'est
pourquoi le souci de la couleur locale (qui est une préoccupation scien-
tifique) ne saurait que l'entraver. Il faut qu'il soit libre à l'égard de l'espace

et du temps, et de tous les personnages, vrais ou légendaires, et de toutes les situations psychologiques possibles.

Or, to put it differently, with Mr. Abercrombie:

Reality, for poetry, consists in nothing more, but in nothing less, than *being alive*: in poetry sense, intellect, and spirit all equally give reality.[10]

Not that in this highest type of tragedy, *Othello* or the *Oedipus* either, there is anything fantastic or extravagant, as in Dryden's *Conquest of Granada* or the romantic vein of Calderón. As I have elsewhere said, 'The hero does not, like Almanzor, do wonders and perform miracles with sword or tongue; there is no irresponsible witchcraft or supernatural intervention in the story. . . . At every point except that of the villain's arts or the fatal dispensation, which is the initial postulate, it is a fairly real Thebes or Venice and Cyprus.'[11] Objects are magnified, emotions are intensified, but except at the point of indulgence agreed upon, the proportions and relations, the outlines and colors, of life as we know it are preserved. For as Freytag, who was both a dramatist and an excellent technical critic, has remarked:

But not this poetic truth alone is needed in the drama. The spectator gladly surrenders himself to the invention of the poet; he readily accepts the presuppositions of the drama, and is in general quite inclined to approve of the invented human relations in the world of beautiful illusion; but he is not able entirely to forget reality, the picture of the real world in which he breathes. He brings with him before the stage a certain knowledge of historical relations, definite ethical and moral requirements of human life, presages and some clear knowledge of the way things go in the world. To a certain extent, it is impossible for him to renounce the purport of his own existence; and sometimes he feels this very strongly when the poetic picture contradicts it.[12]

That the picture should not openly contradict it is a matter of artistic tact, of which, to be sure, Sophocles and Shakespeare are exemplars.

---

[10] *Progress in Literature*, p. 32; and cf. above, p. 40.

[11] *Art and Artifice in Shakespeare*, p. 28, with some adaptations to the case of the *Oedipus*.

[12] Freytag, *Technik des Dramas*, Werke (1897), XIV, 46.

8

Thus in the two tragedies, though after different fashion, the improbable is made probable, the hero having been exposed to, though as much as may be preserved from, the charge of stupidity for the sake of the great situation which the improbable story affords. And thus in the two tragedies both the purpose and the precaution to safeguard it were misapprehended by critics when the center of interest changed. It has for the most part not changed again (though, as we shall see, it is now beginning to do so); in Ibsen, in stage drama generally, high-class or mediocre, the secret is kept, the situation is not permitted to be so improbable, and the characters are, as far as may be, held within the limits of psychological reality. Yet criticism, meanwhile, has profited by historical and comparative methods. Sarcey and Lemaître, in the present instance, did not apply the historical test to the earlier criticism that they opposed; but both knew and appreciated the whole range of drama as Corneille and Voltaire did not. They were not prejudiced either as playgoers or as playwrights; and they endeavored to judge a play according to the intentions of the writer and the natural expectations of his audience. Unlike the dramatists, they had no formula of their own; but they had principles and — what was one of them — kept open minds. After the primary question, Why am I pleased or displeased? came that which was recognized by Arnold as characteristic of Frenchmen in his day (also Sarcey and Lemaître's), the secondary question, Am I right in being so? Such knowledge, with such open-mindedness in the use of it, the English-speaking critics who have mistaken Othello have not abundantly enjoyed.

9

The issue is not a dead one. This more audacious, wider-ranging, and higher-soaring art of the theater, practised by Sophocles and Shakespeare, is by Sarcey and Lemaître not taken to be antiquated; and essentially, despite appearances, it is not. Browning the psychologist, the impressionist before his time, achieved what is perhaps his greatest situation, in *In a Balcony*, after a really similar fashion, at equal cost to probability, when Constance persuades her frank and noble lover Norbert, out of love for him and gratitude to the Queen, to declare to their mistress that all his service has been prompted by his love for her. The improbability lies not only in the success of the deception but also in the willingness of Constance and Norbert to take the risk; nor is it overcome by all Browning's careful preparation and motivation. The improbability, the deception, is, as in *Othello* (and indeed in the *Oedipus*), the price still necessarily paid for a superbly ironical *contretemps* such as that when the Queen, who though married had never known love, rushes to Constance, apparently for confirmation of the news, but really to tell her what love is like, bid her once the time comes give up everything for it, and, when Constance reminds her of obstacles in the way, cry out, as if not to her but to the stars,

> Hear her! There, there now — could *she* love like me?

> Hear her! I thank you, sweet, for that surprise.
> You have the fair face: for the soul, see mine.
> I have the strong soul: let me teach you here.

'Les grands sujets,' says Corneille, himself not always remembering it, 'doivent toujours aller au delà du vraisemblable.'[13]

Moreover, the complaint, which elsewhere, in connection with Corneille and Racine, was made by Voltaire himself, and in the same connection was echoed by Sarcey, that 'nos pièces ne font pas une impression assez forte,' that they lack force and fire,[14] seems of late to show signs of bearing fruit. Ibsen, in his preoccupation with psychology and the 'problems,' narrowed the scope of the imagination and weakened the impact of the emotions. Plays that are nearly puzzles like *Little Eyolf*, plays in which you do not greatly care for hero or heroine either, like almost any of Ibsen's, somewhat defeat their purpose. The only Hamlet on the stage that moves us is not the spiritual cripple of the critics. And the long reign of realism, of literalism, shows signs of ending. Ibsen in *Ghosts*, O'Neill in *Mourning Becomes Electra* have fallen back upon the ancients and adopted a modern equivalent to the ancient fatality. Yet this is personal, internal: sympathy, with admiration, the prerogative of

---

[13] See above, 'Reconciliation in Tragedy,' p. 73.
[14] 'Appel à toutes les Nations' (1761), *Œuvres* (1879), XXIV, 218–19. Sarcey, *Quarante Ans*, III, pp. 308–309.

the ancient and the Shakespearean hero, has not thus been regained for the modern. And only by means of poetry, not psychology, whether of the conscious or the subconscious, can it well be, as in plays like Hauptmann's *Arme Heinrich*, which are lifted above the narrow restrictions of realism. The medieval story of the leper cured by the blood of a virgin involves not only superstition and a miracle but great dangers to the heroic quality of the hero who accepts the sacrifice; yet the dramatist thereby gains access to finer thoughts and vaster passions than any plausible story could offer; and such are his dramatic and poetic resources that the dangers are avoided and the work of his hands becomes an emotional success. Heinrich finally yields to the maiden's urgent prayer as one who has fallen under her spell, and whose cynical and despairing soul has been cured by her already; yields because life as he is means nothing to either of them, because the fulfillment of her vow of sacrifice can be her only happiness, and because there is nothing left for either but life or death together. He is somewhat like a man who marries a woman to whom a child may mean death, but for whom life itself would be death without him. But the fabulous story has greater possibilities than any real one; and as artist and poet both, Hauptmann (or Hofmannsthal, D'Annunzio, Rostand, or Maeterlinck either) would not have misapprehended *Oedipus* like Corneille and Voltaire, or *Othello* like Rymer and his followers.

CHAPTER VII

Iago

I

ITH IAGO I have dealt several times before,[1] though less with the character in himself than as a part of the structure. *Magna pars,* in his case, for he is not only the impelling but also (to use Coleridge's word) the 'credibilising' force in the fateful action. Without him, as we have seen in the two preceding chapters, there would simply be no tragedy; and only by the fiction of Othello's open, undefended mind and Iago's impenetrable, all-prevailing one is the hero brought to ruin. The slanderer is sagacious and 'honest,' not only in the eyes of the hero but of every one else in the play; therefore in believing him the hero is not to be thought — a quality inappropriate in a romantic hero — either gullible or suspicious. What the dramatist was seeking was, as usual, the intensest situation, the most striking and significant contrast; what he was seeking was, as usual, not primarily to present character as its own destiny, but to arouse our sympathies to the uttermost, produce the most overpowering emotional effect; and to that end, as he did elsewhere, he somewhat distorted and exaggerated reality instead of reflecting it, both ennobled the character of the hero and blackened that of the villain in the original story, leaving the former in this instance with scarcely anything that can be called a 'fault' and the latter with scarcely anything that can be called a virtue. After the fashion of the Greeks he raised his tragic structure, as the highest must be, on the broad and solid foundation of melodrama.

Like the hero himself, moreover, the Ancient, though one of Shakespeare's most remarkable creations, is not to be treated as a definite psychological entity. If it may be admitted that in the epic,

---

[1] *Othello* (1915); *Shakespeare Studies* (1927), pp. 382–92; *Poets and Playwrights* (1930), pp. 127–29; *Art and Artifice in Shakespeare* (1933), Chap. II.

and (what is more) the novel, psychology or even a plausible motivation is not indispensable to a character, Iago, meant only for the stage, is (though a highly convincing one) a devil in the flesh, who plays the part of an honest and friendly fellow before the other characters and (except momentarily) shows the devil in him only to the spectators. His is a double role, like Richard the Third's and Hamlet's, far finer than the one, less fine than the other but almost as attractive to the actor, and equally poetical (which in Shakespeare means individual) in conception and utterance. And like Richard the king and Aaron the Moor, Iago is a development of the Elizabethan stage villain, who had had a long and rather chequered history. Indeed, like many of the greatest figures on the stage or in literature, such as Shakespeare's own Falstaff, Molière's Harpagon, and Goethe's Mephistopheles, he is an imaginative composite or 'condensation'; himself derived from the medieval Vice, the Senecan hero-villain, the Plautine or Terentian intriguing slave, or *fallax servus*, and the Machiavel. This last is the caricature of the great Italian philosopher in which Kyd and Marlowe had, after the true popular dramatic fashion, incorporated the current mythical notion of that dire menace to the Northern faith and *mores*. Iago both professes and exemplifies the veritable Florentine principles of egoism, simulation of the virtues because of their usefulness, and glorification of the will; but he has, besides, most of the highly colored or picturesque traits or ways of the established stage figure — the frank delight in intrigue and open avowal of hypocrisy, lust, and murder, the league with hell and enmity against Heaven, the honest and merry manners in the open and the menaces and bloodcurdling malice in colloquy with the catspaw and (still more frankly) in soliloquy and aside. His chief point of superiority lies in the subtlety of tone or contour. The violence of Richard and Aaron is now dissembled: to look at him this is no 'lion' at all but wholly 'fox.' Here is none of Aaron's bluster and yet none of Richard's slime. The hypocrisy of the Ancient is not egregious or fulsome; and it is Richard's more disarming manner, his bluffness and cynicism, that he especially affects, modified and seasoned with bonhommie. For the present undertaking he produces human motives, but, except the inadequate and superficial one of Cassio's being promoted above him, they are manifestly trumped up.

The psychologists are not justified in providing him others of their own; particularly any so feeble or neutral, unmoral or merely human, as a craving for activity and sensation, an artistic taste for intrigue, a delight in a sense of superiority and in the pain of his victim only as proof of his power. These are traits of his rather than his motives, and of them he is little aware. To the psychologists he is a mate for their Hamlet, with pretexts (though for action, not inaction) conjured up to overcome an 'inner resistance'; and with even a 'safety-valve' — caustic and cynical speech to relieve him of 'the discomfort of his hypocrisy,' like the feigned madness to relieve the Prince of his pent-up emotions and save him from madness itself. Of such resistance or discomfort, either, there is no discernible evidence, and it is a notion that would have troubled both dramatist and spectator. At bottom Iago is moved by simple 'hatred,' 'this fairy-tale hatred,' as Mr. Murry calls it, which he flatly avows at the outset and reiterates again and again; he revels in villainy and welcomes the help of 'all the tribe of hell,' of 'hell and night'; and so far is he from really deceiving himself that, when once[2] he dallies to play at that game a bit, he cannot keep from chuckling at the humbug. The accumulation of inadequate motives, the acknowledged uncertainty and flimsiness of his suspicions, but show the hellishness of his purpose.

Still less are the sentimentalists justified as they make him out to be a victim of circumstances and environment, 'warped out of humanity by misfortune or the world's injustice'; and least of all, as they make him out to be honest and friendly by nature, 'a prince of good fellows,' 'the most popular man in Venice,' who 'would not have trod upon a worm had it kept out of his way, and would rather have done a service than an injury.' So Tieck, to Goethe's disgust, thought Lady Macbeth a tender, loving soul and as such to be played.[3]

In either sort of criticism, the psychological or the sentimental, there is something like the spirit of monism or Christian Science, to which your villain is on principle unacceptable. Shakespeare, living in a world where evil was very real and terrible, positive not

---

[2] II, iii, 356: 'Divinity [theology] of hell!' etc.

[3] From my *Shakespeare Studies*, pp. 382–92, comes most of the material in this and the two preceding paragraphs.

negative[4] (not, however, as has recently been thought, the world of St. Thomas Aquinas or of Aristotle, either, but of the common man then and today), makes, like the other Renaissance dramatists, his villain positive enough to be the motive force in the tragedy; and out of him psychologists and sentimentalists alike proceed to extract the poison and the sting. Criticism, rightly practised, is primarily, if not ultimately, interpretation; interpretation, once mere difficulties of medium are disposed of, is mainly 'a study in emphasis.' The sentimentalists seem not to comprehend the medium, indeed not to have attentively read the play; the psychologists have read it, but mysteriously, esoterically, and set the emphasis awry. Neither sect or party does what is demanded of criticism, by the very voice of reason — put itself at the author's point of view. Neither gives the impression of appreciating the significance of the villain's feigning or of the reputation for honesty arbitrarily established for him: the sentimentalists taking the 'honest' and genial chap for the real Iago, sinned against as well as sinning; the psychologists taking the superficial or incidental traits of a craving for activity and a delight in superiority for the fundamental ones. Neither sees, what was evident to the earlier critics, as well as to Coleridge and Lamb, the dramatist Freytag, and in more recent days, George Woodberry, J. J. Chapman, W. L. Courtney, Lytton Strachey, and John Palmer — what indeed the dramatist has made sufficiently plain, not only by the characterization itself, but by the villain's own avowals at the outset and the hero's and Ludovico's recognition at the end[5] — that, under all the appearances of humanity, Iago is little or nothing

---

[4] See Croce, *Ariosto, Shakespeare, and Corneille* (1920), pp. 143–54.

[5] 'If . . . not too hard for my wits and all the tribe of hell,' I, iii, 364; 'Hell and night must bring this monstrous birth to the world's light,' I, iii, 409; 'Divinity of hell! when devils will the blackest sins put on . . . as I do now,' II, iii, 356; and Othello, last scene, 'I look down towards his feet,' etc., 287–88; 'demand that demi-devil,' etc., 301–302; Ludovico, 'hellish villain,' 368. All this, to be sure, might be only the strong language of tragedy if it were not for the manifestly diabolical nature of Iago in both principle and conduct. For the still more numerous and pointed remarks by and about Aaron and Richard, see *devil, devilish, hell, hellish*, in Bartlett's *Concordance*. Mr. G. W. Knight is justified in finding in the tragedy a continual rhythmical recurrence of the words or notions of *hell* and *devil, heaven* and *angels*. However, he presently blurs his contrast and confuses his harmony by making the evil rather negative, and Othello sometimes sentimental. See above, Chap. V, p. 210.

short of a demon. And neither sees that not only in characterization but also in the avowals and the recognition this devilishness is a direct development out of the more crudely drawn and more glaringly colored Aaron and Richard III.

2

At one of these opinions — whether sentimental or psychological let the reader determine — I will have a glance. Professor Tucker Brooke, following the line of Professor Bradley (though taking issue with him), and more especially of Hazlitt (though not mentioning him), develops the notion of what he startlingly, yet perhaps not inappositely, styles a 'Romantic Iago.'[6] Mr. Bradley, rightly abandoning for the moment his opinion that evil in Shakespeare is negative, compares 'the prince of villains' with Goethe's unromantic and anti-romantic Mephistopheles as he says, 'Here there is something of the same deadly coldness, the same gaiety in destruction.' Of the coldness Mr. Brooke will have none, arguing (from the success of his imposture, apparently) that he is a man of 'warm, sympathetic qualities.' His diabolism is an accident, thrust upon him early in the play, 'when in seeking to convince Roderigo of his hatred for Othello he convinces himself likewise'; and having a materialistic philosophy, 'he suddenly finds himself over head and ears in the depths of his own egoism, vaguely conscious that he is being used for the devil's purposes, but incapable either of shaping the direction or checking the progress of his drift.'[7] Thus, instead of being the impelling force he is himself impelled: he is a less noble (though not irresolute) Hamlet of the true psychological cut. Suffering from ennui, he preys upon Roderigo 'to spice his life'; and upon Cassio, Othello, and Desdemona, to provide himself 'narcotics' or 'anodynes.' This is his tragedy (as well as theirs!), but, still more

[6] *Yale Review*, January 1918.
[7] This is somewhat like the notion that, in his desire to get on, Iago, almost without malice, is, as it were, wrenched from his moral moorings and swept out to sea (cf. my *Shakespeare Studies*, p. 386). It probably arises from Iago's being the source of all evil in the play and therefore constantly wickeder as this accumulates; and from his not revealing definitely (for purposes of suspense) all his plans from the outset. But 'Hell and night' (I, 3, end) places him.

strangely, it is not altogether that. In the midst of his villainy, as
Emilia vows

> I will be hang'd if some eternal villain,
> Some busy and insinuating rogue,
> Some cogging, cozening slave, to get some office,
> Have not devised this slander,

he wakes up, 'sees himself in a new spiritual light,' and recoils
incredulous:

> Fie, there is no such man; it is impossible.

(What other answer was there to that home truth?) And 'last scene
of all, hedged about by the desperate perils which his own *moral
obtuseness* [italics mine!] has drawn upon him . . . he offers as a
chief inducement to the reckless game the new motive of shame':

> If Cassio do remain,
> He hath a daily beauty in his life
> That makes me ugly.

This is the 'moral awakening of Iago' — 'the tragedy of the honest, charming soldier, who swallowed the devil's bait of self-indul-
gence, grew blind to ideal beauty, and in his blindness overthrew
more than his enemies.' But if in Shakespeare's day words, as now
they do, depended for their sense on one another — if context or
situation in story or drama, as now they are, were to their sense of
appreciable importance — then all that the Ancient could have meant
in answering Emilia was summarily to hush her up. 'Speak within
door,' he bids her sharply next moment as she angrily runs on.
And all that he could have meant in referring to Cassio's 'beauty'
was the simple and solid fact (of more immediate interest to our
Ancient than his own blindness to the ideal) that the deposed lieutenant, being now by the Signiory's command deputed in Othello's
place, would unendurably overshadow (or outshine) him, who had
so recently possessed himself of Cassio's. These are among his first
words after appearing on the stage in Act V, scene i; and among his
last on his previous appearance, Act IV, scene ii, were the directions
to Roderigo how to make Cassio 'uncapable of Othello's place' —
'by knocking out his brains.' Strange speech, this, for one who keeps

even a memory of 'the vision splendid'! Such meanings as Mr. Brooke here discovers are 'out of character,' *à contresens*, which phrases have point in drama, regardless of psychology. From beginning to end Iago never ceases to look down upon Cassio or highly to esteem himself; and as for his 'growing blind to ideal beauty' or ever 'awakening' to it, one would naturally expect in the lines some evidence for anything so surprising.

Against Professor Allardyce Nicoll's rather similar theory that objection cannot be urged because of his fundamental principle — of the unrevealed in Shakespeare as equally important with the revealed. Here the critic has great need of it. For he is reducing the dimensions of Iago's wickedness still further, making him not only the victim of self-deception and of circumstances after the action begins, like Professor Brooke, but also before that. He is 'soured' by 'lack of birth and education' (not in the lines, but no matter), his cynicism 'is a kind of perverted idealism,' and there is 'something pitiful,' since he 'might have been so great,' in his 'final doom.' Gratiano's, Ludovico's, Othello's own very different feelings on that subject, definitely 'revealed,' do not count, although Shakespeare 'beyond a shadow of a doubt has a perfect sense of the theater.'

3

Appreciably closer to the text, as is to be expected, is the opinion of Professor Kittredge, who, within the narrow limits of an introduction in a one-volume edition of the plays (1936), takes issue with Coleridge and Lamb as they speak of the 'motive-hunting of a motiveless malignity.' Without a motive Iago would be 'monstrous' or 'maniacal.' But Shaw's Richard Dudgeon, for his good deed, 'had no motive.' And to Iago neither Coleridge nor Lamb would really deny one. He both hunted and found.

First it is the grudge about the lieutenancy, warranted or not. Then Othello has been too familiar with Emilia; then even Cassio has been so and he himself desires Desdemona; then Cassio also does. That these are pretexts is apparent to the audience not only from the way that they bud and pullulate in the Ancient's brain but also from his own explicit comments. Sheer hatred, avowed four times in Act I, and also, according to Roderigo, before the act began, is what

impels him; and the reason for it comes out in the same act near the
end. 'I hate the Moor,' he mutters in soliloquy:

> *And it is thought* abroad that 'twixt my sheets
> He has done my office.

The pretext, apparent even in the expression, is like the others,
immediately laid bare. 'I know not if 't be true [Othello's adultery]
but I *for mere suspicion in that kind* will do as if for surety' — 'to get
his place [Cassio's] and to *plume up my will* in double knavery' —
'not out of absolute lust, though peradventure I stand accountant for
as great a sin, but *partly led to diet my revenge.*' 'For mere suspicion'
is only in the same inverted vein as the following sentence: 'He holds
me well; the better shall my purpose work on him.' In this forcing-
bed, moreover, suspicions quickly become convictions.

In the second soliloquy (II, i) the 'revenge' is no longer for
thwarted ambition but for the adultery, the thought whereof now
(though in Act I he knows not if it be true) 'doth gnaw my in-
wards.' Yet here are both the first and the last we learn of that, and
of his lust for Desdemona and his conjugal jealousy of Cassio as well.
It is the notion that Othello will be happy with Desdemona, apparently, which provokes him; the only means that occurs to him —
slandering her — leads to a momentary notion or pretense that he
has some reason; and the plan thus to have 'our Michael Cassio on
the hip' summons up a parenthetical suspicion to support it —

> Abuse him to the Moor in the rank garb —
> *For I fear Cassio with my nightcap too* —
> Make the Moor thank me, etc.

And the same progress in 'wishful thinking' appears now in his
thought of Desdemona and Cassio's guilt — 'I do well believe it.'

In the third soliloquy he obviously does not believe it, and evil
frankly becomes his good as he resolves to 'turn her virtue into pitch
and out of her own goodness make the net which shall enmesh them
all.' What Professor Vaughan says of Seneca's Medea is far truer of
Iago; 'She does not commit crimes for her designs, she forms designs
that she may commit crimes.' And the audience are left in no doubt
about it. Not only does the Ancient both avow and betray his
motive-hunting, he also frankly invokes 'hell and night,' acknowl-

edges the 'divinity of hell' he is practising in the defense of his hypocrisy, and several times in soliloquy and in colloquy with Roderigo expounds its portentous principles. Here are his temper and his point of view — both diabolical. His own lascivious desire and Cassio's designs upon Emilia he touches upon but once, Othello's adultery but twice. As Professor Bradley notices, he takes no particular pleasure in Cassio's place once he has got it; and in neither his endeavors nor his achievements does he demean himself like an injured husband or an envious libertine. His imagination is 'habitually licentious,' and when with his victim, inflammatory, but (except with hatred) not itself inflamed. 'The whole point of Iago,' as Mr. John Palmer observes, 'is that his evil is evil for its own sake'; he enjoys it, is not tortured by it; and to this fine dramatic critic the demon's motive-hunting is 'simply an intellectual exercise.'[8]

What is more, the audience would themselves see that for his resentment, as for his suspicions to support it, there is little if any basis. There is manifestly nothing wrong between Desdemona and Cassio, and the Moor takes no interest in Emilia, nor is he at all the sort of person who would have been guilty of such an offense. Nobody else in the play is aware that the Ancient has a grievance or a cause for one, not even in Cassio's lieutenancy; that Cassio is a poor soldier, a mere 'technical theorist,' nobody else seems aware, including Othello and the Senate; and if in the first scene a spectator should be momentarily impressed with Iago's presentation of his case, he would soon be set right by Roderigo's own complaint of being cheated as well as by the plain evidence to that effect, by the Ancient's disloyalty to his General produced as proof of loyalty to his present employer, by his wanton tormenting of old Brabantio under cover of darkness, and by his hypocritical solicitude for Othello's well-being as the next scene opens. This conduct, together with his malign intentions upon the unoffending Cassio and Desdemona, no normal audience is in danger of mistaking for anything like 'resentment for injustice,' whatever the original basis for the complaint. That there should be no real basis is, moreover, essential to the structure of the play — to Iago's imposture and to Othello's, Desdemona's, and Cassio's reputation for discernment.

[8] *Studies in the Contemporary Theatre* (1927), p. 78.

To be successful a slanderer and intriguer must obviously be above suspicion of a grievance.

4

Criticism, evidently, is a delicate undertaking: a good critic, as poets themselves have said (what would that in Stratford have said had he read any?) is rarer than a good poet. 'Interpretation apart,' said Mr. Housman, who was both the one and the other, 'criticism does not exist'; and shall we think that he had not in mind the criticism of Shakespeare — or had? Interpretation, mainly a study in emphasis, is, if worthy of the name, in faithful response to the emphasis of the poet; and if in popular performances wicked characters like the Scottish Queen and the Venetian Ancient appear in such a light as to Tieck and Mr. Brooke or Mr. Nicoll, this must be due to the fact that there has been criticism instead of interpretation and that the primary moral and emotional impression has been missed or ignored. But even those who earnestly endeavor to respond will often go astray in their subsequent analysis. In my earlier discussion I failed to perceive, as M. Legouis[9] has done, the relative importance of the Vice in the Ancient's make-up as well as in Aaron's and Richard's — failed duly to appreciate the positive advantage of tradition, both at that particular point and in general. In my impatience with the vagaries of sentimentality and the irrelevance of psychology I insisted over-much on the features of that later accretion, the Machiavel, such as his frankness about his own wickedness and devilishness, his appeals to the infernal powers in league with him, and his hostility to God, or, in the current phrase, his 'atheism.' Not that there is any mistaking of these, but in Iago they are made to serve also the higher purposes of art.

'La seconde utilité,' declares Corneille, after considering that of moral 'sentences,' or apothegms,

la seconde utilité du poème dramatique se rencontre en la naïve peinture des vices et des vertus, qui ne manque jamais à faire son effet, quand elle est bien achevée, et que les traits en sont si reconnoissables qu'on ne les peut confondre l'un dans l'autre, ni prendre le vice pour vertu. . . .[10]

---

[9] Legouis and Cazamian, *History of English Literature*, I, 156.
[10] 'Le Poème dramatique,' *Œuvres* (1862), I, 20.

'Naïve,' of course, here means 'true and faithful'; but that, the context shows, was to Corneille and his time not what it is to us. In the tragedy of the time, at any rate, the clever villains must *not*, as in life they did and do, ordinarily speak of themselves and their purposes as good or sensible, and of good people and their ways as hypocritical or foolish. And the record bears him out. For with frankness about their own wickedness and with remarkable fairness to the goodness of others does not only Corneille's Cleopatra in *Rodogune* express herself, but also Racine's Mathan and Aman; though thereby moving the French Academy (in 1730), as well as Fontenelle and Houdart de la Motte, to demur to such 'aveux' as 'peu vraisemblables.' However, though Corneille's reason for adopting (or rather continuing) the method is the primary one — that the wickedness and the goodness may be clearly distinguished and not taken the one for the other — it is not the ultimate and highest reason.

That, with all these dramatists, ancient, Elizabethan and Bourbon, is the rousing of the passions in their intensity. With the Greeks and Shakespeare, as I show in Chapter I, tragedy (and in some measure comedy, too) is a system and rhythm, a contrast and harmony of the passions. The secret is not kept; in Shakespeare the incentive of suspense is sympathy, as in Ibsen it is curiosity, the response being immediate, not, as in Ibsen, delayed. And the spectators' emotions are ampler and more intense when there is a moral element in them, the sympathy linked with admiration and love for the hero and with fear of the villain or dread of a malignant fate. It is another matter when wickedness is instinctive, is permitted its bias or prejudice or is indulged because it is the fruit of heredity or environment, as in Ibsen and the Naturalists; and if we are to judge by the tragedies that have so far been written, in order rightly and fully to arouse the emotions of the audience there must be a perfectly clear distinction between the good characters and the bad, by way of chorus or comment, or else in soliloquy or (the ordinary French tragic equivalent) the *confidence*. These serve for the excitement and also the guidance of the spectators' emotions, not the exercise of their wits; and for that purpose they must, when the speaker is as a simple matter of fact in a position to know, contain the truth, not represent the speaker's bias. Such is the nature of the medium, the tradition of the stage; and though, like Mathan, Iago is a liar, he must not be, as by one great critic he has been, found lying to the audience, to himself. If he were, the audience, accustomed and attached to the tradition, would be not moved but bewildered, the last thing in the world an audience should be.

5

So far, however, this is a matter of technique and medium, of the dramatic language (as it were) rather than the substance or content; and in content tradition is, for imaginative and emotional effect, of perhaps still greater importance. As we have noticed in the chapter on Shakespeare and Jonson, the highest art deals, in a familiar way, with the familiar. In the drama above all, which depends for success upon mass emotion. Hence the value of the component elements in Iago — the Machiavel, the Senecan hero-villain, and especially the indigenous Vice. In Iago appeared the original combination of the comic and the tragic, of temptation and slander, of dissimulation and hypocrisy, of a motiveless malignity and the league with the infernal. This portentous figure must have fired the Elizabethans' imaginations and roused their emotions as no novel but more natural one could when he at last stood before them realized, perfected. The response must have been immediate and unanimous. That response we cannot, of course, appreciate today: we have not both heard and seen Kyd's Lorenzo, Marlowe's Guise and Barabas, Shakespeare's own Aaron and Richard, the prototypes. But the audience at the Globe were here delightedly coming upon the villain that they were looking for, 'the perfect Vice,' says Miss Boddy, 'returned to the world to sport with hearts and souls.'

It is, in general, the imaginative and emotional figures on Shakespeare's stage that owe most to tradition; and the figures owing most to tradition are often those which arouse the emotions that are deepest. This is especially true of the supernatural; ghosts and demons, the Weird Sisters, the sprites or fairies and the moon-calf Caliban, all of which strike root in popular superstition, are presented in keeping with it, and therefore, even in an age which does not accept it, affect us in a way that literary or classical spirits and specters, like the Senecan — Chapman's, Jonson's, or Marston's — or those which appear to Posthumus, by no means can.

Thy bones are marrowless, thy blood is cold, —

at that, in imagination, the veriest sceptic shivers. And the Vice is a devil, really. But the emotional appeal of tradition is strong also in the purely human Hamlet, Macbeth and Lady Macbeth, the romantic young woman in love, Falstaff, and the Fool in *King Lear*, though Othello and Lear himself, in whom the traditional element is less apparent, are poetic and emotional, to be sure.

It is the purposes of imaginative and emotional effect that tradition serves, not those of a psychology; and where there are so many traditional elements, both primitive and logically incompatible, as in Iago and Falstaff — the latter, not only a picaresque rogue, but a clown, a parasite, a satyr, and a *miles gloriosus* — it is evident that there can be no thoroughgoing mental coherence, that the individuality lies nearer the surface — in traits, not motives, in tone and manner rather than a consistent point of view, and in the immediate impression. The two are not true to life, and still less are they done from life, though both have been declared to be the one thing and the other; yet they are what is the all-essential thing, alive, are 'persons,' as Mr. T. S. Eliot has said, 'whom we can see and hear,'[11] though not comprehend or analyze. Or, as Mr. Forster says of fiction in general, the characters 'are real not because they are like ourselves (though they may be like us) but because they are convincing.'[12] In other words, a character is such because he has form and shape or, as M. Hankiss has phrased it, solidity ('dont la vérité consiste dans sa solidité'); because he has a life of his own, or, as Mr. Grigson calls it, 'organic tensity.' Jonson's characters are less like us than Shakespeare's ordinarily are, but the best ones, as Mr. Eliot has it, are, though less varied and complicated, as much 'alive,' and Envy and Sylla's Ghost as much so as those of Jonson which pretend to be human. The same is to be said of Shakespeare's ghosts and sprites; and Caliban, the moon-calf, and Iago, the demon, are even more alive than characters less unlike us. The figures in the modern novel and theater are in structure more of a transcript, more consistent, comprehensible, and analyzable than the Elizabethan, but less distinct and vivid, less moving in voice or feature. In them tradition is less apparent, and must be. Faithful studies, food for thought rather than stimulants for the imagination and the emotions,

---

11 Cf. above, p. 88, and *Selected Essays* also, at pp. 130, 137.
12 E. M. Forster, *Aspects of the Novel* (1927), p. 87.

they are more nearly original. Otherwise they have no reason to exist. But they cannot, like the great traditional figures, content us with the novelty of perfection, with the 'slight novelty' or the 'fine excess' of poetry — poetry, which in subject, as Wordsworth remarked, like Pope before him, is familiar, and as Rossetti declared, like Keats before him ('almost a remembrance'), should seem to the hearer to have always been present to his thoughts but never before heard. So Iago had never been heard, although muttering for a generation. Mr. Shaw is certainly right as he declares that 'the fitful attempts to make him something better than a melodramatic villain only make a hopeless mess of him and his motives'; but he does not appreciate the fact that this of Iago's is the supreme melodramatic villainy, nor remember that the highest or most effective forms of art are popular crudities developed and refined.

6

What confirms me in the opinion that the greatest drama is emotional rather than psychological is not only the parallels which I have traced in the ancients as well as in so-called psychologists like Racine,[13] but also the pronouncements which I have recently come upon, of open-minded and (what is almost the same) poetical-minded critics, like Mr. Eliot as quoted above, Swinburne and Henley, Lytton Strachey, and (most important of all to reassure me) the actor, producer, and dramatist Mr. Granville-Barker. Swinburne, who never went in for psychological interpretation as practised in his day and afterwards, but treated Shakespeare as an Elizabethan dramatist and poet, not a Victorian novelist, touches on his 'oceanic harmonies of terror and pity.' And what Henley and Strachey and Mr. Granville-Barker have to say bears on the particular point of Iago's character now in hand.

Henley, in his essay on *Othello*, first printed in 1903, presents a conception of the tragedy, similar to mine, of which some notion may be gathered from the quotation, page 52 above. In saying, 'Iago *apart*, the interest of *Othello* is entirely and unalterably emotional,' the critic is possibly thinking of the deadly coldness which has since been denied him; but this is a positive and penetrating, not

---

[13] See the chapters 'Reconciliation in Tragedy,' '*Phèdre*,' 'Oedipus and Othello,' 'Art and Artifice in the *Iliad*.'

a negative thing, is, to use Iago's own words, 'a poisonous mineral,' a hatred like that of 'hell pains,' and certainly Henley would acknowledge the emotional reaction he produces in the audience.

Mr. Strachey, in an unfinished essay on *Othello* recently published, makes clear that, in creating the villain, Shakespeare was concerned not with psychology at all but the great situation — with intensity of effect. To that end he changed Cinthio's murder story, in which the Ensign had a motive — unrequited love:

> . . . the tragedy must be enormous, and unrelieved. . . . If Iago had been led to cause this disaster by his love for Desdemona, in that very fact would lie some sort of comfort; the tragedy would have been brought about by a motive not only comprehensible but in a sense sympathetic; the hero's passion and the villain's would be the same. . . . The whole story depends upon his plot, which forms the machinery of the action; yet, if the Desdemona impulsion is eliminated, what motive for his plot can there be? Shakespeare supplied the answer to this question with one of the very greatest strokes of his genius. . . . He determined that Iago should have no motive at all. He conceived of a monster, whose wickedness should lie far deeper than anything that could be explained by a motive — the very essence of whose being should express itself in the machinations of malignity . . . and, when the moment of revelation came, the horror that burst upon the hero would be as inexplicably awful as evil itself.[14]

The motivelessness was, we have seen, a characteristic of the Vice, but only as an incidental part of his make-up: by the great dramatist it is made a point of. What was at hand, but dormant, is turned to dramatic account — a capital instance of the advantageousness of tradition. In Shakespeare generally there is no paltering with morality; there are no justifiable or glorious crimes, and, of course, no neutral or ambiguous motives like *ennui*. There are not even any ethical or psychological studies of either villain or hero. Elsewhere he has deprived villains (or villain-heroes) of motives, furnished in the source, simply to deepen the wickedness of their nature, as in Richard III, Goneril, Don John, and the Oliver of *As You Like It*; or of their deeds, as in Macbeth and his Lady;[15] and, as in the present

[14] Lytton Strachey, *Characters and Commentaries* (1935), pp. 295–96 (by permission of Harcourt, Brace and Company).

[15] Cf. Sir Arthur Quiller-Couch, *Notes on Shakespeare's Workmanship* (New York, 1917), pp. 18–24, for Macbeth.

instance, he has done it to heighten the contrast and intensify the situation, to let loose passions in villain or victim beyond the reach of ordinary human nature, to arouse the emotions, not to satisfy the intellect, motives seeming rather to be excuses or palliatives, which blur the contrast, deaden the impact. Like other Elizabethans from the time of *The Spanish Tragedy* and the old *Hamlet*, he had little use for them in a villain pitted against a nearly faultless hero. But nowhere else has he turned on the spotlight — the searchlight — making the villain trump motives up, invert them, trifle with them or jeer at them, and thus only expose the fiendishness of his intention. The only real occasion or provocation for his hatred, his being passed over in the matter of the lieutenancy, which replaces the thwarted love in the *novella*, is, like Macbeth's grievance at the designation of Malcolm as Prince of Cumberland, or Hamlet's 'oblivion' of the duty laid upon him, or Lear's vexation with Cordelia, a 'superficial motive,' for the conduct of the story. How the scope and stature of Iago's wickedness (and of Othello's virtue) would be limited by any adequate grudge! How the contrast would be weakened by evil in the villain that was merely negative, and by a temper in the hero that was credulous, suspicious, or (as has been thought of late) sentimental!

And as for Mr. Granville-Barker, of Lady Macbeth's invocation —

> Come, you spirits
> That tend on mortal thoughts, unsex me here,
> And fill me, from the crown to the toe, top-full
> Of direst cruelty —

he observes: 'Note the ultra-human pitch, hit and sustained.'[16] Presently he insists on 'the dramatic need for ultra-human force.' Lady Macbeth, after the Weird Sisters (another force ultra-human), fills the place of Iago in the tragic economy; intensity of effect is peremptorily secured at the expense of psychology — she does violence to herself as Iago is to do to Othello, while (as he also does to the Moor) the Three mislead under the spell of a 'fatal hallucination'[17] her brave and honorable husband; and yet our contemporary

---

[16] *Companion to Shakespeare Studies* (1934), p. 78.

[17] The phrase of Sir Arthur Quiller-Couch (*Notes on Shakespeare's Workmanship*, p. 24, by permission of Henry Holt and Company). The critic himself, though

dramatist looks on in approval. In a longer essay Mr. Granville-Barker too would no doubt have remarked the advantage here of tradition; for the appeal is imitated from Seneca's *Medea*, or, more directly, from *The Misfortunes of Arthur* (1587), or *The Warning for Fair Women* (1599).[18] The earlier dramatists, having similar emotional purposes, had felt the same 'need'; and the supreme one profits by their example.

7

A fiend, then, though in human form, with a convincing accent and individual manner; and in this tragedy a fiend he must be to fill his role, which, at bottom, is not so much that of the Elizabethan or Senecan villain as of the ancient Fate. Like Fate, though without any Aeschylean elements of justice or retribution, he is malignant, motiveless, and inscrutable, is mocking or ironical. Like Fate, he holds the reins all in his hand and, till near the end, disposes of everybody. Now except in the background, as an object of apostrophe or as a rhetorical figure, that venerable entity had no existence on the Elizabethan stage, no meaning for the Elizabethan consciousness. It was a classical, mythological fiction. Seeking, then, whether he knew of it there or not, the great effect in ancient tragedy of a noble spirit doing dreadful deeds, Shakespeare naturally seized upon the Vice in the Elizabethan stage villain as the motive force available. The Weird Sisters, to be sure, are a sort of Destiny; but to make them acceptable and interesting he had to embody them as Elizabethan witches. And the Vice, though he retained the gross and comic element, he intensified and exalted, to fulfill a loftier and larger function. Unlike Aaron and Richard, Iago has, as we shall see, an infernal philosophy and not only their devilish hatred but also a Satanic pride.

8

A fiend, but in form quite human, and a great part, unquestionably, for actors. If our interpretation of ancient and Elizabethan

---

without going farther, compares Othello's delusion as he tells the story of a young woman who cried out from the gallery, 'Oh, you great black fool, can't you see?' But Macbeth's delusion is by no means so complete or exonerating.

[18] Cf. the passages quoted in the old *Variorum Macbeth* (1821), pp. 64–65; *Medea*, ll. 9–12; and my *Shakespeare Studies*, pp. 361, 107–108.

drama is justified by the lines, it is mainly by means of those who have to speak them. Even today actors demand, and rightly, not psychological studies but emotional roles (though with many sides or facets), the greatest of which are found in Shakespeare and the ancients, or in Racine and Ibsen when most like them. Iago is such a one; in his sub-zero, antipodean region he is, when roused, almost as intense as Othello, and far more various, in this respect comparable to Hamlet. Like him he has both humor and wit, both prose and poetry, and much of the time wears a mask — plays the honest man and is dishonest, plays the passionate man and is cold and calculating, though with a coldness deadly and devouring as a fire. 'Iago seems to be the author's favourite,' says Mr. Chapman, agreeing with Coleridge. 'Shakespeare is perfectly enchanted with Iago. . . . Yet Iago is not a human being at all; he is not even a true stage character; he is a demon.'[19] With him Shakespeare was enchanted as Richardson was with Lovelace or Goethe with Mephisto, other beings who could never have walked the earth. And why? Much as actors are — and Shakespeare was one, we remember — by the changing and flickering flame within him, by the multiplicity of his being, and the quality and identity, the content but not the psychological significance, of his speech:

Is there in the whole history of cynicism anything comparable to the eloquence and magical perfection of Iago's talk? Real cynicism is sad; Mephistopheles is a dried-up, middle-aged clubman; Milton's Satan is a rhetorician. But Iago is a black angel, full of leaping, spontaneous, electrical vitality. He is, in truth, the Spirit of Evil, with no passions and no habitation; and he ought to have been shown with horns and a tail. But the world has never noted this circumstance. The world accepts Iago as a man, and shudders, feeling nevertheless a little mystified and prejudiced against the play.[20]

With the phrase 'no passions' we need not quarrel, since this is plainly a malignant and destructive Spirit of Evil; the Elizabethan audience,

---

[19] *A Glance toward Shakespeare* (1922), p. 46 (by permission of Little, Brown and Company). Cf. Coleridge (Mackail's ed., p. 206): 'It was in characters of complete moral depravity, but of first-rate wit and talents that Shakespeare delighted. . . . Richard III, Falstaff, and Iago.'

[20] *A Glance toward Shakespeare*, p. 47 (by permission of Little, Brown and Company).

we may be sure, guided by the tradition, were not mystified. And Mr. Chapman's perception of Iago is evidently in keeping with Mr. Shaw's, quoted above, except that like Coleridge, like Shakespeare and his audience, he delights in him.

And the villain is to be acted accordingly. Convinced that 'to compare any character in Shakespeare to any real character is absurd,' and (for the moment outdoing Mr. Shaw) that 'all our pains-taking discussion of Shakespeare's people as human characters must go by the board,' Mr. Chapman declares that 'the plays should be acted largely, as they were written. I think that even Salvini and Irving would have done better if they had been less conscientious and intentional. Richard should be played genially and with gusto, and without so much regard to a supposed inner logic of character as to the blatant outer logic of stage effects.' And since, like Mr. Shaw, Mr. Chapman insists on the staginess of the Venetian tragedy, he would no doubt have said much the same of the way the villain there should be acted, though blatant would scarcely be the word.

9

The character in the situation, then (not the situation from out of the character), in the lines (not between or behind them or in some fanciful hypothesis erected upon them); and to him there, in his dramatic and poetic immediacy, we now tardily turn. At the outset the venomous and deadly Ancient is, as for the audience's sake he must be, fairly himself, though not too completely so. He is warding off Roderigo's complaints; and Roderigo is, conveniently, enough of a ninny and also of a catspaw to be confided in. Both speakers are in a measure serving the dramatist's purposes of 'exposition,' but the villain derives a perilous pleasure out of skating on thin ice and almost giving himself away. His native note is distinctly struck, though it is to ring out fuller and clearer in the soliloquies; before the catspaw it need not be muted or muffled as before the other characters it must.

And what note is it? Hard and sharp, jeering and sneering, lively and penetrating, haughty and contemptuous, yet (for this too is part of him) even here a little veiled in indirection and understatement, hypocrisy and deceit. Now, in his superiority, he can afford himself the luxury of indifference or magnanimity — until, as his plans define themselves and Brabantio appears in the darkness, he lets, for a moment, his vindictive vivacity and malicious glee break loose. Now he is soldierly and cynical, harsh and free-spoken, not, as presently with Othello and the other respectable people, rather manly and honest. Now he is humorous and cunning, not yet sly, gloating, or terrific. And, properly, he and Roderigo are speaking verse — prose comes later, as they get down to business, and serves to relieve the lofty flights of tragedy — for at the outset, as a poetical, though demonic figure, Iago must be rightly 'placed,' though not completely revealed. Without verse the finest effects, both here and afterwards, would be unattainable.

Comment in general, however, is idle — we must endeavor to catch his accents. Roderigo complaining that Iago had assured him of his hatred for the Moor, he replies:

> Despise me if I do not. Three great ones of the city,
> In personal suit to make me his lieutenant,
> Off-cápp'd to him; and, by the fáith of mán,
> I knów mỳ príce; I am worth nò wórse a pláce.

How the digression of the last two lines, with the asseveration and understatement, the poised but swaggering spondees, embodies his mingled pride and self-restraint, in due preparation for the sneer! —

> But he, as loving his own pride and purposes,
> Evades them with a bombast circumstance
> Horribly stuffed with epithets of war,
> And in conclusiön
> Nonsuits my mediators.

And how the half-line, pronounced as by the Elizabethans, and with the long *u*'s in 'conclusion' and 'nonsuits,' sets the tune of his contempt, his voice and eyebrow at the same time lifting and falling! The very 'he,' which means Othello, and presently Cassio, itself turns into a sneer through the repetition and emphasis, underscored by the *ee* sounds in 'Certes,' 'Florentine,' 'mere,' 'beleed,' as well as accented by another curt half-line, in what follows:

> for 'Certes,' says he,
> 'I have already chose my officer.'
> And what was he?

> Forsooth, a great arithmetician,
> One Michael Cassio, a Florentine)
> A fellow almost damn'd in a fair wife;
> That never set a squadron in the field,
> Nor the division of a battle knows
> More than a spinster, unless the bookish theoric,
> Wherein the toged consuls can propose
> As masterly as he. Mere prattle without practice
> Is all his soldiership. But he, sir, had the election;
> And I, of whom his eyes had seen the proof
> At Rhodes, at Cyprus, and on other grounds
> Christen'd and heathen, must be be-lee'd and calm'd
> By debitor and creditor; this counter-caster,
> He, in good time, must his lieutenant be,
> And I — God bless the mark! — his Moorship's ancient.
>
> I, i, 17–33

And what of the metallic short *a*'s in 'damn'd,' 'battle,' 'masterly,' 'bombast,' 'prattle,' 'practice,' and 'counter-caster'? In tune as well as in thought and rhetoric was there ever such contempt or derision?

To be much ruffled, however, is a confession, a defeat; and in that key Iago is too supple and superior to play long. Sympathy, from 'such a snipe,' is an irritation, an impertinence, and he puts it by with his easy magnanimity and condescension —

> Why, there's no remedy. 'Tis the curse of service . . .

and takes to the refuge of the haughty, which is understatement —

> Now, sir, be judge yourself
> Whether I in any just term am affin'd
> To love the Moor.

'I would not follow him, then,' whimpers the not unlikable ninny:

> O, sir, content you:

another wicked half-line, where more is meant than meets the ear, look and gesture filling out the pause.

Thereupon Roderigo and we are treated to a taste of the opportunist's philosophy —

> I follow him to serve my turn upon him —

but with far more of relativity and psychological appropriateness in
it than in the subsequent soliloquies. These must, as we have seen,
be reserved for the truth itself; and for Iago's self-praise at the
present moment there is (if he needed it) some provocation. He is
compensating himself for the slight put upon him or for the inferiority of his position. 'Honest' is used in scorn as equivalent to
'foolish': it is such as Iago that 'have some soul.' The phrasing and
imagery are in the sneering vein that later is worked abundantly —
'asses' and 'daws,' 'duteous and knee-crooking knaves,' are of the
same stamp as 'flies,' 'baboon,' 'guinea-hen,' and 'such a snipe';
but as his baleful eye rolls inward upon him it softens, his voice
mellows, the cockles of his heart are warmed:

> Whip me such honest knaves. Others there are
> Who, trimm'd in forms and visages of duty,
> Keep yet their hearts attending on themselves,
> And, throwing but shows of service on their lords,
> Do wéll thríve by them, and when they have lín'd their cóats
> Do themsélves hómage. These féllows have sòme sóul.

His fidelity to the dupe before him he proves even by exhibiting his
falseness to his chief, and at the same time he is, safely enough,
revealing his antipodean inner nature:

> I am not what I am.

'I am that I am,' God said unto Moses.

From the contemplation of these his personal virtues, however,
he is soon brought down by Roderigo's repining at Othello's happiness; and he cries out, not only to distract Roderigo's attention
from his grievance but to satisfy his own sheer malice:

>   Call up her father,
> Rouse him. Make after him, poison his delight,
> Proclaim him in the strèets. Incense her kinsmen,
> And, though he in a fertile climate dwell,
> Plague him with flies!

What devilish envy in the figure of speech, what venomous vivacity
in the rhythm of the whole! Here is the leaping, spontaneous, elec-

trical vitality of which Mr. Chapman has spoken. And what bright eagerness in the long *i*'s of

> Do, with like timorous accent and dire yell
> As when, by night and negligence, the fire
> Is spied in populous cities.

His craving for activity and his gaiety in destruction are unmistakable, springing out of something considerably more positive and dynamic than 'ennui.' And presently he lets go like a hoodlum, unable to hold himself in or quite keep out of the impish fun:

> Awake! what, ho, Brabantio! thieves! thieves!
> Look to your house, your daughter, and your bags!
> Thieves! thieves!
>
> .   .   .   .
>
> Even now, now, very now, an old black ram
> Is tupping your white ewe. Arise, arise!
> Awake the snorting citizens with the bell,
> Or else the devil will make a grandsire of you.
> Arise, I say.

With that, he subsides into prose, gleefully and obscenely jesting with Brabantio at his expense. Shakespeare's infernal angel, of whose intellectual elevation and inglorious grandeur we have now seen a little, has also the tastes and instincts of the gutter. In one sense his gross and lascivious merriment may be a relief to the 'discomfort of his hypocrisy' — not that he minds the hypocrisy but that this is a more abandoned pleasure! Even the Devil, the father of lies, would surely once in a while relax and 'be himself,' as we say.

10

Before Brabantio descends and reënters, Othello's 'honest' subaltern must needs take his leave; yet not without first egging Roderigo on against the General, while he touches again upon his own bottomless animosity, lightly, in a subordinate clause, as a matter now to be taken for granted, and finishes with a pleasantry:

> Though I do hate him as I do hell-pains,
> Yet, for necessity of present life,
> I must show out a flag and sign of love,

Which is indeed but sign.   That you shall surely find him,
Lead to the Sagittary the raisèd search;
And there will I be with him.

Loyally at his side! And how admirably arranged, for a comic
yet disquieting contrast, as, within a score of verses, at the beginning of the next, immediately following scene, the traitor reappears,
with other tones and gestures, in the full tide of honest talk! No
more slyness or sneering or spitting of poison now, but only the
blunt, plain man of war! Shakespeare's unparalleled power lies in
the differentiating of the speech of one character from that of another, and in then modifying it to suit time, place, and occasion;
but here, as in Hamlet, he has the further task of adapting it to suit
a changing role. Play-acting, Iago is, as he should be, still recognizable. He keeps his hard and incisive manner, as well as his gift
for understatement, and though Othello does not see it nor is meant
to, his humor: 'I lack iniquity sometimes to do me service' — 'with
the little godliness I have I did full hard forbear him.' The best roles,
at least the most attractive to both actor and audience, have feigning
in them; and the most effective feigning, such as Hamlet's or Rosalind's, is of a part not too remote from (or else sharply opposed to)
the character's own. Thus it becomes the extension or variation of
the character himself, and the dramatic current is not impeded.
Since Iago lacks the fulsomeness and unctuousness of Aaron and
Richard, he does not seem gross or clumsy, nor Othello gullible;
and it is deeply disquieting for the audience now to hear him make to
the noble and generous Moor, whom he hates like hell-pains, dis-
avowals that are so nearly avowals, with an apparent honesty that is
so close to the genuine:

> Though in the trade of war I have slain men,
> Yet do I hold it very stuff o' the conscience
> To do no contriv'd murder.   I lack iniquity
> Sometimes to do me service.   Nine or ten times
> I'd thought to have yerk'd him here under the ribs.
>
> *Oth.*   'Tis better as it is.
> *Iago.*   Nay, but he prated,
> And spoke such scurvy and provoking terms
> Against your honour
> That, with the little godliness I have,
> I did full hard forbear him.

'Yerk'd him here under the ribs' — how readily Iago would have done it to Brabantio on the slightest provocation, or at that moment to Othello without it! The phrase, in its gritty simplicity, betrays him. In fact, a loyalty that repines at not having gone the length of stabbing your father-in-law for 'prating' is of itself suspicious; here, as somewhat even in the previous scene, Iago is posed for the *optique du théâtre*, and like Aaron, Richard, and Shylock, as well as Webster's White Devil, though still more like Tartuffe,[21] he is made now and then to seem the hypocrite that he is, but would, of course, not seem to be. Of this there is something later, particularly at the inquiry after the uproar on the watch, and even in the Temptation scene.

When, after the hearing before the Senate, Desdemona is by Othello given in charge to 'honest Iago,' we both start at the danger and are also impressed by the confidence the dishonest man inspires; and thereupon the plot thickens, as after the departure of the others and in response to the whimpering of his catspaw and creditor, 'what shall I do?' the villain, dropping into prose after the high poetry of the Council, but still speaking a poetry of his own, tells the gull, both openly and mysteriously, what it is he shall do and what will come to pass. It is a notable scene, in which Iago talks half to Roderigo like a bulldozing swindler, half to himself like the infernal angel that he is as well, looking into the seeds of time and saying which grain shall grow, which shall not. In either capacity he utters more of his atheistic-Satanic philosophy, not only of life but of love, and as if from the podium or the tripod:

---

[21] Cf. below, in the chapter on *Tartuffe*, the dramatic principle of the *optique*, whereby, for dramatic effect, Tartuffe somewhat appears to be the hypocrite he would not appear to be. There it is for comic effect, here more often for a tragic one, to heighten suspense. The mere fact that there has been controversy about Webster's Vittoria is proof of her two-sidedness. In her 'innocence-resembling boldness' at the trial Lamb a little overemphasizes the former quality at the expense of the latter; Hazlitt speaks of the 'sincerity of her sense of guilt.' Her sense of guilt is to me undiscernible, and her innocence is nearer to impudence, her boldness to brazenness. When charged, she knows not the meaning of the word 'whore'; when sentenced, she cries 'A rape! a rape!' Sometimes she stands on her dignity almost like Hermione; but oftener she rails and gibes, and, informed of her husband's death, in which she is implicated, she jests about it. In the colloquies with Brachiano her playing a part need not be so evident because Flamineo or the maid is there for comment, aside.

O villainous! I have look'd upon the world for four times seven years; and since I could distinguish betwixt a benefit and an injury, I never found man that knew how to love himself. . . .

Virtue! a fig! 'tis in ourselves that we are thus or thus . . . but we have reason to cool our raging motions, our carnal stings, our unbitted lusts, whereof I take this that you call love to be a sect or scion. . . .

It is merely a lust of the blood and a permission of the will.

And in the long speech beginning with the last-quoted sentence, the oracle is fairly rapt in a tragicomic 'enthousiasmos' as he sways and fluctuates, in both thought and word, from Desdemona's changing to Roderigo's drowning, from that to putting money in his purse and back again, the note of prophecy or destiny continually asserting itself:

The food that to him now is luscious as locusts, shall be to him shortly as bitter as coloquintida. She must have change for youth; when she is sated with his body, she will find the error of her choice; she must have change, she must; therefore put money in thy purse. . . . If sanctimony and a frail vow betwixt an erring barbarian and a supersubtle Venetian be not too hard for my wits and all the tribe of hell, thou shalt enjoy her; therefore make money. A pox of drowning thyself! it is clean out of the way. Seek thou rather to be hang'd in compassing thy joy than to be drown'd and go without her.

And after that:

If thou canst cuckold him, thou dost thyself a pleasure, me a sport. There are many events in the womb of time which will be delivered. Traverse! go, provide thy money.

And then, as a finishing touch for the swindler:

Go to; farewell. Do you hear, Roderigo? (What say you?) No more of drowning, do you hear?

This is not a slice of life, or any that I know of; the gull has had wit enough to complain of Iago's bleeding his purse at the beginning, and these reiterated orders to replenish it after his unblushing avowals of duplicity would make even an idiot prick up his ears. It is no probable imposture, but is the poetry — for such it is, though not in verse, and not like Othello's, ample, noble, highly colored — is the poetry or rhapsody rather than the reality of deluding and diddling; as Antony's repeated 'honourable men' is of demagoguery,[22] and somewhat as Falstaff's story of the knaves in buckram and Kendal Green is of bragging. The corpulent cavalier's is frankly extravagant, a bit of exuberant horseplay; this is art of a higher order, and is of value to the structure as an exhibition of Iago's personal prestige and dominance and also as a preparation for the Temptation scene. Money, the villain intimates, opens every door; and under the hypnotic spell Roderigo is not free to consider what is behind the words. In the effect on us the chief value of the speech reposes — in the lyric elevation and prophetic exhilaration of a humorous swindler: sneering, gloating demon and vulgar cheat in one. Its very texture is lyrical, with its repeated themes and inverted phrases — 'she must have change for youth . . . she must have change, she must' — and yet the verbal rhythm, as always in Shakespeare, is true prose rhythm, such in quality as only Shakespeare ever framed. The high style is not out of keeping with the low in the scheme of alternation, for a grimly comic effect is intended. 'Shall be to him shortly as bitter as coloquintida,' which spurtles as from a darting and forkèd tongue, blends well enough with 'If thou wilt needs damn thyself do it a more delicate way than drowning.' And if there is a finishing touch for the swindler there is another afterwards for the 'black angel' as he rises into a paean of unholy triumph —

Thus do I ever make my fool my purse, —

and in hatred lifts up his eyes to hell and night. The demon in the scene heightens expectation like Lady Macbeth's invocation to the spirits 'that tend on mortal thoughts'; and the comedian is not entirely diverting. Logically or poetically, though not psychologically, Iago is one of Shakespeare's most consistent characters; unlike most of them he has a 'philosophy,' or point of view, of which we have had some inkling already; and now his portentous figure fully appears. The ending of the scene is at the same time both lyrical and intensely dramatic. The final, blood-curdling couplet

I have't. It is engend'red. Hell and night
Must bring this monstrous birth to the world's light.

[22] Since it comes so early in the speech to the prejudiced Citizens, actors are warned against irony or sarcasm; but, Hudson says, always, so far as he has observed, to no avail.

was prepared for by the quiet-disquieting, oracular words

There are many events in the womb of time which will be delivered.

He is Satan, though without a God.

II

Thus, speech by speech, syllable by syllable, I could follow Iago throughout the play; but, craving company, I will touch only upon the more important moments and the new traits as they make their appearance.

At the end of Act II, scene i, on the quay at Cyprus, Iago has another talk with Roderigo, this time inculcating his doctrine of the tender passion and female frailty — 'when the blood is made dull with the act of sport' — not so much in general as in particular and detail. Desdemona and Cassio will be in love, and are. In the previous colloquy the Ancient had certain feeble sentimental objections or scruples of Roderigo's to meet, which now, as he becomes so specific, are a little stronger; yet he meets them as before, not by evidence or argument but assertion and reiteration, not by overcoming but overriding. Again the situation is not so much a parallel to that of the Temptation scene as a preparation for it. At bottom Roderigo is predisposed, as in the matter of providing Iago with more money he wasn't; fatuously hoping himself to seduce Desdemona, he is really inclined to accept Iago's opinion of her frailty, as Othello isn't. But the method of the slanderer is, after making allowances for the comparative smallness of the undertaking and the inferiority of the subject of his arts, somewhat the same. Here, as there, Iago plays upon — imposes upon — the imagination, and speedily, dexterously takes for granted the thing he is pretending to prove.

. . . Very nature will instruct her in it and compel her to some second choice. Now, sir, this granted, — as it is a most pregnant and unforc'd position — who stands so eminent in the degree of this fortune as Cassio does? a knave very voluble; no further conscionable than in putting on the mere form of civil and humane seeming, for the better compassing of his salt and most hidden loose affection? Why, none; why, none; a slipper and subtle knave, a finder of occasion, that has an eye can stamp and counterfeit advantages, though true advantage never present itself; a devilish knave. Besides, the knave is handsome, young, and hath all those requisites in him that folly and green minds look after; a pestilent complete knave, and the woman hath found him already.

(*Rod.* I cannot believe that in her; she's full of most bless'd condition.)

Bless'd fig's-end! The wine she drinks is made of grapes. If she had been bless'd, she would never have lov'd the Moor. Bless'd pudding! Didst thou not see her paddle with the palm of his hand? Didst not mark that?

'Villainous thoughts, Roderigo!' he adds in a moment, wringing the neck of Roderigo's romanticism; and Iago is the same chuckling and cajoling, button-holing and overpowering fellow that said, 'If thou wilt damn thyself, do it a more delicate way than drowning. — Do you hear, Roderigo? . . . No more of drowning, do you hear?' With his employer Iago has the manner of an American political or criminal boss with an underling.

Hitherto we have seen in him the infernal angel and the swindler, whether as the affable but condescending mentor or the blunt and honest man of war. Now, on the watch, he is the good companion. He is polite, expansive, familiar; and with Cassio is genial and open-hearted before his disgrace and sympathetic afterwards. He calls him 'man' before and after the latter is drunk: 'What, man, 'tis a night of revels. . . . What, man! there are more ways tò recover the general again. . . . You or any man living may be drunk at a time, man.' Roderigo he had addressed as 'Sir,' and then, as he advanced in contemptuous condescension, as 'noble heart,' 'silly gentleman.' Cassio he now addresses as 'lieutenant,' as 'good lieutenant' when drunk and in need of humoring; and as 'good lieutenant' again, though one of any sort no longer, when he sounds him on the subject of Cassio's confidence in himself, about to suggest his approaching Desdemona. And as before that they clink their canakins Iago — a stroke of genius! — sings, and more than a single song. Goethe's Mephisto, too, lifts up his voice, long after; Marlowe's doesn't nor Milton's Satan; neither does Richard, Aaron, Barabas, nor Kyd's Lorenzo; and it is a surprising but appropriate trait in Shakespeare's ampler yet subtler conception of the diabolical incarnation that he should break into a rollicking, traditional and unobjectionable ale-house ditty, with a wicked purpose, indeed, but with hearty satisfaction in the singing itself. A jolly 'good *fellow*' (look at Tammany!) is the honestest sort of disguise. Shakespeare's Caesar distrusts Cassius, who hears no music and seldom smiles, and even Hamlet seems somewhat startled on finding one can smile and smile and be villain. But this is another point at which Iago's feigning is but an extension or exaggeration of his natural disposition, and, as usual, he profits by it in his effect upon us. A convivial, a congenial villain! 'A pestilent *complete* knave,' as he has slanderously but enviously called the kindly Cassio!

A man's man, too — the handsome and charming Cassio he despises! — and therefore still fitter for the dramatist's purpose. He is not, as in Cinthio, made beautiful; he is neither attractive nor attentive to Desdemona or any other 'hen.' To be either would have interfered with his intrigue; a Lothario or a Lovelace would have been suspect. Before an Anglo-Saxon audience at least an Adonis or anything of a lady's man would have difficulty keeping up his reputation for honesty and sagacity.

In the inquiry after the uproar Iago is bid by Montano to tell the truth, as he is a soldier; and then, if ever in this world it did, dishonesty rises to the occasion:

> Touch me not so near.
> I had rather have this tongue cut from my mouth
> Than it should do offence to Michael Cassio.

That asseveration, with the solemnity of the full baptismal name, is as imposture better than his words about the quarrel before this:

> And would in action glorious I had lost
> Those legs that brought me to a part of it!

There the hypocrisy is apparent, as when, just before, he looked 'dead with grieving.' Here too it is perceptible, as for the effect on the audience it should be; but by 'touch me not so near' Iago has now, if not before, earned his honorable title. And yet — what of that glittering glance at the General, new come from the bridal chamber, in the first words of his reply?

> Friends all but now, even now,
> In quarter, and in terms like bride and groom
> Devesting them for bed.

Cassio he envies his charms, Othello his happiness.

12

The soliloquies, eight in number, are pretty progressively devil-ish. As Mr. Chapman says, they fulfill the function of the Greek chorus, 'punctuating the story with explanations' of the complex details of the intrigue; but they fulfill another of its functions. The chorus is the *raisonneur*, fairly, in the long run, the voice of the dramatist; and here that must be heard, not explaining the intrigue but applying to it the accepted moral values, in order, in this system and rhythm of the passions, rightly to arouse the sympathies of the audience. In this tragedy there is a special need and justification, despite the cost to realism. To credibilize his imposture Iago, unlike Aaron and Richard, enjoys a reputation for honesty with everybody in the play: to save the reputation of his chief victim with us Iago must rob himself of his own. The need that he should do this is the greater because elsewhere he is at this point presented with realism: in his conversations, particularly with Roderigo, he tampers with the moral values, speaking well of himself or his like and contemptu-ously of others. And the need that he should do this is greater still because, being a wit and a humorist, he is at times to all appearances a 'good *fellow*.' Without the soliloquies, why should he not be taken for such (and with the accent shifted) by the plain and simple souls in the audience as he has been by the wise and subtle with the text before them? So Falstaff has been, another wit and humorist, and really a good fellow (with the emphasis on 'fellow' still), but, as he confesses, a thief, coward, deadbeat, and embezzler; for to merely literary people soliloquies do not mean much. To the audience (as they should) they mean a good deal, and therefore in speaking of himself to himself — to the audience, under cover — Iago's black and boiling heart must, as it is, be wholly laid bare for the excite-ment and direction of their sympathies and emotions; and his pur-poses and his eagerness to carry them out must, as they are, be made steadily more apparent for the sake of suspense.

It is a different matter with Browning's monologues, whether separate, like *My Last Duchess, The Spanish Cloister*, and *Bishop Blougram*, or connected, like Guido's in *The Ring and the Book*. These are to be read, not delivered: there is no action to be sup-ported, no mass emotion to be aroused, no prolonged suspense, whether of anticipation or curiosity, to be excited or sustained, no tradition of the hypocritical villain to be observed. Hence, when a soliloquy, the monologue is not, as with Aaron, Richard, and (far less frankly and crudely) Iago, a confession or exposure; and when addressed to some one person or to several, it is not an apology or defense. In either, the principles of psychology can be respected; and like the criminal in Lombroso, the villain thinks well of himself — in any case speaks well of himself and familiarly and confidently of God.[23] In the process, to be sure, he continually gives himself away. As Hutton[24] and others have noticed, he is so contrasted with a noble or lovable person — the Duke's wife, 'Brother Lawrence,' Pompilia, or Caponsacchi, whom he despises or detests — or with his noble position or profession — husband or ruler, priest or artist — that his approval and disapproval, his arguments and excuses, recoil upon him. Of the marriage into which he had entered with the ineffable Pompilia, whom he has murdered, Guido speaks as of buying a young hawk for a falcon at the market:

> I have paid my pound, await my penny's worth,
> So hoodwink, starve and properly train my bird,
> And, should she prove a haggard, — twist her neck.

But so he is in character. There is no *optique du théâtre*. And in Iago soliloquizing there is less of it than in Aaron and Richard. He does not, like them, frankly and flatly call himself a villain, does call Othello an ass, a fool, and his own diabolical nature he lays bare indirectly — for some learned readers too indirectly — as he trumps up motives and from 'mere suspicion' acts as if from 'surety.' But the situation is still artificial, theatrical, as not in Browning. Like Aaron and Richard, Iago is a 'true villain,' a conscious impostor. He wears his soldier's profession as a loose cloak of disguise; in Browning it would have fitted him closer. The hypocrisy of Browning's prelates is second nature.

13

Like the colloquies with Roderigo, the soliloquies are in preparation for the great Temptation scene. But there, as in the soliloquies

---

[23] Cf. my *Shakespeare Studies*, Chap. VII.
[24] R. H. Hutton, *Literary Essays* (1896), p. 196.

and not in the colloquies, the Ancient is wholly the hellish angel wrestling for a soul, not also the swindler, for a purse. And he puts on his more honest disguise, nothing now of the devil being permitted to peep from under it. Yet at moments the feigning is perceptible. At the beginning he is still the honest officer and faithful plain-spoken subaltern that has been his cue; but he is on the whole slyer and more sinuous, and steadily becomes more so. Really his conduct is suspicious, and it is only by virtue of the convention of the calumniator credited that he is not suspected or refused a hearing. An honest man who undertakes to tell you that your wife and friend are too familiar makes at once a clean breast of it, does not twist and turn, advance and retreat, tease and tantalize.[25] This one plays upon Othello's imagination as he has done upon Roderigo's; but both more freely and elaborately and also much more in defiance of the probabilities and proprieties, since he is having to do with an intelligent and naturally prejudiced subject, his superior, whom he has no right thus to address. Or rather, it is Shakespeare himself, working out freely and rhythmically the *motif* of deception by suggestion and repetition, and letting the deceiver take the role not so much of an honest man as of a slanderer and hypocrite:

Iago. Indeed!
Oth. Indeed! ay, indeed. Discern'st thou aught in that?
Is he not honest?
Iago.   Honest, my lord?
Oth.   Honest! ay, honest.
Iago. My lord, for aught I know.
Oth. What dost thou think?
Iago.   Think, my lord?
Oth.   Think, my lord!
By heaven, he echoes me,
As if there were some monster in his thought
Too hideous to be shown.

He plays upon him as upon an instrument.

In itself, to be sure, this method of suggestion[26] is psychological, but for realism it is here too little adapted to the circumstances,

---

[25] Cf. my *Art and Artifice in Shakespeare*, pp. 9–10.

[26] This obviously, is a different use of the words from that in Chap I, p. 22, where I deny Shakespeare a 'suggestive method' in characterization.

carried with too high a hand; and if it were not for the convention,
together with the unimpeachable prestige of Iago's reputation for
honesty and sagacity, the General must needs soon perceive in his
disquieting counsellor the intruder and intriguer that he is and drive
him off and knock him down. It is poetically, theatrically, that this
development of the *motif* of suggestion to the limit (and beyond the
limits of psychology) is effective; like that of Iago's apparent hypocrisy, its complement, which gives the suggestion scope. On the
stage, as not off it, the tempter should, as he does, beat about the
bush, 'contract and purse his brow,' and then, as he prospers, domi-
nate his victim. So he is less to the taste of Henry James or William,
but more to that of Molière or Sophocles as well as of the average
man who saw their plays. The appropriately simple and honest role
would lend itself less to the development of contrasts and offer
fewer opportunities for the excitement of the audience, both directly
and through its effect on the Moor. Drama is not a matter primarily
of psychology nor of logic; and mere poetry is that still less. When
Satan plays the hypocrite before Uriel the poet must avail himself
of not only this convention of deception —

For neither man nor angel can discern hypocrisy —

but also (even here!) the *optique du théâtre*, making Satan pretend a
desire for knowledge and a yearning adequately to praise the Creator
as the motive of his voyage and wind up his speech with a demurely
sanctimonious droop of voice and eye:

wise are all his ways.

For the emotional advantages of neither convention can be ex-
ploited — the contrast and irony cannot be fully developed —
except as the two conventions are combined; that is, the innocent
person made unable to penetrate — not merely a pretense that is
almost imperceptible — but one that is now and then apparent.
What is the use of the fiction of a greater credulity than in life if there
is not, before our eyes, something more than in life to be credited?
And the theatrical, emotional development now in question appears
more markedly later, as, growing bolder, Iago openly takes the
reins and delivers himself in loftier style:

Oth.   Nay, yet there's more in this.
    I prithee, speak to me as to thy thinkings,
    As thou dost ruminate, and give thy worst of thoughts
    The worst of words.

Iago.   Good my lord, pardon me.
    Though I am bound to every act of duty,
    I am not bound to that all slaves are free to.
    Utter my thoughts? Why, say they are vile and false;
    As where's that palace whereinto foul things
    Sometimes intrude not? Who has a breast so pure
    But some uncleanly apprehensions
    Keep leets and law-days and in sessions sit
    With meditations lawful?

Oth.   Thou dost conspire against thy friend, Iago,
    If thou but think'st him wrong'd and mak'st his ear
    A stranger to thy thoughts.

Iago.   I do beseech you —
    Though I perchance am vicious in my guess,
    As, I confess, it is my nature's plague
    To spy into abuses, and oft my jealousy
    Shapes faults that are not — that your wisdom yet,
    From one that so imperfectly conceits,
    Would take no notice, nor build yourself a trouble
    Out of his scattering and unsure observance.
    It were not for your quiet nor your good,
    Nor for my manhood, honesty, and wisdom,
    To let you know my thoughts.

Thoughts, thoughts, meditations and apprehensions — it is as if he had them there in his hand, half opened it, then held it behind him, and in the last slow tantalizing line half opened it again, lest they might after all be forgotten.

This is as Iago mounts in stature and authority before us — which on the carpet he would not do so rapidly or to such a height, but fortunately does on the stage. The scene is a signal example at once of external movement and internal development; for poetic and dramatic, but not any psychological or realistic, effect Iago rises and dilates like Satan confronting Gabriel,[27] in order that he may be fit to cope with his heroic and struggling victim; and the infernal one

[27] *Paradise Lost*, IV, 985–87.

more and more declares himself as he harps on the subject of 'good name,' and hints at the shame of cuckoldom, the misery of jealousy, seeing with a demon's vision what his victim cannot see but trembles, is 'affrighted,' to hear of. The rapidity and the extensiveness of the change, in tempter and tempted both, are made plausible by the art of preparations and gradations — almost anything in drama may be made plausible by that. Towards the end of the .cene, when Othello reënters, altered beyond recovery, the villain can become more definite and specific, no longer inflames but torments and tortures the Moor's imagination, and, though not so barefacedly, is almost as domineering and insulting as with Roderigo. As with him, he unbends and is humorous, but vindictively. Othello demanding proof or 'satisfaction,' Iago, in no pretty way, inquires whether he would wish actually to catch the pair *delicto flagrante*,

> It were a tedious difficulty, I think,
> To bring them to that prospect —

and it is thus now continually that he satisfies not his General but himself.

14

His humor is involved in the *optique du théâtre*. This, as applied to those who are feigning, may seem to belong to comedy, not tragedy. Sainte-Beuve and the other French critics discuss it, so far as I remember, only in connection with Tartuffe;[28] and Lamb, who in his essays on *Some of the Old Actors* and on *Stage Illusion* recognized it before them, though in histrionic art rather than in the dramatic, insists that it is misplaced in tragedy. Still he notes its importance in the acting of comic villains and intriguers.[29] From the beginning Iago is comic as well as tragic; and yet, as we have seen, his betraying his true nature, or his hypocrisy, in the presence of Roderigo and more particularly of Othello, often serves a purpose not comic at all but to excite our anxiety and heighten the suspense. So it is at times with Hamlet playing the madman, as he gives himself away before the King in the Nunnery scene or at the 'Murder of Gonzago,' though a closer parallel to the tragic effect of the Vene-

---

[28] Cf. the chapter on *Tartuffe*, below, p. 341.

[29] For further discussion on this matter, see my *Shakespeare Studies*, p. 468, n.

tian's villainous feigning as it betrays itself is in Richard III. Really, the *optique* is only a form of irony, which likewise requires repetitions and reminders of the contrast involved; and irony may, of course, be either tragic, or comic, or both together, as it is with Iago and Hamlet, Richard and Titus, or comic only, as it is with Portia and Rosalind, or comic and pathetic, as with Viola and Imogen, who also momentarily speak up in their true character, out of their disguise.

As for Bensley, whom Lamb declares to have been the only endurable Iago that he remembers to have seen:

No spectator from his action could divine more of his artifice than Othello was supposed to do. His confessions in soliloquy alone put you in possession of the mystery. There were no by-intimations to make the audience fancy their own discernment so much greater than that of the Moor — who commonly stands like a great helpless mark set up for mine Ancient, and a quantity of barren spectators, to shoot their bolts at. The Iago of Bensley did not go to work so grossly. There was a triumphant tone about the character, natural to a general consciousness of power; but none of that petty vanity which chuckles and cannot contain itself upon any little successful stroke of its knavery — as is common with your small villains, and green probationers in mischief. It did not clap or crow before its time. It was not a man setting his wits at a child, and winking all the while at other children who are mightily pleased at being let into the secret; but a consummate villain entrapping a noble nature into toils, against which no discernment was available, where the manner was as fathomless as the purpose seemed dark, and without motive.

As for Bensley, I say, and the acting of the part, Lamb is certainly right. What I have been noticing has to do merely with the lines, in which the Ancient, as certainly, does betray himself, and to which the actor should add nothing of his own. Othello must neither be a dupe nor appear to be such, and mainly to avoid that result the dramatist has availed himself of the convention of slander and provided the slanderer with a reputation which nobody on the stage can question; but even so, probability is for him here, as everywhere else, a secondary interest, emotional effect (tragic or comic) the foremost. And that interest — for the imagination rather than the intellect, of immediate impression rather than inference — is served by Iago's 'a little deserting nature,' showing now and then his wicked cunning rather than that plain and perfect honesty which logically we might expect of him, and playing all the stops of the Moor's sensibilities more audaciously and successfully than in reality he would do or could.

15

Now with Iago, as not with Tartuffe, this *optique du théâtre*, or transient self-betrayal, depends in large measure on his humor, and his humor in some measure on the *optique*. For he really is a humorous figure, the other only a comic one. Iago goes much farther in feigning and masquerading, in hoodwinking and manipulating, and this he enjoys partly for its own sake. Tartuffe betrays himself unintentionally; for Iago it is but playing the game to show himself now and then almost in his true features and colors and yet not be caught. And he can adjust himself to the person and the occasion — face to face with the purblind, infatuated Roderigo pull the mask of sturdy honesty nearly off, with the General (after he is excited) lower it a little now and then, but more and more. The catspaw cannot be supposed to perceive the irony when Iago declares to Roderigo that the latter 'is sure of him,' nor the General when with a clear sad brow he inquires,

> Who has a breast so pure
> But some uncleanly apprehensions

and the rest. Here the character, if not the actor, may be conceived to be 'in secret correspondence with the audience' or else merely with himself. It is little that Roderigo would appreciate (and no matter how much) of Iago's demure references to his superior, as in 'And there will I be with him'; or as when, after the discussion of his designs upon the Moor, in which for forty-five verses his name has not been mentioned, he refers to him with the 'cool, off-hand, slighting' pronoun, noted by Cowden Clarke:

> Meet me by and by at the citadel: I must fetch his necessaries ashore.

Besides, Iago is a humorist in his own right, apart from hypocrisy and play-acting. More than most Shakespearean characters and than any other Machiavel he has a philosophy, a point of view; and still less would Roderigo appreciate the 'twisted wit,' to use the phrase of Miss Manley — the cool and complacent inversion of all moral values in 'These fellows have some soul,' whereas they haven't any, or in 'By the mass, 'tis morning, pleasure and action make the hours seem short,' the hours (for they that are *bad* shall be happy!) of the night he ruined Cassio! But the audience would be responsive; and it is only because readers believe laughter to be human, and humor to be kindly, that they are not responsive too. In form the humor is human, and there is no high and wintry derision of the Creator or his creation. The Ancient, who drinks and sings, likes money and company, and goes so far as to keep a wife, has no thoroughgoing, universal grudge. But how naturally unnatural are his 'have some soul,' 'make the hours seem short,' and 'since I could distinguish betwixt a benefit and an injury, I never found man that knew how to love himself'! And towards the end, after his grip on Roderigo has tightened, he can unmask his ghastliness pretty completely, as, in Act IV, scene ii, he tells him nothing is so important as the removing of Cassio. 'How do you mean, removing him?'

Why, by making him uncapable of Othello's place; knocking out his brains.

That, surely, is 'gaiety in destruction,' and the audience both laughs and shudders.

In the Temptation scene the Ancient must be warier — so he is, in both play-acting and wit. But still he has a little game for himself and the audience. 'Men should be what they seem,' he murmurs to the General, seeming so obviously what he isn't. His wit is true to the situation and to his nature. 'I do not think but Desdemona's honest,' groans the Moor.

Long live she so! and long live you to think so!

and once granted that Iago may say it and his chief may hear it, what delicate thrust could go deeper? It is the thing, he knows, that the impassioned man now cannot do — like what is next suggested:

My lord, I would I might entreat your honour
To scan this thing no farther; leave it to time.

The insidious innocence! And at the first, innocence is his cue. Then it is astonishment and regret at the commotion he has caused — 'Is't possible, my lord? . . . Is't come to this?' Then, as we have seen, once he controls the situation more securely, it is a condescending spirit, as he produces proofs and torments with more definite suggestions. But still it is innocence. He is careful not to go too far — for the safeguarding of tragic effect the dramatist himself is careful — and the villain retreats or pulls the mask tighter. In his oath of fidelity —

> Witness, you ever-burning lights above —

as it echoes Othello's, his hypocrisy is just apparent; and it is pretty imperceptible as he makes his self-denying surrender:

> My friend is dead; 'tis done at your request.
> But lét hèr líve.

'Sine effusione sanguinis!' in the traditional sanctimonious phrase of death-dealing evasion.

16

These conventions of calumny and the *optique* may seem something of a load for the audience to carry. The conventions of disguise or the aside, which are more definite and concrete, we perceive and acknowledge; we accept the improbability of Rosalind's not being recognized in man's clothing by Orlando, who fell in love with her yesterday, nor by her father, when she meets him in the forest, and of Iago's not being overheard and noted by Cassio and Desdemona (nor by Montano and Emilia) as he mutters menaces on the quay. Yet these of calumny and the *optique* and those of the aside and mistaken identity are really of the same nature and order. All alike are in themselves superficial and transparent deceptions; all alike, subjected to the test of realism, imply stupidity in the one deceived. This last, as I show in the preceding chapters, is the charge wrongly brought against Othello and Emilia. The same, on similar grounds, could be brought against Orlando and the Duke, or Bassanio and Gratiano, who at the trial do not recognize their own newly wedded ladies; and on almost the same grounds it has been brought against Oedipus and the Chorus. They cannot read the book of Fate in the oracle and recent disclosures any more than the Moor and Emilia can in Iago's character and demeanor. And the convention of slander, in its own day, the audience accepted as naturally and readily as disguise; in fact, unlike a sophisticated, psychological audience at present, more readily, for with the former, as not with the latter, they needed not distrust their own eyes and ears. Really it is only nowadays, as in narrative or drama motives are more strictly regarded, that the convention is clearly apparent; in Elizabethan times and earlier it was the simple and natural thing in a story to believe what one was plausibly told. And here, in this tragedy, acceptance is, still more decidedly, the path of least resistance. For the striking situation and its great emotional effect the improbability is incurred, and then, as far as may be, made probable. From the outset Iago's formidable power is fully exhibited: by gradations his ascendancy over Othello, Cassio, and Desdemona is established, his unimpeachable reputation borne in upon us. And then, momentarily, for another effect, of heightening the suspense and irony, the process is reversed, and he is permitted, before his victim, furtively to show his hand and betray his tricks, to lower the mask and give the audience glimpses direfully reassuring.

17

As in Act IV his ascendancy more and more establishes itself, the demon gives rein to his deeper inclinations, taunts and torments more than he jests, and somewhat more unstintedly than a true friend and experienced counsellor may or can. He plays more frankly with foul imaginations; as, in scene i, with kisses, with the precious handkerchief and Cassio's use of it, with blabbing and the cuckold's horns, making light of these as Othello is far from doing or is meant to do. Or he reverses the process, as when Othello, grieving over the Desdemona that is now for ever lost to him, dwells on her charms one after the other. 'And then, of so gentle a condition [disposition]' — 'Ay, too gentle' — 'Nay, that's certain. But yet the pity of it, Iago! O Iago, the pity of it, Iago!' — 'If you are so fond over her iniquity, give her patent to offend; for, if it touch not you, it comes near nobody.' The deadly coldness, the frigid, acrid wit, thus conspicuously appear. No poohpoohing or banter now; but in the Moor's deluded and inflamed condition the thrust infuriates him only against the object of his jealousy. 'Get me some poison, Iago; this night.' Here, too, is the high note of destiny again, that of the prophecies already fulfilled — 'shall be to him shortly as bitter as coloquintida . . . there are many events in the womb of time which will be delivered' — as the deemster ordains:

> Do it not with poison; strangle her in her bed, even the bed she hath contaminated.

'Even' and 'hath,' not 'has,' are the inevitable words.

And it is in this Satanic vein that he meets his end. Othello but wounds him, saying:

> If that thou be'st a devil, I cannot kill thee;

whereupon, through his teeth, Iago retorts with an avowal of his identity —

> I bleed, sir; but not kill'd.

And no little one he proves himself, too, when he pulls himself up to his height, and locks his lips.

> Demand me nothing; what you know, you know.
> From this time forth I never will speak word.

Shakespeare, Mr. Edward Mayo aptly says, is here making a dramatic virtue of necessity, shrouding in infernal mystery what, for most critics (except as they supply it), is wanting in the character's structure. But since there is really no defect, the dramatist is only making the fullest use of his medium. Othello here at the close had asked the wonder-stricken question

> Why he hath thus ensnar'd my soul and body,

to show there *is* no reason why. And Iago must not make even such answer as he can, the trumped-up motives being already familiar to the audience. For Iago as a stage figure his end is proper and complete.

So it is for him as a character. It is a 'bad end,' manifestly — not one of relief from tedium or ennui, or even from 'the infinite vexation of man's own thoughts,' which should be his if he were the mere bankrupt idealist or disillusioned worldling that he has been taken for; nor one of any 'moral awakening,' either — it is a bold bad end that he is making. But of its sort there could not be a better. 'What,' rejoins Lodovico, 'not to pray?' and, neither praying nor replying, Iago rises above the vulgar valedictory blasphemies and imprecations of Barabas, the Guise, and Aaron. This impenitent and contumacious spirit is necessary to the logic of the conception, not only as handed down by tradition but (still more) as previously presented in the text. At first glance the villain may here seem to be drawn according to the latest principles of criminal psychology: he lacks a moral sense, and like Browning's Guido feels no penitence or remorse. But this before us is (again) a positive, not a negative, matter; and while Guido or the ordinary murderer considers himself good and others evil or unjust, Iago is at enmity with the good and wedded to evil. At heart he is like Barabas, the Guise, Aaron, and (really) Richard, undeluded and defiant; but more like the Clytaemnestra of Aeschylus and the sinners of the *Inferno* (unknown, apparently, to Shakespeare), who, though also haughty and impenitent, maintain their dignity.[30] It is a matter not of psychology but (once again) of emotional intensity and continuity. He is Satan still, and at his greatest. Great actors, as Mr. Woodberry aptly remarks, are 'likely to be nearer to the spirit of Shakespeare than the critics.' Though Edwin Booth made him 'outwardly amiable . . . inside, he had no doubt, Iago was the spirit of hate. . . . And perhaps in that most difficult moment of the role, the climax of Iago's fate, the elder Booth was right in making the expression of this intense enmity dominant in the Parthian look which Iago, as he was borne off, wounded and in bonds, gave Othello, — a Gorgon stare, in which hate seemed both petrified and petrifying.' Not 'perhaps' but 'certainly'; for how could the evil spirit, in league with hell and night, and deliberately denuded of all motives but deadly point-blank hatred, make his exit in any other way?

18

Why 'outwardly amiable,' however? Why given the sociable graces, wit and humor, popularity and a good reputation, for which

[30] *Hibbert Journal*, October 1931, 'The Dignity of the Damned,' by F. MacEachran.

such beings are not distinguished? Why, above all, the combination
of haughty demon and vulgar swindler, unless deliberately to
justify Christopher North in saying the character 'is a riddle' and
tease the critics with it. Richard, then, must be another. To quote
Mr. Chapman:

> The character of Richard has caused the literary people many wakeful
> nights. No one has ever seen a man like Richard III; and yet he is nearly
> perfect as a stage villain. He is glowing with wit and humor, and in his
> seven soliloquies he expounds himself like a prologue. One thing how-
> ever is clear: had Richard been gloomy, the play would have become a
> bore. We should have cried, 'Oh, here he comes again, that dreary
> criminal!' I doubt whether Shakespeare troubled himself much about the
> question, Do such persons exist? or built up his characters out of observa-
> tion. He evolved them rather through stage experience.[31]

Yet the combination of villainy and humor was also evolved before
him, a matter of tradition as well as his own experience; and Shakespeare, as he created Iago, was not dutifully regarding the nature of
reality but doing far more effectively what others had, not ineffectively, done already. In life itself there is an affinity between cynicism[32] and swindling, jesting and licentiousness, and that was enough
for Shakespeare — for poetry and drama.

Riddles are not for drama, we have seen. In delineating such a
figure he was concerned, if with psychology at all, not with that of
Iago or Richard so much as with that of his audience; and really
not with their psychology either, but with their taste, which at bottom was his own. The purpose and end of all art is, of course, to
create something that the spectator can love or be delighted with,
or (as in this case), however he hate it, in some way admire. And
as the dramatist Freytag says of Iago compared with Richard, 'he
was a more difficult and repulsive subject than the prince, the general
to whom environment and his great purpose imparted a certain
importance and greatness; and therefore Shakespeare endowed him
more copiously with humour . . . which has the unique advantage

---

[31] *A Glance toward Shakespeare*, p. 30 (by permission of Little, Brown and Company).

[32] Mr. Chapman (above, p. 247) says that 'real cynicism is sad,' but he must then
define and restrict the meaning of the word. Was not Voltaire a cynic, and Anatole
France, and Pope?

of throwing an attractive light upon even the hateful and vulgar.'
It is a principle, a tradition, followed by Richardson in his Lovelace,
Goethe in his Mephisto, Browning in his Guido, even (in the form of
sarcasm) by Milton in his Satan.

Corneille, defending himself for presenting in a tragedy a murderess, Cleopatra, and in a comedy a liar, le Menteur, declares that
we cannot but admire her greatness of spirit and his presence of mind
and vivacity.[33] And both the one thing and the other we may say
for Iago. Like Shakespeare's Richard and Edmund, Macbeth and
Lady Macbeth, he has courage and energy, pride and dignity, intellectual and imaginative compass as well as (like the Menteur and all
other great rogues in literature) vivacity and address. With his
dignity, as we have here and there noticed, his vivacity and variety,
like the very nature of his wicked role, somewhat interfere; like
Dante's sinners, he can enjoy only the willful 'dignity of the damned';
and even that, obviously, cannot, without disturbing the dramatic
equipoise, fully assert itself in the presence of Othello. The soul of
dignity being on the stage, Iago must not, here at the last, be given
scope, but only — 'Demand me nothing' — pride and reticence.
And in thus presenting his 'demi-devil' the English dramatist was
not, primarily, meeting the requirements of realism or morality any
more than the French dramatic moralist and dialectician himself.
'The poetic value of a character,' says De Sanctis, 'lies 'not in his
morality and faith but in his vital energy.' These artists, like the
Greek dramatists, are morally solid and sound; and, though following traditions so different, are nevertheless at one in serving the purpose of art, which is to please, and in yielding to the power of the
imagination, 'which reveals itself in the balance or reconcilement
of opposite or discordant qualities.' In poetry is the 'reconcilement';
and when the 'qualities' are in little need of that, poetry cannot
exercise or demonstrate its fullest power.

Nowadays we demand in art less of the 'artificial,' more of the
'natural' and 'true'; and in dramatic figures we seek for the reconcilement in a framework or mechanism of motives. Our villains,
in so far as we can be said to have any, are rather like those of the
late eighteenth and early nineteenth centuries, who bear resentment
against individuals for injuries, against the world or society for in-

---

[33] Œuvres (1862), I, 32.

justice, but are not so much wicked as 'unfortunate,' are sentimental, not hard and witty, melancholy, not merry. They are not in love with evil, and are prompted by motives, not raised above them. Shakespeare's and Webster's villains, Corneille's and Racine's, on the other hand, like also the less noble of Shakespeare's heroes, Coriolanus and Timon, who more than most of them are the cause of their own undoing, are made human, or else attractive, not so much by traits that explain their conduct — motives, circumstances, or previous experiences — as by other, added traits that adorn or redeem them in our eyes. With the Plebeians Coriolanus is nearly insufferable, and what restores him to our sympathy, apart from the admiration for him from everybody but his contemptible enemies, is the fact that he is not always arrogant and vainglorious but is a good son and husband, a true friend and generous enemy, a loyal subaltern and valiant warrior, a big spirit who will not stoop to deceit. It is a matter of emotions, again; of sympathies or acceptable antagonisms, or of imaginative and poetical dignity not of the understanding or the judgment; of creation, not of imitation and consistency or verisimilitude. And yet the greatest villains of the eighteenth and nineteenth centuries, such as Lovelace, Mephisto, and Guido, are more like Shakespeare's than like Schiller's, Byron's and Hugo's. They too are hard, witty, and merry; live and have their being in poetry rather than in any faithful imitation of reality or sound structure of motive; and 'can be seen and heard.' Like Shakespeare's they hold and fascinate us by their accents; and Guido, though at no one point indebted to Iago, is like him in his jeering and cynical tone, ugly imagery, piquant phrasing, energetic and vivacious rhythm.

19

The Duc de Broglie, as a Frenchman, is, in an interesting essay on *Othello* justly praised by Furness, little concerned for a psychology but much (as indeed he should be) for the integrity of the role. Like the modern spectators as Mr. Chapman understands them, he is mystified by the merging of demon, swindler, and petty revenger. 'The Devil has neither humour nor honour; he has neither rancour, nor rage, nor covetousness; he is a disinterested person; he does evil because it is evil, and because he is the Evil One.' The Duke would preserve 'decorum,' would keep unimpaired the logic and rationale of the role. His objection is characteristically French, like that of Lemaître to Tartuffe and of Legouis to Rabbi Busy, though also (I must admit) like that of Schücking to Cleopatra. The amplitude of the characterization offends them, the dignity mingled with vulgarity.[34] The Elizabethan standard of 'decorum' is not so narrow and rigid. The same objection may be made to other characters, particularly Shylock, who at times wraps a mantle of biblical dignity about his vindictiveness and cunning. But these are all poetic and dramatic successes; and what would become of Shakespeare's devil in an atmosphere so rarefied as this of the Duke's? Even Satan could not breathe it, still less Mephisto. The critic is dealing with the principle of evil like a metaphysician, not like Shakespeare, who is none — that is (as Burke has it when writing of your metaphysician as himself akin to a wicked spirit), with 'incorporeal, pure, unmixed, dephlegmated, defecated evil.'[35] Iago is not incorporeal, not defecated, if we know him. The concreteness and many-sidedness, the breadth and richness, the wit and humor, the vulgarity and very obscenity of him are among the transcendent virtues of the part. In no tragedy, I fancy, is there a place for so thoroughgoing, undisguised, and uncompromising a devil as the Duke demands, certainly in none of Shakespeare's; and this devil, like every other of his creatures, however fantastic, appears to us only clad in the plausible, changeable vesture of humanity, planted on the earth, and (as in this case he should be) in the dirt. If Wordsworth could say in a preface:

I have wished to keep the Reader in the company of flesh and blood, persuaded that by so doing I shall interest him,

how much more the dramatist, still readier to follow 'wheresoever he can find an atmosphere of sensation in which to move his wings'!

20

The fundamental justification, however, for Iago's humor and vulgarity is structural. The principle or practice of alternation in

[34] Cf. the chapter on Tartuffe, p. 343; and as for Schücking's opinion that Cleopatra is inconsistent, at first a vulgar harlot and at last a sublime queen, cf. my *Poets and Playwrights*, pp. 12–13, 24. On Shylock, *ibid*, pp. 132–33.

[35] Letter to a Noble Lord.

tension, which we have already noticed, particularly in the first chapter, here prevails. Iago must unbend, at least in England, in Shakespeare. He cannot be permitted to keep to the high pitch of tensity in his soliloquies and his final defiance, as the Duke would have him do, or he would be unendurable and fail of effect. And for him to unbend there is no other good and plausible way. That of pathos, manifestly, is not open to him as it is to the heroes — to Othello, Hamlet, Lear, even to Macbeth. Neither pathos nor romantic melancholy is open to him as it is to Milton's or Marlowe's Devil. There must be, and there are, no retrospect or prospect, no forlorn or wistful touches such as

'Tis true, I am that spirit unfortunate,

with 'its stately and melancholy music-roll,' or as

Think'st thou that I who saw the face of God . . .?

for they would not only be incongruous but imperil the position of the hero. Moreover, as by the best comic effects or other relaxations in tragedy generally — those of the Porter scene or the martlet scene — there is thus provided variation rather than relief. Iago's very wit and humor make us shudder; his pleasantry is a menace. And, as we have seen, the Ancient can thus unbend in another sense — be, after his feigning, himself again, with Roderigo or alone. In short, his humor is indispensable.

21

In another villain, Edmund, Shakespeare somewhat approaches the modern attitude and method; Webster, in his Bosola, approaches it more nearly; and a word or two of comparison with both may make somewhat clearer the art employed upon the greatest of all. In Edmund tradition is far less apparent, though he slanders his innocent brother with as little evidence and, since with less skill, in even greater reliance upon the convention of credulity. Being in the under-plot, he plays a smaller role, and is not the chief motive force in the tragedy: the burden of villainy he shares with the two daughters of Lear. Fatality, as in Gloster's utterance about the flies and Kent's about the stars, plays a part as well, and, at the outset, the impetuosity of Lear and Kent, not to mention the uncompromising spirit of Cordelia. An infernal angel, then, is not required; and the bad man of the story is given a more adequate motive, a real grievance. But it is one at that time not so appealing as today. A bastard, he is therefore in disrepute and without valid claims. He is not ill-treated or impoverished; the objects of his resentment, his father and his brother, are, the former, kindly to the point of heroism, the latter, wholly generous and noble; and his illegitimacy, like that of Don John and others in Elizabethan drama, like Richard's physical monstrosity and Shylock's racial one, is meant to be taken as an indication of villainy rather than an extenuation of it.[36] Embittered by the baseness of his birth, he is eloquent in his resentment; but he is cynical and sceptical, vindictive and cruel, and shows no sign of affection thwarted or blighted. Like Iago's, and even Shylock's, though less so, his villainy is far in excess of his injury. The means whereby he is made acceptable or endurable are still, as with the Ancient, not psychological or sociological; they lie mainly, that is to say, in the management of the story on the stage and in his eloquence and poetry, his sarcasm and wit. He is not justified or explained, but made interesting, and kept from being repellent. He is not present at the blinding of his father, just as Iago is not at Desdemona's death (though in the *novella* the Ensign was); and he is not permitted to look upon him afterwards, in his mutilated state. His wit or humor is less inhuman than Iago's, but though not so abundant, almost as original: 'Fut, I should be that I am had the maidenliest star in the firmament twinkled on my bastardising.' So it is when he hears of the death of the sisters, who were rivals:

> I was contracted to them both. All three
> Now marry in an instant . . .

and when he looks upon their bodies:

> Yet Edmund was belov'd!
> The one the other poison'd for my sake,
> And after slew herself.

'And Hell itself is not without its supreme satisfactions.' Of a finer, nobler nature the hints are slight, and all of them are at the end.

---

[36] See my *Shakespeare Studies*, p. 300.

To Edgar, who bows before the nemesis that has come upon his father, he addresses the great words:

> Thou'st spoken right, 'tis true.
> The wheel is come full circle: I am here . . .

which are not beyond his reach. If he be to blame, his progenitor is more so; comic irony differs from the tragic only in degree, and at its best a sense of humor includes a sense of justice or retribution. On such terms even Milton's Satan deigns to blame himself.[37] And moved by Edgar's tale, Edmund sends the countermand to the prison. These traces of humanity, like the blot of bastardy, somewhat restore him to our sympathy, but they do not explain his conduct. They are, again, only emotional amends.

In Iago such as these are lacking. There are spirit and fire, the sparkle of his wit, the glitter of his humor, the artfulness of his playacting in a role not always alien to his nature; above all there are the unmistakable voice and semblance of an individual, human or inhuman: but not a shred of virtue, not a drop of human pity or tenderness. In his behalf nothing at all is pleaded in mitigation or extenuation — at the center of the action a sharper contrast and steeper intensity are demanded — and the only indulgence is by way · of humor and poetry. He is like one of Velásquez's villains, acceptable in painting as he could never be in the flesh. He 'fascinates, and is intolerable.' Edmund, sinned against as well as sinning, is not beyond the pale.

22

Webster's villains, Flamineo and Bosola, are in some respects far nearer to our time, are almost of the Romantic Age. Like Edmund they have no demonic, essentially malignant quality. Like Edmund but unlike Iago, and like Milton's and Marlowe's devils as well as Byron's and Hugo's, Goethe's and Schiller's villains, they have a past; like these Romantic creations but unlike the two Shakespearean, they are at times sympathetic and compassionate, melancholy and gloomy, laboring under a sense of guilt. They have more wit and humor than the Romantics — Flamineo, Mr. Lucas rightly says,

[37]
> He gave it me,
> Which I as freely give. — iv, 380.

has more than Iago, and though he has some pangs and twinges, is the gayest of the lot. Bosola is more Romantic, and his humor is of a macabre and gruesome turn, not, like Iago's, of an infernal. His philosophy of life is warped, but not self-centered and sensual, perverted or inverted, wicked or impious, like Iago's and in some measure Edmund's; and he has a feeling for the miserable and sorrowful mystery of human existence, both in general and as represented by the Duchess and Antonio, his victims. These qualities he possesses in his own right, not by any feigning. Yet he fulfills his function of hired torturer and cutthroat, with rare and only momentary relentings, as obediently and unflinchingly as a Sultan's mute, with no motive for it but one still more superficial and inadequate than Iago's or Edmund's for their voluntary villainy — his poverty and the Duke and Cardinal's gold. In his make-up, as in theirs, there is a contrast but less of a 'reconcilement'; there is, indeed, a cleft. Until after the climax thought and conduct have little in common. The emotional and imaginative amends are too far-sought. The scruples beforehand and the remorse afterwards are questionable and insufficient means of reconcilement, less needed (to be sure) for Flamineo, whose meditations are more cynical, less lofty. In both alike, as in Iago and Edmund, the identity is established, not through a psychology but the poetry, the tone and manner, the idiom and imagery; yet, psychologically no more plausible and consistent than the Shakespearean villains, they are poetically, dramatically less so, and are by no means so intense. Superficially they are more poetical; their speech is studded with imaginative utterances; but these are less thoroughly in character or of the situation. Flamineo's or Bosola's identity — their improbable roles — are less continuously and perfectly preserved than Edmund's, and Edmund's less than Iago's. The Venetian (and the bastard too perhaps) betrays no obvious moral incongruity, which is far less acceptable on the stage than the psychological; and psychologically the least consistent or conceivable of the four, he is poetically and dramatically the most so — alive, active, identical in every thought and syllable.

CHAPTER VIII

The Tempest

Which of you did I enable
Once to slip inside my breast?
BROWNING, *At the Mermaid*

I

THERE is always a particular interest attaching to the last work of a great author; and in an especial degree this has been true of Shakespeare. If *The Tempest* was not his last play, it would seem that it ought to have been. The action now and then lags a bit, and gives the people on the stage or in the audience a chance to ponder; which the chief character once does to such effect that his speech, of purest and highest poetry, might serve for the 'conclusion of the whole matter,' *der Weisheit letzter Schluss.* And there are meetings and leave-takings, and glances into the past and at what is to come.

Yet, as I have several times elsewhere indicated, I cannot believe that there is any allegory (which, as in Spenser's *House of Pride*, says one thing and means another), or symbolism (which, as in Tennyson's *Ulysses*, means the thing it says and suggests another), or even 'veiled biography' here. *The Tempest*, like every other Shakespearean or popular Elizabethan drama, stands like a tub on its own bottom, is a story in its own right and for its own sake; and unless the intention of the author be of no primary importance, and meanings be not derived from the text but imparted to it, this must be only a rather simpler story of his than usual, a romantic fantasy, precious, not indeed because of the structure or situations, but because of the characters, the poetry, and the rich and dreamy spirit which informs it. That the story is slight is no proof that there is another within or behind it. And Prospero is not Shakespeare any more than (as fewer think) he is James I, except in the sense that the dramatist, not the

Scotch monarch, created him; his 'potent art' of magic is not the art of poetry; Ariel is not genius, or the lawless imagination, craving liberty but kept in service; Miranda is not the drama; Caliban not the vulgar public; Milan not Stratford; and the enchanted isle not the stage, or London, or the world.

What strange opinions a student of Shakespeare has to contradict! The late Stuart Sherman once said that he was 'sorry' for those who do not believe something of the sort; and though thus I am doing only what he was doing, as well as all other people who venture to pity the benighted, I am tempted in turn to be sorry for those — despite their name and number — who believe it. Drama, and character, and poetry do not content them; Shakespeare himself, I fear, does not content them; and with the same noble simplicity 'that the author writ' they will not read. They have a medieval or late-Roman taste for an inner meaning, such as that which allegorized Virgil; or the latter-day taste for an inner meaning, which runs into the biographical or symbolical; and particularly in a last work, but in any of moment, they expect to find a 'message.' Not only do I think such an interpretation unwarranted by the text and the spirit of the poet, I also think it actually troubles and disturbs the artistic effect.

Above all is this true of the characters, especially the mythical ones most eagerly seized upon — Ariel and Caliban. Where does the beauty or greatness of these creations lie if not in their reality? They are not single abstractions personified, but many-sided conceptions incarnated. They are not spirits such as are to be found in Shelley's verse dramas, but beings more actual and convincing than Miranda and Ferdinand themselves. In short, they are not dull, shadowy, or puzzling as the supernatural and allegorical in poetry generally are. Each has his own accent, and personal air, and point of view. Each is interesting in his own right, not by a sort of reversion. And never has the plastic power of the poet asserted itself more emphatically and fruitfully than here, where he had no models in nature to follow. It is as with the fairies in *A Midsummer Night's Dream*, the Weird Sisters and the ghosts in *Macbeth* and *Hamlet*. 'Certainly the greatness of this author's genius,' says Nicholas Rowe, Shakespeare's earliest editor and himself a competent dramatist, 'does nowhere so much appear as where he gives his imagination an entire loose, and raises his fancy to a flight above mankind and the limits of the visible world.' For, above mankind (or, in Caliban's case, beneath it), these creations are, though fashioned after its similitude. To be works of art, Shakespeare's ghosts, fates, and sprites, like the angels and demons of Dante and Milton, and the gods and goddesses of Homer and Virgil, are made human, though proportionately.[1] And how by allegory these clear outlines would be troubled, these solid forms dissolved!

Besides, like the ghosts and the Weird Sisters, these two beings are plainly indicated as developments out of popular superstitious conceptions, which are concrete. If Shakespeare meant allegory or symbol he strangely misled his audience, thinking only of the critics to come. In Ariel the tradition is double: he is a sprite like Puck, who gladly serves the king of fairies; and he is the 'familiar spirit' of a magician, whom he serves unwillingly. And Caliban is a mooncalf, offspring of a witch and a devil, a conception still current as late as Dryden's day. Unlike and contrasted as they are, they have, as the simple denizens of earth and air, some traits in common: an aversion to labor and a longing for liberty; a primitive sense of humor and a fondness for tricks and pranks; a childish pleasure in tastes and sounds, sights and lights; a spontaneous and unsophisticated love of nature; and (deeper within them) a fear of a higher power, on the one hand, and a craving for affection and approbation, on the other. Thus the contrast between them is heightened.

2

Ariel is like Puck before him in the enjoyment of his own will-o'-the-wisp performances, and of their effects on mortals. He mimics Ferdinand 'cooling of the air with sighs, and sitting, his arms in this sad knot'; and it is with delight that he tells of Stephano, Trinculo, and Caliban pricking up their ears and lifting up their noses like colts at the music, by which they are led through briars and thorns into the horsepond. As with Puck, it is by mimicry that he misleads them — that of dogs barking, cocks crowing, a cow lowing or a horse neighing; of drums beating, bells ringing, or people singing or

---

[1] Lessing (*Hamburgische Dramaturgie*, Stücke 11, 12) complains of the ghost in Voltaire's *Semiramis* that it is not poetical — human — enough.

calling. (What but the mimicry, indeed, can make this a fitting employment for a personification of Shakespeare's genius?) And like Puck and the other fairies he rejoices in movement, drinks the air before him, and cries, 'I go, I go,' eager as the wind. Yet this is the celerity, not of thought, but of a sprite, swifter than the moonës sphere.

He is more spiritual, however, than the fairies; more 'delicate' than Puck. He is not naughty or mischievous; the conspirators whom he pesters deserve what they get. Still he pities them, or comes as near to doing so as a careless sprite well can. He is kept a bit aloof, like Nature herself. He does not laugh at lovers —

Lord! what fools these mortals be! —

for he is not of the earth — a 'lob of spirits' — but of the air; as, indeed, his name, falsely etymologized, would signify, as Prospero explicitly remarks, and as his sports and occupations clearly indicate. He runs, if need be, upon the sharp wind of the north, but prefers the bat's back, after summer merrily. He flies and sings invisible, and flames amazement with St. Elmo's fire. He palpitates with eagerness,

What shall I do? Say, what. What shall I do?

and again and again, as a child does, craving reassurance, he inquires,

Do you love me, master, no?

His work is play, and yet he is continually longing for liberty. He is a wild thing, though by fear and gratitude he has been a little tamed. As is observed by Coleridge[2] (to whom, as to Hazlitt, Ariel is a myth and no more), he represents a power of nature, like wind or water, harnessed for the time to man's service, and delighting in it, yet ever ready to break loose. In service and at liberty alike he is eager and impetuous — he is the wind blowing, the stream flowing. Prospero will miss him but he will not miss Prospero. 'My bird,' Prospero calls him; but the cage opened — the spell broken — he at once and for ever takes flight. And though in the mysterious making of him there has been some process of abstraction, this is a poet's, a myth-maker's creation, which cannot stop short of a full corporeal

---

[2] See Raysor, *Coleridge's Shakespearean Criticism*, II, 176. I have a bit modified the poet's thought.

existence, as with Shakespeare's personifications time and again. Witness, in a single scene:

> And *pity*, like a naked new-born babe
> Striding the blast. . . .
>
> Vaulting *ambition*, which o'erleaps itself
> And falls on the other. . . .
>
> Was the *hope* drunk
> Wherein you dress'd yourself? Hath it slept since?
> And wakes it now, to look so green and pale?

As Wordsworth would keep the reader, Shakespeare would the spectator, 'in the company of flesh and blood.'

Sprung, now, out of a creation of popular superstition (though refined and vivified anew), and taken to be a myth of nature by the Elizabethans, by one of the greatest of modern poets, and for that matter (though in simpler fashion) by any schoolboy who can read, Ariel, who earns his freedom and blissfully wings his way back to the elements, has, by the accepted interpretation, been turned into something which, according to all the poets' testimony, takes flight, to be sure, but never by their permission! And were he imagination or genius, would he bury himself in the bosom of nature, to sing, unlike the skylark, songs nevermore to be heard? Or if in this character he is to be conceived as the spirit of earth and sky, visiting and inspiring the soul of a poet, is not that an idea fit for a Romantic like Wordsworth or Shelley —

> Make me thy lyre, even as the forest is! —

rather than the playwright? If external, his genius resided in the world of men.

3

The chief and determining cause of this indifference to the probabilities of the case and the poet's purpose is the other matter, already touched upon, which likewise escaped the poetical perception of Coleridge and Hazlitt, though not of our all-discerning age — that Prospero is the poet himself and his magic no magic at all. It is the poet's art. The apostrophe to the elves, by whose aid he has bedimmed the noontide sun and waked sleepers from their graves, is his farewell to it; the breaking of the wand and burying of the book, his abandonment of the stage; and the Milan to which he is triumphantly returning, Stratford. This opinion is now pretty nearly a dogma. By Masefield, Lytton Strachey, and Schücking it is not accepted; but in some form or other it is by most of the other Germans — Ulrici may have been its originator — and of course by the biographical-minded Brandes and Harris, as also by Lowell, Dowden, and Churton Collins, and even by Chambers, Bailey, and Mackail,[3] present-day critics of great and merited renown. Sir Edmund then goes so far as to suggest that Ariel, though also the agent of an inscrutable Providence, may be a symbol of the spirit of poetry found pegged in the cloven pine of pre-Shakespearean drama;[4] which reminds us of Miranda as the drama, of Caliban as the public, and (quite recently, for of this among Shakespeareans, and worse still, Baconians and Oxonians, there is no end) of Cordelia as the Shakespearean plays, Kent as the author, and Lear (*mon Dieu!*) as Elizabeth![5] There, is the trouble with the criticism by hypothesis or impression (rather than interpretation) which still prevails. Everyone having a right to his own opinion, Ariel must be anything that he is taken to be, and consequently, in the upshot, is nothing at all. Thus criticism becomes a contradiction in terms. Thus meanings are no meanings, but labels attached; and a work of art is no longer art — a means of expression — but an arbitrary emblem like the flag or the eagle, the cross or the crescent. Yet is not a critic (κριτικός) a judge, who does not explore his own consciousness, but determines the author's meaning or intention, even

[3] Professor Mackail and Mr. Bailey, however, have misgivings, and make reservations in keeping with their general antipathy to such a critical process. Cf. *Approach to Shakespeare*, pp. 104–105; *Shakespeare*, in the 'English Heritage' Series, pp. 204–205.

[4] Chambers, *Shakespeare: A Survey* (1925), p. 310. It is only fair to notice that Sir Edmund is here not so confident as in the matter that Prospero, when bidding farewell to the elves and breaking his staff, is Shakespeare. See below, p. 291.

[5] See the review in the *Times Literary Supplement*, August 1933, p. 522. By the same author Audrey too is made 'the plays,' and Perdita, 'the lost plays,' which the Old Shepherd, Shakespeare's father, has found (see my 'Detective Spirit,' *Saturday Review of Literature*, May 8, 1937). 'What is a symbol?' says Mr. Belgion. 'Something by which one is led to recall something else' (*Criterion*, January 1930, p. 215). Mr. Allen recalls, but is not led.

as if the poem were a will, a contract, or the constitution? The poem is not the critic's own.

If it is not, there is little basis for the idea, pivotal in the accepted interpretation, that Prospero is the poet. And why should London, or the Globe theater, or 'Man's universe,' be a 'desert' (or *uninhabited*) isle, peopled only by Ariel, Miranda, and Caliban; and Stratford and repose be adumbrated by Milan and the duchy which the poet, 'Duke of Stratford,' is again to govern? The audience (and in Shakespeare's lifetime there were for this play no readers) would have been very considerably at sea! Allegory or symbolism cannot, like dreams, go by contraries; and is the dreariest of failures if, even at the time, it do not fit. Or if, in lieu of that, it be not supported by a long-established convention, as with the shepherd's trade for the poet's ever since the days of Theocritus; and there is nothing of convention here. Magic has no such traditional association with poetry. How is this to be taken for anything else than what it is manifestly intended, and would certainly be understood, to be — the magic (though the *white* variety) of the time of James I (author of the *Demonology*, hunter of witches) with its paraphernalia of robe, wand, and book; the magic in Greene, Marlowe, Dekker, Jonson, Middleton, Ford, and Rowley, in Lope and Calderón, which, like Prospero's, but Shakespeare's by no means, must be 'abjured'? Nowadays we do not believe in it as an 'art' (and for that if for no other reason we here turn it into a metaphor); but nearly everybody so believed in it then.[6] Nowadays 'magic' and 'spell,' 'enchantment' and 'incantation,' 'witchcraft' and 'witchery,' are stock metaphors in the critic's vocabulary; but they were nothing of that sort then. Of the farewell to the elves Wolff remarks that 'the poet gives back to the elements the genii who for twenty years have been in his service.' 'Where,' asks Schücking, 'do we find Shakespeare or one of his circle speaking of his dramatic abilities as genii?' And the raising of the dead had been a function of sorcery since the days of the Witch of Endor; this particular reference to it, like the apostrophe as a whole, is taken from the *adjuration* of Medea, in Golding's Ovid.[7] How strange that Shakespeare, if renouncing a novel and metaphorical magic, should, without a hint of the difference, have

---

[6] See my *Shakespeare Studies*, the chapter on the Ghosts.

[7] *Metamorphoses*, vii, 192–219 (Golding, 258–88).

adapted the retrospective formula of one who is renewing her practice of the real! Did he not greatly care to be understood, until these latter days?

The strangest thing of all, however, is the application of the theory to the Epilogue, as undertaken by Dowden, Luce, and a few others. One hopes that those sorry lines are not by Shakespeare; but whether they be or not, they rather show that in his own time no such understanding was intended. An address by the actor of Prospero begging for applause, the Epilogue is nothing more than a series of wire-drawn conceits on the subject of pardon and indulgence, and with Shakespeare's own personality and present situation seems to have nothing to do. Yet if anywhere in the play the poet were making his farewell, here, surely, was the place for it, and for his clearest and most telling utterance besides. That for himself the prince of dramatists should make so pitiful an exit, until now no one suspecting that it is his!

As for the play proper, apart from the objection that the interpretation does not fit the text, there is the other that it is alien from the spirit of Elizabethan popular drama, and of Shakespeare. The popular dramatists — such as Marlowe, Middleton, Heywood, Beaumont and Fletcher, who also did not print their plays — do not write allegorically, and, except satirically, do not refer to other dramatists, still less to themselves. Such writing would have been out of place, and (except the obvious sort sometimes found in Dekker, which is mere Morality) highly perplexing. Allegory then, as symbolism now, was not for the popular stage. Lyly's *Endymion* was a Court play, and a mythological one — *The Tempest* is neither — in which compliment and allegory were naturally and traditionally expected. In the *Midsummer Night's Dream*, which, like *The Tempest*, indeed, has some of the characteristics of a Court entertainment, there is the compliment to the 'imperial votaress'; yet that is not allegory of the abstract (or autobiographical) and recondite character we have been noticing, but is concrete and unmistakable. And as Creizenach said of Shakespeare and the Elizabethans in general, and Mornet, of Molière and the *grand siècle*, they did not choose materials which offered occasion for personal confessions in the style of Goethe. In *Faust* the poet indubitably appears; but Goethe, as the late Mr. Henry M. Alden once said to me, could not have created an Ariel.

Why not? Mr. Alden said it was because he would have given him an ethical turn — which is the same as saying that the poet was too self-centered, too little of a myth-maker to conceive a sprite. He could not like Shakespeare forget himself to the point of thus entering into the soul of a phenomenon of nature. His Ariel would have been more like Milton's Attendant Spirit in *Comus*, as contrasted by M. Legouis. 'Both spirits leave the earth when their tasks are done, but while the Miltonian angel ascends to heaven amid moralising mythological visions, his last words a plea for chastity, Ariel takes flight like a butterfly.'

Ibsen likewise was too self-centered; over his stage his grim spirit ever broods, while Shakespeare's, like a god's in his own world, is, though everywhere, nowhere; and yet as I have said in a previous discussion, I cannot conceive of the Master-Builder, first erecting churches, then homes for human beings, then castles in the air, as an allegory of the author's artistic development — from his early romantic plays, through the social dramas, to the poetical, symbolical ones at the last. Such an idea, like that of Ariel imprisoned in the pre-Shakespearean drama or of the dramatist's farewell — though far less alien from the mind of the poet concerned, equally so from his art — robs the play of its general and human significance. Though it deals with poetry and drama, it is not poetic or dramatic itself. Indeed, it is not relevant to the story. A scholar, a biographer, more especially the particular one who invented it, might find it interesting, but what audience could?

It is for students and readers, and those, I must think, who for the moment (for bad moments we all have) are not the most poetical-minded, either. On the stage even today it would not be acceptable as applied to *The Tempest*. The drama is in fact seldom performed: there is too little suspense, and the conjuring tricks pall upon us. But a Prospero who, after mysteriously freeing the spirit of poetry from the cloven pine and then mysteriously bidding farewell to it — and to the elves as spirits of poetry, too, rather superfluously before that — is now for riding back for good and all to Stratford, would make almost any audience yawn, except one made up of a Shakespeare Society or an Educational Association at a centenary anniversary.

How much more so at the Globe, on the Bankside, where Shakespeare's plays were delighted in but not taken to be literature, and

the author of them (when he was thought of at all) was not hailed
as a genius, nor was so esteemed by himself.[8] He had worked for a
competence, and was now retiring to enjoy it. Though he had still
nearly five years ahead of him he did not take the trouble to see the
better half of his plays, still in manuscript, safely into print, or even
to correct the garbled versions of the others. In his will he mentions
none of them, no books from his own pen or any other, though concerned who should receive money for mourning-rings, who his
sword, his silver-gilt bowl, his very clothes and beds. He thinks to
be remembered by his friends and for himself, not by the world or
the poets, for his poems. And it is in such a spirit that he writes.
He is not personal. His songs, in the vein of folksong, are perhaps
the most objective and dramatically appropriate that ever were
penned. And when he did undertake to write of himself it was in
sonnets. In style they are so sweet and poignant that they have
piqued the curiosity of critics for three hundred years; but in content
they are so traditional, or so veiled and obscure, that they have only
baffled it. He is not concerned for his reputation — is not conscious
and critical, logical, orderly, or correct. He frequently falls into
bad taste — in his greatest plays as in the least — and in the later
ones lapses at times into the primitive devices of the first. He frequently falls into contradictions, as we saw in Chapter I, not only
in matters of time and place, but of fact and circumstance, and even
of motive. Here in *The Tempest*, Luce has observed, the incidents
of the wreck as witnessed in the first scene and as reported or
discussed by Prospero, Miranda, and Ariel in the second, do not
harmonize, like numerous details of the intrigue and background —
witness Bradley's appendices — in the four great tragedies. They
are for an audience, not for print, and the writer is an opportunist.
But the abundance is not a chaos; the mind that produced it in some
fashion or other informs it, puts life into it. What is partly carelessness is partly instinctive artistic cunning. The shipwreck is not
meant to be real — it is the work of magic — but it is real enough
to be exciting. And defect is turned to commodity by the dramatist's 'short time' and 'long time,' the scene now here now nowhere

[8] For Shakespeare's obscurity as a literary figure in his lifetime and as late as the
time of Addison, see my *Shakespeare Studies*, pp. 11–12, and J. J. Jusserand, *A Literary
History of the English People*, III (1909), pp. 180, 347–55.

in particular, the 'naïve perspective' and 'veiled confusion of motive' noticed above.[9] His development, throughout his career, in structure, style, and meter, which is continual and enormous, is not according to conscious principle or for mere novelty's sake. There is scarcely a rule in grammar, rhetoric, meter, logic, or dramaturgy, whether of his own time or ours, that he has not broken, many of them over and over again, in his impetuous effort for fullness or adequacy of expression. For it is a work of nature as much as of art, and the expression becomes richer, subtler, and more various as the conceptions within him take their resistless way, each craving, like a soul when descending upon the planet, a body, not quite like any other before or after, of its own. And on these, not the applause of posterity, or the sanction of antiquity, or the fine figure that he is cutting in his own eyes, he is intent. He enters into them; so did his audience after him; and then there was none of our questioning what he was like himself. He was the better for that. He was lost in his creation, as only the very greatest are. *He* could conceive an Ariel,[10] and a Caliban.

And how impossible to believe (what one of the greatest living Shakespeare critics finds it 'impossible to doubt') that one so lost and silent in his work, and personally so little noticed where Jonson and Bacon, Beaumont and Fletcher, were heeded and honored, should, when he sat down to write *The Tempest*, utter a solemn valediction, as if he were the darling of the metropolis, the acknowledged king of poets, and boast that he had bedimmed

> The noontide sun, call'd forth the mutinous winds,
> And 'twixt the green sea and the azur'd vault
> Set roaring war; to the dread rattling thunder
> Have I given fire, . . .

and all the rest? At that even Walt Whitman might have hesitated, or in his worser moments (as when he compares, or contrasts, himself with the dramatist now in question) Mr. Shaw. What was suitable enough for Prospero the magician, addressing the spirits, 'by whose aid' he had done it, becomes, in this metaphorical sense,

---

[9] See Chap. IV, pp. 123, 161.

[10] See my *Shakespeare Studies*, Chap. I, especially pp. 22–38, from which some ideas and expressions here and in the next paragraph are borrowed.

insufferable swagger, preposterous rant. We may turn him into a god if we please, but not have him turn himself into one. The real deity cannot be expected to speak quite like a mortal, and we make allowances for him in *Paradise Lost* and the *Aeneid*; but what a rodomontade not only for but also by the most unobtrusive, elusive, and in the world of literature then unappreciated, of men! Only a Freud could explain it, provided he forgot that the man was a humorist, and that his fellow-playwrights were. *The Tempest* was performed at Court, where Jonson would have seen it; indeed, he afterwards jeered a little at its fairy-tale character; but how could the poet, if he had talked of himself like that, have faced the inevitable and ferocious guffaw? Not only do I think that Shakespeare here had not himself in mind, but also that even if it had occurred to him that any one would imagine he had, he would have instantly erased the words. Schücking objects in general to Shakespeare as Prospero because the magician has no sense of humor. The fundamental objection, I take it, is, that, should the dramatist have meant anything of the sort, he must (like the critics themselves in proposing it) have for the moment flung away his own.

4

It is otherwise with Milton, who certainly here and there appears, under cover of the hero, in another final drama, *Samson Agonistes*. Of himself also he is thinking as blind, among his enemies, the idolaters; and something of his own bitterness against women may give edge to the captive's under the eyes of Dalila. But like Goethe, though after a different fashion, Milton in general was self-centered and a little lacking in humor, loftily treating himself as chosen not only of the Muse but of God, once fairly putting himself (though not necessarily as an equal) in the place of Pindar and, again, of Orpheus. And in his sonnets, instead of hinting darkly and trafficking in riddles, he uttered boldly and frankly whatever he had it in his heart to say. Moreover, in dealing with a Bible character as a prototype of his own, Milton had the warrant not only of the Puritans, who continually called themselves the chosen people, and the prelatists Hittites or Amalekites, but that of homilists for more than a thousand years, as well as even (in relation to the Old Testament) of the

evangelists and apostles. Sermons (like criticism!) have always kept
to the text as a point of departure; and in a sacred drama it was only
to be expected that there should be some inner meaning, or 'application,' as not in a stage play. Anyhow, by thus somewhat associating
himself with the Hebrew bruiser and Nazarite woman-hunter, the
haughty old poet cannot be said to be exalting himself, as here the
self-forgetful Shakespeare would certainly be. In fact he does not
labor the point; and in the tragedy there is nothing that can be called
allegory or symbolism. No one that I know of suggests that Dalila
is Mary Powell, or Harapha Salmasius.

. . . I am wrong, I immediately discover. Turning to William
Vaughan Moody's *Milton* to make sure that for the last name I
should not rather have written *Morus*, what do I light upon but the
following passage, in the now traditional expository formula of
'He too had'?

He too had been a Champion favored of the Lord, and had matched his
giant strength against the enemies of his people. He had sent the firebrands
of his pamphlets among their corn, and slain their strongest with simple
weapons near at hand. He too had taken a wife from among the worshippers of Dagon; he had made a festival with her people over the nuptials
which brought him a loss as tragic as Samson's, — the loss of human
tenderness, a lowered ideal, and a warped understanding of the deepest
human relationships, etc.[11]

There, in the last sentence, if not before, crops up the capital error
of such interpretation, at which we just now hinted, the failure to
take the poet's own point of view, the failure of criticism itself, indeed, to be dramatic. In Raleigh it appears frankly as a principle —
and in connection with this apostrophe to the elves.[12] If the thought
that Shakespeare himself was the wonder-worker occurs to us, why,
then, how much the more to him! But that logic is too simple, and
is prompted by idolatry, which generally results in the distortion
and degradation of its object. There are thoughts which others may
entertain about the greatest but the greatest cannot themselves have
shared. 'No really great man,' says Hazlitt, 'ever thought himself
so'; for all that Milton, Goethe, and Wordsworth did, not to men-

[11] Page xxxii, by permission of the Houghton Mifflin Company.
[12] *Shakespeare* (1907), p. 225.

tion such as Shaw, Whitman, and Strindberg, Strauss and Wagner, as well as many other musicians, philosophers, and 'leaders' in our naked and shameless day. And of Shakespeare the critic declares, in the spirit of Dr. Johnson in his Preface, that 'he appears to have stood more alone and to have thought less about himself than any living being.' Not that it is altogether a matter of his own nature. He comes long before nineteenth-century romanticism and twenty-century anarchism, which made a poet a rebel, a prophet or a propagandist, and the sort of artist that, uncertain of the public's sympathy or approval as Shakespeare was not, must (or thought he must) assert himself.

Mr. Moody, to be sure, would not insist on each detail of his comment but only on 'some such autobiographic second intention'; yet to me it seems about as likely that the never-humbled Milton, even furtively and to himself alone, acknowledged this 'loss of human tenderness,' this 'lowered ideal,' as that Shakespeare thus coolly and openly avowed himself a wonder-worker.

And perhaps all that Sir Walter meant was that Shakespeare thought of it, did not expect others to do so. One critic actually suggests that it was only the subtler few (but among them would have been Jonson!) who would have nodded and understood. To the first suggestion there is little to reply. Art is expression; and where there is no expression, criticism has no warrant to speak. Who, indeed, can limit the author's thought — but who, unaided, can thus disclose it? And if he has not in any way expressed it, how can it concern us? But in the second suggestion, which implies expression, however elusive, there lies the old fallacy of a double — an esoteric and an exoteric — meaning, which troubles today not only the criticism of Shakespeare but of much other literature of a time gone by. It is like the interpretation of Shylock and Falstaff, of George Dandin and of Don Quixote, which I have touched upon elsewhere.[13] There are, to be sure, *nuances* to the characterization — witness our own interpretation of Ariel above! — that the author may not have expected the ordinary audience to notice or appreciate; but that is a different thing from a double, self-contradictory conception, one half for the gross-minded or hard-hearted public of

[13] *Shakespeare Studies*, pp. 331 *et seq.* Cf. Lamb, letter to Southey, August 10, 1825, where he ridicules Landor's Quixote as Charles V and Sancho as 'the people.'

his day, the other for enlightened posterity. What the coarser intelligence could not perceive must have been fairly in harmony, not at variance, with what it did perceive, or the work of art would be incomprehensible.[14] The child's delight in the story of Crusoe or Gulliver, in *Goblin Market* or *Alice in Wonderland*, is shared by the adult, who but enjoys it more. It is a matter of 'degree,' says Burke. With Goethe it is much the same as with Milton. Goethe is Faust or Werther in that he himself had at this point or the other passed through somewhat the same experiences, cherished the same sentiments, or arrived at the same conclusions; but there is no secondary personal meaning to the story, no abstract allegory in the other characters. 'Nothing is more characteristic of Goethe's poetic genius from youth to age,' says Calvin Thomas, 'than his objectivity.' (And more objective is Shakespeare, as all the world knows!) 'His starting-point is always the mental image.'[15] And so it was with Shakespeare, as in Ariel and Caliban. The sage himself said to Eckermann:

Speaking broadly, it was never my way as poet to attempt the embodiment of any abstraction. I received impressions . . . such as an active imagination offered; and I had nothing further to do as poet then than to round out and perfect such visions and impressions inwardly, and portray them vividly.[16]

Shakespeare, if he had been self-centered and self-analytic enough, might have said the same. Ibsen did say it as he protested against philosophical interpretations of his own work; and in general Mr. Archer objects to these: 'I do not believe that this creator of men and women ever started from an abstract conception . . . the germ in his mind was dramatic, not ethical' (Introduction to *Little Eyolf*).

Yet Goethe, with much more reason, but still too little, has been made in the Second Part of *Faust* to undergo much the same sort of criticism as Shakespeare in *The Tempest*.

. . . regarded as didactic through and through. . . . And since there are many scenes and characters which, in a natural reading of the text, show

[14] Cf. W. W. Lawrence, *Shakespeare's Problem Comedies* (1931), p. 15. Cf. *The Sublime and Beautiful*, introd.; Quiller–Couch, *Notes on Shakespeare's Workmanship*, p. 142.
[15] *Faust*, Part II (1901), p. lxviii.
[16] *Ibid.*, p. lxx. 'Speaking broadly,' for in figures like Sorge there is allegory of course.

little trace of any didactic purpose, there was no recourse but to ascribe to these an allegorical meaning. The masquerade was an allegory of society, the sham fire at the end denoting 'revolution'; Helena was Greek art; Euphorion, the logical offspring of classicism and romanticism; Mephisto's insects, the whims, crotchets and theories of mechanical scholarship, and so forth. Or if not allegory, the text was veiled biography:[17]

Prospero, as represented, is the veiled biography; Ariel, Caliban, and Miranda, the allegory; and *The Tempest*, as from the hands of some of the critics we receive it, is another *Zweiter Theil*. For this neither poet is responsible. Personalizing, allegorizing, is simply the besetting sin of criticism: what it has done to Browning, also, both before and after his repeated protest, is evident upon examination of *Childe Roland* and, under that heading, of the *Browning Cyclopaedia*.[18] To warrant such interpretation there must be some hint in the text; as indeed there is for allegory in Tennyson's *Vision of Sin* and *Palace of Art*, and for symbolism in his *Ulysses* and *Merlin and the Gleam*.

With hints enough, there is more of that today, particularly the personal sort. There is Strindberg, who declared that all great art was fundamentally autobiographical, and his own certainly is. There is Richard Strauss, with his Heldenleben, the *Held* being frankly and generously himself! And there were Byron and Poe before them, and (at moments) even Goethe and Ibsen. Artists now are ready enough to lay bare their struggles, all the joys and sorrows of their 'love-life'; and their public, unlike the Elizabethan, is looking for them. But Shakespeare and his audience were not as these; Matthew Arnold was not, either; self-representation is, as he says, not the highest type of poetry:

'A true allegory of the state of one's own mind in a representative history,' the Poet is told, 'is perhaps the highest thing that one can attempt in the way of poetry.' — And accordingly he attempts it. An allegory of the state of one's own mind, the highest problem of an art which imitates actions! No assuredly, it is not, it never can be so: no great poetical work has ever been produced with such an aim.   Preface to *Poems*, 1853

[17] *Ibid.*, p. lxiii.
[18] M. de Reul (*Rice Institute Pamphlets*, XIII, p. 236) is certainly right in denying the presence of any allegory in Browning except possibly in *Numpholeptos*.

In any case, with hints or without, what is the use of our critical exertions to lay the allegory or biography bare? Allegory too is expression: 'its function,' says Mr. C. S. Lewis, 'is not to hide but reveal.' Even in those poems, like the *Fairy Queen* and the *Divine Comedy*, in which it not only is in keeping with the times and the *genre* but is both avowed and apparent, when it is an imaginative success it does not need interpretation — or in its own day did not — and when it does, how dubious and divergent are the results! 'In any case,' says Mr. Drinkwater, a poet, 'this personal-interpretation method is full of snares . . . whenever I read or see [the play], the notion of regarding the lovely closing scenes as a dramatisation of the poet's farewell to the stage strikes me as ludicrous. Really, Shakespeares do not work like that.'[19]

5

And Shakespeare also made Caliban — after the air the earth, or, as some say, alongside the spirit of poetry that of prose! But Caliban is as poetically conceived and expressed as Ariel, and as far beyond the reach of Shakespeare's experience or Goethe's imagination, He fits perfectly into the dramatic scheme as the creature of earth — both a parallel and a contrast with the spirit of the air — but not at all as 'the vulgar public.' It is a state of nature — Prospero and Miranda as human figures coming in between — and what is drama, or the dramatic public either, doing there?

In his own day Caliban, like Ariel, the Ghosts, and the Weird Sisters, had, as we have seen, the advantage with the audience (by the accepted interpretation now taken away from him) of being somewhat familiar, a development out of a popular superstition. Coleridge the poet, forgetting his philosophy and psychology, perceived that the Fates and Furies singly or together would have been ineffective; but merged with witches, though 'different from any representation of them in the contemporary writers, they present a sufficient external resemblance to the creatures of vulgar prejudice to act immediately on the audience.' From the familiar to the unfamiliar — it is the right dramatic and poetic procedure, particularly in dealing with the supernatural: it was followed by Milton when he peopled his hell, not with his own inventions, but with heathen

[19] *Shakespeare*, pp. 115–16.

divinities, such as Moloch and Mammon — followed by both Milton and Dante, indeed, when undertaking to present hell and heaven in the first place. With the mental image Shakespeare began, but in his mind it budded and developed; and like many others of his, superstitious or not in origin, it seized and assimilated qualities of characters somewhat different but compatible and akin. Puck, merged with the magician's jinnee, becomes in *The Tempest* the spirit of the air. So Caliban, a moon-calf, is not only the offspring of witch and devil, but both a sea monster and a land monster, and also a native Indian or 'man in the making,' who quaintly, but decently, wears a gaberdine. Iago and Falstaff, though not in bodily frame or feature, are still other examples of traditional elements in an imaginative merger, in virtue of the poetic license allowed by Bacon, as by Horace before him:

the imagination, being not tied to the laws of matter, may at pleasure join that which nature hath severed, and sever that which nature hath joined; and so make unlawful matches and divorces of things; *Pictoribus atque poetis*, etc. . . . The use of this feigned history hath been to give some shadow of satisfaction to the mind of man wherein the nature of things doth deny it, the world being in proportion inferior to the soul.

And the contrasts or contradictions in the Moon-calf's inner make-up, still greater and more various — his lawlessness and his instinct to worship and obey, his affectionateness and his vindictiveness, his abusiveness and murderousness and his craving and ready gratitude for human comfort and protection, his sensuality and his delight in the pleasures of imagination, that is, in dreaming and in listening to stories and music — all these nevertheless belong together, congruous in their incongruity, within the wide and elastic limits of the primitive mind. Unfamiliar, he is conceivable enough; for like him, once upon a time, by ancestral proxy, were audience and author both, and, though with a shudder, they delight in the combination now.

This is only, so to speak, the structure or anatomy — in Caliban it is more clearly indicated than in most of Shakespeare's characters — and the miracle of creation is yet to come. He is given a voice, his very own. As with the other great characters of Shakespeare the style (or accent) is the man, and here it is completely differentiated

from that of any other in this play or its predecessors. Not that there
is realism. What is more difficult, but therefore the finer, the dramatist keeps within the limits of meter and the established dramatic
convention and literary idiom: and does not let him take to wharf-
rat jargon, like the Hairy Ape; or drop into baby-talk, like Kipling's
Thy Servant the Dog; or speak of himself in the third person, like
the Caliban of Browning. He curses, and yet like the pirates in
Treasure Island is not gross or blasphemous; he is lustful, and yet
*un*like most of O'Neill's characters, not filthy or obscene. He is not
a naked monster, happy in the mire; as Cleopatra is not a naked
prostitute, Falstaff not a mere rogue nor Shallow and Silence mere
bores nor Iago a murderous beast. One and all they are clothed —
in humor, thought, imagination, verbal music, and whatever else is
woven into the magic mantle of poetry.

6

Prospero calls him, and by a felicitous stroke of stagecraft he
bawls out before he enters: 'There's wood enough within.' The
speech both sets the comic tone and gives at the outset the clew to
situation and character. For him wood-carrying is his 'cross,' his
tragic lot, as it still is, I fancy, for many a boy on the farm. It is
continually on his mind, or so to speak, his conscience, and becomes
a measure of his passions — fear or hatred, love or gratitude. Later,
in dread of Trinculo and Stephano as spirits sent to punish him, he
vows to bring his wood home faster; and when shifting allegiance
to the new ruler, or god, who bears the celestial liquor, he will not
only kiss his foot but 'get thee wood enough.' It is at once a comic
device — a repeated *motif* — and a unifying and simplifying artifice
in the characterization.

Six lines are spoken — Ariel, for a contrast,[20] appearing and dis-
appearing, and Prospero repeating his summons — before the moon-
calf, cursing, lumbers in. All the malign and baleful operations of
nature he can think of he now calls down upon the magician and his
daughter, receiving threats in return. Scared by these, he thereupon
takes to the defensive and to grumbling.

I must eat my dinner,

[20] Raysor, *Coleridge's Shakespearean Criticism*, II, 177.

and it is a speech in the same vein as the first. Nothing irritates a servant like being interrupted at that sweet duty, and Caliban stands on his primal rights. Others he remembers forthwith:

> This island's mine, by Sycorax my mother,
> Which thou tak'st from me,

— even as we now unconvincingly say of our Continent, though not born on it, to all newcomers. Then, by an illogical but delightfully natural transition, and in the same childish vein, he casts up to his master his kindness in the past and his own gratitude for it.

> When thou cam'st first
> Thou strok'dst me, and made much of me, would'st give me
> Water with berries in't, and teach me how
> To name the bigger light, and how the less,
> That burn by day and night; and then I lov'd thee
> And show'd thee all the qualities o' the isle,
> The fresh springs, brine-pits, barren place and fertile.
> Curs'd be I that did so.

And from out of the midst of this appealing whimper he falls, despite his memories, to cursing Prospero anew. He must have release, as the saying now is; for he has not yet developed 'inhibitions.' 'His spirits hear me,' he later confesses, 'and yet I needs must curse.' For only with time do punishments deter.

Never, I suppose, was by thought, word, and rhythm, as well as by mental process, a character so instantly created, and — for I have thus far omitted nothing — so perfectly preserved. Not a false note, anywhere. Caliban is the perfect brute, who would be petted and patted, given food and drink, taught to talk and told stories, yet (with this given as the reason) turns vindictive when he isn't. And what follows is, though startling, as true. When he complains of being 'stied in this hard rock,' Prospero reminds him that he had lodged him in his own cell until he sought to violate his master's daughter. Then comes the one sexual touch, with the 'gros rire ignoble,' that Shakespeare permits himself — imagine, with the opportunity, a Joyce or an O'Neill! —

> Oho, Oho! would't had been done!
> Thou didst prevent me: I had peopl'd else
> This isle with Calibans.

No doubt the picture would have been truer with the monster freely wallowing, and art is not morality. It is beauty, however.

7

After the sweet idyllic meeting of Miranda and Ferdinand, and the cynical but rather boresome conspiracy of Antonio and Sebastian, there comes — according to the happy Shakespearean principle or practice of 'vivid contrast between scene and scene swiftly succeeding each other' — one of low life and comic relief, Caliban entering, amid thunder, bowed under the white man's burden, and with curses again pouring from his lips. His second entrance, though similar, is better than the first, and, as repeated *motif*, would instantly bring a laugh. This time we *see* the wood, cause of the cursing. And Trinculo the jester now appearing, he takes him, with his bad conscience, for a spirit dispatched to punish his sloth; whereupon, like an opossum or an ostrich (though not exactly), and like Browning's Caliban seeking to escape Setebos' ire, he falls flat.

The scene that ensues is delectable. Trinculo, after due consideration of the ambiguous phenomenon (neither flesh nor fish) and of the unambiguous weather, arrives at the conclusion that it is an islander struck by a thunderbolt, and there being no other refuge hereabouts, crawls under his gaberdine. Then enters Stephano the butler, half-drunk yet enriched with the drunken man's 'double personality,' trolling catches to his own disappointment, as if they were not of his own choosing and singing, but, after each one, taking to his bottle for comfort. 'Do not torment me, Oh!' cries the moon-calf. . . . 'Do not torment me, prithee; I'll bring my wood home faster.' Stephano thinks him a devil, then a monster of the isle, — with four legs! — 'who hath got, as I take it, an ague.' 'Where the devil should he learn our language?' he cries, with a start. But 'tis a point in common, a tie. 'If it be but for *that*,' he will give him relief, such as he himself is enjoying. *Both* now are having agues, and Caliban also — 'you cannot tell who's your friend,' quoth Stephano — takes the cure. Trinculo, meanwhile, should know that voice — 'but *he* is drowned, and these are devils.' — 'Four legs and two voices,' ponders Stephano, 'a most delicate monster. . . . If all the wine in my bottle will recover it [a test of

charity indeed!] I will help his ague. . . . I will pour some in thy
other mouth.' — 'Stephano!' — 'Doth thy other mouth call *me*?
Mercy, mercy!' The tie is a bit too close, and the butler now is one
of a *second* shaking pair. — 'Stephano! If thou beest Stephano, touch
me and speak to me; for I am Trinculo, — be not afeard — thy good
friend Trinculo.' His fear would dissipate itself and the fear that he
causes, but is met by the sage and apposite reply: 'If thou beest
Trinculo, come forth.' There are solemn and sacred reminiscences in
these reciprocal tremulous adjurations, and, though not instantly,
they have effect. 'But art thou not drowned, Stephano? I hope thou
art not drowned.' The Jester is not jesting, and for his hopes he has
more reasons than one. 'And art thou living, Stephano? O Stephano, two Neapolitans scap'd!' The stage business we divine.

Caliban, meanwhile, all innocence and gratitude — for this water
has more than berries in it — looks on, and, with but a single misgiving, like and appropriately unlike Trinculo's, admires:

> These be fine things, an if they be not *sprites*:
> That's a brave god and bears celestial liquor.
> I will kneel to him.

The god is unworthily absorbed in Trinculo's story of his escape and
his own tale of cask and bottle; but worship never demanded recognition, else there would be none, and the liquor works on within the
moon-calf's veins and brains:

> Hast thou not dropp'd from heaven?
> *Steph.* Out o' the moon, I do assure thee. I was the man i' the moon
>   when time was.
> *Cal.*   I have seen thee in her and I do adore thee.
>   My mistress show'd me thee and thy dog and thy bush.

While his belly warms, his imagination (as then it will) expands;
and, as with most drinkers blest with the faculty, all his romantic
dreams come true. It is so with Stephano as well; but himself being
the dream rather than the dreamer, he would have the monster
swear to his own unsettling words, kissing the book — pulling at
the bottle — which in such fashion he does as to call forth the self-
forgetful admiration of Trinculo. 'Well drawn, monster, in good
sooth.' Caliban himself becomes not only generous but suggestible;

and now he will kiss, not the butler's book, indeed, but his foot, and
show him all his treasures and wonders, nay, work for him, though
by nature so little inclined. Kindness conquers all; and I cannot believe, though a great critic has said it, that only by terror he can be
controlled and made serviceable. If that were so he would be far
less of an artistic triumph.

> I'll show thee the best springs; I'll pluck thee berries;
> I'll fish for thee and get thee wood enough.
> A plague upon the tyrant that I serve!
> I'll bear him no more sticks, but follow thee,
> Thou wondrous man!

These final half-lines — 'I will kneel to him,' 'And I will kiss thy
foot,' 'Thou wondrous man' — are they not each equivalent to a
genuflection or prostration? He is a right worshipper, with motives
mingled — love with fear or hatred, gratitude with desire — and it
is a comic but (as with Shakespeare often) even a pathetic situation
besides, as the poetical native worships the drunken white.[21] Also
he grows confiding and intimate:

> I prithee, let me bring thee where crabs grow;
> And I with my long nails will dig thee pig-nuts;
> Show thee a jay's nest and instruct thee how
> To snare the nimble marmoset. I'll bring thee
> To clust'ring filberts, and sometimes I'll get thee
> Young scamels from the rock. Wilt thou go with me?

Who wouldn't? 'Show thee a jay's nest'! — for there is only one,
and Caliban's have been the only eyes to see it. Like Ariel, he loves
nature, though after a different fashion; indeed, the two mythical
beings alone betray any interest in the island. And now, seized by
the spirit of rum and rebellion, and bidden by the newly chosen king,

[21] L. L. Schücking (*Character Problems in Shakespeare's Plays*, 1922, p. 254) speaks
of Caliban's 'disgusting self-abasement and servility'; both Coleridge and Hazlitt
say the poet has raised him far above contempt; and the artistic principle touched on
above (p. 299) here applies. Boot-licking per se *is* disgusting, but not in a dog,
and not in Caliban half-drunk and moved by gratitude and admiration, in a nobly
written play.

> Was im Leben uns verdriesst
> Man im Bilde gern geniesst —

though Aristotle was the first to say it.

or Lord of Misrule, to lead the way, while Trinculo[22] bears aloft, like mace or scepter, the empty bottle — no empty symbol, however, for 'we'll fill him by and by!' — the monster sings, howls, and hiccoughs his Declaration of Independence, to the tune, not of the Carmagnole, but of the cancan:

Farewell, master: farewell, farewell!

Ban, Ban, Ca-Caliban
Has a new master, get a new man.
Freedom, hey-day! hey-day, freedom! freedom, hey-day, freedom!

In throwing over his old master he has, like all primitive rebels, necessarily taken on another. Some critics, intruding not only their aesthetics but also their latter-day ethics into the sacred text, declare that the play teaches the 'beauty of service': in Caliban it is rather the necessity of it, as, though differently, in Ariel and Ferdinand. 'Let *him* be Caesar!' roars the rabble, after Brutus has justified Caesar's death. Let *Lenin* be Czar!

8

In the next scene where he appears, the monster's tongue, loose enough when last we saw him, is tied, his eyes 'almost set in his head.'[23] And when he comes to himself he is still full of adulation for Stephano, but of hostility against everybody else. He won't serve Trinculo — he's not valiant. Trinculo calling him a debosh'd fish, he turns to the butler —

Lo, how he mocks me! Wilt thou let him, my lord? —

and the insult being repeated, he cries,

Lo, lo again. Bite him to death, I prithee,

for when annoyed not only beasts but children bite. How appealing, like a brute! Resentment is gratitude inverted, is, in the primitive mind, its immediate alternative, and he is still the same creature that had listened wide-eyed to Miranda. Again the insult is repeated, by

[22] It may be Caliban, but Trinculo is carrying it in the next scene.
[23] A phrase misapprehended by both a German and a French critic. 'Deep-set,' they say, like a philosopher's, or a zealot's!

the mimicry of Ariel; and Caliban bethinks him of punishments more suitable to the offense and occasion, wherein he himself can share:

> Give him blows
> And take his bottle from him. When that's gone
> He shall drink naught but brine, for I'll not show him
> Where the quick freshes are —

so I won't! 'I'll bear him no more sticks,' he said of Prospero before. And he ha-ha's like a schoolboy at Trinculo's beating, hoping by and by to beat him himself, though now too busy, as he plots against the tyrant. At that thought all his earthy brutality and superstition assert themselves, in appropriate speech. The deed, he would have it done not too delicately, not in the Borgia or Medici style:

> There thou mayst brain him,
> Having first seiz'd his books, or with a log
> Batter his skull, or paunch him with a stake,
> Or cut his wezand with thy knife. Remember
> First to possess his books,

for they are in Latin or gramarye, and it is by the illiterate that writing and print are held most in awe. In return, he will hand over the daughter; for Stephano is master, he but man, and

> she will become thy bed, I warrant,
> And bring thee forth brave brood.

The words smack enough, but not too rankly, of the age of stone.

Ariel, invisible, now troubles them with his mysterious song and tune, and Stephano cries, 'Mercy on us.' 'Art thou afeard?' asks Caliban, pricking up his ears, for the spell of the bottle has lifted. 'No, monster, not I.' 'Be not afeard,' he answers, like a child; and then comes the celebrated passage about the isle being full of noises,

> Sounds and sweet airs, that give delight and hurt not,

which has, however, sometimes seemed to me to be a little out of character. Yet an imaginative brute may properly like music as well as stroking and stories; by it Caliban has been made to dream, not as (at our best) we do, but as every now and then a simple soul does next to us at a concert; and then to see the clouds open and show riches ready to drop upon him, that when he waked he cried to dream again. And the like of that still happens in every nursery, high or low.

This child of nature, however, is growing up and, to his cost, learning the folly of his choice. His fellow conspirators won't hold their tongues, and are led astray from their purpose by the plunder — the 'trash' or 'luggage,' as Caliban calls it — at the mouth of the cave. What he foresees befalls them. And when at the end he and the rest are by Ariel ignominiously driven in, he has already fathomed their folly and inanity. Setting eyes now on the gentlemen from the ship, and on Prospero in ducal apparel amongst them, he swears, in an outburst of admiration, but by the god of his mother again, not by him of the bottle:

> O Setebos, these be brave spirits indeed!
> How fine my master is! I am afraid
> He will chastise me.

The strangers are spirits to him, as Columbus and his crew were to the Indians, and as a newcomer in town was thought to be possibly a god in disguise by the Homeric Greeks. Rebellion, moreover, is already in full reaction. Prospero is master again, and the servant by his very nature is servant again, to the point that he takes a delight in his master's finery but, by another psychological transition, bethinks him of what is coming next. The transitions of his thoughts, indeed, the succession of his emotions, are among the happiest touches in the role. He thinks like a savage, without uttering all that a savage thinks. But Prospero sets him to work trimming the cell; and Caliban shows that he has already learned his first lesson in the values and limitations of life as he good-humoredly accepts the order, muttering;

> What a thrice-double ass
> Was I to take this drunkard for a god
> And worship this dull fool!

Nature is justified of her child: he acquires something of what she could not transmit but has bestowed the capacity of acquiring — the faculty of Common Sense. His last unromantic, unexpected speech is the most delectable touch of all. Who in the whole world

is like Shakespeare? Why, Chaucer, and Fielding, and Scott, and the
English people.

9

How can, now, a character so full-bodied and full-blooded, so
vivid and various, so beastly and yet appealing, and engaged in so
simple and actual a situation, have a part in anything so contradictory
to its interest and reality as an allegory? Prospero himself might possibly be surrendered to the allegorists, and even (though with a
pang) Miranda; but not Ariel, and still less Caliban. Man in the
making, to be sure, he in a sense is; but that idea does not interfere
with our impression of him as an individual.

So real and vital is he, indeed, that by the murder motive the
comic effect is somewhat disturbed. It is a case, like Shylock's and
Tartuffe's and that of some characters in Russian novels, where the
figure oversteps the comic limits. That is the difficulty with comedy
— it can no more than tragedy be made wholly to square with life.
Caliban, however, does not lose our sympathy, as Stephano and
Trinculo somewhat do, because we remember that he is a monster,
a savage with a moral sense yet undeveloped. The consciousness
of one's own wickedness, present in all of Shakespeare's villains, and
to us somewhat disconcerting, is happily missing here.[24] And even
the disturbance to the comic effect is somewhat allayed by our
remembrance of the conspirators' drunken condition and Prospero's
potent art.

Did Shakespeare mean anything by Caliban? asks M. Gillet.[25]
'Je pense que son but, comme celui de tout vrai poète, a été de
donner une fête à lui-même, de jouer avec ses rêves.' And what is
said applies to Ariel as well: he was giving his imagination the rein.
Indeed, there is, as often with a poet, something in the sport akin to
real dreaming: by the process of 'condensation' things apparently
dissimilar, as according to Horace and Bacon they in poetry may be,
are merged.[26] The Centaur is like a dream; and so are Lamia and
Lilith, the snakewomen. Caliban, offspring of witch and devil, is

---

[24] Cf. *Shakespeare Studies*, Chap. III, §4; and Chap. VII. — Coleridge and Schücking have noted the difference in Caliban.

[25] Louis Gillet, *Shakespeare* (1931), p. 333.

[26] Cf. Professor F. C. Prescott's *The Poetic Mind* (1922).

partly of the earth, partly of the sea, and also, even in the literal sense, a 'caveman.' Ariel, a tricksy fairy merged with a magician's 'familiar spirit,' becomes the genius, not of Shakespeare, but of the air. Both, like much else, as we have seen, in Shakespearean art, grew up in the poet's mind, out of a simple popular conception, by a process of fusion and assimilation, as if it were a living body, into something new, 'rich and strange.' In the process there was of course a guiding thread of thought, or a germinal idea — the spirit of the air in the one, the spawn of the earth in the other — but that worked darkly and under cover. Guided by touch and instinct, the poet, when consciously active at all, was concerned with the life and shape of the imagined creature, not with a meaning inside it. (Or rather with both, for this meaning — this germinal idea — is simple and inherent, not arbitrary and external as in the accepted interpretation — as if in algebra — and the creature and its meaning are one.) And we should be concerned with the same. As M. Gillet remarks after considering some of the most recent interpretations: Mr. Robert Graves's, whereby Sycorax becomes the Dark Lady, now exiled, Ariel Shakespeare's passion for her, and Caliban the friend who betrayed him; and Miss Winstanley's, whereby Sycorax becomes Catherine de Médicis, Miranda the Huguenot sect, Ariel the Martyr King, and Caliban (as a matter of course) either Ravaillac or the Jesuit Father Mariana — as he appositely remarks thereupon, I say, nothing is to be gained by translating a metaphor. Mistranslating I would call it — and what happens then?

Too well we know: of that the history of criticism is in large part the sorry record. And most of it we could have been spared if the critics had observed their primary, self-evident duty of regarding the author's meaning, of attentively reading the text. On principle, generally, they do observe it (though there are some of late who on principle do not, and with the natural, lamentable consequences); but they generally have some formula of self-deception or the subconscious, of allegory or symbolism, whereby, in the end, they can thrust their own meaning upon the poet. Or else they labor under the conviction that poetry is biography or history scrambled together, finding references to the Rizzio and the Darnley murders, the Gun-Powder Plot and St. Bartholomew's Eve — for the case all four are needed! — in each of the tragedies *Hamlet*, *Macbeth*, and

King Lear! And up from the maw of such dragons of error come those reams and bales of print whereupon we are expected to spend the rapidly diminishing number of our dollars and days! Yet everybody in his senses ought at once to see how it is — that the *Fairy Queen* is allegorical, and *Paradise Lost*, except in the story of Satan, Sin, and Death, is not; that Tennyson is sometimes allegorical, sometimes symbolical, and Browning is neither; that the *Master Builder* and the *Wild Duck*, the *Princesse Maleine* and *Pelléas and Mélisande*, are symbolical, and Pinero and Galsworthy are not; and, in contrast, that Shakespeare has only a trace in him of the one quality and none of the other. Manifestly a writer, whatever else he may be without knowing it, cannot, in that dim state of mind, be allegorical, or symbolical, or biographical, such a matter requiring a little effort or attention. Moreover, how can Prospero be both Shakespeare and James I, and Hamlet both James and Essex, 'in a pamphlet in favor of the Scottish Succession,' the same monarch also serving for the Duke in *Measure for Measure* and for Bottom in the *Midsummer Night's Dream*, and the same earl for Caesar, etc., etc., whether in the pages of the same critic or of several? For if one of these identifications be founded, the others are, since there is no internal evidence or external probability for any. In such a debate the affirmer is in no position to deny. But for us, who deny all of them, what is there now left, since words and argument seem to be of no avail, but to fall back upon the desperate remedy of Mr. Max Eastman, who is out of this particular conflict, as he considers the similar criticism of our 'modernist' poets. He thinks we should be tolerant when poets are too childlike but for infantilism in critics there is no defense; and when they are so little developed that they 'do not know the difference *between receiving a communication and making up a fairy-story*' what is left but to 'bundle them into a well-rotted ship and shove them out to sea'?[27]

10

There is much else to be said of *The Tempest* — of Miranda, whose love affair is not exciting, but whose character, though without Perdita's or Imogen's spirit and humor, is not, as some recent critics

[27] *The Literary Mind* (1931), p. 121.

have declared, insipid; of the relations of the father and daughter, which are exquisite; and of the action as a whole, which, owing to the magician's omnipotence, is, for all the good moments, somewhat meager and dull. By some of the Germans Prospero has been taken psychologically, as having lost the dukedom, not really through a brother's treason but by his own withdrawal from reality, and as having mended his ways (like those, I suppose, who learn to skate in summer and to swim in winter) on a desert isle. By Shakespeare his downfall is explained as wholly owing to the machinations of Antonio; and Prospero's failure then and there to employ against him the magic arts which later are so efficacious is not explained at all. This, like other initial postulates in Shakespeare, and in many another dramatist before and after, must simply be granted: and a psychical defect is no more to be discovered in this deposed duke than in that of *As You Like It*, or in the disguised one of *Measure for Measure*, or in the rejected one of *Twelfth Night*.

Like Rosalind's father, moreover, this duke is glad to return to power; (he and his daughter seem much less interested in their uninhabited island than the other and his followers in the wood of Arden). No one seems to delight in it but Caliban, who was born on it (for Ariel is of the elements, and follows summer like a swallow); and indeed the chief reason that I can see for *Milan's* being Ştratford is that from Nature both Duke and daughter seem glad to get away. So for us too the isle is a disappointment, enchanted, but — and here, again, the difference between Elizabethan fact and present-day figure — not enchanting. Only through the limited sensibilities of Caliban do we know it. It is full of noises, but they are Ariel's sweet airs, not the native woodnotes wild. And that it *is* wooded we scarcely should be aware except for Caliban's and Ferdinand's forced labor, Ariel's penitentiary pine, and Stephano's threat to Trinculo of the nearest tree. Shakespeare himself seems uncertain, for in a previous scene Trinculo has crept under the monster's gaberdine because 'here's neither bush nor shrub'; and in the Masque the scenery and vegetation are of field and pasture, not of the wilderness at all. But a virgin forest, on a virgin island, with rocks and flowers and fountains, under unfamiliar and unclouded constellations, encircled by tropical seas! What would not Coleridge, Shelley, or Keats have made of it, Chateaubriand or Heine! Milton would have given it mystery — if not of novelty, then of reminiscence, and of time and space, of light and shade; even Spenser, who, like everybody with a soul, delighted in islands, would have made it into a romantic, though scarcely a wild, primeval spot. Ordinarily, though Shakespeare had less interest than the latter in discovery and the New World, he had far more in Nature unsophisticated, in bird, beast, and flower, river and sea; and before this he had filled the woods of Athens and Arden with life and charm:

> I know a bank where the wild thyme blows . . .

> Under the greenwood tree
> Who loves to lie with me
> And turn his merry note
> Unto the sweet bird's throat . . .

> Under the shade of melancholy boughs
> Lose and neglect the creeping hours of time.

Even the poetry of desolation is missing — 'there let the wind sweep and the plover cry!' — and Prospero and Miranda leave the island to Caliban, with a farewell only for Ariel and the elves.

II

And that leads to a further consideration, the pervading spirit of the play. Since the chronology was established, criticism has delighted in these last works of the poet's pen, *The Tempest*, *The Winter's Tale*, and *Cymbeline*, not only as a farewell to his art but as a revelation of his personal experience. It has found in them, after the darkness and despair of the tragedies, a spirit of serenity and reconciliation; and, in the flowers and pastoral landscape, the gallant youths and pure-minded maidens, something of Stratford again. Even scholars are inclined to think that they must have been written there; on the same principle as that of the tradition that the ghost scene in *Hamlet* must have been written there, hard by the churchyard and the Charnel-House.

An optimism, or a delight in Nature, either, that depends upon the present experience of the poet, would count for little. Moreover, the supposition, as Mr. Sargeaunt says, 'puts a strange construction on an artist's activity. For is it not the irreconcilability, the irrationality of actual experience, which sets him to the creation of life in art?'[28] Even as a man the poet would, more probably, have been thinking of the pastoral in London, from afar. But in fact, as Mr. Lytton Strachey,[29] who also rejects the supposition, clearly shows, these last plays, including the one now before us, are not altogether serene. Dowden and his followers apply to the period of the tragedies the expression 'Out of the Depths'; to that of the dramatic romances, 'On the Heights.' But in this final period there is a measure of ugliness and horror, cynicism and grossness. There are the intended crimes of Iachimo, Cloten, and Cymbeline's Queen, Antonio and Sebastian, and the murderous jealousy of Posthumus and Leontes. And the maidens Imogen and Miranda show a familiarity with unmaidenly ideas, and Prospero insists upon them, in a way that somewhat grates upon us. Why should he warn Ferdinand, about to be left a moment with Miranda, not to break her virginknot, and then, the next moment, harp on the subject again? Why, before that, when, mistaking, she asks him whether he is not her father, should he in reply take to the musty old joke of her mother's word; and then, before the scene is over, as, speaking of Antonio's perfidy, he wonders 'if this might be a brother,' why should the daughter in turn apply it to her grandmother?

Here is still another instance of the critics' not reading but reading *in*; and, as Mr. Strachey says, 'this combination of charming heroines and happy endings [and the flowers, we might add, in *Cymbeline* and *The Winter's Tale*] has blinded the eyes of modern critics to everything else.' Of delight in Nature for her own sake there is in these plays less, it would seem, than in the earlier ones. Prospero himself, as the impersonation of Shakespeare, Mr. Strachey finds to be no compliment to the poet, and complains of his crustiness. And there is some truth to this, though Prospero's harshness is mainly owing to the poverty of the plot. No obstacles opposing his omnipotence from without, one must be raised up within. Since Miranda, the ingénue, is ready to fall into Ferdinand's arms like a brook into the river, he must stand between them with his menaces and tasks; and since Ariel and Caliban have otherwise little personal interest in

[28] *Times Literary Supplement*, December 15, 1932, 'The Last Phase.'
[29] *Books and Characters* (1922). The quotations in the next paragraphs are at pp. 58, 59, 60, 63 (by permission of Harcourt, Brace and Company).

the outcome, he must thwart their longings for liberty or idleness. But Mr. Strachey is right enough in saying that 'it has often been wildly asserted that he is a portrait of the author — an embodiment of that spirit of wise benevolence which is supposed to have thrown a halo over Shakespeare's later life.' For though the critic goes pretty far in declaring that on closer inspection 'both portrait and original are imaginary,' Prospero himself, after all allowances, is too often dull or sour.

The sweet savor, then, of these last plays, and the autumnal glory of them, are not all-pervading, and the poet's own mood is not easily to be ascertained. These dramatic romances, like the contemporary ones of Beaumont and Fletcher, and of Lope and Calderón, and like the nondramatic Greek romances before them, are, in personages and setting, idyllic or fantastic; in time and place, intentionally inaccurate and hazy;[30] in incident, exaggerated and improbable; in plot and denouement, arbitrarily contrived. 'The Bohemia of *The Winter's Tale*,' says Mr. Mackail, 'the Britain of *Cymbeline*, and the island of *The Tempest*, fluctuate between earth and a sort of fairyland.' The evil in the end does no great harm, and we little believe in it; there is pardon for all misdoers, and that is the necessary ending of such a play. 'It is clear,' says Mr. Strachey, 'that such happy endings, such conventional closes to fantastic tales, cannot be taken as evidences of serene tranquility on the part of their maker.' There is, to be sure, a far finer and healthier spirit in Shakespeare's dramatic romances than in Beaumont and Fletcher's; yet it is not easy to say that it is finer and healthier or generally much more exalted than in the comedies or tragedies of his prime. In fact, *The Tempest* is the culmination of his fantasy and *féerie*, and follows the same formula as in the *Midsummer Night's Dream* and the character of Mercutio — as in Peele's *Old Wives' Tale* and Lyly's mythological comedies —

---

[30] With the well-known anachronisms and geographical incongruities in *Cymbeline*, *The Winter's Tale*, and *The Tempest* compare Calderón and Lope, Ticknor's *Spanish Literature*, II, 375. — In keeping with these, monstrous situations, such as Leontes' commands to throw Perdita and Paulina into the flames, Antigonus' being eaten by a bear, and Cymbeline's recklessness with human life in the denouement, are not only not realized and taken to heart, but also the shock of these is often broken by positive comedy. Generally this is not quite happy in effect; but in the first scene of *The Tempest* it is. The shipwreck is kept from unduly alarming us, and yet the humor is not at the expense of kindliness.

the airy contrasting with the earthy, the delicate, lyrical, and fanciful with the coarse, farcical, and grotesque.

A change there has been, of course. A tendency to reverie has grown upon the poet and, with that, a change in the character of his imagery. The plastic, anthropomorphic imagery of his heyday — How sweet the moonlight sleeps upon this bank! — gives place a little to something less vital, less solid and clear-cut. 'The outlines tend to become vast, vague, and wavering, as in a dream — as they will to one whose eyes are resting on the horizon, whose thoughts brood upon the beginning and the end, over "the dark backward and abysm of time." And whereas nature then took on the semblance of man, man's life or work, in its changes, now takes on the semblance of cloud, wind, or water, most fleeting and mutable of things.'[31] Even before the dramatic romances there is an example in the talk of Antony and Eros as the triumvir faces suicide — 'Sometimes we see a cloud that's dragonish. . . .' But the supreme one is, of course, Prospero's speech about the cloud-capped towers, which also it is idle to quote. Perhaps this latter passage, together with the sheep-shearing festival in *The Winter's Tale*, and the dirge in *Cymbeline*, has done as much as the charming maidens and the happy endings to make us think of Shakespeare as now serene and exalted. All we can say, however, is that this spirit, together with a meditative and dreamy vein, is prominent. We cannot infer much concerning the poet in himself. Mr. Strachey, judging from the inequality and uncertainty in the workmanship, the fitfulness of the inspiration, thinks that in these last plays Shakespeare was 'half enchanted by visions of beauty and loveliness and half bored to death.'

12

It is particularly the cloud-capped towers speech, I suspect, that causes critics like Mr. Bailey and Professor Mackail (who have elsewhere resisted the insidious biographical fallacy) to accept Prospero as Shakespeare.[32] And certainly here the supposition nowise entails

[31] My *Shakespeare Studies*, pp. 22–25.

[32] See above, p. 286n. Professor Mackail, *Coleridge's Literary Criticism*, Chap. II, even seems to share my opinion that Shakespeare, like the world about him, was not aware of his own greatness; himself certainly not aware that by the reviewer in

a charge of vaingloriousness as it does in connection with the address to the elves. In this speech, then, is Shakespeare — *ergo*, Prospero is Shakespeare himself! But why, in the first instance? Because the speech comes directly from out of his heart of hearts? Like the apostrophe to the elves, it is deeply and directly indebted to another poet, to Lord Sterling in his *Darius* (c. 1603), as the other to Ovid. The fact is, in life we would have things come pat and neatly, as in a play — though in a play, according to our aesthetic principles, as in life! We know not that *The Tempest* is Shakespeare's last un-aided work — indeed, more than likely one so un-self-conscious and so dependent upon circumstances would not have known it was to be such as he wrote it — but we think such it must be because there are two farewells in it, one to an art, and another, in a sense, to the world; and since it *is* his last work, the farewells must be Shake-speare's own! We would have him, too, making his exit, in the traditional style, with gesture, bow, and 'parting glance.'

The farewells are his because he wrote them. And the speech about the cloud-capped towers is his in a deeper sense than that to the elves because his imagination as he wrote it was more afire; and also because what he says there fits the situation not only of Prospero at the end of his pageant but that of many another serious soul when for the last time the curtain falls, or a leaf is turned. But in this deeper sense all the great speeches, and all the great characters, are Shakespeare's, and especially the nobler ones. Yet this does not mean that through the mask he himself is speaking, or puts his own person on the stage. He is a dramatist, and is the greatest of dramatists chiefly for the very reason that, amid the multitude and plenitude of his characters, he does this less than any other. Goethe, in a sense, is Faust, and, particularly in the next to the last great speech —

Ich bin nur durch die Welt gerannt,—

he tells the story, pronounces the justification, and imparts the phi-losophy, of his life. With a lofty and not unseemly self-consciousness the sage of Weimar bids the world adieu. And it is not unnatural that we should be sorry for those who do not believe Prospero to be Shakespeare. Most of us read biography rather than poetry; and

---

the *Times Literary Supplement* (September 1, 1927) the conception had been already pronounced impossible—despite William Hazlitt and Samuel Johnson!

if poetry, to find the poet. But upon reflection should we not rather be sorry for those who do not see how much more it is in keeping, not only with the man as we know him but with the poetry which is highest, that Shakespeare, perhaps penning his last drama, should write as no one has ever written of the end, not only of man's work but of Nature's, and of life as a dream, and death as a sleep, and yet be thinking almost as much of any other mortal as of himself? Self-forgetfulness is a virtue of the mind — the imagination — as well as the heart. It is what raises the greatness and beauty of the drama above that of the lyric. And the supreme poet, I suppose, such as Homer and Shakespeare, rather than Goethe, Milton, or Byron, is a seer and creator, not a sage, or prophet, or actor, with eyes now and again rolling inward — upward — sidelong. He is an 'extravert,' and in the world of visions. He is 'a poet hidden in the light of thought.'

CHAPTER IX

Phèdre

Un vrai poète, tel que Racine, est, si je l'ose dire, comme
un dieu qui tient les coeurs des hommes dans les mains.

VOLTAIRE, 'Discours historique,' *Les Guèbres*

I

BOUT *Phèdre* there is no question: it is a masterpiece. Hailed as such in its own day, it has been
so recognized ever since; it was the favorite of
the poet himself, no mean critic. And there is
as little question about the leading part; in fact
it stands higher than the play. As a tragedy
Voltaire preferred *Iphigénie*; yet he held that the role of Phèdre 'is
the most affecting and most exquisitely wrought that ever was
penned,' 'the finest ever put upon the stage in any tongue,' 'the
masterpiece of the human mind.' And such it has been accounted
by the actors and the public, after their fashion no mean critics,
either, in a country where the tradition of the stage has never
been broken. What Hamlet is for English actors, Phèdre is for
actresses across the Channel — the part which all have aspired to
play, by which many have won their fame. Champmeslé, Lecou-
vreur, Dumesnil, Duchesnois, Rachel, Bernhardt are numbered
among them.

Why is this, how can it be? Racine is the first undisputed 'psychologist' in drama. Shakespeare's psychology, though of course
not his art, is nowadays in question: Racine's has never been. With
him, says Sainte-Beuve, everything is motived. Corneille, according to Brunetière, often subordinated character to situation — 'invented and constructed the situation first, and then, if I may so
express it, put the character inside.' Racine, on the other hand, has
been thought to subordinate situation to character, 'finding the
characters first, studying them, mastering them, and then seeking

the situations which shall best bring out their different aspects.'[1] This, according to orthodox criticism, is the right way to do; and this, Brunetière explicitly says, Racine did both elsewhere and in *Phèdre*. But did he, there or in *Iphigénie*? The central and pivotal situation — the queen's adulterous and incestuous passion for her stepson, inspired by fate — and much of the ensuing action of slander and revenge were not invented but were inherited from Euripides (and Seneca) in his *Hippolytus*; and something similar, in both origin and structure, is to be said of *Iphigénie*. Story and situation came first in point of time and, what is more, of importance. In *Phèdre* the fatal spell of Venus might have been made only the external representation or the provocation of the heroine's native bent; instead it has fallen upon her as a curse and plague. The Racinian daughter of Minos is *not* 'betrayed by what is false within'; though in the same situation, she is on a loftier moral plane than the heroine of Euripides, and yet the Greek too has, as Professor Vaughan observes, 'spared no pains to make us feel that she is the victim of a force which the human will has no power to resist.'[2] Boileau, in Racine's own day, who, as Lemaître reminds us, 'était un coeur droit et un ferme esprit,' speaks of her 'douleur vertueuse,' and judges that she is perfidious and incestuous despite herself — 'malgré soi.' Lemaître also, equally sound and true, speaks of her conscience 'infiniment tendre et délicate.' And this fact so impressed the great Jansenist Arnaud that he highly approved of the tragedy, taking the role of Phèdre to be a signal example of human helplessness before certain temptations when not succored by God's grace. He is thinking in terms of predestination. Chateaubriand, at a later day, is thinking in those of the correlative reprobation, as he declares: 'C'est la chrétienne réprouvée, c'est la pécheresse tombée vivante dans les mains de Dieu.'

Both here are Christians rather than critics; but even so they are discriminating enough to appreciate the dramatic contrast presented. They can see that this is not a case of

> video meliora proboque;
> Deteriora sequor.

---

[1] *La Loi du théâtre.*
[2] C. E. Vaughan, *Types of Tragic Drama* (1908), p. 71.

There the contrast is not so sharp and clear; it is not so sharp and
clear, we know, when reflected in the human conscience: and it is
this Ovidian situation that is to be found in the modern drama and
novel, where duty and inclination gradually and insidiously merge.
Conscience, particularly before yielding to temptation, cannot be so
authoritative and uncompromising, or one would never yield. And
— what Arnaud and possibly Chateaubriand, too, had no chance to
see but we are in a position to see for ourselves — this is not the
'fate,' as in modern novel or drama again, that is a personification of
the character's own desire. There destiny is not irresistible or resisted. But here it is as in Euripides —

    C'est Vénus toute entière à sa proie attachée —

and to Phèdre her love is a 'crime,' which she shows no such disposition to extenuate. As we shall learn, the extenuating is (through
the supernatural agency, to be sure) wholly on the part of the
dramatist, in the presentation. What makes the supernatural more
of a reality is the fact that at the climax of her passion she calls upon
the goddess to crown her triumph even by smiting Hippolytus,
rebellious to her sway.

2

What, then, have we here? Is it not very much as in the ancients
and in the tragic masterpieces of Shakespeare, a great role instead of
(in the strictest sense) a character, or else a character rather than a
psychological entity — a figure springing out of the situation rather
than the source of it, a noble person doing or desiring dreadful
things, and, as a consequence, an intenser and wider-ranging passion, which awakens a deeper and completer sympathy in response?
This is the reason actresses all aspire to play the part, and the actresses
are right. Aristotle long ago declared for such subordination; the
practice of the dramatists both then and afterwards has been in keeping; and tragedy (as well as comedy) lies not so much in doing what
a person, in purely natural circumstances, of himself would do, but
almost despite himself, 'malgré soi.' To bring that about there has
often been provided, as in both the present tragedy and *Hamlet*,
what Petronius Arbiter calls the 'ministry of the gods.' In *Iphigénie*
the ministry is more in the background than in the direct deliver-

ances to Agamemnon, but it is to the same dramatic purpose and effect. Without the divine intrusion the latter tragedy, in its greatness, is inconceivable; *Phèdre*, really, is so no less.

If the Cretan princess and Athenian Queen, as we hear her in the play, only felt and did, though after a struggle, what her nature bade her, the record might be an interesting though somewhat forbidding study, but not so poignant a tragedy. And it would not, like Hamlet, be, in the actor's phrase, 'a part that you can sink your teeth into.' Only the half of her would be in it, indeed, not her judicial conscience. Instead, she feels and does what her nature forbids her, determined by a more or less irresistible external power, like Oedipus and Orestes, Hamlet, Macbeth, and Othello. Thereby, like these, she can, in effect, be a great criminal, and yet call forth our nearly whole-hearted sympathy and admiration. Thereby the poet secures the indubitable dramatic advantages of adultery, incest, jealousy, or revenge, without the disadvantages; as in Macbeth he has only the advantages of treason and murder, and in Othello those of jealousy and the murder of her whom the hero holds dearest in the world. The Scottish thane hearkens to the Weird Sisters, whose first prophecy is at once fulfilled, and to his Lady; the far nobler Moorish general, to one universally considered the honestest and wisest of men. Hamlet and Lear are not evildoers even in this vicarious fashion; but in them, too, there is, through the improbable situation, the advantage (without the disadvantage) of feigned madness and atrocious revenge, on the part of the one, of paternal wrath and real madness, on the part of the other. In all these tragedies, though in various ways, the situation is condensed, is doubled: in *Phèdre* it is that of a woman in love with her husband's son, yet a good woman nevertheless. The difference between this contrast and that in *Iphigénie* is only in the fact that the latter contrast is simpler and less complicated, more external and obvious, less between feeling and feeling, and more between feeling and doing, as the father piously steels himself to sacrifice his child.

3

How the improbable is made probable, the antipathetic sympathetic, and the unpsychological only the more poignantly dramatic, I now undertake to show only in the tragedy before us. Racine is

here a dramatist primarily, but is as psychological as may be; fatal
influence and a relentless conscience are not enough, are only the
data or premises; and as I trace the subsequent, natural or at least
logical, development from these, the reader of himself will see how,
so far, this secondary motivation becomes both realization and extenuation. To understand, here also, is to forgive.

   At the outset the dramatist makes the most of the unities, and puts
the visitation of the unholy passion some distance in the past. The
passion is rooted and deep-seated when first we come to know of it;
and it seems the more irresistible and the less blamable when we
learn that the heroine, to smother it, had procured the banishment of
Hippolytus and had so borne herself that she seemed to him his
enemy. Now, in his neighborhood, it threatens to break out of control, and she thinks not of satisfaction but death. For three days she
has not eaten or slept. It is with difficulty that she can be brought by
Oenone to reveal the cause of her agony; and when she is, she tells
only of her long vain struggle, the looks and traits of her spouse
continually recalling those of his son. The news arrives of Theseus'
death. This gives her a start; but though the chief barrier is, apparently, now broken, she does not rejoice or let her passion have scope.
It is permitted only to Oenone to appreciate the new state of affairs.
Discreetly, though insidiously, she counsels the Queen to approach
Hippolytus, her enemy, in the interests of her own son, heir to the
throne of Athens; but in his presence Phèdre, swept off her feet,
betrays herself. Shame for both the confession and the repulse overwhelms her, and she would have death again, at his own hand. Yet
the avowal, as well as the tidings, has put a spark of hope into her
bosom. Shame would efface itself. The youth's insensibility must be
owing to his inexperience; and she bids her confidante tempt him
with the crown, with the opportunity to be a father to her son, with
the sovereignty over him, herself, and everything. It is here that
she appeals to the goddess to take vengeance upon the youth, so
indifferent to her worship: Venus' cause and her vassal's are one
and the same. But Oenone returns with no better news than that
Theseus is alive. Death is now certain, but not so welcome. She
cannot meet either her husband or his son; but it is not so much the
brand of dishonor upon herself that appals her as that upon her children. Suicide, the confidante declares, would be a confession, and

the Queen is besought to prefer charges instead of awaiting them. She refuses to blacken innocence; yet since her friend is so sure that the king will spare his own flesh and blood, she, in bewilderment, suffers Oenone to take the matter in hand. Hearing, however, that he has cast his son off with imprecations, Phèdre comes to the rescue. Yet before she gets so far as to make her confession she learns from Theseus himself that Hippolytus has not been so insensible as she has thought, but loves Aricie. This overpowers her, 'the words of truth are frozen on her lips,' and in her subsequent colloquy with Oenone she at last gives passion the rein, as she imagines the happiness that the lovers have enjoyed while she was in torment. Not knowing of the death which the Prince, under a father's curse, is meeting, she would have such a fate for her rival. Still, even in that moment her conscience recoils, and, as never before, she realizes the horrors of crime (though really it is but criminal intention) that have accumulated upon her. Oenone would have her yield to passion as her destiny, but this Phèdre now takes into her own hands and waves the woman indignantly away. When next she appears it is with poison in her veins, to make to her husband a complete avowal, her last thought and word being of the purity that she has stained.

Thus, the initial premise of a fatal influence and a clear-seeing conscience being granted, the play — and the character as part of it — becomes plausible enough. That once granted, we have indeed 'la suite logique, la liaison ininterrompue des idées et des sentiments' of Sainte-Beuve.[3] Every imaginable extenuating circumstance or provocation is discovered, yet every conceivable development and manifestation of the criminal passion is produced. Phèdre thinks evil, but against her will and — which is important to our sympathies — without doing evil. All the dramatic virtue of the evil is extracted, and is alone retained.

The situation is less external, to be sure, than in Euripides and Seneca, particularly than in the former. Venus there actually treads the boards; her power is made more manifest and precise. It is directed primarily, moreover, against Hippolytus, in Euripides the leading figure, who has scorned not only love but the goddess of love; and it is his nemesis to appear a hypocrite and die under the charge of seducing his stepmother. That is a situation of a different

[3] *Portraits littéraires* (1876), I, 79.

sort. Yet it too has been psychologized and humanized, allegorized and moralized, away. 'The Love-goddess,' says Professor Gilbert Murray, 'is a Fact of Nature personified . . . her bodily presence is evidently mere symbolism.' So the critic thinks the hero 'a saint in his rejection of the Cyprian,' and says it is 'absurd to talk of his impiety.' Like most critics, Professor Murray is evidently bent upon deriving the action from the character and is concerned about a 'tragic fault.' Certainly it is absurd to find that in his impiety; and as certainly the hero had chosen the better part; and yet, on the other hand, he did not need to go so far as to 'revile' the goddess (l. 13), making her his enemy. For that this is so and that she is a real being, the mainspring of the action, appears plainly in the text from beginning to end. It is no more possible to make her a personification than Athena when she bids Achilles stay his hand in his quarrel with Agamemnon. Professor Vaughan is truer to the text as he approves of Seneca's and Racine's keeping the goddess off the stage because she 'robs Phaedra of her freedom.' He acknowledges that the goddess's power 'softens the horror' of the heroine's subsequent action (in Euripides before she kills herself she accuses the hero in writing) but thinks the price too 'heavy.' Psychology he somewhat prefers to emotional effect. Yet Professor Murray himself, as well he may be, seems a little staggered by the outcome of the hero's simple preference for the higher life — 'suicide, malediction, and murder.'

4

A priori it might seem that the heroine's character as the Frenchman presents it would be unedifying and in effect immoral; indeed, the eighteenth-century Jesuits thought it so, if only to contradict the Jansenists. Even Schlegel was of that opinion, though in his Teutonic hostility to French manners and art he can scarcely be taken at his word. But no unbiassed student of drama, and no normal and natural audience, would be so inclined. If by nothing else, they would be hindered by Phèdre's own horror and that of the other characters, and by the calamity that descends upon her, as, at all three points, is true also of Macbeth and his Lady. But still more they would be affected by the selective refinement, already intimated, in the presentation. Like Shakespeare's tragic criminals, and (as we shall see) still more than they, she moves not in a world of the senses but of thoughts and imaginings, and those not of delight but of anguish. Like them, and not as in nature, she is occupied less with incentives and temptations than with deterrents and the sin. Her conscience is as rigorous and as external as the Scottish thane's. Though the motive — ambition in his case, and erotic passion in hers — must be sweet, it is, in the presentation — and there lies part of the improbability — turned to bitterness. She has fleeting glimpses of what happiness with Hippolytus might be, but only from afar, and mostly in envious imagination of what it has been to him and his chosen love. And even so there is nothing voluptuous or corrupting about it:

> Les a-t-on vus souvent se parler, se chercher?
> Dans le fond des forêts allaient-ils se cacher?
> Hélas! ils se voyaient avec pleine licence.
> Le ciel de leurs soupirs approuvait l'innocence;
> Ils suivaient sans remords leur penchant amoureux,
> Tous les jours se levaient clairs et sereins pour eux.
> Et moi, triste rebut de la nature entière. . . .

Was ever jealousy less vindictive, less gross and sensual? It is, as in art the passions in some sort should be, only the essence or distillation of reality: Cleopatra's passion is not directly voluptuous or seductive on the page. Othello's jealousy, comparatively, *is* vindictive, gross, and sensual; the dramatist avails himself to the uttermost of the great advantages of the passion. That does not alienate us because the hero's fate is at his elbow, and with our own eyes we have seen him, in his nobility of soul, step into its snare; his passion, artificially produced, is also love performing an act of justice. It is not tainted with perversion — but by that the French dramatist, in turn, is in a position to profit.

In treating the impassioned Queen thus rigorously and austerely Racine is proceeding no more ignorantly than Shakespeare himself. As Lemaître notices, who is not concerned with the issues we are now raising, and apparently considers her a psychological unity, the other blamably but naturally impassioned women — Roxane, Eriphile, and Hermione — are untroubled by a conscience. And so it is, as regards the grand passion, with women in modern novel and drama, and in history and the life about us. So it is, too, with

Shakespeare's Cleopatra, despite his Lady Macbeth. Neither dramatist, that is to say, followed a formula. But even Shakespeare's villains Richard and Iago, whether coolly or desperately, at times confess their own villainy; and it is only towards the less heinous offenses
that the perpetrators of them keep a strictly psychological, a relative
point of view, and judge themselves according to their prepossessions. The frankness of villains or of the Macbeths and Claudius, as
of Phèdre, is partly owing to the traditional, absolute conception of
conscience (cherished by his public, if not by the dramatist) as a
nemesis, the voice of God or Devil rather than of one's own better
nature, the worm that never dies; but it is still more owing to the
dramatic method, particularly as applied to the villain himself. In
Shakespeare's tragedy, which, like the ancient, is a system and
rhythm of the emotions, both a contrast and a harmony of them,
motivation, which in effect is extenuation, plays a far inferior role;
and approval and disapproval, sympathy and antipathy, are aroused
and directed either by the admiration or the condemnation of the
numerous subsidiary characters. Now in order that the reputation
of the hero, such as Othello, may not be damaged, the villain, who
takes him in, must be esteemed and praised; and therefore the villain must himself reveal his nature to the audience. That is especially
needed when, like Iago, he is made not only outwardly wise and
honest, but witty and fascinating; or the open-minded spectator's
sympathies may go astray.[4] Even in Racine, when there really is
a villain, such as Mathan, he too, though with less dramatic justification, is made to reveal himself in his naked hideousness in order to
heighten the spectator's concern. This before us, however, is a
matter of hero or heroine, such as Macbeth or his Lady; Phèdre's
conscience, like theirs, and unlike the unmitigated villain's, is a
torment, meant to arouse our sympathy, not provoke our condemnation; and for that purpose as well it is an indispensable element of
the ample, indeed double, situation that is the center of energy in
the play.

For Racine's tragedy, also, is a system and rhythm of passions,
though more of a clash than a contrast, and within a narrower range
than the Shakespearean or the ancient. His psychology, like theirs,
though generally more carefully articulated, is only such as an audi-

[4] See above, Chap. I, p. 27; and Chap. VII, pp. 239–40.

ence of itself can immediately comprehend and value; and with him apparently it played no such part as it does in the present-day theory of dramatic criticism, whether applied to Racine himself, to Shakespeare, or to modern drama. 'Une action simple,' he says in the preface to *Bérénice*, 'soutenue de la violence des passions, de la beauté des sentiments, et de l'élégance de l'expression'; such is his ideal, and of psychology or character, even, there is not a word.

If there is little tampering with ethics, still less is there, as we have already intimated, with theology. Questions (or rather doctrines) of predestination and free will are no more the dramatist's concern than the poet's. 'A great writer,' as Mr. Murry says, 'does not really come to conclusions about life; he discerns a quality in it.' Or, as Mr. Eliot answers the query what the dramatist thought of this or that, 'Did Shakespeare think anything at all? He was occupied with turning human actions into poetry.'[5] Jansenists and Jesuits go as far astray in their concern for dogma as the Germans who investigate and argue the subject in relation to Macbeth. What seems to them a philosophy is really the tragic framework and structure. There are certain ways of doing, if not of thinking, in which no one has ever improved upon the Greeks — the making of a statue or a temple, a lyric, an epic, or a tragedy. Voltaire, who praises *Phèdre* so highly, was certainly not thinking of it when, in echoing Saint-Evremond, he declared that, in comparison with the ancients and Shakespeare, 'Nos pièces ne font pas une impression assez forte; que ce qui doit former la pitié fait tout au plus de la tendresse; que l'émotion tient lieu de saisissement, l'étonnement de l'horreur; qu'il manque à nos sentiments quelque chose d'assez profond.' Mesnard, to be sure, in the *Notice* to his great edition, strangely suggests that in his encomiums Voltaire may have been preoccupied with the beauty of the verse and diction, to the point of forgetting that among Racine's masterpieces there is no other in which the 'peinture de la passion soit aussi énergique, aussi profonde, d'un aussi extraordinaire effet.' Mesnard himself here forgets, or perhaps half remembers, the above quotation from Saint-Evremond! And as certainly the capable dramatist and more capable critic was not thinking of *Phèdre* when, praising Racine as the most

[5] J. M. Murry, *The Problem of Style* (1922), p. 27; T. S. Eliot, *Selected Essays*, p. 115.

nearly perfect of our poets, he made these reservations and quali-
fications: 'Si on peut condamner en lui quelque chose, c'est de
n'avoir pas toujours mis dans cette passion toutes les fureurs tragiques
dont elle est susceptible, de ne lui avoir pas donné toute sa violence
. . . de n'avoir que touché le cœur quand il pouvait le déchirer.'[6]
It is in *Phèdre*, if anywhere, that he *is* heart-rending. There the *pitié*,
the *saisissement*, the *quelque chose d'assez profond*, the *extraordinaire
effet* is, if ever, unquestionable; and that, so far as the mere mechanism
is concerned, is owing to the dispensation of a malignant providence
upon an unoffending mortal, herself appalled. Dryden, in the very
year of *Phèdre*, laments that in his *All for Love* 'that which is wanting
to work up the pity to a greater height was not afforded by the story;
for the crimes of love, which they both [Antony and Cleopatra]
committed, were not occasioned by any necessity, or fatal ignorance,
but were wholly voluntary.'[7] But here the pity both can be and is
worked up to that greater height, and the terror too. We spare
Phèdre because the hand of the god is heavy upon her — because
she spares not herself.

5

If there is little tampering with ethics or theology, of the psychology can as much be said? M. Lanson[8] seems to hold that in this
there is really no more fatality than in Racine's other tragedies or in
Corneille's. 'La tragédie est mue par des passions humaines.' And
yet, again, he says, 'fatalité interne, non externe.' If by that he means
only 'prédestination secrète au malheur ou au crime,' we have no
cause to quarrel: the goddess herself does not descend. But if he
means that Phèdre sins merely because of what she is, as if she were
in a George Eliot novel, we have cause indeed. The tragedy is moved
only by human passions, but the dark and nefarious one was instilled
into the heroine's bosom, or else (which is not according to the evidence) the incompatible conscience was. How much better for
Racine's reputation to follow the text, and acknowledge that, to
procure passions of greater scope, he deliberately so contrived and
arranged the matter at the beginning and complied with psychology

---

[6] Voltaire, *Œuvres* (1879), XXIV, 219; *Œuvres* (1880), XXXII, 297.
[7] Preface (1678). Necessity is, of course, *necessitas*.
[8] *Esquisse d'une histoire de la tragédie* (1920), pp. 88–90.

afterwards, than that he consciously or unconsciously played fast
and loose with it all through! To be sure, Racine 'ne croit pas aux
dieux,' whether here or elsewhere. But neither does Shakespeare in
the Weird Sisters, nor, very probably, in 'the true villain' Iago. It
is likely that O'Neill does not, either, and certainly not all of his
audience do, in the Freudian fatality of heredity, as in *Mourning
Becomes Electra*. And yet this up-to-date mythology, replacing
that of Aeschylus, he finds as necessary for the highest tragic
effect as the Athenian his own. The fatal visitation and possession
are even made visible and tangible, as in Racine they aren't,
when the Mannons assume the mask and walk woodenly like
puppets. How much finer the effect, though still by no means
Aeschylean, than that of the same combination of adultery, incest,
and murder *without* the ministry of the gods, in *Desire under the
Elms*! *Phèdre*, without it, could not, in the hands of a Racine, have
been like the play of O'Neill; but a stricter psychology would have
as much impaired our sympathy as it does in the sordid and hideous
Desire — as much as it does in *Hedda Gabler* in comparison with
Ghosts and *The Master-Builder*.

Indeed, psychology — realism — has made sad work of tragedy,
and turned the appellations hero and heroine into misnomers. Being
the architect of his own misfortune, the character must be a mixed
one, that is, both hero and also fate or villain together; and then he
alienates our sympathy. Or else he must be a victim, leaving the
role of fate or villain to society or environment; and then he loses
our admiration or respect. He is either abnormal or subnormal, a
criminal or a weakling, an enemy of society or its prey. On the one
hand, there are Borkman, Hedda, and Rebecca; on the other, such as
Oswald, in *Ghosts*, and as Falder, in Galsworthy's *Justice*. And as we
go down the list of contemporary drama from Pinero to Milne, from
Sudermann to Molnar, it is the same story, probability at the cost of
sympathy or tragic effect. The crimes themselves are commonplace
or contemptible — deceit and adultery, embezzlement or forgery,
bribery or treason; for the 'tragic fault' must fit the person, and to
keep our sympathy the person himself must be not too bad, too
unlike ourselves. And on the stage there is shame or humiliation
rather than grief and anguish; in front of it, pity rather than
sympathy; and there is no fear. The spectacle becomes before the

end an ignoble or distressing one in *Borkman* and *Justice*, *The Thunder-bolt* and *Mid-Channel*. Or if the deed be more truly tragic, as when Masefield's Nan (or to turn to the novel, Hardy's Tess) stabs her lover, why then, to keep our sympathy, the character must, as of old, be above it, and there is, despite the preparations and provocations, as real violence done to her integrity as if Virgil's Alecto had flung the viper into her bosom. I, for one, cannot believe that as a psychological entity either fine, sweet, and unresentful woman had, in the circumstances, recourse to the knife. Ibsen's Hedda and Rebecca are not, like these, superior to their conduct, but they repel us, may indeed interest us, yet leave us not so much trembling as shivering; and though a passion for playing with people's souls and shaping their destinies provides motivation for murder, it is an exceedingly specious one. In short, the highest tragic effect and a strict psychological probability are ordinarily incompatible; 'Les grands sujets,' says Corneille, and in the spirit of Aristotle and Longinus, 'doivent toujours aller au delà du vraisemblable'; and since the highest effect is the aim and end of this as of every other art, how much better frankly and honestly to adopt a convention, a simplification or short cut, in order to secure it!

6

In the ultimate analysis, then, Racine's heroes or heroines, particularly Phèdre, are, like Shakespeare's and those of the Greeks, sometimes not wholly consistent; their own unity is impaired in the interest of the emotional effect of the tragedy as a whole; yet an external and poetic unity is imparted to them, as to Shakespeare's. His are more highly individualized in the mere turn and mannerism of their speech. Blank verse lends itself to the purpose more readily than the Greek and the French measures: so does the Elizabethan liberty in vocabulary and diction, not to mention stage deportment and demeanor. Tricks of repetition or parenthesis, colloquialism or familiarity, wit or fancy, incisiveness or circumlocution — traits of dignity or violence, tenderness or gaiety, eagerness or indifference, distinguish Hamlet, Othello, Macbeth, and Lear. In Racine, where the characters all are elevated, speaking within the narrow range of the *style noble*, in Alexandrines of which the syllables are always twelve, the accents four and two of these fixed, and the masculine and feminine couplets alternating, no such striking and various distinctions as Shakespeare had at his disposal are possible. Phèdre, no doubt, has a different accent from Roxane and Hermione, from Monime and Andromaque. Yet for the most part her individuality lies in the consistency (once the premise of fatality and a quick conscience is granted) of her mental and emotional portrayal, her temper and disposition, her attitude and point of view — in the matter comparatively more than in the manner of her speech.[9] Her passion possesses her, her imagination torments her, her sin is ever before her. Once only does she give the fury within her the rein, and then with what a recoil! Throughout, her passion is its own punishment; and in true French style the identity of the character appears mainly in the logic of it, less distinctly in the concrete realization, the phrasing and the rhythm.

That is to say, once the premise is granted and the arbitrary situation is established, Phèdre, in the direct presentation, resembles the other characters of Racine (and also of Corneille), whether this situation is troubled (however heightened) by an alien intrusion or not. 'Le procédé,' says Sainte-Beuve, 'en est d'ordinaire analytique et abstrait; chaque personnage . . . au lieu de répandre sa passion au dehors en ne faisant qu'un avec elle, regarde le plus souvent cette passion au dedans de lui-même.'[10] It is Shakespeare's that pour out their passions instead of analyzing them, that look out rather than within, and that keep much of the color and flavor of reality and of the irregular movement and individual mannerism of credible speech. Of realism there is little in either the French characters or the English, but verbally, colloquially, there is a greater approximation to it in the latter. There is the transforming power of poetry, of the imagination, in all alike, in Shakespeare's far more of it. But in these there is synthesis rather than analysis, the concrete rather than the abstract. And it is by their imaginings rather than their reasonings, their feelings rather than their ideas, their accent rather than their attitude, that we know and remember them. 'Je pense, donc je *sens*,' says Sainte-Beuve, is the phrase that applies to Racine's characters and, we may add, to Corneille's. Indeed, the phrase

[9] See above, Chap. III, pp. 90ff.
[10] *Portraits littéraires*, I, 106.

might equally well be reversed: 'je sens, donc je pense.' What is felt is translated into terms of thought; in expression it is not, to use Croce's phrase, the 'immediate passion,' however much this may be refined and transmuted into poetry, as in Shakespeare it is. Nowhere is the contrast more striking than in the great moments when the hero or heroine contemplates the plight where he or she is placed. Shakespeare's looks abroad, as when Othello, speaking instinctively of his wife, realizes that now he has no wife,

> O heavy hour!
> Methinks it should be now a huge eclipse
> Of sun and moon, and that the affrighted globe
> Did yawn at alteration;

or as when Macbeth cries out, his eyes on the blood-stains,

> Will all great Neptune's ocean wash this blood
> Clean from my hand? No, this my hand will rather
> The multitudinous seas incarnadine,
> Making the green one red;

or as when Lear appeals for comfort to the heavens — 'if you yourselves are old.' Shakespeare's hero is like the Prometheus of Aeschylus when in his first outbreak of agony he appeals to sky and earth, the springs of rivers, and the innumerable smile of the ocean waves. Corneille's or Racine's looks within, into the tangle there:

> (Oenone.   Ils ne se verront plus.)
> Phèdre.   Ils s'aimeront toujours.

> (Oenone.   On vient; je vois Thésée)
> Phèdre.   Ah! je vois Hippolyte.

So Chimène, asked what she intends to do now that Rodrigue, to save the honor of his father, has met hers in a duel and killed him:

> Le poursuivre, le perdre, et mourir après lui.

In all these there is the effect of concentration. But Shakespeare's characters, as M. Jaloux has it,[11] speak with their hearts in their

[11] See *Cahiers du Sud*, no. 154. *Théâtre Elizabéthain*, 'L'Esprit Elizabéthain.' M. Jaloux finely traces it in other Elizabethan tragedy, but attributes it, in the spirit of Taine, to the social conditions of the time. The individual, enfranchised and isolated,

mouths, and link their feelings to those of the universe about them. When Phèdre becomes so imaginative she is more self-conscious, yet more strictly relevant, as when she thinks of appearing, with all her sins upon her, before her sire, the judge below:

> Que diras-tu, mon père, à ce spectacle horrible?
> Je crois voir de ta main tomber l'urne terrible.

What a shudder! But her horror is all the greater because, like Othello and Macbeth, she is a noble spirit, the victim, not the author, of her destiny.

7

In *Phèdre*, then, Racine, always unquestionably French, is not 'too French' or modern. In the essentials of his art he is here not unlike the ancients and Shakespeare — dramatic rather than imitative, emotional rather than psychological. He too is here intent upon the powerful and fruitful situation rather than the character; he is concerned not so much for verisimilitude as for imaginative excitement; he would elicit sympathy rather than — much as he would and does do this besides — satisfy the understanding. And both the one and the other he is able to bring about more abundantly than anywhere else because he overleaps the narrow limits of probability and motivation; like the ancients and Shakespeare, he proceeds from an arbitrary premise or postulate — of a fatal influence and an uncompromising conscience — and precipitates instead of developing a situation. By the two hostile forces he produces it. Unlike Shakespeare, but like the Greeks, he does not have recourse to fate in the interests of condensation and celerity; keeping the unities, he does not let us witness the process of laying the mine but only the ensuing explosion and destruction. This — consequences, not causes — he thus has a chance to present fully and exactly. The past taken for granted, he can again be psychological and analytical, where the Greeks and Shakespeare are more summary, more purely emotional and imaginative. But nowhere else is Racine so emotional and imaginative; for nowhere else has he so big and rich a material to

---

turns to Nature for sympathy. Yet it is to be found in Greek tragedy, and really is part and parcel of the emotional and imaginative method of all early tragedy, the synthetic as opposed to the analytic of Corneille and Racine.

present. He has both the passions of a very good woman and (in effect) of a very bad woman upon which to play. Even in the character he has his contrast, his situation. Like Shakespeare with Macbeth, and above all Othello, he has the enormous dramatic advantage of dealing with a soul that is not naturally — tediously, harrowingly, or ignominiously — degenerating, but stricken and possessed.

CHAPTER X

Tartuffe, Falstaff, and the Optique du Théâtre

I

TARTUFFE is perhaps, as many critics think, Molière's masterpiece; in any case it is (what may or may not be equivalent) his best stage play. No one could be a better judge of this matter than Sarcey, who had seen it not a dozen or a score but hundreds of times; and he insisted that of all the plays of Molière, to say nothing of the plays of all the *genres* and all the countries of the world, it is the only one which equally amuses everybody, however and wherever performed. As Henley says of *Othello*, 'it can be played in a barn' — 'dans une grange et en habit de ville' — 'or at a fair.' When half a dozen conservatory students gather to give a soirée at Etampes or at Fouilly-les-Oies, they choose *Tartuffe*; when strolling players undertake a gala performance, they choose *Tartuffe*. The year that the theaters were liberated there was an orgy of *Tartuffe* on all the stages of Paris; and not because of the traditional animosity, either, of the French against the Jesuits. It was because of all the works of Molière *Tartuffe* is widest and deepest in its appeal — 'la plus accessible, la plus émouvante, celle qui était la mieux taillée soit en forme de mélodrame, soit en forme de vaudeville.'

What is the reason for this perennial popularity with both high and low, and under whatsoever circumstances? Sarcey has himself suggested it. The play is boldly and broadly shaped, is both a comedy of manners and a melodrama, both a study of character and a drama of situation. Like Shakespearean tragedy and the ancient, which contain elements of melodrama and comedy, like Shakespearean comedy, which often verges upon tragedy, *Tartuffe* is of no narrow scope or limited range. It, too, verges upon tragedy, which is in the background and at times looms up before us. To this fact is due in some measure even its comic force. When in the fourth act Orgon breaks from cover and cries out at the traitor,

Ah! ah! l'homme de bien, vous m'en voulez donner!

laughter, Sarcey remembers, bursts out in every corner of the house; yet this is no innocent, unmingled hilarity, but, as he says, 'un rire de vengeance, un rire amer, un rire violent.' It is the laughter of nemesis, as again and again it is at *Volpone* or the *Alchemist*. 'Le *Tartufe*,' observes Sainte-Beuve as he passes the comedies in review, 'qui réunit tous les mérites par la gravité du ton encore, par l'importance du vice attaqué et le pressant des situations.'[1]

2

The force and impact is unmistakable; and it is this, not the study of manners or of character, fine and firm though it is, that from generation to generation keeps the play upon the stage. And the force derives from the situations, from the structure, though that indeed would be impaired if the characters were inadequate. Plato long ago pronounced the genius of tragedy to be the same as that of comedy; and, curiously enough, in this greatest of Molière's comedies the central situation and mechanism are much the same as in one of Shakespeare's greatest tragedies, the Venetian. Iago, like Tartuffe, is a hypocrite, an impostor, though in a very different story; and with him as with the other, the author has secured the striking and fruitful situation of a good and intelligent man put in a wicked man's power. In both plays the impostor is very clever (though Iago is far more so), but in real life no one of sound mind and soul could, with so little reason or inclination, be led to turn against his own dearest and highest interests; and consequently, in both plays, the dramatist has to redeem the victim's reputation as best he may.

In *Othello*, as I have shown, the villain works within an ancient convention, that of the calumniator credited (and of hypocrisy impenetrable), whereby a normal person may to his damage be led to believe what he is cunningly told. And the prestige of the impostor, as well as the reputation of his victim, is supported by the confidence

[1] *Portraits littéraires*, II, 35.

reposed in him by everyone else in the tragedy. The Moor is not a gull, otherwise all the other clever people in the play would seem to be. Moreover, his reputation for intelligence and nobility of nature is established positively, not only by the presentation, both before and after he is misled, but also by the admiration of everybody in the play except the villain himself. So the jealous change in him — and that is part of the effect — is not questioned or doubted but wondered at and deplored.

In *Tartuffe*, not a tragedy but a comedy, and a satirical one at that, in which the victim's reputation is not so urgently important, and therefore the impostor's prestige is not either, the dramatist proceeds in a similar, though in some respects opposite, manner. Orgon is a gull. Everyone distrusts, instead of trusting, Tartuffe, except Orgon and his mother, Mme. Pernelle. That, indeed, is part of the comedy; unlike Iago, Tartuffe pretends not to honesty merely but to piety and, for comic effect, he must in part act like the hypocrite that he is. This would not do in *Othello*, until once the hero is excited — and very little then — for there we ourselves see him fall into the villain's toils; and the improbable influence is necessarily made probable — the temptation exceedingly cunning and artful — in order to be tragic. In *Tartuffe* it is otherwise. There we do not see the influence first brought to bear, and it is intentionally made not probable but actual and absurd. There it is not a matter of a 'free and open nature' tempted and misled, but of an obsession; not of confidence abused, but of an infatuation, which, from the outset, is a settled fact. The comedy keeps the unities, and presents only the results and consequences of the obsession, not the beginnings. Indeed, Tartuffe himself does not appear till the third act; but up to that point, by way of the concern of Orgon's family and the differences and difficulties between them on the one hand and Orgon and his mother on the other, the fact of the amazing ascendancy he has secured over his patron is, though not explained, completely presented and established. Explained it could not be if Orgon is to be a character worthy of consideration, a gentleman who has, except in this one matter, the regard of his family, including the fine and clever Elmire, his wife, and has merited the favor of his king. But it must be affirmed and confirmed, as both established and accepted, a fact 'aussi vrai qu'il est inexplicable,' or the consequent developments of the action would lay no hold upon our interest.[2] The audience need not understand — here as in *Othello*, though in far greater degree, they cannot, and analysis would only arouse distrust of the author — but, as there, they must, 'for the moment,' be led to believe; and their poetic faith is in both cases owing not to the psychological art of the presentation but to the dramatic manipulation and (largely) to the impression made on the victim's friends. As Sarcey says, Orgon's infatuation is the pivot of the piece; and the audience must be persuaded into accepting this improbability, like that of Othello's confidence in Iago and Iago's apparent deserving it, as an initial postulate, with the difference, however, that they are to laugh, not to shudder. So only after elaborate preparation, and then in all the fulsomeness of his piety, does Tartuffe first come upon the stage. The magazine must be loaded to have the explosion; the battery must be charged to produce the spark.

The spark or explosion is the dramatist's prime purpose, for in comedy psychology is no more demanded than in tragedy. In this one, as in satirical or critical comedy generally, the motive force is not sympathy but antipathy — against the designing hypocrite. Orgon, not analyzed or explained, arouses only so much sympathy as a worthy comic figure may, a little in the role of a victim, considerably more as he drops it.[3] Sympathy is rather with his family; so far as he is concerned it is mainly but the complement of the antipathy and even provokes or exacerbates the laughter. The duped is an object of mirth as well as the duper. In the third act, after the scoundrel, overheard by Damis, has, in conversation with Elmire, betrayed himself, and only by recourse to hypocritical magnanimity can defend himself, laughter at both villain and victim drowns out, says Sarcey, sympathy with the latter and indignation against the former. The pious rogue takes refuge in Uriah-Heep-like general self-abasement:

> Oui, mon frère, je suis un méchant, un coupable . . .

and Orgon, who has spontaneously cried out in natural astonishment and horror, and might thereupon be expected to demand answers

---

[2] Sarcey, *Quarante Ans de théâtre*, II, 144.

[3] Meredith, in his *Idea of Comedy*, speaks of the way we are led 'to put faith in Orgon's roseate prepossession,' which we share 'by comic sympathy.'

more to the point, turns, instead, without preparation or any intimation of a change within him, against his son:

> Ah! traître, oses-tu bien, par cette fausseté
> Vouloir de sa vertu ternir la pureté?

Then the house bursts into a roar. But it is not the *rire amer* — this, in the spirit of mirth without mercy, is yet to come, at Tartuffe's entire expense. The earlier laughter is only because the spectators are thus fully convinced and made sensibly aware of the worthy Orgon's improbable obsession; because they now see in him, to use Bergson's phrase, a jack-in-the-box, whereof Tartuffe knows and readily touches the spring. The *rire amer* does not come until as, danger pressing into the foreground, the laugh is turned against the manipulator — at Orgon's crying out from under the table in indignant rage, and, again, at the officer's springing the surprise of the arrest:

> Et vous, suivez-moi tout à l'heure
> Dans la prison qu'on doit vous donner pour demeure.

Before that Tartuffe is laughable, indeed, for his artfulness or for his egregious sanctimoniousness; but Orgon is still more so for his folly.

In *Othello*, though there is the same contrast between the victim's character and his conduct, the same external influence to produce the situation and lead the character thus astray, there is no such stiffness or automatism; and but momentarily and incidentally is there any effect of comedy (not connected with the hero, moreover), as in *Tartuffe* there is but momentarily and incidentally any effect of tragedy. On the contrary, in *Othello* there are overwhelming sympathy and pity, terror and horror. To that end we actually see the hero fall into the villain's power, as Orgon we do not —

> quae sunt oculis subjecta fidelibus et quae
> Ipse sibi tradit spectator.

Therefore the villain must play the honest man, and his hypocrisy and diabolical villainy be laid bare in the soliloquies or (but slightly) in colloquy with the tool Roderigo.

In either play, however, with or without the process disclosed before us, the villain produces a delusion or infatuation; and thus the dramatist accumulates a store of emotion that in the sequel repeatedly explodes. For the power of tragedy lies, as certain few critics from Aristotle to Henley have discerned, in the emotions generated and discharged, as if by a dynamo; and of great comedy, like *Tartuffe* and *Volpone*, the same is true, though the effect is different. There the audience *reacts* instead of responding, laughs instead of trembling or weeping. Some critics have said that emotion is alien to comedy; but the words apply principally to its effect. There is little genuine emotion, to be sure, in artificial comedy like *The Way of the World*, or *The Importance of Being Ernest*; but Orgon's outcries, cited above, are as emotional as Othello's. The difference is that they awaken no sympathetic echoes, provoke only a revulsion in the house.

Being, then, a skillful and powerful contrivance or engine to generate emotion, tragedy or comedy, when at its highest potency, is not primarily a study of character. Character is presented not for its own sake, in the interest of strict verisimilitude or internal consistency, but in the higher or more urgent one of tragic or comic effect. It is treated poetically rather than psychologically or logically; verisimilitude and consistency are for the minor characters, not those at the center of the action; and for the latter at times there is consistency only on 'the surface of the mind,' in the manner of thought and utterance. Psychology, as we have seen, is interfered with in the victims, who are led to act in a way contrary to their noble or sensible natures. As this interference concerns Othello and other Shakespearean personages, besides those of Sophocles, Racine, and Homer, I have discussed the matter at length in other chapters; in this I undertake to do the like with *Tartuffe*, not the victim but the villain.

3

Here again he is like Iago. For the full tragic effect the depths of Iago's villainy and hypocrisy must be revealed to the audience; and since they cannot be to any one on the stage, that service is performed in soliloquy. In the process there is some wrenching of the psychology: it is contrary to nature for one so evil, and so manifestly rejoicing in it, to think or speak evil of himself. Likewise, though the process and purpose are not quite the same, there is wrenching of

the psychology of Tartuffe. For the full comic effect the egregious-
ness of his hypocrisy must be revealed to the audience; but since
comic effect is, unlike the tragic, a matter primarily of the deception
— the sharp contrast between fact and appearances, not the dire
consequences of it — the hypocrisy must, improbably, manifest
itself, display itself, in the very presence of the victim or his friends.
It must be open and palpable enough to make the audience laugh,
and the other characters chafe, as Orgon and his mother are taken
in. It must also be extravagant and picturesque enough to make the
audience laugh at it as a specimen of human vice and folly, and as the
fulfillment of the expectations aroused in the prolonged exposition.
The audience must be permitted to see and judge for themselves; and
in comedy the judgment takes the form of hilarity. Before the
hypocrite appears we learn, through Orgon, how in the sanctuary
he distinguishes himself by the ardor of his devotion, kneeling,
sighing, and kissing the ground, everywhere makes scruples of
trifles, and the other day reproached himself for having too angrily
killed a flea caught whilst saying his prayers; and we learn through
Cléante, Orgon's judicious brother-in-law, and also the other characters, that he is a whited sepulchre of specious zeal, given to lifting up
his eyes and groaning, and to covering his resentment with the cloak
of Heaven's interests. Sighs and glances, except as thus reported,
count for little on the stage. There we must have speech and conspicuous action. Hence it is that, when Tartuffe makes his long-
expected appearance, his *début*, he cries out, perceiving Dorine, to
his footboy, like the hypocrite he is but would not appear to be,
'Lock up my hair shirt and my scourge and pray heaven ever to
enlighten you — if I am asked for I am distributing alms':

> Laurent, serrez ma haire avec ma discipline,
> Et priez que toujours le Ciel vous illumine.
> Si l'on vient pour me voir, je vais aux prisonniers
> Des aumônes que j'ai partager les deniers.

Then, taking notice of Dorine, and of her bosom, liberally bared
according to the mode,

> Ah! mon Dieu, je vous prie,
> Avant que de parler prenez-moi ce mouchoir.
> (Comment?) Couvrez ce sein que je ne saurais voir.

Which prudery provokes the soubrette to declare, with a truly Gallic pointedness and candor, that she for her part is not so sensitive or susceptible; and thus there is no mistaking the hypocrisy or escaping its comic effect.

4

Tartuffe would fain have all this mistaken for piety; yet not only with Orgon, who is infatuated and blinded, but with Cléante, Elmire, Damis, and the rest, he continually thus betrays himself. Now from the time of La Bruyère the critics have been troubled by this conduct, cavilling at it or justifying it. La Bruyère's Onuphre 'does not say my hair shirt and my scourge, for then he would be taken for what he is . . . he acts so that it shall be thought, without his saying so, that he wears the hair shirt and uses the scourge.' In general he makes of his piety less parade, and his villainy he holds in check. He does not presume to make advances to his patron's wife unless he should feel certain of her, nor undertake to deprive the direct heirs of their heritage. Against the collateral are his designs.[4]

Whether La Bruyère intended to reflect upon Molière's artistry or merely to set the reader right should he take the stage figure for the real thing, Sainte-Beuve was, so far as I know, the first to make tenable distinctions, and justify both the writer of 'characters' and the dramatist, the one as a painter of portraits, the other, of 'tableaux.' Like Dumas *fils* and Sarcey after him, he insisted upon the *optique du théâtre*. 'To be truer, more real, La Bruyère's hypocrite, at moments, smiles or sighs and does not make answer; and that is perfect, it is subtle; but it would not take you far at the theatre.' The point is that with Molière still more than with any other French comic dramatist it is not a matter of copying or imitation but of a new creation, a comic one:

Chez Molière, plus que chez aucun auteur dramatique en France, le théâtre, si profondément vrai, n'est pas du tout, quant aux détails, une copie analysée, ni une imitation littéralement *vraisemblable* d'alentour; c'est une reproduction originale, une création, un monde. Molière n'est rien moins qu'un peintre de portraits, c'est un peintre de tableaux; ou mieux, c'est un producteur d'êtres vivants, qui sont assez eux-mêmes et assez sûrs de leur propre vie pour ne pas aller calquer leurs démarches sur

[4] *Œuvres* (1912), II, 154–59.

la stricte réalité. Essentiellement humains dans le fond, ils n'ont d'autre loi pour le détail et pour l'agencement que le comique dans toute sa verve.[5]

Dramatic and comic effect, then, is the chief thing, not a nice and faultless adjustment to reality; and of Tartuffe's first and second speeches, quoted above, Sainte-Beuve further observes that, after all this preparation and expectation, they afford the character his necessary and perfect *début* on the stage:

Que La Bruyère dise tout ce qu'il voudra, ce *Laurent, serrez ma haire* . . . est le plus admirable début dramatique et comique qui se puisse inventer . . . le second n'est pas moindre, c'est surtout le geste ici qui est frappant . . . cela n'est pas vraisemblable, dira-t-on; mais cela parle, cela tranche; et la vérité du fond et de l'ensemble crée ici celle du détail. Voyez-vous pas quel rire en rejaillit, et comme toute une scène en est égayée?

For comedy, like tragedy indeed, is not description or exposition; and Dumas *fils*, in the preface to his *Père prodigue*, ranges himself with Sainte-Beuve, as against La Bruyère and Fénelon, in favor of 'high relief.' Of the former he says:

. . . un écrivain que je révère plus que personne . . . qui a inondé le monde de vérités qu'il eût été incapable d'énoncer au théâtre, parce qu'il aurait gravé en creux là où il faut sculpter en relief.

5

By this (though in his own day the great realist Tolstoi said the same),[6] Lemaître is not convinced, avowing that he thinks Tartuffe at his best where he is nearest to Onuphre. He, too, finds an improbability in the play, but one less to the credit of the dramatist's art. Taking, evidently, the center or source of the action to be not the situation but the leading character, he considers the improbability to be within him, not in the relation between him and Orgon, and sees no justification for it. He does not acknowledge the far higher

[5] *Port-Royal* (1878), III, 292–93.

[6] Contrasting the novel and the drama, he remarked of the latter, 'Everything must be clear-cut and in high relief,' etc. (Quoted in Barrett Clarke's *Study of the Drama*, 1925, p. 50.)

emotional and comic effect ensuing once this ascendancy has been established, premised. Concerned only for the psychology, he notes that Tartuffe is a gross hypocrite and guttler at the outset, then, in order fitly to solicit the hand of Orgon's daughter and the favors of his wife, a clever and finished rake. He does not here take account of Molière's finesse: how the grosser and cruder manners and practices, the guttling, tippling, and belching, the genuflections and grimaces and too choleric killing of fleas when at prayer, are only reported, not presented on the stage, how it is off-stage that this hypocrite is a Stiggins. The comic effect of the character, in short, he judges to be somewhat objectionable, and even discovers there the root of the difficulty. What is ridiculed in him is the forms of devotion in general, the apparatus of piety, religion itself; and to this satirical purpose Molière has sacrificed the unity of his principal personage. What is funny about Tartuffe? Not his hypocrisy, which would be tragic:

Certes, on ne rirait pas de Tartuffe, on n'en aurait nulle envie, *si on ne riait que de Tartuffe*.

. . . Il n'a pas pris garde que ce qu'il ridiculisait, en somme, c'était l'appareil même de la piété, et plus particulièrement de la piété populaire et monastique. . . . Je suis tout près de penser qu'il a réellement voulu, en bafouant les 'gestes' de la piété, atteindre la piété même, et, pour tout dire, la religion . . . Molière s'est volontairement arrangé de façon que le ridicule ne pût être limité à une seule catégorie de dévots, et que c'est même à ce dessein qu'il a sacrifié l'unité de son principal personnage.[7]

And thus Lemaître ranges himself in the controversy by the side of Bossuet and Bourdaloue, Brunetière and Faguet, indeed, but also by the side of the very hypocrites, who, unlike the Marquises and the Précieuses, the Doctors and the cuckolds, did not, says Molière himself, understand 'raillerie.'

Yet this was a wit, a poet, a dramatist, and that Lemaître was a great critic everybody knows. His error (as I take it) lies in his approach, not only in forgetting that the play or situation is more important than the character but in presuming a philosophic bias or purpose. Molière himself, translator of Lucretius and possibly pupil of Gassendi, may have been 'peu chrétien' or even *libre penseur*; as

---

[7] *Impressions de théâtre* (1892), IV, 45–47 (italics the author's).

such he may possibly even be present in his own play; but since there was every reason that he should not be and no need that he should, it is no likelier that he is there than that the husband of Armande is in *L'École des femmes*, and by examination the supposition is confirmed. This is drama, not propaganda, *comédie humaine*, not religious or sceptical polemic; indeed any intentional satire of sincere piety in a piece to be performed before the Most Christian king and his court and the honest, appreciably more Christian though decidedly less penetrating bourgeoisie of Paris, is something of a slur, not only on the courtier's address and the manager's common sense — and who in this world ever had more of it? — but even on the dramatist's art. Satire in comedy is only for recognized or recognizable follies and vices; and Lemaître's misconception is, so far, pretty much that of the *cabale*, the *Compagnie du Saint-Sacrement*, the *président du parlement* M. Lamoignon, who belonged to it, the Archbishop of Paris and the multitudinous other bigots of the city, who for five years pretty successfully obstructed performances, to the amazement of right-thinking people then and since. Molière himself, in the preface and the *placets* to the King, insists on the distinction between true piety and false; this is amply supported both by the explicit discussions of the matter on the lips of Cléante and by the way the hypocrite is presented. One of the chief reasons for making Tartuffe's hypocrisy so obvious is to preclude this very misconception; and thereby not only a comic purpose is served — the comic issue must be clear-cut and decisive, of course, or there will be no laughter — but a moral one. Concerning the wickedness of Tartuffe, the dramatist declares, the spectator is left not a moment in doubt:

> Il ne tient pas un seul moment l'auditeur en balance; on le connaît d'abord aux marques que je lui donne; et d'un bout à l'autre il ne dit pas un mot, il ne fait pas une action qui ne peigne aux spectateurs le caractère d'un méchant homme, et ne fasse éclater celui du véritable homme de bien que je lui oppose.

6

The strangest error of the critic, however, is in misapprehending, what ordinarily he knew so well, the spirit of comedy. Hypocrisy not comic? It would, rather, be tragic? For the moment Lemaître belies his own nature, his nation, one might even add, his race. Ben Jonson's Rabbi Zeal-of-the-Land Busy, I suppose, his Ananias and Tribulation Wholesome, might become for us tragic or even pathetic characters — if we paused and wondered about their past, their parentage and environment, their struggles and hardships, as, if the comedy is to remain such, we must by no manner of means permit ourselves to do. So Shylock (though with more warrant than Tartuffe, for *his* wrongs are touched upon) has been interpreted *à contresens*. Almost any comedy can, by our taking thought, be turned and twisted into a tragedy, and particularly high comedy, with its large dimensions and far-reaching issues, like Molière's and Jonson's.

Lemaître seems to have been led astray by his wits — a malady most incident to critics, as Molière in his day knew. Dealing with ingenuity of a different sort, he is well aware that a play makes little appeal to our wits but much to our imagination, our humble senses and passions. 'Ne consultons,' says Dorante in the *Critique de l'École des femmes*,

... ne consultons dans une comédie que l'effet qu'elle fait sur nous. Laissons-nous aller de bonne foi aux choses qui nous prennent par les entrailles, et ne cherchons point de raisonnements pour nous empêcher d'avoir du plaisir. ... Vous avez raison, Madame, de les trouver étranges, tous ces raffinements mystérieux. Car, s'ils ont lieu, nous voilà réduits à ne nous plus croire; nos propres sens seront esclaves en toutes choses (sc. vii).

Here, though in a comedy, it is the same principle that Corneille in his *Discours* nine years before expressed in defense of his frank and clear-cut presentation of villainy in tragedy — 'la naïve peinture des vices et des vertus ... qu'on ne les peut confondre l'un dans l'autre, ni prendre le vice pour vertu.' In their criticism both dramatists are concerned for edification more than for aesthetics; but in practice each recognized the fact that in his own sort of drama, which arouses not curiosity but the emotions, there must be no doubt in the mind of the audience who or what is right or wrong. Of comedy that is still truer than of tragedy, for there the judgment of the audience — 'pas un moment en balance' — must be instantaneous and unanimous; in *Tartuffe*, moreover, the hypocrite must clearly betray himself in his conduct because, unlike Corneille's, Racine's, and Shakespeare's villains, he does not do so in soliloquy or *confidence*. Yet it is not the bare knowledge of the hypocrisy that is needed, but the visible, audible impression. Even Iago, to sharpen the contrast and heighten the suspense, and for comic effect besides, thus betrays himself a little now and then, not only with Roderigo but also, momentarily, in the presence of Othello and his friends. For the same reason most feigning on the stage does this, somewhat like Rosalind's and Hamlet's; the contrast thus presented involves irony, whether comic or tragic; and essentially it is the same principle of *optique* in ancient tragedy when the characters 'speak and act not just to the purpose of the immediate situation but always, for the audience, in the full context of the whole circumstances.'[8]

It is only as comedy and tragedy, both, are replaced by drama, and character-drawing by psychology, and the sympathetic emotions by curiosity, that the *optique* can be dispensed with. Even in Elizabethan times was the beginning of this; and Luke Frugal, in Massinger's *City Madam*, is the sort of villainous hypocrite that La Bruyère and Lemaître would have preferred. Until near the end he is so plausibly hypocritical that no one in the play sees through him, and since he makes no avowals in soliloquy or *confidence* not many in the audience would do so. Until near the end he is an interesting study rather than an effective stage figure; curiosity gets the upper hand of sympathy or antipathy and the comic or tragic effect of his hypocrisy is meager and dubious. '*Il* tient l'auditeur en balance.'

7

And Voltaire, what shall I say of him, with whom I am (naturally) almost as loath to differ on the subject of comedy as, on that of theology, a good Catholic might be with the Pope? But as there is a greater than the Pope, so is there than Voltaire, even the supreme master of comedy to whom we were listening a moment ago; and here is another critic who has reasoned himself out of his pleasure.

---

[8] E. T. Owen, 'Sophocles the Dramatist,' *University of Toronto Quarterly*, January 1936, p. 239. — For the reminders of Rosalind's, Portia's, and the others' sex and real character in the midst of their disguise, see E. E. Kellett, *Suggestions* (1923), pp. 8–9.

Speaking of absurdities mingled with vices, he declares that we are
delighted by the portrayal of them but experience only a pleasure
that is serious:

Un malhonnête homme ne fera jamais rire, parce que dans le rire il entre
toujours de la gaieté, incompatible avec le mépris et l'indignation. Il est
vrai qu'on rit au *Tartuffe*; mais ce n'est pas de son hypocrisie, c'est de la
méprise du bonhomme qui le croit un saint, et, l'hypocrisie une fois
reconnue, on ne rit plus: on sent d'autres impressions. [9]

A dishonorable or ignoble man not move us to laughter? — philosophically, *a priori*, that may be. But not as we read or remember.
Has Voltaire forgotten the parasite and the *fallax servus* of Latin
comedy, the rogues, scamps, dissemblers and hypocrites there and
on the comic stage ever since, as well as in the picaresque novel?
Has he forgotten Aristotle, who holds comedy to be an imitation of
men worse than the average; or, as he avers that *gaieté* is incompatible
with contempt and indignation, has he forgotten even himself, with
his store of acrid or caustic wit? Has he forgotten Tartuffe and
Harpagon on the stage?

8

Sarcey and Sainte-Beuve stick appreciably closer to their 'propres
sens,' their immediate perceptions, as well as to the spirit of theatrical
art; and their opinions are supported, I think, by some comparisons
apart from those already considered. It is particularly in Renaissance
and ancient drama that the minor figures are most readily recognizable as the images of life; and it is the major ones, for the reasons
already adduced — the requirements of situation and a range of
passion — that present difficulties. This is true not only of comedy
but of tragedy, not only of Othello, Macbeth, and Hamlet, upon
whom fate or villainy intrudes, but of Romeo,[10] Lear, and even Coriolanus (as when he intends to burn Rome), who are not controlled.
And it is true of comedy, as in Falstaff and Shylock, Jonson's Rabbi
Busy, and in Molière apart from Tartuffe. M. Legouis complains of
Jonson's Puritan that he is 'an arrant hypocrite and an enthusiast as
convinced as ridiculous. [The dramatist] should have chosen one or

---

[9] *Œuvres* (1877), III, 444.
[10] See 'Romeo and Juliet,' in my *Shakespeare's Young Lovers*.

other of these alternatives.'[11] I myself (and apparently others too) am not persuaded that these are artistically (however psychologically) inconsistent, still less that either alone would have been more 'completely diverting';[12] and here is the same amplitude in the characterization, a similar complaint from the critic. Harpagon is another case, as baffling to the psychologist and sociologist as Tartuffe. L'Avare is one of Molière's great comic successes; and some critics speak of the 'profondeur d'analyse.' There is breadth rather than profundity or consistency. Grandet, says Sarcey,[13] is all of a piece and in harmony with his surroundings; but this wretched miser keeps a big establishment, servants, coach and horses — accessories which serve only to produce comic contrast and variety. Psychologically Harpagon is to Sarcey incomprehensible. But, as Sarcey also clearly sees, the horses he keeps in order to get up nights and steal away their oats; the servants, to stint them and worry them — to bid one not to rub the furniture too hard, another to turn the hole in his breeches to the wall, another to cover the oil stain in front with his hat, and all of them to keep the wine from flowing freely and to take off their blouses only when the guests arrive. (For — unreasonably enough! — he entertains, and what is more, is on the point of marriage — to a beautiful young woman without either property or thrift!) These domestic and social connections he must have, which your true miser would dispense with, to vary the effect of his avarice and throw it into relief. The other characters, on the contrary, who are not at the center of the action, such as Cléante, Valère, Elise and Mariane, are, though slightly treated, as consistent as they are in Tartuffe and (excepting their unanimous respect for Iago) in Othello.

---

[11] History of English Literature, I, 291. — In justifying his strictures, M. Legouis (Revue anglo-américaine, February 1936) makes use of Purecraft's and Quarlous' evidence that Busy was a hypocrite consciously; which is going farther than Lemaître (see above, p. 343) as he makes use of report to prove Tartuffe inconsistently both a gross hypocrite and guttler and also a finished rake: 'Ni Shakespeare ni Molière ne feraient cela,' says M. Legouis of the incompatibility of the traits, forgetting the elder critic. And he takes too little account of the difficulty in presenting hypocrisy on any stage, at any time, especially in a day when subjective behavior was not even attempted (see above, Chap. III, p. 86) and all hypocrisy, like Iago's, Tribulation's, and Tartuffe's was pretty conscious. The only error here is Busy's admitting that he is confuted by the puppet, at the end.

[12] See above, 'Shakespeare and Jonson,' p. 105.

[13] Quarante Ans de théâtre, II, 129-30.

9

So far as range of comic effect is concerned one of the best parallels to Tartuffe is Falstaff, who has been equally misapprehended, though (unlike the other) psychologically exonerated. He is bigger, not in body only but in spirit — a coward and a braggart, a parasite and a sensualist, a deadbeat and an extortioner, on the one hand, and king of cronies and companions, on the other. He is not a hypocrite, though by most of the critics since Morgann's day he has been drolly taken for one — of an inverted sort, a little like what simple Cecily, in Wilde's *Importance of Being Earnest*, fears that Algernon may prove to be:

I hope you have not been leading a double life, pretending to be wicked and being really good. That would be hypocrisy!

The fat rogue a sheep in wolf's clothing! But really there is some-what the same method in the presentation. He exposes himself, and acts like the traditional coward and braggart, as Tartuffe acts like the hypocrite and false bigot, that each of them disavows and (if off the stage) would more sedulously endeavor to conceal. In most respects he is, of course, still more like Molière's Sganarelle in the *Cocu imaginaire*, also a coward, and many another medieval and Renaissance *miles gloriosus* or *gracioso*, who in soliloquy both confess to the indictment and the next moment shake it off with their merry but craven sophistries about the folly of honor and the wisdom of 'discretion.' Tartuffe holds no soliloquies and has no humor; in particular none of that sly gammon about religion on the lips of medieval and Boccaccian, Ariostian and Machiavellian clerics, which is nearest akin to Falstaff's and Sganarelle's about chivalry. Yet he is essentially in the same dramatic tradition, fulfills the same broad comic and dramatic requirements. Falstaff, too, is in an improbable situation — not that of a humble and (till recently) unknown man of God parading his piety and maneuvering to seduce his patron's wife, marry the daughter, disinherit the son, and take possession of the property; nor that of a wretched old miser keeping up a great establishment and wooing a poverty-stricken young girl; but that of a coward taking, like a Dick Turpin, to the road, boasting ludi-crously (though a wit) after his failure, and, later, with a bottle in

his holster for a pistol, voluntarily going to the war, where in battle
he falls flat as in robbing he ran away. In the coward's boasting and
lying, to be sure, there is, superficially at least, nothing improbable:
that illogical situation has lain embedded in human life from the
beginning and been exhibited on the stage for a couple of thousand
years. But one who is also a wit, and who has just openly shown the
white feather, would, if at all, brag with greater moderation and
wariness. And a coward, even with the Prince and Poins to support him, would not take readily to highway robbery; if he could
be got into battle at all, he would go armed to the teeth; and in either
business he would be too much preoccupied and agitated for jesting.
But thus disconcerted Falstaff, like most other such stage figures of
his time and many afterwards, is not; and therefore is no coward,
many modern critics hold.

The chief similarity, however, is in the way that his cowardice,
together with the natural and traditional accompaniment of bragging, is, like Tartuffe's sanctimoniousness, made obvious upon the
stage, particularly at the outset. We remember the hair shirt,
the scourge, and the handkerchief for the chambermaid's bosom at the
hypocrite's first appearance; — is not this all to the same effect and
purpose, though differently treated, as Falstaff's conduct after Gadshill, with his story of the knaves in buckram and Kendal green, his
hacked sword and bloodied garments? Both characters have been
previously analyzed and discussed and their conduct described or
predicted, Tartuffe amply and in general, Falstaff more particularly,
with regard to these vices of cowardice and bragging; and now, by
what they do and what they say, they fulfill every expectation. 'Cela
parle, cela tranche,' though 'cela' n'est pas 'vraisemblable.' Both
characters are clever; in Tartuffe, as we have seen, the psychological
inconsistency or logical contradiction is recognized; but in Falstaff
it has not been and in some measure still isn't.

10

I have no intention of opening up the question as a whole. If
my argument thirteen years ago[14] be, as Professor Cazamian would
have it, 'in a way irrefutable,' and yet Professor Bradley's intuition,

[14] *Shakespeare Studies* (1927), Chap. VIII, where the reader may find evidence for
the statements in the two previous paragraphs. To the numerous parallels to Fal-

which it attacked, remain profoundly true, 'because they do not meet
on the same plane,' [15] why, then, there is no prospect of profit in
much further discussion. Even could I contrive to be so unanswerable
on his higher plane, the critic would, I fear, take wing to another.
It is the old opposition of faith and reason, of feeling and understanding, *Vernunft* and *Verstand*, the limitations of a spectator and the
privileges of a reader; and M. Cazamian seems only to be bringing
up to date Morgann's '*secret* impressions of courage' in 'actions of
apparent cowardice and dishonour.' If this transcendentalism means
only poetry, in allegiance to that, I, as a student of comedy and
tragedy, yield to no man. In the past I have said that Falstaff is a
poetical character, and I say it again; so is Tartuffe as well, though to
a lesser degree; and it is in poetry or in (what often comes to that)
terms of dramatic effect, but not in psychology, that the contradictions of Falstaff and most of Shakespeare's other characters are
resolved. The dramatic effect is, moreover, an immediately perceptible one (not, if there be any such, one concealed), with the
individuality of the character preserved in his ways of thinking,
feeling, and fancying, of speaking and acting, which cannot be
comprehended within a psychology, a harmony of motives. Above
all, the individuality is preserved in the speech, in the manner and the
accent; and there Falstaff, far more than Tartuffe or Harpagon, is
continually convincing. But the eminent critic, who also insists
upon poetry, is not content with it, and for once in his life is not
blamelessly faithful to the muse. He wanders after philosophy and
psychology (psychology not only of the conscious but the subconscious, not only Falstaff's but Shakespeare's own in the making of
him), and away from the exceedingly plain and pointed meaning of
the sixteenth-century stage play and the sixteenth-century comic
figure in it to considerations of the relativity of morals and the trans-
valuation of values. *Raffinements* certainly *mystérieux*, and neither
comic nor dramatic.

---

staff there produced from Renaissance and ancient comedy — lying braggarts,
ingeniously excusing but ingenuously betraying themselves, falling flat before a
sign of danger, as on Shrewsbury Field, but undauntedly confronting another coward, like Pistol or M. le Fer — I wish to add Braggadochio, *Faerie Queene*, II, iii,
whom I took account of but too cursorily. Cf. Janet Spens, *Spenser's Faerie Queene*
(1934), p. 66.

[15] Lecture before the Tudor and Stuart Club, Johns Hopkins, 1934.

However, M. Cazamian has, at least on my terrestrial plane, accepted my unpretending and (one would think) superfluous contention that Falstaff is a coward and a braggart, is, as Addison said, both a wit and a butt, as well as a dishonest recruiting-officer;[16] and this concession suffices for our present purposes of comparison with Tartuffe. Braggart and butt he is in the story of the rogues in buckram and Kendal green, and here poetry — the comic muse — is asserting itself. It is a *quasi* lyrical, good-humored, and exuberant development of the familiar and time-honored situation of reckless boasting after pitiful behavior, in fine keeping with Falstaff's high spirits and his fantasy, but not, except very short-sightedly, with his wit. M. Cazamian, too, says that it is 'poetical lying,' but he means a different thing. Poetry he makes of it but leaves the lying out. He will not, after all, and despite his admissions, have the character psychologically inconsistent — here for the moment a butt or dupe, the coward giving his fancy the rein in the effort to cover up his cowardice. Like Mr. Bradley, he thinks that Falstaff, 'free from all utilitarian motive,' does not expect that any one will believe him, and that here we have 'the pure, the philosophical joy of transcendental audacity . . . a clear intelligence [understanding, perception?] of the relativity of things, a mood of free experimenting in the interversion of the real and the fictitious . . . a duality of mental planes, and an indirect mode of expression, the actual intent offering itself in disguise — that is to say, the very conditions of humour.' Philosophy, for a farcical roguery scene in a tavern? Transcenden-

---

[16] At this last, naturally enough, M. Cazamian hesitates; and of Falstaff the deadbeat, cheating his landlady, his tailor, and his host, as well as of the 'whoremaster,' he says nothing at all. Faintheartedly and without definite approval, he refers to Mr. Draper's opinion that Falstaff's chicanery in recruiting was 'just what an Elizabethan audience would expect of a professional army officer'; which is like Mr. Draper's opinion that Iago was pretty much justified by the *mores* of the Renaissance. That officer himself avows that he has 'misused the king's press damnably.' In the army nowadays there is no such corruption; but there is as much in professional politicians, both American and French, and an honest man, such as M. Cazamian and I alike take Shakespeare to be, would not be so indulgent to it. Later some such consideration seems to be borne in upon the critic, for of the recruiting business he says that 'the psychological interest is waning'; and still later, that Falstaff is a 'dishonest soldier.' And yet after all that he winds up his discourse by accepting Mrs. Quickly's aposiopesis of admiration, 'but an honester and truer-hearted man — well, fare thee well!' To such a pass does a critic of comedy come in 'transcending the plane of good and evil'! It is poor Quickly that is really transcending it, in her comical infatuation!

talism, in a den of thieves? Free from all utilitarian motive, he who 'roared for mercy, and still run and roared, as ever I heard bull-calf,'[17] sweating to death and larding the lean earth as he ran, and who, like other Renaissance cowards, has just now hacked his own sword, tickled his nose with spear-grass, and bloodied his garments? Only playing a pretty little transcendental comedy, this confessed (or well-known) thief, deadbeat, extortioner, glutton, winebibber, and libertine, lying now as he always does when he can anywise profit by it — would, then, the dramatist not really have him understood? After that interpretation what can one do but refer the baffled reader or spectator (who is surely beginning to 'ne se plus croire,' to doubt his own senses, and is for shutting the book or quitting the theater) to the simple and solid sense of the colloquy between the Prince and Poins beforehand:

The virtue of this jest will be the incomprehensible lies that this same fat rogue will tell us when we meet at supper; how thirty, at least, he fought with; what wards, what blows, what extremities he endured; and in the reproof of this lies the jest.

And then to the pointed and justified gibes on Gadshill:

Fal. 'Zounds, will they not rob *us*?
Prince. What, a coward, Sir John Paunch?
Fal. Indeed, I am not John of Gaunt, your grandfather; but yet no coward, Hal.
Prince. Well, we leave that to the proof.

Could anything be more explicit and insistent in advance, or more exactly and obviously verified and justified in the sequel, and is it all in vain? Or does it point in the opposite direction? The method[18] doesn't elsewhere in comedy, as in the gulling of Benedick and Beatrice by their hopeful friends and of Falstaff by the Merry Wives

[17] M. Cazamian, of course, does not go the length of Morgann — 'think he does not roar' though the Prince himself says the above-quoted afterwards and Poins cries 'how the rogue roared!' at the time; nor attribute these words and the prediction of his later conduct to Poins's 'malice'; nor in general proceed in his criticism, like Morgann and his followers, as if Falstaff were a *real* person, who had been inadequately or incompletely represented in the play (*teneatis risum!*) and concerning whom he had information of his own to furnish.

[18] Cf. M. I. Wolff, 'Shakespeare und sein Publikum,' *Shakespeare-Jahrbuch* (1935), p. 103; and above, Chap. I, p. 16.

of Windsor; nor in tragedy, as in the machinations of Iago and
Edmund; but it serves for effects of clearness and excitement in
either, in comedy more indispensably. There, obviously, expectations of laughter in any particular form or quarter, once aroused,
must, though at the expense of plausibility, not be disappointed or
but partially fulfilled. The procedure, of anticipation and exact fulfillment, is precisely the same as that of the French lords in *All's
Well* in their exposure of another coward, Parolles, the only difference being that *his* 'quick evasions' and 'easy escapes' (as by Dryden
and Johnson Falstaff's are rightly called), his lying and slandering,
are not good-humored and witty. But what is the point of evasions
if there is really nothing to evade? As I have said before, 'in the
cowardice lies the whole point of twitting him with his boasting lies
and excuses — if in fun Falstaff had run away or lied where would
be the fun of confuting him'?[19] Or as Mr. John Bailey has, not
knowing it, said after me:

where would be the humour of 'a plague of all cowards' if the speaker
were a brave man? Where would be the fun of the 'plain tale' that put
his preposterous boastings down if, as we are told, he never meant to be
believed? Where that of 'Lord, Lord, how subject we old men are to
this vice of lying' if the speaker were as truthful as the Duke of Wel-
lington?[20]

Good sense who but Coleridge and Wordsworth, the arch romantics, severally declare to be a property of all good poetry;[21] and
that is still truer of drama, of comedy. The eighteenth century, the
age of good sense, and Falstaff's own century, which ought to
know him — Thomas Fuller, Oldmixon, Dryden (twice explicitly),
Nicholas Rowe, Addison, Lewis Theobald, Samuel Johnson, Tom
Davies, Edmund Malone — as well as Baretti, Mézières, and
Courthope afterwards — had no doubts of our artful dodger's
cowardice. Johnson, the incarnation of good sense, who knew

[19] *Shakespeare Studies*, p. 421; and for Tom Davies (1785) and Richard Stack (1788)
to the same effect, p. 445, n. 85.
[20] *Shakespeare* (1929), pp. 127–28. In the excellent Variorum *Henry IV* (1936)
this book is ignored.
[21] Preface to the *Lyrical Ballads*. *Table-Talk*: 'Poetry is certainly more than good
sense,' says Coleridge; 'but it must be good sense, at all events: just as a palace is more
than a house; but it must be a house, at least.'

Shakespeare well and also not ill the ways of the imagination, made answer to Morgann, as quoted by Malone, that 'all he should say, was that if Falstaff was not a coward Shakespeare knew nothing of his art.' And Courthope, in our time, who has the wider view of an historian of literature, not thinking it necessary to argue the point, finds 'his cowardice absolutely transparent.' 'Not a coward *in fact*,' asserts Professor Kittredge. But 'the appropriate business of poetry,' says Wordsworth, is to treat of things not as they are but as they appear; the stage, says Archer the dramatic critic, 'is the realm of appearances'; and if some of the appearances are false the difference must be perceptible in the play itself. Here, indeed, it is — between the fighter and the coward, the boaster and the liar! Now this is the essence of comedy — the sharp, abrupt contrast between appearance and fact and the swift transition from one to the other. But if the fact *itself* should thereby turn out to be appearance, what of laughter then? 'Transcendental audacity and a clear perception of the relativity of things'? Why, the ground must be solid beneath us, the right must, as we think, be clearly with us, and in a bewildering Einstein world we could not laugh at all. In a comedy as in life the man in question must, in the upshot, be the rogue, hypocrite, miser, or coward depicted, beyond all doubt. There are no hazy debatable lands in comedy. And that cowardice is the particular question here the remarks of the Prince and Poins, of Bardolph and Falstaff himself make so evident that there is no justification for recent criticism like Mr. Priestley's[22] in declaring the question 'unimportant' and avoiding it. A comedy that raises questions which are 'unimportant,' or any without answering them, is crazy.

---

[22] *The English Comic Characters* (1925), p. 92 (*Variorum*). — A strange state of criticism, in which a man of Mr. Priestley's intelligence and literary experience must be reminded by one of mine that Falstaff is not flesh and blood, necessarily a mystery! Only if he were, could there be 'many Falstaffs,' not only the running and roaring or sprawling artful dodger, but also the sceptical philosopher of Morgann and his followers, the 'big-game hunter, his last shot fired,' of Mr. Charlton, and the varieties in between; just as there are (to choose a convenient but manifestly otherwise inapt comparison) several Hitlers now, in and out of Germany. Which is the true Hitler only his maker could tell us: which is the true Falstaff his maker has told us, in plain English and by way of the unmistakable comic technique at his disposal. The question of cowardice which Mr. Priestley thinks 'unimportant' is clearly put and answered; the question which is the funnier, real cowardice (with boasting) or the pretended, is Mr. Priestley's own, unimportant to the play.

Criticism may be indulged in the discovery of shades of meaning undiscerned by an ordinary audience or insufficiently appreciated by the dramatist, but not of a wholly new meaning like M. Cazamian's, which contradicts the primary one, manifestly the dramatist's own. Criticism cannot be indulged in the discovery of a transcendental comedy which undermines or overwhelms the apparent one, despite the forecast exactly fulfilled, despite the natural and immemorial association of bragging with cowardice, and of cowardice with excuses and evasions, despite the want of any explicit evidence of definite indication to the contrary — all in a drama where the author finds it necessary even that the Prince, who as roysterer is really playing a part, should twice[23] be made to tell us so. To such criticism on the part of another, M. Cazamian would — in similar circumstances who wouldn't? — deny the title and name.

I have elsewhere suggested[24] that Falstaff fulfills predictions to overflowing in much the same fashion as Benedick and Beatrice, two other clever people, who so overstep probability in living up to the predictions of their friends and the expectations of the audience that they betray all the traditional external symptoms or pretenses of lovesickness, such as melancholy and toothache,[25] in utter forgetfulness of their desires and intentions to cover it up. Just so Falstaff produces the 'incomprehensible lies' — 'gross as a mountain, open, palpable,' the Prince calls them as they come — and the circumstantial details that Poins had expected. Like Benedick in anticipating — justifying — the quality of his reception, he persuades his followers to hack their swords and bloody their garments, so that even Bardolph 'blushed to hear his monstrous devices.' Indeed, so far as origins are concerned, there is here something of the self-descriptive or 'emblematic' technique, widely observable in the medieval portrayal of character, whether comic or serious, whether on the stage or off it: such as St. Lawrence with his gridiron or St. Catherine with her wheel, in sacred painting; Hope with her anchor, Jealousy with his lattice, or Modesty holding her hand upon her

---

[23] *Henry IV*, Pt. I, I, ii, 160, 217–end; II, iv, 599.

[24] *Shakespeare Studies*, p. 439.

[25] 'He is troubled with the toothache, for lovers ever are' (quoted from Beaumont and Fletcher by Nares). And cf. Marston's *Dutch Courtesan* (1605), II, ii, 68, where Malheureux hides his lovesickness under the same pretence. — For Benedick's anticipation see *Much Ado About Nothing*, II, iii, 244f.

gentle heart, in Spenser; the forsaken lady 'with a willow in her hand,' the melancholy or distracted one with her hair down, or the malcontent with his arms folded and his hat pulled upon his brows, in Elizabethan drama time and again; the poltroon with a lath for a sword, like Falstaff with a bottle for a pistol, in many a Continental comedy; the hypocrite with his breviary, as in Aretino; or with the hair shirt and scourge, as in Molière.[26] And surely what is so primitive and traditional in its origins and still so external in effect does not lend itself to transcendentalism. It is M. Cazamian himself that is in the mood of 'free experimenting in the interversion of the real and the fictitious,' as he transforms Falstaff's discomfiture into a triumph, a secret one, of which neither he nor any one else on the stage becomes aware, and turns the jest — still no one aware! — against Poins and the Prince. His only triumph is, as usual, open enough, by way of his 'evasions' and 'escapes' — 'I knew ye' and 'instinct' — to mask his retreat and cover his discomfiture, to hide him, as the Prince has it, 'from this open and apparent shame.' And the evasions and escapes themselves, like those in soliloquy, are such so apparently not only because of the situation but because they are, in substance or in the very wording, similarly employed, whether before or immediately afterwards, in other comedies of the time. In at least three,[27] 'I knew ye' performs the same service; and in Shakespeare himself 'valour' and 'discretion' are likewise satirically reconciled in *Midsummer Night's Dream* (V, i, 235–57), *Coriolanus* (I, i, 206), and (see Bartlett) elsewhere. To the force of tradition at this point, as well as in Falstaff's whole deportment (so like that of other cowards on the stage, whether ancient or immediately preceding), the audience, even if so disposed, could not be insensible. Had the dramatist intended to break with tradition, as Farquhar did with Wildair and Shaw with Bluntschli, he would have had like them to make it clear, and — in face of this boasting and lying, running and roaring, falling flat and playing possum, stealing, cheating, and whoremongering — very clear. He would have had to cross out 'coward,' written large, and put pacifist there instead.

Such *secret* triumphs and *undivulged* jokes, such riddles and cryptograms, are unknown to the stage, and certainly would miss the mark

[26] Cf. my *Shakespeare Studies*, pp. 434–36, for other examples.
[27] *Shakespeare Studies*, p. 443.

in the theater, particularly when the one person presumed to be enjoying them gives not the slightest sign of it. The old rogue is far from relishing his situation or lingering over it as Morgann and Bradley, Cazamian and (apparently) Pearsall Smith fondly do. 'No more of that, Hal,' cries the fat knight, laughingly but coaxingly and wheedlingly, 'an thou lovest me.' Here, in the tight place and the embarrassment, is, as Dryden, Addison, and Johnson clearly recognized, the center of interest; and here is the point of the *belle response* — the *bella risposta* — of self-extrication.[28] 'I knew ye,' 'Hostess, I *forgive* thee,' and the like are triumphs of wit and agility, to be sure, but also, as the speaker himself well knows, of effrontery and impudence. But the later critics are not so hard-hearted, so simple-minded: 'of that' *their* Falstaff cannot have enough, and transcendentally — masochistically — delights in the twitting and jeering. Thus the positive counts for less than the negative, high relief for less than low, speech than silence, and the requirements of dramatic expression are contradicted or ignored. *Their* Tartuffe would be another Onuphre, who 'does not make answer,' but with this difference, that no La Bruyère is there beside him plainly calling our attention to the fact; and even in our day of subtleties, when eloquence and rhetoric are, as not in Shakespeare's, under a cloud, holding one's tongue counts, as in J. J. Bernard's Martine, who, *unlike* Viola, really 'never tells her love,' only after the most elaborate preparations and indications, a point being made of it.[29] *They*, to be sure, have been '*Reading Shakespeare*,' not (as in the process we are by every dramatist, even by Milton in his *Samson*, expected to do) putting him on the stage of their imaginations; or not so much reading as rewriting him, 'making up fairy stories,' and as they con the page their eyes wander to the 'red-leaved tables' of their own hearts. 'In the reproof of this lies the jest,' says Poins to the Prince beforehand, and when they return, all Eastcheap, including the rogue himself, agrees with them. 'Not so,' say Morgann, Bradley, and Cazamian, after the lapse of centuries. 'Gross, open, palpable,' cries the Prince. 'Subtle, secret, impalpable,' cry Morgann and his followers without a word in the play to support them. What a state of affairs! Looking hard at the joke, they decipher,

[28] Cf. *Shakespeare Studies*, p. 445.
[29] Cf. John Palmer, *Studies in the Contemporary Theatre*, pp. 97–100.

underneath it, a finer one, on Hal and Poins — unexpressed! In art there is no such; in art, obviously, there can be nothing of any sort, however suggestively, unexpressed. In real life a man can keep a secret, even a joke, to the very end; but I know not how he well can in a story, from spectator or reader. The 'transcendental farce,' when there is any — as at the end of Dunsany's *Glittering Gate*, where Jim and Bill, jemmying the Gate, house-breaking even into the Beyond, find 'only stars,' 'blooming great stars' — is expressed, and it is amid abysmal laughter off-stage (still in the play, however) that the curtain falls. Indeed, when there is any doubt about the joke, either what it is or whom it touches, why, then, for spectator or reader and particularly the former, there is no joke at all. A dubious joke, unlike a 'questionable' one, is a contradiction in terms, a philosophical fiction.

Or if the finer joke, on Poins and the Prince, be really, though elusively, expressed, for those who have senses tenuous enough to perceive it, how then with the company and their audience? What a state of discomfort and discord among them instead of the desired and required hilarious unanimity! What company would under-take the play, what actor the leading role? Part of the audience would laugh at the apparent joke, part (a slender, uncomfortable one!) at the transcendental — that at Falstaff's cowardly duplicity, this at the Prince's censorious stupidity — while still others, not laughing, would be frowning or fuming; or else the audience would between the jokes rest suspended, silent if not solemn, starving like Buridan's ass between the two bunches of hay! 'The audience,' Professor Kittredge himself once said, 'is never to be perplexed.'

What this transcendental comedy really is, I must confess, remains to me a mystery. Despite his admission that Falstaff is a coward on the lower plane, M. Cazamian seems actually to think that not only in the extravagant boasting at Eastcheap but in running away and roaring, larding the lean earth and sweating to death on Gadshill, beforehand, he was playing a game of make-believe. 'With the fourth scene of Act II Falstaff rises to new heights of paradoxical extravagance. . . . The farcical comedy which he had been playing for the pleasure of his *companions and for his own*,' etc. That out-Morganns Morgann. Such humor is elaborate and costly, is, to my thinking, itself ridiculous — chimerical, incredible, inconceivable —

transcendental, perhaps, but nothing more. And Falstaff? 'So much the worse for Falstaff,' says Mézières, who had not Cazamian or Bradley either to cope with, 'if he needs so much explaining. Sancho Panza does not need it.'

II

Argument in criticism is of as little avail as in religion, particularly when it touches Shakespeare. But Frenchmen are less fixed and rigorous than Englishmen in their doctrine, particularly when, as here, their deity is only being exalted; and Sarcey, I feel certain, would have assented to much that I have said of the 'gorgeous old ruffian,' as Mr. Galsworthy calls him, and so, I think, might Lemaître, who had the heaven-sent grace to recant his sentimental interpretation of George Dandin and to mock at his own verses on him. And I do not quite despair (so may he not of me!) of M. Cazamian. He has the grace — the sense of humor — not to condescend, like Mr. Priestley and Mr. Ridley, to Dryden and Addison, to Johnson and Morgann's other opponents, in their sense of humor, nor airily toss the 'supposed cowardice' of the 'complete professional soldier'[30] aside. He sees, I think, as Mr. Priestley and Mr. Ridley fail to do, that not Falstaff's reputation only but a fundamental matter of dramatic interpretation is at stake.

Argument serves only to reach those minds (and such, till now, has been M. Cazamian's) for which criticism is no mere matter of vague impression and personal inclination, but only of interpretation. Our traffic, moreover, has been not in argument so much as in analysis and comparison, which, as Mr. T. S. Eliot has justly remarked, are a critic's chief tools. His concern is with the ways of poetry and drama as they are, not as they, perhaps, ought to be, and with the likenesses and differences in the authors' purposes, methods, and effects — not with reality primarily but with the way reality is presented. To these I have endeavored to draw the reader's attention; and I hope I may have succeeded in showing that, particularly

[30] 'If only we can get that idea into our heads!' cries Mr. Ridley impatiently, *Henry IV* seeming to be a work and not a play! And finding the 'soldier' to be indisputably a butt in the *Merry Wives*, Mr. Ridley, without stopping to think, turns in exasperation upon Shakespeare himself (New Temple *Shakespeare*, introd. vol., p. 74). Whose Falstaff, then, is he?

in *Othello* and *Tartuffe*, the form and substance of tragedy and comedy are more akin than they are ordinarily taken to be. Both proceed from the situation rather than the character, both accumulate a store of emotion and discharge it, though with an opposite effect, upon the audience. Both, moreover, as they do this, intensify, simplify, or (though in the interest of the play as a whole) even distort the delineation — with none of this effect, however, upon some readers! Because of the *optique* Othello and Iago, Tartuffe and Orgon, and Falstaff too are misunderstood. But thus these dramatists moved men (which is their main purpose and duty) whether to anguish or to laughter. Though their leading characters are at times not wholly consistent, they speak (especially Shakespeare's) if they do not act or think, consistently. 'A living character,' says Mr. Eliot, 'is not necessarily true to life' — but I respect the reader's memory. 'Tous les livres de valeur littéraire,' M. Thérive and M. Benda assert together,[31] 'sont composés dans le dessein de plier les faits aux exigences de l'art.' All great art is calculated less to transcribe or imitate, and more to force us to think and feel; but of drama, which demands compression and intensity, this is truer than of the novel, and especially of the leading characters, at the center of the action.

[31] *Nouvelles Littéraires*, February 8, 1930, p. 1. — Further discussion of the Falstaff problem (if really there be one) is to be found in my article 'Recent Shakespeare Criticism,' *Jahrbuch* (1938). I there take up the moral confusion of the Falstaff lovers. This would not be so surprising in leftists, who do not believe in property rights or military duties. In Morgann, Bradley, and M. Cazamian, however it be with Mr. Charlton, it must be wholly owing to idealism or sentimentalism, to reading and pondering instead of seeing and responding to the play.

CHAPTER XI

Art and Artifice in the Iliad

The Poetical Treatment of Character in Homer and Shakespeare

I

I T IS quite old-fashioned thus to couple the names of Homer and Shakespeare. Here there is no question of sources, for I shall not take up *Troilus and Cressida*; or of influences, for, in any natural sense of the word, there are none. It is unlikely that Shakespeare read Homer in Greek, and likely that he did not even in translation, but got the very story of Troilus at second hand. Moreover, the *Iliad* is an epic, and as a writer Shakespeare came no nearer to that than *Venus and Adonis* and the *Rape of Lucrece*. With, then, neither a source nor an influence up my sleeve, how can I lift up my voice on such a subject before scholars? Out of my own mouth I am condemned, and my manuscript the editors of nearly all the learned journals in the country would remorselessly turn down. Our literary historians nowadays, at least those with Ph.D's, trace the development of types and *genres*; they strictly distinguish and separate epic, lyric, and drama, even Shakespeare's tragedy from his comedy; often you find one poet's work in half a dozen separate chapters, and for a complete impression of his genius you must piece the *disjecta membra* together. Yet the historical or generic formula is not all-embracing. It is profitable, in fact indispensable, that we should know Shakespeare or Ibsen as tragic and comic dramatists both, and Goethe or Hugo as dramatist, lyrist, novelist, and epic poet, all in one. The same genius reveals itself in its different activities, and the activities are related. These have influenced or reacted upon one another: they now serve to explain one another. And it is profitable to view contemporary writers together, apart from the types or *genres*. They too have influenced or reacted upon, and now serve to explain, one another. In a measure Marlowe, Shakespeare, and Jonson each wrote as he did not only because he was what he was but because the others were writing differently. Thus each found his own field to cultivate, or, if I may change the figure, his own instrument in the orchestra to play. And it is even profitable and enlightening to compare poets far removed in time and place who have never come into contact. They too may serve to explain one another if we view them aright.

This is particularly true of the very greatest writers, in the essentials of their art. On the same level there is no one to compare with Shakespeare in the Elizabethan age; and comparison and analysis, as Mr. T. S. Eliot has said, are the critic's main resource. Or as Mr. Abercrombie puts it, feelings cannot be defined but only related. So there is no one to compare with Homer in Greece, or with Virgil in ancient Rome, or with Dante in medieval Italy. In point of technique we may compare Shakespeare with his contemporaries profitably enough — in structure of plot and scene, in style and meter, in types and even in methods of characterization, in all matters that made them variously acceptable to the public of their time. But Shakespeare and Homer, Virgil and Dante, rose above their fellows, transcended their time. Not that any of them had his eye on posterity, speaking a language, or conveying a message which only posterity could rightly comprehend. That way, for the critic — or his reader! — madness lies. But in any art meant to move the imagination at any one period, there are, when it arrives at perfection, certain elements and features common to the same or a similar art at other periods. The great master speaks the artistic dialect of his day, but on his tongue that is a language which, when the local and temporary features are explained and allowed for, is comprehended by the public of any day. Homer and Shakespeare still touch and delight us, as their contemporaries, to whom they are indebted, seldom do. One, to be sure, is classic, the other romantic. One is simple and chaste, the other often complicated and gorgeous; one is direct and unmannered, the other sometimes ingenious and fantastic; but both alike are fiery and free, each creating, not copying, his own world, and dealing boldly with the greatest emotions. And not only do Homer and Shakespeare tower above their own time; they are also nearer to each other than to any poet of ours, even as the Renaissance is nearer to the great age of Greece.

Why, then, not compare Shakespeare with Aeschylus and Sophocles, whose art is of the same *genre*? I have done that above. There is, moreover, a special reason for the comparison with Homer. In the *Iliad*, as in the *Odyssey*, there is more time covered than in an Hellenic tragedy, a greater fullness of plot and variety of character presented; in tragedy the action begins with what would ordinarily be Shakespeare's fourth act or the fifth. Besides, there is no necessary, fundamental difference in either cause or effect — that is, when in the hands of masters — between tragedy and epic, or, for that matter, between these and the lyric and the novel. There is often something of the drama or of the lyric (the simplest but not the most condensed form) in all of them. Aristotle himself constantly treats Homer alongside the Greek tragic poets, and indeed as the greatest of them, declaring the structure of the epic to be (as at its best it has ever been) like that of the drama. Addison once showed how in the great epics the essential unities, those of time and action, are, proportionately, observed and, as much as possible, the story is presented through speech and dialogue.

In so saying Aristotle was not thinking of psychology or motives; and Shakespeare's treatment of character is essentially more akin to Homer's than to Ibsen's. Like Aristotle himself, Homer would have understood, as the learned do not but, in effect, the simple tailor in the gallery does, when Hamlet reappears from banishment meditating, and not on revenge. It is drama, for, as we know, there is a plot against him and presently the plotters will appear; it is poetry, for he broods, unwittingly, over the grave of her who was dear to him, and under death's spread hand. To that imaginative and emotional though 'Gothic' situation Homer would have responded. Like Aristotle, he would not have sat exploring his own consciousness, and judging that, if sound and healthy and quite what he ought to be, the Prince would be acting instead of thinking, or at least thinking of something else, elsewhere. He would have understood this highly poetic, comparatively external and unpsychological treatment of character.

2

My point of departure is Horace and De Quincey in their diverg-
ing judgments upon Achilles. Insisting on the ideality of the hero,
De Quincey recounts how once, when he observed to Wordsworth
that of imagination, in the poet's own sense, he saw no instance in the
Iliad, the poet replied, 'Yes; there is the character of Achilles.' 'Character,' he adds, 'is not properly the word nor was it what Wordsworth meant. It is an idealised conception. The very perfection of
courage, beauty, strength, speed, skill of eye, of voice, and all personal accomplishments are embodied in the son of Peleus. He has the
same supremacy in modes of courtesy, and doubtless, according to
the poet's conception, in virtue.' And thus the critic comes to comment on the astonishing blunder of the Tiburtine when he describes
the hero as spirited, hot-tempered, ruthless, fiery, disowning law as
never meant for him, claiming the world as the prize of arms:

> Impiger, iracundus, inexorabilis, acer,
> Jura negat sibi nata, nihil non arrogat armis.

'Was that man "iracundus," ' cries De Quincey, 'who, in the very
opening of the *Iliad*, makes his anger, under the most brutal insult,
bend to public welfare? . . . Because his own brutality to a priest
of Apollo had caused a pestilence, and he finds that he must resign
this priest's daughter, [Agamemnon] declares that he will indemnify
himself by seizing a female captive from the tents of Achilles? Why
of Achilles more than of any other man? Colour of right, or any relation between his loss and his redress, this brutal Agamemnon does
not offer by pretence. But he actually executes his threat. Nor does
he *ever* atone for it; since his returning Briseis, without disavowing
his right to have seized her, is wide of the whole point at issue.
Now, under what show of common sense can that man be called
iracundus who calmly submits to such an indignity as this? Or is that
man *inexorabilis* who sacrifices to the tears and grey hairs of Priam
his own meditated revenge, giving back the body of the enemy who
had robbed him of his dearest friend? Or is there any gleam of truth
in saying that *jura negat sibi nata* when, of all the heroes in the *Iliad*,
he is the most punctiliously courteous, the most ceremonious in his
religious observances, and the one who most cultivated the arts of

peace? Or is that man the violent defier of all law and religion who submits with so pathetic a resignation to the doom of early death?

> Enough, I know my fate — to die, to see no more
> My much-loved parents, or my native shore.

Charles XII of Sweden threatened to tickle that man who had libelled his hero Alexander. But Alexander himself would have tickled Master Horace for this infernal libel on Achilles, if they had happened to be contemporaries. I have a love for Horace; but my wrath has always burned furiously against him for his horrible perversion of the truth in this well-known tissue of calumnies.'[1]

I, too, have a love for Horace, and of course a high opinion of him as a critic; nevertheless De Quincey seems to me right, though not altogether for the reasons he alleges. The Latin poet has most classical scholars on his side, even recent ones like Lang, D. B. Monro, Gilbert Murray, and C. M. Bowra; but De Quincey has the modern poets, Goethe, Wordsworth, and Shelley, despite their ethical bent and humanitarian sympathies. Horace was too much of a Roman to understand Achilles, not merely because of inherited Trojan prejudices, but also because of ingrained regard for discipline and patriotism, reverence for law and order. Besides, he here betrays the ethical bias in criticism that is frequently apparent in the *Ars Poetica* and sometimes perceptible even in his master Aristotle;[2] and he seems to commit the error of which the master is never, but classical scholars like most modern critics are generally guilty, that of viewing the character apart from the action or, indeed, as the source of it. 'We maintain,' declares the Stagirite, 'that the first essential, the life and soul of tragedy is the plot, and that the characters come second.' It is as true of the epic. The foundation and the framework, naturally enough, precede the edifice.

3

De Quincey takes his stand partly upon historical grounds, partly upon the privileges of the imagination. 'According to the poet's conception' — that is, other times, other manners. Revenge, as is

---

[1] *De Quincey's Works*, ed. Masson (1897), VI, 81–82.

[2] Cf. Bywater, *Aristotle on the Art of Poetry*, pp. 213–16; also 'Reconciliation,' above, p. 69; F. L. Lucas, *Tragedy*, p. 34.

well known, in ancient times as in those less remote, was not only what it still is, a satisfaction, but also a duty, a matter of honor both to him who inflicts it and to the dead. Hence Achilles proves himself a devoted friend of Patroclus when he mutilates the corpse of Hector and refuses it burial, just as he does when he slays twelve Trojan captives by the funeral pyre. He is prompted and guided, though he goes to extremes, by an ancient and widespread religious instinct. And as for the withdrawal from battle, that is a matter of retaliation as well; the least Achilles can do is thus to assert himself and protect his honor once the goddess Athena stays his hand. Honor was not yet sublimated, as the honor of woman was not in the Middle Ages; and like that it was still a matter of people's good opinion, one's due share in the booty being the indispensable sign of this. So it is in other early epics, and as in them — Old French, Old German, or Anglo-Saxon — the worthies boast freely in order themselves to uphold their honor, and like Achilles rage when it is sullied. Whether the son of Peleus was justified in his insubordination and withdrawal can be determined, not by history, but only by the evidence of the poem. For even in Homer's day this was no ordinary war. These heroes are kings themselves, the tie between them being an alliance to recover the wife of one of them; and by Agamemnon's conduct Achilles holds the tie to be severed. The other leaders seem to think that he has the privilege of withdrawing if he likes; none of them reproaches him for it or himself appears, at this or any other time, to be animated by a patriotic or a feudal fealty. Nestor is simply of the opinion that Achilles should not strive with one who is a king over a larger country; and later Phoenix, when ample amends have been offered, avows that were it not for these he himself would not bid his friend cast aside his anger and save the Argives in their sore need.

In historical matters, however, De Quincey is not explicit, and he dwells on the injustice of Agamemnon, the magnanimity of Achilles in the sequel, and his rare qualities in private as distinct from public life. These the classical scholars would admit, and they acknowledge his eloquence and his charm. But they blame him for 'sulking in his tent,' cannot forgive him for the 'crime,' as they call it, of refusing the offers of reconciliation and atonement, hold him responsible for the death of Patroclus, which they take to be his 'punish-

ment,' and look upon his later generosity to Priam only as the fruit
of penitence and an inner change. As they see it, he develops and
reforms. With them, as with Horace, it is chiefly a matter of ethics,
though in the end the hero is purified.[3]

4

De Quincey is on surer ground, incomprehensible as this may
appear, when he takes his stand simply on the ideality of the character. There he ranges himself with Shelley in his *Defence of Poetry*:

> Homer embodied the ideal perfection of his age in human character;
> nor can we doubt that those who read his verses were awakened to an
> ambition of becoming like to Achilles, Hector, and Ulysses: the truth and
> beauty of friendship, patriotism, and persevering devotion to an object,
> were unveiled to the depths in these immortal creations: the sentiments
> of the auditors must have been refined and enlarged by a sympathy with
> such great and lovely impersonations, until from admiring they imitated,
> and from imitation they identified themselves with the objects of their
> admiration.

So Goethe speaks of honoring Achilles as one of the gods, and his
Tasso would meet him in Elysium as one of the greatest souls. But
Goethe, Wordsworth, Shelley, De Quincey, arrayed against Horace
and classical scholars so aesthetically gifted as Andrew Lang and
Professor Murray, with no basis of mediation between them? These
last-named cannot be wholly in the wrong. Reason, indeed, and
common sense, after all due allowances for the 'rugged individualism' of the Homeric age, are on their side. De Quincey and the
modern poets respond more sympathetically to the epic poet's intention (which, since in poetry, is not that of mere reason or common
sense); but they give an inadequate account of it. They use the
word 'ideal,' which ordinarily has moral implications; and in some
serious regards, if he is to be judged merely by his conduct or even
also by some of his sentiments, Achilles is immoral — lawless,
implacable, cruel. Yet the modern poets are right in their admiration of him, echoing the admiration of his creator; and all, I think,
that is wanting to justify them is a distinction between the realistic

---

[3] Cf. Andrew Lang, *Homer and the Epic*, pp. 137–39; C. M. Bowra, *Tradition and
Design in the Iliad* (1930), pp. 20–21, etc.

and rational, the ethical or psychological, treatment of character and
what may be called the poetical.

5

What is the poetical treatment of character?[4] There are, of course,
many sorts, but what I am now thinking of is the structural or
functional service of poetry in drama or epic. This is not a matter
of meter or of diction, or of the characters themselves talking poetry,
though all these may greatly contribute to it. Nor is it a matter of
the fantasy, calling up specters or giving birth to chimeras in human
form, like Shelley at times, without much relation to human nature.
It is that enlarging and intensifying, simplifying but liberating
method employed by the greatest poets, whether epical or dramatic,
particularly as applied to their leading personages, in order to secure
the maximum of emotional effect; Othello, Hamlet, Macbeth, Lear,
Phèdre, the chief figures of Aeschylus and Sophocles, the Homeric
Achilles and Odysseus are examples. These are not psychological
studies or even faithful images of reality. Questions of motive and
ethics are, when need be, subordinated, the passions are in a sense
let loose, set free; and of these last the characters become the centers,
the vortices and wellsprings, 'the pleasurable excitement of the
emotions' being, as Aristotle thought it, 'the end and aim of tragedy.' And as such, the characters 'exceed nature,' are, as Longinus
would have them, 'greater than human,' and run to extremes.
The tragic complication, or contrast, is an emotional one and comparatively external. Placed in a plight which for the most part is
not of their own making, they are led into conduct averse not so
much from their better natures as from their real natures; becoming
cruel, vindictive, and outrageous like Hamlet and Othello, Lear and
Macbeth, and Achilles himself, who have not been so before. As
the modern tragic heroes more seldom do, they, in these extremes,

---

[4] Only when ready for the press have I become acquainted with Mr. Santayana's
'The Elements of Poetry,' in *Poetry and Religion* (1900), of which the following
sentences might well be on the title page: 'The construction of characters is not the
ultimate task of poetic fiction . . . in master poets, like Homer and Dante, the characters, though well drawn, are subordinate to the total movement and meaning of
the scene. . . . Aristotle was justified in making plot the chief element in fiction'
(pp. 272–73, 280, by permission of Charles Scribner's Sons).

pass beyond the bounds of decorum and propriety — curse, rage, shed blood, or, like Achilles and Hamlet, pursue revenge even beyond the limits of the grave. And to bring about this terrible, exorbitant situation, and then in turn make it acceptable, that is, to relieve the character of much of the reponsibility and to retain the admiration essential to the rousing of our fuller sympathy, the poet has recourse to artifices, or as Goethe says of a painter thus intent upon effect — the effect, however, not of any detail, we must remember, but of the whole — he proceeds to fictions, 'er schreitet zu Fiktionen.'

What are these? The chief one is the instigation or intervention of the gods, or, as Petronius Arbiter designates them together, the 'ministeria deorum.' Since there were no devils in the Hellenic mythology, supernatural mischief must needs come from one or other of the gods themselves; and that there were ordinarily no villains in Hellenic poetry is owing to the fact that to produce dramatic situations a more potent agent — fate or a deity — was at the dramatist's disposal. It is Hera that brings about the quarrel between Achilles and Agamemnon at the outset, as she puts it in Achilles' mind to summon the council; so, though at the prompting of Hera, it is Athena, not the personification of wisdom (for in Homer she is often far from being such)[5] that stays Achilles' hand when he draws his sword, assuring him of due honor at the last. And it is the instigation and intervention of the goddesses that keeps, or should keep, our admiration and sympathy for Achilles in the quarrel and his subsequent resentment, somewhat as it is the will of Olympus that, as, answering the prayer of Thetis, it makes the fortunes of war go more and more against them, heightens our admiration and sympathy for the fighting Greeks. After the reconciliation both warriors acknowledge their enmity to have been the doing of Zeus, who sent Ate down upon them. But it is Achilles, the hero, that is thus exonerated; and the fault is repeatedly recognized, by the Greeks and the gods and, shortly after the quarrel as

[5] She is, on the contrary, intriguing and deceitful, and to quote Professor Murray, treacherous and bitter. And when, in the *Iliad*, allegory is intended, it is unmistakable. Cf. my *Art and Artifice in Shakespeare*, pp. 60–61. Also J. D. Bush, *Mythology and the Romantic Tradition* (1937), p. 206, n. 15, for the earlier version of the Judgment of Paris; and C. S. Lewis, *Allegory of Love* (1936), p. 52, on the *truly* allegorical intervention of Pallas in the *Thebaid*, ii, 682–90.

well as later, by Agamemnon himself, to be wholly on the latter's side; nor is there any evidence[6] that, as one ethical-minded scholar insists, Achilles is of a quarrelsome disposition or that he and Agamemnon have had trouble before this. Thus little blame attaches to the son of Peleus, as, for the same reason, little attaches to Othello in responding to the instigation of Iago, less than there might be to Macbeth in responding to the instigation of the Sisters, none at all to Hamlet in responding to the Ghost. And thereby is here secured what may be held to be the biggest situation in all narrative, and certainly one of the finest, the hero withdrawn from the foreground soon after the beginning but looming up on the background continually more important, ever remembered and more needed or more dreaded, till he bursts upon the battlefield like a tropical tempest four books before the end.

Plot comes first, says Aristotle, earliest and wisest of critics and therefore the most misunderstood. As in *Hamlet*, the hero is held until the end in leash. But in the *Iliad* his inactivity is made in some ways more plausible. It is not merely a matter of story, of anticipation or expectation, or of leaving the ground free for the achievements of such as Diomed and Ajax, Agamemnon and Ulysses, who with Achilles on the field would have been overshadowed — with him on it, to be sure, there would be no story and never a reason for defeat — but it is also a matter of character, of drama, not only in the outcome, the hero returning for a reason he has little anticipated, but even at present, the hero 'yearning for the war-cry and for battle'[7] and continually more interested in its fortunes. He says he will go home to Phthia, where, according to the prophecy, he shall live long, but, abiding here, shall perish; yet he stays.

This last stroke still farther enlarges the situation or exalts it. From the beginning the paladin's fate has been involved in the fall of Troy, and we are continually more reminded of it, by the words of Zeus, Thetis, and other gods, of Hector, the steed Xanthos, and Achilles himself, as we near the end. From the beginning he has made the choice of glory rather than life and happiness; and now that he can change his mind, he does not. This conditional doom, another fiction, familiar in myth and ancient poetry and tragedy,

---

[6] Excepting Peleus' admonition, referred to below.
[7] I, 492.

ennobles Achilles' conduct.[8] 'Mother,' he cries, after the quarrel, looking over the great deep to the goddess, 'seeing thou didst of a truth bear me to so brief span of life, honor at the least ought the Olympian to have granted me, even Zeus that thundereth on high.' Not for honor merely is he pleading, but for what to him is as life itself, and both the goddess and the Father acknowledge the justice of his plea. No doubt the hero would have been more exemplary and edifying had he risen above all personal considerations, but he would have been less fitted for the purposes of tragedy. Sheer idealism, like any other perfection — witness in the matter of fortitude Hector, considered below — leaves too little scope to human nature, subdues instead of developing the passions, puts an end to a story at the start.

6

The chief reproach brought against the hero is for his conduct when, in Book IX, he repels the offers of reconciliation and atonement; in that situation are involved the artifices already mentioned and another presently to be. Here, above all, is the 'crime,' as Lang calls it, to be 'punished' by the death of Patroclus. But in Book VIII, without reference to the embassy or its possible outcome, Zeus declares to the gods that the war is to go against the Greeks until Achilles shall be roused by Patroclus' death. To Zeus and the other gods this latter calamity is not a nemesis upon the son of Thetis, for his and his mother's prayer, nor is it to any of the mortals, but only, for a brief space, in his misery, to the hero's own generous mind. Moreover, on the one hand, Agamemnon, in making amends, does not, as De Quincey observes, admit that he had no right to take away the maiden Briseis; and on the other hand, the deportment of the hero now in declining to be reconciled, as in surrendering her to the heralds in the first place, is the perfection of courtesy. If irascible, he is so in no petty ways and on no small or merely personal occasions, but only — after the outrage, yet before he himself has been designated as the object of it — against Agamemnon, and (in case his later godlike avenging wrath be reckoned as anything akin) against Hector and the Trojans, who have slain his friend. Not that pride

---

[8] See Mr. J. A. K. Thomson's fine book on *Irony*, Chap. VIII; but the author seems to think that the irony of the story is all that saves the character.

and wrath are foreign to his nature: Odysseus now reminds him of Peleus' warning against these failings.[9] But if really *iracundus*, and depicted with psychological consistency, he would have had to show the trait with the ambassadors Odysseus and Ajax, who are speaking so plainly: and then he would have been more like Shakespeare's Coriolanus, who thus verges sometimes upon the comic. Coriolanus is far more like the Achilles whom Horace is indicting than that Achilles is like Homer's; nevertheless, though not wholly, he keeps our sympathy in similar fashion, by not being irascible and arrogant continually and by showing many other qualities which redeem him in our eyes. But the Greek is on the level of Lear, a many-sided poetic creation, and not by nature what the Reverend Stiggins would call a 'man of wrath'; as Othello is not the incarnation of the deadly sin of jealousy, nor Hamlet of melancholy and sloth, as if the creations of Jonson. Achilles keeps our sympathy as these truly Shakespearean characters do, but would not if they followed the scheme and abode a rigorous analysis.

When the embassy approaches, he is sitting before his hut, singing, to the lyre, of the renown of heroes. Renown he is now losing, but in the ensuing colloquy he disclaims it, declaring that nothing in the world is of such worth as life itself. Since, however, he does not return to Phthia, as he thinks of doing, we remember of what he sang. And what is prompting him to refuse reconciliation but renown of a negative sort, his honor? His conception of this, as of that which prompts him later to revenge, is too extreme and exorbitant for our present *mores* and perhaps for the Homeric. Yet the ambassadors, though they think him stubborn and implacable, understand and somewhat sympathize with his motive. Phoenix, who remains with him, only begs Achilles to give way in time.

7

Now honor, in its various forms, some of which we have seen already, permeates the poem; and there again is an artifice. Like other great poets, such as Shakespeare and Dante, Homer has created his own world; and this convincingly hangs together. It is for honor

---

[9] *Iliad*, IX, 254-58. Cf. XI, 786ff., where Nestor reminds Patroclus that Peleus meant him to be Achilles' counsellor.

that the heroes, especially the Greeks, are fighting: Hector is fighting also for his country, but the Greeks, particularly Achilles, are not, and most of the time scarcely have Helen or their oaths, the principles of conjugal or social fidelity, in mind. Like Hotspur (and Prince Hal, too) at Shrewsbury and Coriolanus at Corioli, like Sir Thomas Malory's and Edmund Spenser's knights and Charlemagne's in the *Chanson*, they are playing the glorious game of chivalry. It is a point of honor, moreover, with Greeks and Trojans alike not only that they should have their due share of the booty, nor endure the reproach of having it taken from them, but that as victors they should in general conspicuously appear to be such, sparing the lives of the conquered, or surrendering a captive, only for a ransom, and taking not merely a life for a life but also the armor as a trophy and the corpse to mutilate or refuse it burial. The sublimated, transcendental honor which the modern reader demands, sinking personal grievances in concern for the common good, would not only kill the story but, even in a minor character, would be incompatible with it. Something like that, but not altogether, comes, and can come, only at the end. Meanwhile, no one, as we have seen, disapproves of Achilles, however much regretting his conduct, for withdrawing from the field, and still less for dishonoring Hector's body. He does to Hector only what Hector had endeavored to do to Patroclus, and what Patroclus, in turn, had hoped to do to Sarpedon; the other Greek heroes also wound Hector's body, and throughout the war the corpses of the fallen are as much a matter of honorable contention as the armor upon them. That the gods protect Hector's and finally interpose is not so much on abstract principle as because the hero has been devoted to their worship.[10] And what, near the beginning, Achilles, in defense of his personal honor, does to Aga-

10 Both Professor Murray and Mr. Bowra take notice of the fact that the poet himself, in passing, pronounces upon the impropriety of Achilles' treatment of Hector's corpse and of his slaying the captives (22, 395; 23, 24, 176). This disapproval may be owing to interpolation in order to satisfy the morality of a later age, but is not out of keeping with the poet's own purpose, as I conceive it. If Achilles did not go farther than the other Greeks did, or than Hector or Patroclus would have done, we should not feel how much greater was his love or grief. Mr. Bowra and others, however, insisting on the ethical interpretation, think Achilles 'half-mad,' really the victim of Ate, not only in the quarrel but afterwards, and consider that he has 'avenged his friend at the price of his own honour and chivalry' (Bowra, *Tradition and Design in the Iliad*, pp. 19, 199).

memnon, is far less than Agamemnon (though later, by his noble avowals and his own big achievements he retrieves himself in our opinion) has done to him. Angry (unlike the son of Peleus) as one is likely to be when in the wrong, for the injury to his honor in being (though at the dictate of the oracle) deprived of his maiden, he wreaks himself by taking away the hero's own. Yet, however much this spirit of retaliation, whether for blood shed or for booty taken, may be representative of the Homeric age, it is not altogether so; the individualism is certainly too rugged and too consistent; and it is clear that the poet has made the other characters share Achilles' standpoint, and approach his conduct, for a purpose.

In the poet's world Achilles, larger than human, is of it. If he insists so extravagantly upon his personal honor and carries out his revenge for his friend upon the enemy's unoffending body, others do somewhat the same; if he goes to greater extremes, that is the measure of his greater nature and passion. Also a matter of honor is his prayer, through his mother the goddess, to Zeus at the outset that the war should go against the Greeks till it reaches the shipping; yet this notion of satisfaction again is not in the first place his own, but, as we have seen, Athena's when she bids him stay his hand. The great god, moreover, hears and grants the prayer; and if the additional slaughter of the Greeks thus incurred appals us, that is no more what Achilles is thinking of than Zeus himself and the other immortals as, like the Hebrew deity in the Old Testament, they, for their own ends, make the fortunes of battle sway now this way now that throughout the poem. At the beginning does not Apollo bring down a deadly pestilence, not upon Agamemnon, the offender, but the whole Greek host, simply in answer to Chryses' supplication? This is a world of warfare, human and divine; fighting is men's business, 'the noblest mysterie,'[11] life counting as nothing in the scale; and honor is their aim. Yet as the story proceeds (and that is the heart of the story), honor, which the hero had chosen instead of life and happiness, gives way, but only to a higher honor, and this to what is higher still. His own claims, against Agamemnon, yield to those of his friend who is dead, which call for vengeance, even upon the body of his enemy; these, in turn, to reverence for the gods, to sympathy and pity, as face to face with Priam beseeching him for

[11] Spenser's *Mother Hubberd's Tale*, l. 221.

the body of his son, he bethinks him of his own father, to lose his son forthwith. Such, I take it, is the 'purification,' without 'penitence' or 'amendment,' one passion prevailing over the other, though the first, and still more the second, was not wrong.

8

The best critics recognize that great art creates its own world, and this some of them, notably Alexander Pope, have readily acknowledged in the *Iliad*. But, like Professor Murray, they do so in the vague or loose sense of its being a consistent world of poetry or of the marvelous, with mortals 'exceeding nature' in point of strength or courage, and immortals aiding or thwarting them. They do not admit of the heroes' exceeding nature in point of morality, whether of their own day or of the poet's, as I think they are bound to do if they respond to his purpose, which, especially with the hero, is to give the passions scope and play. They are shocked not only by Achilles' conduct but by his sentiments. His hunger for glory reaches such a pitch that in his enthusiasm, but also his anxiety, he bursts out with the wish, as he bids farewell to Patroclus, that not a single Trojan now alive might escape death, and not a single Argive, if only they two might escape destruction and capture Troy together.[12] That is Homeric hyperbole, and means, as Mr. Sheppard says, 'I care for you more than all the Greeks and Trojans in the world.' It is like his wish after Patroclus' death that Briseis, whom he indubitably loves, though less than he does Patroclus, had perished the day he captured her,[13] rather than that he and Agamemnon had quarreled; and like Priam's that his sons, who have been tardy in making ready for his departure to the Greek camp, had all been slain in Hector's stead. But it is not hyperbole altogether, and Achilles' ambition for himself and Patroclus is that of Hotspur,

> To pluck bright honour from the pale-faced moon
>
> . . . .
>
> And to the fire-eyed maid of smoky war
> All hot and bleeding will we offer them.
> The mailed Mars shall on his altar sit
> Up to the ears in blood;

[12] XVI, 97f.   [13] XIX, 58.

and that of Coriolanus when before Corioli or when bent on burning Rome, both of them drinking delight of battle, thoughtless of human suffering, both children of honor and renown. Not, of course, that in the *Iliad* there is anything like a central idea, a thesis or problem, a 'study' in the subject. But if Achilles is ruthless and revengeful, for honor ahunger and athirst, the other Greeks and Trojans are as well, and therefore it is not strictly to be reckoned against him. Still less is there any positive revolutionary turn; there is no new ethics, or anti-golden rule, and Achilles is not justified in wreaking himself on the corpse of Hector just because Hector had intended against Patroclus the same. It is somewhat an aesthetic, that is, a narrative matter, rather than a moral one. We are not in Hellas or Ionia, but in the *Iliad*; and there is, as I have said, an artifice. Achilles is not egoistic and atrocious, for then all the other Greeks and the Trojans would be so too; just as Othello is not stupid or gullible, for then all the other characters, who think Iago wise and honest, would be so too; and what we have in the epic, as in the tragedy, is verily 'a legitimate poem, the parts of which mutually support and explain each other.'

For Homer this may seem too complicated and ingenious, too intellectualized and sophisticated: but of course the poet did not reason it out, and it is a matter of imaginative grasp and tact, of the poise and harmony to be found in the greatest artistic creation. The parts support and explain each other as they do in a Greek temple. Drama is imitation, as architecture is not; but, as in the greatest writing, it is not so much a matter of harmony with reality as within the work of art itself. It is a matter of equipoise,

And earth self-balanced on her centre hung.

Yet, for all this remoteness, there is in this world the 'semblance of truth.' By art or artifice Achilles is not entirely exonerated. Like Othello, Hamlet, Lear, and far more Macbeth, who also are subjected to strong external influence and placed in an environment which makes this plausible, he has had some share in bringing the disaster upon himself and his friend, or, indeed, his story would disappoint, not to say repel us. It would be too unnatural, too little in accord with our notions of reality and justice, and, moreover, it would spoil the intended effect of his conduct as a measure of his passion or a contrast with it. His conduct must pain us a little, as it does, or we should not appreciate his passion. But the hero does not by any means carry the weight of a 'tragic fault,' the burden of the tragedy. Not his character is the source of the action, but, in a sense, his passions and the fate behind them. The wrath and pride and atrocity, like the wrath and pride of Lear, the atrocity of Othello and Hamlet, subserve the tragic purpose. The poet enjoys the aesthetic advantages of their violence without the disadvantages.

This is no mere aestheticism, however; nothing like art for art's sake. It is, as I suggested, a sound as well as effective narrative method. The passions which 'exceed nature' — love of honor and love of a friend, wrath for the loss of one and revenge for the loss of the other — are still natural, and struck responsive chords in the hearers as they strike them today in the readers. The excesses of the hero are 'supported' by the similar excesses of the other characters in the poem, but not warranted by them. They are warranted only by his own far greater feelings, and as the less noble of these gives place to the more. And such excesses as Achilles' — a pride and a love that are implacable but each in turn breaking down before something higher, the gods themselves provoking or participating — do not, in exceeding the bounds of morality put him beyond the pale of the hearers' or readers' approval.

In epic this last is still more important and indispensable, it would seem, than in tragedy. In the *Iliad*, the *Odyssey*, and the *Aeneid*, in the *Nibelungen* and the chivalric romances, the worthies are relieved of responsibility or disgrace by divine or else magical or demonic intervention. And in the *Chanson de Roland* the hero's fault is mitigated in our eyes even without it, but as in the *Iliad* and in *Othello* there is a manipulation. For not sounding his horn it is only Olivier that blames him — not Turpin, nor he himself, even in his dying moments, nor Charlemagne afterwards. As M. Bédier says, he does not cry, like Augustus, 'Vare, redde legiones!' For, though in death, there has been a victory. The Saracens have been routed, and what seemed to be foolhardiness has turned out the height of courage, the pinnacle of chivalry.

9

The central situation, then — the plot — comes first and foremost, with its great effect of the hero kept out of the combat (while, on the whole, it goes against his countrymen) till near the end. But this situation would, though interesting, be comparatively unexhilarating if it were a mere matter of wrath and pride withholding him. Wrath and pride are unsympathetic and unattractive, witness Shakespeare's Coriolanus: the Greek, unlike the Roman, is relieved of the one stigma by the intrusion of the deity, and of the other by the similar conduct of the estimable characters about him. Besides, as we have noticed, it is made clear, by his conduct above all but also by the attitude to it of both mortals and immortals, that ordinarily he is not irascible or quarrelsome, but, on the contrary, is distinguished for courtesy, sweetness, and charm. His dire and painful passions not only serve to put and keep him out of the combat, but are a measure of the noble passion which at the slaying of his friend swallows them up or sweeps them away. Wrath and pride kept him off the field whilst he yearned for the war-cry and the battle; they cannot do so now. Suddenly he is become indifferent to any amends from Agamemnon: suddenly he forgets not only his enmity but his desire to live, his thirst for fame. And atrocity? That now is the measure of a new and higher wrath and pride which springs out of the loss of his friend and his desire to do him honor. In the words of De Quincey:

His friend perishes. Then we see him rise in his noontide wrath, before which no life could stand. The frenzy of his grief makes him for a time cruel and implacable. He sweeps the field of battle like a monsoon. His revenge descends perfect, sudden, like a curse from heaven. We now recognize the goddess-born. This is his avatar — the incarnate descent of his wrath. Had he moved to battle under the ordinary impulses of Ajax, Diomed, and the other heroes, we never could have sympathized or gone along with so withering a course. We should have viewed him as a 'scourge of God,' or fiend, born for the tears of wives and the maledictions of mothers. But the poet, before he would let him loose upon men, creates for him a sufficient, or at least palliating, motive. In the sternest of his acts we read only the anguish of his grief. This is surely the perfection of art.[14]

It is the biggest of situations, as I said.

---

[14] *Works*, VI, 90–91.

10

Here is the climax, and how has the poet realized it for us, or justified De Quincey's account of it? Achilles is a demigod, by far the
greatest of warriors, and how does the poet make us feel the fury
of his onset and satisfy our prolonged and eager expectations? For
one thing, by letting him do wonders above all that had been done
by Ajax, Diomed, or Agamemnon before him. He contends with
gods and with the river Scamander, and sweeps the plain like a
whirlwind or a fire. Yet that is not enough. Death at a demigod's
hands is no worse than at a mortal's: he must be endowed with powers more than physical or natural. He must afflict the Trojans'
spirits as well as their bodies, must frighten and appal as well as
wound and kill; and it is an effect approaching that of Milton (who,
however, is here imitating) as the rebel angels fly from before the
Son of God, who 'into terror changed his countenance.' The panic
begins even before Achilles receives his new armor, when, with the
flaming cloud that Athena set there upon his head, he shouts three
times by the trench, and three times the Trojans, seeing and hearing
him, are confounded and recoil. And the climax of the climax,
which is the meeting with Hector, slayer of Patroclus, how shall
that be marked and signalized if not in similar but still more powerful fashion?

Hector's flight round the walls is an example, in little, of the
whole poetic method that we have been considering. Here it is not
the passion we have been having — wrath, pride, or revenge — but
terror; and it is not Achilles that feels it but the worthy who, practically, is the hero for most modern readers, and possibly was —
alas! — for Horace. Hector has the ethical qualities, all the domestic
and civic virtues, in which Achilles may seem to be wanting, and
ordinarily his passions do not carry him to extremes. He is a stain-
less knight, and though a patriot, is lamented by Helen, his sister-
in-law, as one who, with cause enough, had never given her a bitter
word. And Lang, characteristically, cannot read of the flight without shame and sorrow; in a saga or *chanson de geste*, he declares, an
Arthurian romance or a Border ballad, it would have been an impos-
sibility. It would have been, in more senses than one.

This is a passage among the finest even in Homer, the *scène à faire*, the rencounter to which we have been looking almost from the beginning, and like the two paladins themselves, more eagerly towards the end; but as it is handled it is a plain case of plot or emotional effect coming first and foremost. Though the real hero does not himself feel the dread as he has felt the wrath, pride, and spirit of revenge, it is for his behoof that another does. Again the poet sacrifices psychology, even character, for suspense and surprise, or rather to satisfy a higher, overruling requirement or expectation. And such a poet must needs have been something more than a blind harper — or, indeed, several harpers one after another — as by those scholars who both raise and answer the 'Homeric question' he has been taken to be!

Before the Scaean gate Hector takes his stand, despite the entreaties of his father and mother, alone, unchallenged, while yet he might enter with honor, after all the other Trojans, even as a captain last to leave his ship. 'As a serpent of the mountains upon his den awaiteth a man, having fed upon evil poisons, and fell wrath hath entered into him, and terribly he glareth as he coileth himself about his den, so Hector, with courage unquenchable, gave not back.' And he ponders, Achilles meanwhile advancing, how his honor is at stake, and how futile now would be a parley or any proposals of peace. 'Better is it to join battle with all speed: let us know upon which of us twain the Olympian shall bestow renown.' But when at last Achilles bears down full upon him, brandishing his spear, the hero flies. The courage unquenchable is quenched.

His flight, the high-souled paladin Hector's flight, is the measure of the fear that the Achaian inspires, and the price paid for that effect is Hector's reputation. And yet not altogether so, for a poet, if a psychologist cannot, may save it. Mr. Bowra evidently has read Morgann and Bradley on Falstaff; and (though thus he is turning their statement round)[15] he discovers in Hector, even at that early day, the 'principles' rather than the 'instincts' of courage. Instead, it is a matter of sheer poetical skill, a superb example of preparations and gradations in an emotional development, of sympathy putting the reader in the character's place. 'The sickening dread of Achilles' distant oncoming,' says Professor Murray, 'grows as you wait, till

---

[15] *Tradition and Design*, p. 202.

it simply cannot be borne. The man must fly; no one can blame him.'

And why not? Mere waiting is a greater strain and a severer test of one's courage than any activity; and, in the redundancy and supererogation of gallantry, Hector has taken his stand while Achilles, misled by Apollo, is still afar. The dread grows as we wait by the brave man's side. And we behold the terror of the Trojan plain, as it approaches, with the eyes of Priam and Hecuba as well as their son. 'Him the old man first beheld as he sped across the plain, blazing as the star that cometh forth at harvest time, and, plain seen, his rays shine forth amid the host of stars in the darkness of night, the star whose name men call Orion's dog. Brightest of all is he, yet for an evil sign is he set, and bringeth much fever upon helpless men.' Thereupon the king implores his son, and Hecuba after him. 'Yet they persuaded not Hector's soul, but he stood awaiting Achilles as he drew nigh in giant might.' 'Out of the greatness of his soul he could not be persuaded,' like Grenville, who would not flee before the overwhelming numbers of the Spanish. Then come the meditations — and 'sore troubled he spake to his great heart.' But as he ponders, 'nigh on him came Achilles, peer of Enyalios, warrior of the waving helm, brandishing from his right shoulder the Pelian ash, his terrible spear, and all round the bronze on him flashed like the gleam of blazing fire or of the Sun as he ariseth. And trembling seized Hector as he was aware of him, nor endured he to abide in his place, but left the gates behind him and fled in fear.'

Thus, poetically (though my rough sketch can give you no adequate idea of it) the poet motives, justifies, or at least extenuates, the flight. Motives it, that is to say, externally, not internally; and Hector (how else could he be an epic hero?) is kept intact, has both the principles and also the instincts expected. The cause, in the poem at least, is made adequate to the result: from before the face of such terror it is no dishonor to flee. In taking his stand Hector has not underestimated his own pluck but — and that is the point — what it was to meet. And in what follows everything is done to safeguard his reputation. 'Valiant was the flier,' sings the poet, 'but far mightier he who fleetly pursued him.' And the Trojan himself, when at last he halts and turns, calls out frankly yet nobly, 'No longer will I fly thee, as before I thrice ran round the great town of Priam and endured not to await thy onset. Now my heart biddeth me stand up against thee; I will either slay or be slain.' His fear itself becomes the measure of his courage. Athena, to be sure, has intervened, bidding his enemy stand and take breath, and, in the semblance of Deiphobus, promising Hector aid. But this he neither asks nor receives. The Father has hung his golden balances, Hector's lot sinking down; Phoebus Apollo has left him; his fate, he owns, has found him. Yet, despite all, he does his best, and 'noble Hector,' 'Hector of the glancing helm,' he is again as he fights; and 'noble Hector' he soon is even on the lips of the vindictive Achilles. The good account he gives of himself with his weapons, the manly sentiments he utters, and not least the treachery of Athena and her assistance to the Achaian, which add to the odds against him, restore him (if indeed he was ever quite lost) to our respect and sympathy.

Is the above account, I wonder, far from the meaning of Aristotle as he says: 'but the error may be justified if the end of the art be thereby attained . . . if, that is, the effect of this or any other part of the poem is thus rendered more striking. A case in point is the pursuit of Hector. . . . In general, the impossible must be justified by reference to artistic requirements, or to the higher reality, or to received opinion' (*Poetics*, 25).

II

Of this particular effect — cowardice in one meant to excite our admiration — there can, says Lang, be nothing in Northern poetry, and, one might think, least of all on the popular stage. Even for the Romans it would not do, or else Virgil did not here appreciate Homer's art; for while he makes Turnus, near the end, flee like Hector from Aeneas, it is only after the sword has broken in his hand. But Virgil is not so dramatic, does not, like Homer, create situations; and the courage that, the greater the danger, only rises the higher (as in the Anglo-Saxon *Battle of Maldon*, in Milton's meeting of Satan and Death, and in Browning's *Childe Roland*) presented by way of description, does not lend itself to drama. There unfaltering fortitude, if sufficiently developed to produce imaginative and emotional effect, becomes so likewise at the cost of the psychological; for it demands self-description, and then it is open to the

charge of self-consciousness or ostentation, as in Ford's Calantha,
before her heart breaks —

> When one news straight came huddling on another
> Of death, and death, and death, still I danced forward;

and as, less happily, in Shakespeare's Brutus, who, pretending he had
had no news of Portia, can say, on being told of her death, winning
admiration for his virtue,

> Why, farewell, Portia. We must die, Messala.

Lamb and Swinburne, preoccupied like the dramatists themselves
with poetic and dramatic effect, admire Calantha; but Hazlitt and
Archer, preoccupied with psychology and motives, complain, as
they might of the Roman's, of her 'funereal affectation.' Not
description is the medium of drama, but movement and change,
action and contrast; and there is no good way in drama — or in
epic when dramatic, witness Spenser's Britomart, or Tasso's Tan-
cred, confronting the flames — of conveying the impression, at one
and the same time, of great danger and great courage but by a
momentary faltering. Macbeth, certainly a brave man, shrinks from
Macduff. This is to show the impression upon him of Macduff's
disclosure (which is the oracle's fulfillment) that he was not of
woman born. So Hamlet's words at the end of the first act,

> O cursèd spite,
> That ever I was born to set it right,

serve, like the lamentations of Orestes before the matricide in the
Choephori, to mark the tragic situation. So do the outcries of Prometheus, most heroic of heroes.[16]   And there is a closer parallel, though
not in subject-matter, where Romeo goes to the ball, not as in the
source, to find a substitute for his obdurate mistress, but to prove
her more beautiful than any. By his outburst there, in faithless forgetfulness of Rosaline, the power of Juliet's beauty is demonstrated
like that of Achilles' terror. But though it is not in drama, and is
still farther removed in the quality of the situation, the closest parallel

---

[16] Cf. Chap. II above, p. 67. In fact there is no *other* way to mark the situation
when he first speaks and when he hears the fluttering of wings, not knowing it is the
daughters of Ocean on their way (l. 126). He is alone.

is in the sacred story. Without the cry 'let this cup pass from me' in the garden and the cry 'why hast thou forsaken me?' on the cross, the agony of the passion would escape us.

12

The Trojan's flight is a surprise; but in Homer, as in Shakespeare too at his best, the surprises are not total. There are preparations, as there should be. Hector's courage is kept really unquestionable; Lang and the others who are troubled by his conduct now have rightly responded to the poet's presentation of it in the past. And yet on several previous occasions[17] the champion retires before too great odds, not to mention those when he is rescued by a deity, bows to the will of one, or yields to a weakling heart put within him. Others (but not Achilles) do somewhat the same, and it is only part of the poet's plan to keep the greatest on either side from a decisive clash with those on the other — to keep them alive and their reputation, particularly that of the Greeks, untarnished, till near the end. But in Book VII Hector is afraid (and therefore how much the more when it is Achilles!) when Ajax approaches, and he would fly if he well could; and this poetic presentation of character is like that of Macbeth, who refuses to return to Duncan's chamber and quails before Banquo's Ghost, and of Othello, who loses a little of his equipoise and judicial temper when he comes upon the uproar among the soldiers on the watch. This may seem an approach to what is now generally considered the true dramatic method; but it is rather the perfection of the poetic. The characters must not seem to be puppets, the creatures of the situation; like Romeo in his impetuosity, Lear in his imperious irascibility, Hamlet in his aversion and hesitation, Oedipus in his temerity, they must have some perceptible part in bringing the misfortune upon them.

13

In the later stages of Achilles' career we need more than ever to remember that this is a world which exceeds nature, and is one of heroic warfare, of chivalry and the vendetta. His fury is aroused,

---

[17] Cf. my *Art and Artifice in Shakespeare*, pp. 103–104.

and his ferocity excited, by grief and his desire to do honor to the dead. But still the poet is careful to make distinctions, as in the matter of wrath and pride. Frequently, and long before the death of Patroclus, there have been incidental references to Achilles' clemency and his readiness to give quarter when in the field; and of these, directly or indirectly, we are now reminded. Before the combat with Hector he engages with Lycaon, one of Priam's sons, whose life he had once spared; but there is no sparing now. For it is not only his friend's death that he is avenging but (what widens his scope) 'the slaughter of Achaians whom at the swift ships ye slew while I tarried afar.' This is an episode admired by Lang, who has a kindness for Achilles once he rejoins the host. 'Die thou too, my friend; why thus lamentest thou? Patroclus too is dead, who was a better man than thou.' And he tells the youth how he himself is soon to follow. As the critic says, here finely appreciating the poetical treatment of the character, it is 'a passage of the most painful grandeur and beauty, full of ruthlessness, justified by a sense of the ruthlessness of life.'[18] And it is a truly and highly tragic situation: not a matter of justice, nor of logic or common sense, nor of recognizable or verifiable psychology, but of a noble impulse leading to extremes.

From the death of Patroclus on, this sharp contrast (but with an inner connection) of poignant love for his friend and ruthless cruelty to the enemy furnishes forth the tragic situation, until at Priam's visit the hero's natural humanity, which meanwhile we have not been permitted to forget, reappears. Reappear it must, to right the balance; yet, as it should, still dramatically, not in the vein of mere sentiment or pathos. It comes, so to speak, under cover, in the guise of the thought for his own father, soon to be childless too. In Book I and frequently afterwards his filial affection has been made manifest; and now twice of late, as he mourned for Patroclus, he has remembered Peleus, whom, by his return to the conflict, he has tragically chosen never again to see. There is irony in the parallel and contrast as the king stretches forth his hand to the beard of the slayer of his son, and either, mourning for his dead, considers the hapless lot to which he or his has brought the other. But with a natural situation, arising merely out of the character, the poet is

[18] Lang, p. 208.

even here not content. There has been another intervention from above: Thetis has conveyed to her son the mandate of Zeus. As in Aeschylus and Sophocles, as in Shakespeare but not in Corneille and Racine, there is no struggle or inner debate; and the method is illustrated in Priam himself, who, as a suppliant, has obeyed a corresponding behest brought by Iris. Were it otherwise, there would, in a sense, be some dwarfing or dulling of the passions: for Achilles there would be some breaking of faith with Patroclus, to whose *manes* he has devoted Hector's corpse. But though there is no outer or inner contention or hesitation, twice the flame underneath bursts through. Once when the Trojan king declines a seat in the hut, and begs the hero to give him straightway Hector's body. 'Then fleet-footed Achilles looked askance at him' — it is the same formula as for his wrath with Agamemnon at the beginning, τὸν δ'ἄρ' ὑπόδρα ἰδών — 'and cries, "No longer chafe me, old sire; of myself am I minded to give Hector back to thee, for there came to me a messenger from Zeus. . . . Therefore stir my heart no more amid my troubles, lest I leave not even thee in peace, old sire, within my hut."' So he bids the attendants wash and anoint the body of Hector within, lest, seeing it, Priam should not refrain the wrath at his sorrowing heart when he should look upon his son, and lest Achilles' heart be vexed thereat and he slay him. And again, after he has yielded, when he groans and calls upon his dear comrade by name, 'Patroclus, be not vexed with me. . . .' In the previous instances the intervention of the deity relieves the hero of moral responsibility; in this (from our ordinary point of view) it deprives him of the moral credit. But in all instances alike we should thus be lifted, above ethical considerations, into the sphere of the hero's passions.

Now Shelley several times insists that poetry rises above morality, and declares that in his Satan (and I would add his Belial) this bold neglect of a moral purpose is the most decisive proof of the supremacy of Milton's genius. But Milton, immortal poet though he is, is not the palmary example of the liberty and immunity of poetry; and though what Shelley means to convey is not quite clear, certainly it is not that the highest poetry is indifferent, however superior, to moral considerations. A sense of justice fulfilled at the end of play or poem is not unworthy of art; and by Shakespeare, Sophocles, and Homer it is not neglected. Our imagination would not, as we have

seen above and in the second chapter, be satisfied if Oedipus or
Othello, Antigone or Cordelia, Romeo or Hamlet, did nothing at
all to bring their fate upon them. So with Achilles. Although, like
them, he has no 'tragic fault,' he too has his failings. He is proud and,
though on great occasion, terribly angry and revengeful. And certainly there is irony in his prayer to Zeus to do him honor fulfilled
in other sort than he desired.[19] But both in ancient and in modern
tragedy, as also in the modern novel, there is plenty of irony without
a moral significance; the blindness of mortals is a loftier and more
piteous theme for poetry than their folly; and Achilles is not responsible for Patroclus' death. He reproaches himself, but he has no
sense of a crime recoiling upon him, and his sorrow is not that of
repentance. Certainly, if wrath is his besetting sin, he does not now
put it from him — is not 'purified' — as he confronts the Trojans
and Hector, or, except as the gods interfere, Priam himself. And
therefore our sympathy with him, or at least our admiration for
him, is the greater. He is not confined *within a sense of guilt*; like
Hamlet above all, like Lear, like Othello, who blaming himself as
we cannot, yet lifts up his head towards the end, and even like
Macbeth, who, deep in crime, still keeps his poetic vision. So
Achilles' soul remains free to look abroad, and turning to Priam, he
can say of life as they both have found it: 'This is the lot the gods
have spun for miserable men, that they should live in pain; yet
themselves are sorrowless.' It is well-nigh the sentiment of Zeus
himself as in pity he looks down at the immortal horses of Achilles,
who are mourning for Patroclus, to whom their master had lent
them, and wonders why he had given them to Peleus. 'Was it
that ye should suffer sorrow among ill-fated men?' In Homer, as in
Shakespeare and Sophocles and also in the best tragedy today —
that of character and environment and their fateful consequences —
justice is not the primary consideration. Tragedy is now represented, and so it should be, as inherent in the nature of things.

14

The poetical conception of character becomes clearer when we
compare Achilles with Hector, to whom, though in the matter of

---

[19] See Lang, p. 196, etc., who makes much of this.

the flight he too is treated poetically, ethical and psychological judgments more consistently apply. It is only then, confronting Achilles, that he fully enters the maelstrom of the action where, whether off the stage or on it, Achilles ever is; it is only there that his conduct must, in a sense, exceed nature, as Achilles' frequently does; and certainly he is a good son, brother, brother-in-law, husband, father, soldier, and patriot. The other day I overheard Professor W. L. Phelps discoursing on the *Iliad* over the radio, and the Trojan he lauded and applauded, leaving the Greek out in the cold. No doubt the speaker understood the limitations of his audience, who in their hearts, or at least their souls, would prefer to Hamlet Horatio or (short of his perfidy) Laertes, though they would scarcely prefer to play him. But the Greek hero is not a disappointment, the epic not a failure. To Achilles the word 'good' does not apply, as, indeed, not to Hamlet, Lear, Othello, and still less Macbeth. Though these are alike subject to the requirements of the plot, or rather of the central situation, that is, of the play as a whole, the subjection has, in the hands of the master, become a charter of freedom.

Achilles is a larger nature than the faithful and irreproachable husband of Andromache, and leads an intenser and more varied existence. He loves and hates, thinks and acts, upon a grander scale; has more thoughts and feelings one after the other or at one time together: in short, is, if strict mental consistency be not implied, a more poetic and dramatic character. He pities old Priam, and yet he is fearful, as he remembers Hector and Patroclus, that he might do him violence. And what a range, on the one hand, from his childlike dependence on the goddess his mother to a man's love for Briseis, deep tenderness for his old father, and passionate affection for his comrade, and on the other, from his stout resentment of personal injuries to an all-devouring revenge for the dead that in the thought of his honor makes him forget his own! He weeps or groans, he shouts or gives his terrible cry, he sings and touches the lyre, he speaks more eloquently than Odysseus and plays the part of the host as naturally as that of the warrior; and it is the same man that stretches forth his hands over the sea to his mother, presently receiving her caresses, and that lays upon the breast of his dead comrade his man-slaying hands, moaning very sore, even as a deep-bearded lion whose whelps some stag-hunter hath snatched away.

Magnanimity, despite his passionateness and vindictiveness, is his virtue: without amends he makes it up with Agamemnon, and without a request he is thoughtful enough to grant Priam twelve days' truce for the funeral. Magnanimity, which, according to Aristotle, is the first of the virtues, and 'containeth in it them all'; and the greatness of his spirit appears, if nowhere else, as he pours out the flood of his feelings, whether to his mother or Patroclus or before the ambassadors, the warriors, Priam, and even his steeds. 'Xanthos and Balios, famed children of Podarge,' he cries to them in the words beloved by Matthew Arnold: 'in other sort take heed to bring your charioteer safe back to the Danaan host . . . and leave him not as ye left Patroclus to lie there dead.' Hector later, in almost the same circumstances, does not think of them, or speak to them. The soul of Homer has not wholly passed into his bosom, does not thus overflow. Hector generally is the hero's foil, like Horatio. And it is Homer's conception of a hero, less stoical and even more emotional and dramatic than the Northern poet's, that prompts Achilles' reply to Xanthos' prophecy of approaching fate. He does not 'defy augury'; he does not say 'the readiness is all. . . . Let be.' 'Sore troubled,' does the fleet-footed answer him, for he loves life, even now; and yet 'with a cry among the foremost he held on his whole-hooved steeds.' He can still be heroic while he gives feeling the rein.

In both Achilles and Hector, however, in the Greeks and the Trojans alike, Homer rouses the passions, regardless of motive or in defiance of conflicting traits, indeed only thus profiting by the conflict. And thus he is in the company of Shakespeare, of the Hellenic tragic dramatists and the Elizabethan. The great dramatists absolutely must be poets, have small need to be psychologists. Racine has been called a psychologist, but in *Iphigénie* and, above all, *Phèdre*, he is primarily a poet. And 'un vrai poète, tel que Racine,' says Voltaire, 'est, si je l'ose dire, comme un dieu qui tient les coeurs des hommes dans les mains.' (Reverent and hesitant, is not the great mocker an inspiring sight?) It is a far cry from the court of Louis XIV, farther than from that of Elizabeth, to the halls where blind Maeonides recited his verses. Culture and sophistication, philosophy and theology, ethics, dialectic, and psychology, intervene. But in its highest, most powerful manifestations the nature of drama —

of poetry — had, with the process of the suns, not changed, nor had its power much increased or diminished. For of the Ionian Father, if Voltaire knew it, he needed not to have hesitated to say that as a poet he held men's hearts in his hands.

15

There is still other art or artifice in the *Iliad* which resembles that in the Greek tragic poets and in Shakespeare: if nothing else, a musical development or ebb and flow, and a method of repeated themes or *motifs*. For this (though in the preparations and gradations we have seen something of it already) I would not have you take my word, but that of Mr. J. T. Sheppard, the great Cambridge scholar, who does not draw the Shakespearean parallel, in his *Pattern of the Iliad*. What heightens the effect of the incomparable story, and at the same time deepens and subdues it, is the harmony and rhythm not merely of rhetoric and meter but of the whole structure and arrangement. Its course is in three stages or movements (the first two of them divided by Achilles' refusal in Book IX); and from there, with many subordinate fluctuations, the tide sweeps impetuously on to the Greek rout and the death of Patroclus, then rolls back with a roar to the very gates of Troy, and at last subsides and acquiesces, 'in tenderness and inexpiable sorrow,' with Hector's body surrendered, an armistice granted though not requested for his funeral. Achilles' own death is not told; that has been sufficiently indicated as presently to come, at the Scaean gate, by the hand of Paris and Phoebus Apollo; not his career is the subject of the epic but his wrath and its appeasement. And something like this is the tragic course in Shakespeare, with a tranquil and reconciling close which is certainly *not* due to the want of a front curtain. Like the Greek tragic poets also, he 'raises and afterwards calms the passion';[20] the sublime and tumultuous music descends and diminishes to the tonic chord, a rest tone. But where in all literature is there a musical development — a crescendo and a diminuendo — so vast and various as this?

And the whole poem is a rhythm of themes and *motifs*, reappear-

---

[20] Dryden's 'Virgil and the Aeneid.' Like the orators, too: cf. Cicero, *De Oratore*, I, v, 17.

ing, like *honor*, in varied form but with heightened effect. Above all, the *motif* of fate on the lips of gods and mortals, Greeks and Trojans, so far as it concerns the city and Achilles; and by pronouncement or omen it becomes towards the end ever clearer and more emphatic. Then there are bits of action, gesture, or outcry; or important objects mentioned as on the field or, by way of comparison, afar. There is the shouting, which begins the second movement, as Eris, or strife, enters the battle, and which culminates as Achilles, not yet again provided with armor, three times shouts by the trench and the Trojans as often recoil. That is not the last of it; but the note now changes, from defiance to avenging grief. Once he is ready to fight with his hands, not his breath, it is crying a 'terrible cry' that he goes down the beach of the sea to rouse the Achaian warriors; and then, mounting his chariot and hearing from the horse Xanthos, who by the goddess has been given speech, the prophecy of his death, it is with a cry among the foremost that he holds on his whole-hooved steeds. There is Patroclus' striking of his thighs with his hands when he hears and sees the Trojans by the ships and makes way to tell Achilles; and the first ship taking fire before he has yet got into the conflict, Achilles himself strikes his thighs and (the sulker!) calls out to him, 'Up, Zeus-born Patroclus,' for his own blood is rising with the gesture (as is ours!). Go, if thou must: would I could go! And there are many prayers to Zeus in the story, but the climax of them is the hero's, with a solemn and ceremonious libation, for Patroclus' safe return. Likewise (on the battlefield) the oak, the wild fig-tree, and, above all, the Scaean gate, whereby Andromache, early in the poem, would have Hector make his stand and at the last he does so, awaiting Achilles, and whereby the victor himself is in turn to fall, repeatedly loom up before us as the trysting-places of destiny. Moreover the abundant similes are taken from a few subjects, frequently repeated but constantly varied and sometimes combined or accumulated — storm, cloud, wind, and wave, fire in city or forest, woodcutters and falling trees, and beasts such as jackals, the wild boar, above all the lion, which last appears over thirty times. In similar fashion are treated matters like omens and prophecies; human motives like the hero's love for his father, as we have seen, and, as we have not seen, Hector's for his country; epic formulae like 'then fleet-footed Achilles looked askance at him'; and standing epithets such as 'fleet-footed Achilles' itself, or 'wide-ruling Agamemnon,' or 'ox-eyed Hera,' of which the repetition is not pointless or idle.

To what purpose this musical development, most of all? The art of the theater, in every age, is the art of preparations; and the art of the epic, witness both the *Iliad* and the *Odyssey*, the *Aeneid* and *Paradise Lost*, is as well. But contemporary drama is mostly in prose, providing preparations mainly by way of explanation; and this last concerns character and environment and its fateful consequences. Contemporary drama has less kinship with the art of the *Iliad*. But Shakespeare's has much, as in the gravediggers scene in *Hamlet*, the sleep-walking scene in *Macbeth*, the *finale* of *Othello*. There and in the *Iliad* this musical method naturally and happily conspires with the presentation of the passions, rather than of character. It is the quintessential language of poetry, simple and sensuous, as in the lyric. Certainly it contributes to 'the pleasurable excitement of the emotions' in the audience, which was 'the end and aim of tragedy' for the Greeks, as for Shakespeare. The various repetitions of Achilles' terrible cry move us more, and mean to us more than many times the same number of words in analysis. Even in that modern prose drama which excites the emotions most profoundly, such as Ibsen's *Ghosts* and *Master-Builder*, with their repeated *motifs*, the musical method reappears. But farther from reality, in the world of poetry where the emotions have freer sway, where beauty is not always truth and when they clash truth gives place to beauty, the world of Shakespeare, of Greek tragedy and epic, it especially and particularly belongs.

CHAPTER XII

The Tragic Fallacy, So Called

I

ODERN serious drama is mean and depressing, declared Mr. Krutch a few years ago, in a depressing though high-minded essay;[1] and there was and still is some reason for his judgment. Ibsen, by his genius, rises above his contemporaries, but in comparison to his peers or betters before him he presents uninspiring situations and unsympathetic souls within them. These have not the sweetness or the greatness of poetry. Male and female alike, they are not, as the Shakespearean and the Hellenic figures are, blessed with an imagination that comprehends the world about them or their own experience; nor are they richly dowered with virtue or its dramatic equivalent, largeness of life. His leading male characters — like Mr. Krutch, I do not call them heroes — have something of the flincher or deserter in them, witness Bernick, Borkman, Peer Gynt, and Solness, and at the same time, of the trampling, devouring egoist; or they are meddling, floundering idealists, such as Allmers and Gregers Werle; hypocrites, such as Helmer in *The Doll's House*; sentimentalists, such as young Ekdal in *The Wild Duck*; or victims of degeneracy or disease, such as Oswald in *Ghosts*. Most of his leading women are deficient in charm if not in virtue; and the murderesses Hedda, Rebecca, and the Empress Helena are not naïve or impulsive but scheming and calculating. It is the minor figures, like Little Eyolf, Hedvig in *The Wild Duck*, and Hilda in *The Master-Builder* (in the creation of whom the dramatist shakes off the burden of ethics or psychology) that are attractive or appealing; the chief figures on his stage are mostly the worse for the wear — grim and

[1] 'The Tragic Fallacy,' *Atlantic Monthly*, November 1928; reprinted in *The Modern Temper* (New York: Harcourt, Brace, 1929).

ungracious, bad-mannered and forbidding, the interest lying in the situation, whether external or internal, in the character as a study, not as an object of our affection or admiration. And that is the direct opposite of what we find in Shakespeare, despite the greater coarseness and crudity of deportment in Elizabethan life, somewhat reflected in the drama. For on an anxious sympathy, not an excited curiosity, Elizabethan and ancient tragedy depends.

What, then, shall we say of other modern serious plays, English or French, German or Spanish? If the characters are often more attractive, they are seldom more noble; if the situations are less ugly, they are seldom so intense. The English drama is the most familiar; and let the reader summon up in memory Pinero's *Second Mrs. Tanqueray* and *Iris*, *The Thunderbolt* and *Mid-Channel*, sordid stories every one. The leading women are, however attractive, frail or shallow creatures, and the men with whom they have to do are given even less virtue or distinction. The serious situations do not rise to the level of tragedy. The evil deeds are petty or ignoble, or are done in such a spirit. 'The pleasurable excitement of emotion is the end and aim of tragedy'; but there are scenes, as in *The Thunderbolt*, where the pleasure is conspicuously lacking, the shame of the character for her own misdemeanor — the destruction of a will — being fully shared by the audience and eliciting not much more sympathy in their bosoms than in that of the really magnanimous injured party on the stage. In O'Neill's *Strange Interlude*, *Desire under the Elms*, and *Mourning Becomes Electra* there is a return to what may be called tragedy, at least so far as the doings of the characters are concerned; they commit crimes above the level of cheating or forgery, crimes possibly of Aeschylean dimensions, but not of Aeschylean dignity; and the perpetrators awaken more horror than terror, and pity for the most part only as specimens of the *genus humanum*. Certainly tragedy is now often fairly unrecognizable if our notion of it is only as it was in its prime.

2

Is there a reason for this state of affairs? Mr. Krutch discovers it in our philosophy or in the life that we lead. It is because living is for us so mean and ignoble that our art is such. We bow or stumble under the load of our enlightenment. We have lost faith in God and even in man, and therefore it is impossible for us to make a hero of him on the stage. 'We do not write about kings because we do not believe that any man is worthy to be one, and we do not write about courts because hovels seem to us to be dwellings more appropriate to the creatures who inhabit them. . . . We can no longer tell tales of the fall of noble men because we do not believe that noble men exist.'[2] The tragic conception has become for us 'a fallacy.'

There are, I think, several serious defects or shortcomings in the theory. The fundamental one is that the critic fails to remember the principle, which he incidentally, yet explicitly, acknowledges, of art as no mere imitation but a new creation. Since, as is admitted, art is no record, is no document, little or nothing can be proved by it; since art is a reflection of the taste of the time, not the life of the time, it continually changes; and therefore the Spirit of Art is often, quite as Mr. Binyon finds it, 'against the Spirit of the Age.' The fact that there are no ideal heroes in the theater is no definite indication that man has lost faith in God or himself. Against poetic tragedy there has, necessarily, been a great reaction, while in all drama there has been a great decadence; but in England both these changes began even in early Stuart days, in France after those of the *Grand Monarque*, in Germany after Schiller and Goethe, and all long before the age of materialism, scepticism, and general disillusionment that Mr. Krutch, like the rest of us, regrets. In fact tragedy such as Mr. Krutch is speaking of has appeared but rarely on the planet. There have been only five great periods, the Periclean, the Elizabethan, the Bourbon, the seventeenth-century Spanish, and the late eighteenth-century German; and it is no considerable blot on our scutcheon that on the stage there is nothing of the same magnitude appearing now. Mr. Krutch is like Mr. MacEachran[3] (though the latter is less despairing) who, also thinking tragedy quite dependent upon a belief in the dignity of man, labels certain ages as non-tragic, such as those of Marcus Aurelius, the Italian Renaissance, and the eighteenth and nineteenth centuries, these being 'naturalistic,' not 'humanistic' as they really ought to be. Michelangelo, in the Italian

---

[2] *The Modern Temper*, pp. 133, 137 (by permission of Harcourt, Brace and Company).

[3] 'The Roots of Tragedy,' *Bookman*, April and May, 1930, pp. 129–37.

Renaissance, he considers 'an exception'; but what of Raphael, Leonardo, and the rest of the brilliant company of artists and thinkers, certainly examples of that dignity and no doubt also believers in it, what of Goethe and Schiller, who were also rather notable tragic dramatists, and of all the other great and weighty personages of the eighteenth and nineteenth centuries who, though not tragic dramatists, certainly equal in dignity those of the seventeenth (after 1616 at least) who were? This is another instance of the violence done to history — the confusion of literature and life — which I have commented upon elsewhere, and of that explanation of literature and other art out of our knowledge of the period, which has been criticized by M. Baldensperger, the knowledge being mainly or entirely derived from the literature or art to be explained. More is needed (if indeed in any century it is wanting) than a sense of human dignity, or than 'humanism' either, for the making of tragedy — not only a free stage but a responsive audience, and, for this last, a development or evolution, a deep-rooted and continuous tradition of conventions in writing and acting, the means of communication between author and audience without which a Sophocles or a Shakespeare could not have been. From the days of Sheridan until the last forty years there had, on the popular stage in England and America, been no drama, tragedy or comedy either, worthy of consideration; and the recent product, formed on foreign models, was so foreign and so completely formed that the common people have not yet developed much of a taste for it. At bottom there is no blame, nor even a satisfactory explanation. Art has its periods, its ups and downs; and these must be recognized, not bewailed.

Moreover, art does not quite repeat itself. Differences in excellence are no less inevitable than those in kind. Elizabethan tragedy, of course, differs from the ancient, otherwise it would not be Elizabethan; and ours differs from that still more, for reasons not so disparaging to us as Mr. Krutch is disposed to think. The mechanism of Elizabethan tragedy, whereby the noble and ideal action was supported and made acceptable, has long since broken down. A system and rhythm, a contrast and harmony of passions, not a study of character or society; dependent, for effect, on sympathy, not on curiosity, on anticipation, not surprise; as such, tragedy required, and made use of, certain superstitious conceptions — the malignant fate or the villain in league with Hell, ghosts, omens, and fore-bodings, irony, *hybris*, and nemesis, which are now fairly meaning-less, metaphorical, or outworn. Only by external instigation or intervention can Hamlet, Othello, and Macbeth come to do their bloody deeds and at heart not remain, as psychology would require, atrocious, jealous, traitorous. Only by those external agencies can they produce their supreme emotional effect, their stark contrast and overpowering impact. It is enlightenment that has cut us off from practising this highly imaginative and artistic though somewhat naïve dramaturgy; but no age could produce or appreciate another Shakespeare or Sophocles any more than it could a Homer or a Dante. And, like the fluctuations in art, enlightenment must not be bewailed. 'Panta chorei!' — all things flow, quoth Heracleitus, even before Sophocles; but the ancient, who likewise was contemptuous of his generation, was nicknamed by the cheerful and healthy Greeks 'The Weeping Philosopher.'

In one respect Mr. Krutch exaggerates the emotional differences between early tragedy and the modern. Neither the Hellenic nor the Elizabethan is so exultant and exhilarating as he makes it out to be, nor is the modern so abject and depressing. The critic is under the sway of Hegel and Bradley, finding in the earlier tragedy tran-scendental consolations that transcend even the dramatist's text and purpose; but he ventures farther than Bradley (who says that it does not matter what happens to Cordelia, all that matters is what she is), and even avows he is 'glad that Juliet dies, and glad that Lear is turned out into the storm.' I do not know whether Mr. Krutch twists the comic into the tragic or pathetic, as sentimental criticism has done with Shylock, Falstaff, and Malvolio, not to mention Molière's Harpagon, Dandin, and Arnolphe; but to me it seems a like sort of aesthetic wilfulness or perversity. There is some point, of course, to the remark about Juliet, that tragedy having not in-aptly been called a triumphal hymn of love; and for the sake of his argument Mr. Krutch has chosen his examples. He is not glad, is he? (where he has greater need to be) when Cordelia is hanged, Desdemona smothered, Antigone walled up in the rock. If he is, he is thwarting the purpose of the dramatist, turning what the latter has, by every means and resource at his disposal, endeavored to make a tragedy, a thing wholly of terror and pity, into a nameless something deprived of the dominance and equipoise of both. In fact, he goes so far as to declare, contradicting the aim and purport, not to say the very nature of tragedy, that 'all works of art which deserve their name have a happy end.'[4] Let him point out a single good example in the tragedies of Sophocles and Shakespeare, to which in a general way he is continually alluding. The only ones of Sophocles that might be cited are the *Philoctetes* and the *Electra*, but in these there is no reason that the hero or the heroine at the end should suffer. In the *Oedipus* and the *Antigone*, after the direst atrocities of nemesis, the consolations offered are in the vein of 'call no man happy until he hath crossed life's border free from pain'; 'come, cease lamentation, lift it up no more, for verily these things stand fast'; 'reverence towards the gods must be inviolate.' As for Shakespeare, who, Mr. Krutch asserts, 'justifies the ways of God to man,' candid critics, who read him, instead of piously but resolutely remolding him nearer to the heart's desire, have even complained of the want of reconciliation or consolation, of moral interpretation and adjustment.[5] Like Sophocles he ends on a quiet note, a rest tone; like him he gives a final impression of harmony, not of discord; like him he implies a state of order and solidity, not of chaos, in the normal life to which the surviving characters are returning; but, still like him, he never suggests such satisfactions as the memory of the beauty and virtues of those who have suffered and perished. In tragedy it is, as usually in the experience or criticism of art, a question of due proportion and emphasis. Such a memory the spectator or critic should have and keep, but only to break the shock of the tragic current, not to interrupt or divert its trend. He should be affected somewhat indeed like Mr. Krutch, but less definitely and pronouncedly, and more like Mr. Huxley,[6] who finds most fitting expression for his feelings in the lines of Wordsworth:

> Our friends are exultations, agonies,
> And love, and man's unconquerable mind;

yet thus he should feel only in reaction from the tragedy. By the mere beauty and grandeur of the presentation such a reaction is made

---

[4] The quotations in this paragraph are from *The Modern Temper*, pp. 123, 125.

[5] P. H. Frye, 'Sophocles and Shakespeare,' in *Romance and Tragedy* (1922).

[6] Aldous Huxley, 'Tragedy and the Whole Truth,' *Virginia Quarterly Review*, 1931, p. 182.

possible, his emotions in the end made pleasurable. 'The effect of tragedy is not a simple thing,' says Mr. Lucas, 'but a struggle of opposing feelings — our sense of the splendour and of the despair of human life.'[7] But the spectator is meant to respond to the tragedy — 'the tragic pleasure,' says Aristotle, 'is that of pity and fear,' not (though that too plays a part) of admiration — and the reaction, the rebound, should occur in his own mind, not so much in the play itself.

In modern serious drama, on the other hand, the ugly, as in *Ghosts* and *The Power of Darkness*, the humble and sordid, as in *The Weavers*, are not, as Mr. Krutch seems to think them, wanton and gratuitous, but really contribute to the aesthetic effect. The tragic muse now flies lower, when it flies at all. I, too, greatly prefer *Macbeth* and *Othello*, as I do a Michelangelo or Raphael to the best up-to-date Paris or Munich artists, who paint harlots, slums, and dump-heaps; but as Hans Christian Andersen said long ago, every-day life has its tragedy. It is a different conception of the *genre* that is now prevailing, which has borne some good fruit and will, no doubt, bear better. It is not that of the fall of princes or of the in-trusion of supernatural or alien personages, of great crimes know-ingly or unknowingly committed and the nemesis which descends upon them — in short, not that of a tragedy lifted above ordinary experience, on the wings of poesy high in air. The prevailing con-ception is that of tragedy 'inhering in the nature of things rather than in the deeds of men,'[8] or in men's relation to their physical and social environment, rooted in the earth. Poverty and ugliness, humble and low life, hovels and disease are a part of it, and in the right hands, like Ibsen's, Tolstoi's, and Hauptmann's, are sometimes made to yield situations which nevertheless elicit pity and terror, as a poten-tate deposed or wailing in a prison cannot now. A king somewhat more than an ordinary mortal, in whose mental and physical misery there are keener pathos and irony simply because he is a king, fallen from his high estate, as in Marlowe's *Edward II* and Shakespeare's *Richard II*, cannot now move us except as we strain and tax our imaginations. An anointed and sceptered monarch is another bit of tragic furniture, like fate, ghost, and villain, well stored away in the

---

[7] F. L. Lucas, *Tragedy*, p. 48.

[8] Ludwig Lewisohn, *Modern Drama*, p. 6.

theatrical lumber-room; but are we spiritually or imaginatively much the poorer for that?[9]

3

The chief difficulty, however, with Mr. Krutch's theory lies in his not acknowledging that the less noble and sympathetic quality of our present-day dramatic situations and characters is owing to our regard for probability (or rather actuality) and psychology. 'With Shakespeare the villain, with the Greeks Fate, bears the burden. But now that the villain is no longer credible or acceptable, and the cause of the trouble has been seated in the hero himself, it is not so much our smaller opinion of man that makes our modern tragedy mean and depressing as our imperious craving that the presentation of the character shall be real and true. We see, indeed, more clearly that a man bears his fate, or at least the germ of his fatal passion, within him; but we demand that we shall see this in the play.'[10] That and, as we have noticed, the influence of environment, which Shakespeare and the ancients ignored; and thus the most highly emotional situations — at least that are known to us, as in the *Oedipus* and in *Othello* — are no longer attainable. But our art must, naturally enough, be not too far removed from our knowledge, or it will not be ours, or indeed be art; and 'though much is taken, much abides,' however little of this has as yet, for the purposes of art, been discovered.

That it is the demand for realism, for psychological veracity and circumstantial probability, which makes our modern heroes less appealing, is plain enough when we see how the Elizabethans, when they themselves attempted such effects, abandoned them in the falling action of the play. This is in the 'histories,' such as Marlowe's *Edward II* and Shakespeare's *Richard II*, *Antony and Cleopatra*, and *Coriolanus*, where there was little opportunity for the usual mechanism of fate or villain. Of Marlowe it has been said, rather complainingly, that he 'hedges,' 'juggles with the springs of the emotions,' in

---

[9] See my *Poets and Playwrights*, p. 93.

[10] Since this article was published I have come upon Mr. Lucas's retort to 'The Tragic Fallacy,' Warton Lecture (1933), p. 24: 'As if Ibsen had not wrung more tragedy out of a wild duck in an attic than out of the fall of the whole ancient world before Christianity!'

other words, shifts his ground; but the reason for this has not been given. The dramatist undertook to present the hero as the cause, through his folly, of his own misfortune; unlike Hamlet, Othello, King Lear, and even Macbeth, he is, as the accepted criticism now demands, made the victim of his own 'tragic fault.' That conception serves well enough in the earlier part of *Edward II*, while the king is prosperous: there our sympathies are with the misgoverned barons and the neglected queen. But in the latter part the emotions called forth by the king's meeting with his deserts would not be sufficient for Elizabethan tragic purposes. There would be even too much 'justice' and 'motivation,' too little pity or fear, and the effect would be 'depressing,' or modern. Consequently the queen and Mortimer are made cruel and treacherous as they were not before, and Edward attractive and appealing as he was not before. The hedging or juggling arises perforce when the dramatist drops the (so far) psychological or ethical method: the complaint of the critics arises because they keep their psychological point of view. And what Marlowe did in *Edward II*, Shakespeare, after his own fashion, did in *Richard II*, making the king in his fall manlier, more poetic and eloquent, and arousing for him the sympathy of those subjects who had turned against him. The same he did, towards the end, with *Antony and Cleopatra*, emphasizing their generous traits, obscuring their mean and petty ones; and *Coriolanus*, in the latter part of the play, rising to heights of filial devotion and generosity, loses the testiness and resentfulness prominent in the earlier. Ibsen, on the other hand, in *Borkman* and *Hedda Gabler*, stands stoutly by his psychology, by his logic, draws conclusions only from his premises; but thus almost the only quality in the hero and the heroine that at their end elicits our sympathy or admiration is the pluck with which they seek or meet it. Truer, more rational, Ibsen is less tragic.

4

'In these days [those great days!] the finest tragedies,' says Aristotle, 'are always on the story of some few houses, on that of Alcmaeon, Oedipus, Orestes, Meleager, Thyestes, Telephus, or any others that may have been involved, as either agents or sufferers, in some deed of horror'; and evidently it is such a deed that is the important thing, not the rank of the characters or even the familiarity of the story. Presently the sage declares his preference for such a deed when within the family — murder, or the like, of brother by brother, of father or mother by son, or of son by father or mother, and done in ignorance. He would have, in short, the most terrible of situations, with little or nothing in the agent's own character to produce it. The Elizabethan dramatists at their best likewise presented the good and fairly innocent man in a situation that calls forth the uttermost of pity and fear; and this the modern, restricted by regard for probability and psychology, can, at such a pitch of intensity, seldom do. By the tragic fault or psychical defect the dazzling contrast is blurred. At their highest the pity and the fear are complementary and interdependent — we fear for the imaginary beings because we love them, we pity them because we fear for them; but the moderns generally attain to one effect more than the other. Sometimes, as in *The Thunderbolt, The Doll's House,* and *Borkman,* the misdeed is of modest dimensions, like forgery or embezzlement, for to that a good person can, under the mere stress of circumstances and temptation, be more plausibly brought than to homicide; and thus there is a loss in fear. Sometimes, as in *Hedda* and *Rosmersholm, Desire under the Elms,* and *Mourning Becomes Electra,* there are deeds of horror, but to such a pass the fairly good person must then be brought by some psychical abnormality or perversity, the pressure of heredity or subconscious impulse; and thus, however we allow for human irresponsibility, there is a loss in pity. Whatever our principles or convictions, perverts, degenerates, or fantastics cannot but somewhat repel us, certainly do not attract us as truly tragic figures must; and we pity them, without love, only as victims of the physical or the social order.

When, on the other hand, the modern author, as in Masefield's *Nan,* Stendhal's *Le Rouge et le noir,* and Hardy's *Tess,* would have pity and terror both, would keep the character noble or innocent and yet guilty of a great transgression, why, then, he undertakes something as improbable as ever Shakespeare or Sophocles did, but without making it so probable, and, apparently or actually, falls into melodrama. Stendhal is a penetrating and impartial analyst, before the deed and after; but as is generally acknowledged, there is no adequate motive for the tender and noble Madame de Rênal's sending the disparaging letter which (when he learns of it) provokes Sorel to rush off and shoot her, and none for his taking such vengeance or not suspecting that she was under undue influence or coercion. The deed of horror is called a *'folie pour rien,'* the author being 'entranced by the *bravura* of this senseless piece of brutality.'[11] It was, however, in the original story; and, in being attracted by it, Stendhal would have been understood by Shakespeare and Sophocles[12] though they would have proceeded differently. The deed and the letter both are justified only by the situation that ensues — the ecstasies of penitence and devotion, self-renunciation and heroism, for which in more natural circumstances there would have been no occasion. Never had he known how much she loved him as now when, wounded, despite scandal, she visits him in prison; never had she had such a way of showing it.

Nan and Tess, likewise, are sweet and patient, brave and loving creatures, and the deed of horror is warranted by no motive such as self-defense or the defense of another, but only by an accumulation of injury. In the flesh either woman would have turned her back on the man and faced life anew. But with that ending, of course, such passions could not be let loose in the story, nor such emotions of pity and fear in spectator or reader. What Tess has done and what she is to suffer are what makes the scene at Stonehenge so poignant. Her seducer's death and her own are the measure of the 'happiness' which she her whole life long had missed, and now, after bloodshed, has for a moment attained. And this terror there must be, as the price of that pity which we unquestionably feel.

5

Once we are given, however, something that approaches the ancient and the Elizabethan, we are troubled by it, and thus show the root of the difficulty to be not in our own philosophy or experience

[11] E. Rod, *Stendhal* (1892), p. 116; Lytton Strachey, *Books and Characters*, p. 272.
[12] Even by so advanced a modernist as Mrs. Woolf, though she thinks 'the extremes of passion are not for the novelist.' See her 'Notes on an Elizabethan Play' (*The Common Reader*, 1925, p. 76), where, without my knowledge, she had expressed the principle upon which I have been insisting in this book and in my last: [of the function of plot among the Greeks] 'It shall agitate great emotions; bring into existence memorable scenes; stir the actors to say what could not be said without this stimulus.'

but in our realistic taste. We cavil at the 'melodrama,' are ungrateful for the tragedy. What the author of 'The Tragic Fallacy' thinks of the novel now under discussion I do not know; but *Tess* is not 'depressing,' though *Jude* may be. *Tess* Mr. Joseph Warren Beach discusses, in his fine book on Hardy,[13] under the chapter-heading 'Pity,' and *Jude* under that of 'Truth'; but while he exquisitely responds to the effect of pity and skillfully analyzes it, he has misgivings about the way it is brought about. He deprecates, and must needs apologize for, an 'offence against realism.' What is that? In the chapter on 'Truth' he intimates a preference for *Jude* because of its 'complete freedom from melodramatic features like the seduction of Tess and the murder of Alec.' In the persons of Jude and Sue 'we recognize the human nature of our unheroic experience. . . . The reader fresh from Ibsen and Flaubert and Tolstoi may even prefer the drab and biting realism of *Jude* to the shimmering poetry of *Tess*. He will probably find it to be a more characteristic expression of the time.' (The taste of the time, I should say, the reader being 'fresh from Ibsen, Flaubert and Tolstoi.') But 'truth,' 'biting realism,' is, perhaps, not the most precious quality achieved in novel or drama, certainly not in Shakespeare; and two years before he published *Tess* Hardy himself, after considering Turner 'in his maddest and greatest days,' concluded, 'Art is the secret of how to produce by a false thing the effect of a true.'[14] The word melodramatic, which is here and elsewhere used as equivalent to 'wanting in psychological motive,' should it not rather be used as equivalent to 'wanting in narrative motive,' that is, 'sensational,' the sensation being procured at the expense of the whole? Except in this meaning of the word Shakespeare, like Sophocles, is melodramatic time and again: most of the sensations in *Hamlet*, *Lear*, *Othello*, and *Macbeth* only heighten and enrich the effect of the whole.

In the main discussion, however, the 'artistic offence' or 'melodramatic feature' insisted upon, is the seduction by Alec at the outset. 'Her responsibility is represented as practically *nil*.' 'It is here if anywhere that we hear the creak of the machinery. [The critic suspects a concession to Victorian prudery.] . . . "A slight in-

---

[13] *The Technique of Thomas Hardy* (1922).
[14] Florence E. Hardy, *The Early Life of Thomas Hardy* (1928), p. 284 (by permission of The Macmillan Company).

cautiousness of character, inherited from her race," which is all that Hardy will admit in her, can hardly amount to the tragic fault in a protagonist . . . would not suit the purposes of Sophocles, of Shakespeare, of Hawthorne, or George Eliot.' This is certainly true of the latter pair but not, I think, of the former; and here plainly appears the great difference between the two pairs of writers, and between early and modern fiction in general. If Tess at the end were more nearly getting her deserts, were more clearly the cause of her own undoing, the effect would be perhaps more natural, doubtless more edifying, but unquestionably less pitiful; and innocence at the beginning is as necessary to her as to Othello and Hamlet, and as the calamity that descends upon them is to all three, in order to arouse noble, not merely jealous or vindictive, passions in the characters, and the deepest and most unqualified feelings in reader or spectator. The depressing 'truth' is preferred, in *Jude*. But if justifiable that is only because *Tess*, too, is a novel, not a tragedy, in prose, not verse, and is in language and circumstance too little removed from reality to give the poetic conception full sway, or warrant the violence done to the psychology.

Critics even decline to accept tragic poetry in its purity, that is, the passions with no more than a superficial, a narrative or epical, rather than psychological motive, as offered by the writers of the past. Mr. Krutch himself is so much of the age which he deplores that he cannot accept them in *Hamlet*, will not have the hero a healthy and ideal character, and, dissatisfied with the merely narrative motives for Hamlet's delay — his doubt of the ghost, his unwillingness both to kill a man at prayer and also thereby send this particular one to Heaven — goes so far as to 'invent one' — that the hero 'was hesitating between two worlds, the medieval and the modern'[15]— with a candor and simplicity which inspires confidence in him less as a critic than as a citizen, and leaves the youthful Dane as the dramatist conceived and produced him (which is really the sole point in question) quite without any motive at all. Even if the invention were not thus acknowledged, such a motive could have no direct bearing upon the tragedy, not only for the weighty reason that there is no trace of it in the text, but for one almost as weighty — that it would not be dramatic, has to do with the *Zeitgeist*, not the present story,

[15] *The Nation*, June 26, 1935, p. 730.

and is another of those Taine-like generalizations by which literature is treated as the mirror of the age or (rather) of the critic's own conception of it. If by any canon of criticism we are at liberty thus to interpolate our own ideas, however alien to the author's or his public's way of thinking, they should at least not be alien to the life and spirit of drama. 'Between two worlds, one dead, the other powerless to be born' — let Mr. Krutch or any other put Matthew Arnold, who in those words is describing himself, into a drama, Elizabethan or modern, if he can!

And Mr. Shaw, freely delighting for once in Shakespeare to the point of forgetting himself and also his rather rigid ideal of a dramatist, soon rallies and remembers both, to the point of wishing (as we noticed in Chapter V) that Desdemona were more nearly the 'supersubtle Venetian' that Iago makes her out to be. In itself he appreciates the poetry, but not as an element of construction — how by art or artifice, by the potent and enchanting presentation of Othello as 'noble,' Desdemona as 'gentle,' and Iago as diabolical but apparently 'wise and honest,' on the one hand, and by the convention of slander believed when skillfully imparted, on the other, passions are awakened in the hero and the heroine and emotions produced in the audience that, with any appreciable measure of responsibility in hero or heroine either, would be considerably diminished. Desdemona can no more be supersubtle than Tess can be a little 'sensual,' or the pity will be sadly abated. Deliberately, and felicitously, she is given all the 'incautiousness' of unsullied innocence.

It was Corneille that first (at least among great dramatists) consciously turned against the precept of Aristotle and the practice of the ancients in preferring ethics and psychology to pity and fear, and thus influenced all tragic practice and criticism since his day. The tragic deed the Stagirite would have committed in ignorance. Not so the Norman, and thus he secures that effect of internal debate and 'conflict of the passions with nature or of duty with love' which, characteristic of French tragedy, may be highly dramatic, no doubt, but awakens less unmingled and poignant sympathy. What are he and Racine in the scale against Shakespeare and the Greeks?

If there is a double parallel between Shakespeare and Hardy in method and between present-day critics of Shakespeare and of Hardy in their attitude to the method, there is a more striking instance of the same in Shakespeare and Ibsen. Professor Frye[16] objects to *Romeo and Juliet* that it is fate — the stars — which brings about the death of hero and heroine, not, with a greater dramatic economy and exactitude, the family quarrel. So Mr. Lewisohn[17] objects to *Rosmersholm* that it is not the social environment — the hostility and scandalmongering of the press — which breaks the strength of Rosmer, but fate again — 'the dead cling to Rosmersholm' — through the sin committed by Rebecca to save him. A sense of sin eventually overwhelms the enlightened and sceptical Rebecca, as it does Rosmer when he learns of the deed; and 'the play derives its power from a traditional plot and a conventional motive — crime and its discovery, sin and its retribution.' Here, once more, reason and realism are pitted against imagination and poetry; but there is no question which produces greater emotional effect, the family feud and the social environment, on the one hand, or 'the yoke of inauspicious stars' and the 'White Horses of Rosmersholm,' on the other. In Ibsen's play, to be sure, there is no ambiguity; it really *is* the dead — the old established order of Rosmer's house, with its clear and severe distinctions between right and wrong — rather than the scandal and political controversy, that breaks the purpose of the progressive Rebecca and her friend. But that consideration, evidently, would not help the Norwegian much with his critic.

6

Our dramatists, then, cannot mold their situations so simply and boldly as the ancients and Elizabethans, or they will not be appreciated if they do. Yet the outlook is not hopeless. Art may profit by restrictions, by difficulties overcome; and that in this very matter of realism dramatic art has done already. It was not merely realism but a related modern requirement, apparent in Mr. Lewisohn's criticism just quoted — that of originality — which forbade soliloquy and confidence, aside and overhearing, a complicated and ingenious intrigue, and an action scattered out through time and space; and Ibsen and his followers, bowing to the decree, thus secured a structure, if not more concentrated, more plausible than ever before.

[16] *Romance and Tragedy*, p. 298.
[17] *Modern Drama*, pp. 118–19.

Also they have thus been prompted to venture into regions new to drama, both within the soul and without it — its environment, as we have seen, and the subconscious fringe or border. This latter gives not only greater reality but finer effect to self-deception, and it serves not only to replace soliloquy, aside, and confidence, but also, as in *The Great God Brown* and *Mourning Becomes Electra*, to restore to the stage that contrast between the character and his role found in Shakespeare and the ancients, or even that between hero and villain. Of itself it affords a sort of situation.

Who knows but that in seeking this end dramatists may follow Ibsen and O'Neill in falling back upon the ancient technique, and yet outdo them in finding an equivalent for the ancient destiny; or like O'Neill and Hauptmann, D'Annunzio and Stephen Phillips, treat anew, and yet better, old legends such as those of Electra and Heinrich, Francesca and Herod, Tristram and Don Juan? In the novel, the short story, or the narrative poem these reappear, for the same purpose of striking situation. It is curious how, in a day of psychology, writers, unlike the critics, endeavor, as best they may, to circumvent or evade it. (This is especially true of the short story in prose or verse, which, in the nineteenth century and after, somewhat replaced the drama and inherited its technique of contrast and compression.) They take refuge in paradoxes — psychologically interpreted, what else but a paradox can Oedipus or Othello be? — and hence it is that they have recourse to the old legends, to the old devices of deception and mistaken identity (witness Maupassant's tragic yet improbable *Le Port* and *Le Champ d'oliviers*) and (still for a situation) even to ghosts or the evil eye, to trances and dreams. Or else, to abnormality, as in *Porphyria's Lover*, where the man strangles the girl when he knows she loves him; or to roguery, criminality, or special trades or professions, which all have their point of honor; or to life primitive or remote, with different *mores*, like that of Mérimée's Corsicans and Gipsies, Maupassant's prostitutes, Kipling's Hindoos, Browning's Ivan Ivanovitch, O'Neill's sailors, stokers, social outcasts, and West Indians. Here there are plenty of natural or fairly acceptable contrasts and contradictions. Ivan Ivanovitch is, as presented, somewhat like Oedipus and Othello, a good man doing a dreadful deed, without a stain upon him but without a fate or a villain to impel him. Mérimée's Mateo Falcone is a loving father who, not in ignorance and with no hesitation, kills his son; the mistress of the Maison Tellier and its inmates undergo, at the child's first communion, an ecstasy of religious and penitent fervor, and return to their lascivious life with heightened zest: there, surely, is an Elizabethan or ancient juxtaposition or succession of passions rather than an organization and analysis. For the stage abnormality and criminality are obviously not a promising field; but the legendary and the supernatural, the primitive and the remote may yet be fruitful enough.

In any case the modern dramatist has more freely at his disposal something neither subconscious (though possibly involving that) nor remote and questionable — the complications of sex. By Shakespeare and the ancients left almost unexploited, they are almost the richest mine of situation:

> Though worked for another reason — the inherent attractiveness of the material — it lends itself to the purposes of art. Here are contrasts and compression to hand, ironies and paradoxes craving expression. Man and woman become one flesh, one spirit, are even united in the birth of another, though still remaining two. In vain — *nequicquam*, groaned the Roman — is all the ardor of their embraces. Or, thwarted, love turns to hatred, though still love underneath. There you have both contrast and irony, a dramatic struggle. And because in love one is two, and two are one, there is paradox — opposition and apparent contradiction, which are of the essence of drama. 'His honour rooted in dishonour stood.' What in Lancelot's eyes is honor — fidelity to Arthur, abandonment of Guinevere — is dishonor in the eyes of the Queen, and hence in his own. Not easily can so deep a vein of irony and paradox be found in life elsewhere. For it is the peculiar quality of love that the one person should identify himself with the other, and the other in turn with him; that their points of view should for the moment merge and interchange.[18]

When rightly handled, at any rate, this material, though it may fail of terror, does not of sympathy, as cheating and forging do.

And the austere Brunetière likewise celebrates the essential dramatic qualities of the passion:

> In the first place it is to be noted that the passions of love are the most universal and the most individual of all. Many of us have lived without knowing ambition. Few of us have not known love; and every one who

---

[18] *Poets and Playwrights*, pp. 95–96.

has deeply felt it is thereby best differentiated from his fellows. Rodrigue does not love like Polyeucte, nor Roxane like Iphigénie. . . . In the second place, it is to be noted that the passions of love are at the same time the most capricious and nevertheless the most fatal — fatal in their development, capricious in their principle. Does any one know why he loves? And the most heroic effort of will against the power of love generally ends in death; love is strong as death. And in the third place it is to be noted that, being the sweetest of all, the passions of love are also the most disquieting; I mean those from whence arise the most violent agitations, the most cruel sufferings, at times the most irreconcilable hatreds, and the direst catastrophes.[19]

Here again, however, stands our Weeping Philosopher in the way, declaring that love, another illusion or fallacy, is failing us;[20] and so it is if we are to judge merely by the brutalized and bestialized specimens of the passion found in O'Neill, Joyce, and some of the Germans. But literature being no document, we should remember the fluctuations of taste in both writer and public. Romance has had its innings for so long that the primitive and brutal must be given its turn; and what has dropped out of sight is not necessarily gone for good. Aeschylus and Sophocles, undoubtedly, had about them, at their disposal, the same sort of sexual material and knowledge as Euripides, but they made no such use of it; and Shakespeare, who, if we are to judge by the Sonnets, had something rather considerable of the sort in his own private experience, left it, in its complications, almost wholly to Beaumont and Fletcher, Middleton, Webster, and Ford. But at this point, surely, if at every other, the critic need not despair. 'All things flow,' yet some of them not like a river but like wave or tide, recurring. The *jure divino* king and the demonic villain, the arbitrary and personal Fortune or Destiny, the *hybris* which provokes it or the nemesis which is its reply, all are the figments and fantasies of a mythology, swept down the river of time beyond recovery; but the spell that woman casts upon man or man upon woman, with its consequent entanglements, is 'real' if not 'earnest,' ever new however old, never tame however familiar, and can no more than momentarily be eclipsed, whatever the changes from period to period in literary interest. Nature worship, such as Words-

[19] *Études critiques* (1903), VII, 185–86.
[20] See *The Modern Temper*, Chap. IV, 'Love — or the Life and Death of a Value.'

worth's, may have left the earth for ever, but woman worship, with its complement, never will. It may never again be like Shelley's or Browning's, just as theirs was not like Dante's or Petrarch's, but it still bids fair, through the ages, to be deep enough for the making of a lyric, to be mobile, mutable, and poignant enough for the making of a drama or a novel. Or if Aphrodite, like Astraea, is at last forsaking the earth, can we not count upon memory, or imagination?

7

'The future of poetry,' said Arnold at a time when this present tide of scepticism and materialism had already set in, 'is immense.' Wordsworth and Keats said as much, and as buoyantly, before him; and tragedy at its best, as we have been implying, is only the highest, most substantial type of poetry. The question of materials for it, and of a right form for it, is remote and academic — of *that* sort of bankruptcy we need have no fears, however it be nowadays with the other. And as for enlightenment, how many — look about us! — have yet had enough of it to hurt them? It is not enlightenment, certainly, that keeps us where we are, poverty-stricken poetically as economically. 'The objects of the Poet's thoughts,' as Wordsworth says, 'are everywhere'; and as he further says, are in 'science itself.' And if the confines of our life should contract, as by some scientists those of the universe itself are thought to be doing, why then the future of poetry may be all the brighter. 'For poetry the idea is everything . . . poetry attaches its emotion to the idea; the idea *is* the fact.' And as the fact grows less tolerably bitter, poetry will be not one of our early losses but if anything the last. A bird in a cage has one consolation, if only one.

In the meantime most of us no doubt will find life a little worth while; Mr. Krutch himself seems of late to be bearing up pretty well, with so much happiness in the tragedies of the past at his disposal; and Mr. Huxley, no bloodless visionary, is even persuaded that tragedy will be restored to us as a living art. The difference, indeed, between tragedy and the serious drama now practised is pretty much that between 'Pity' and 'Truth,' whether the latter be the depressing truth of *Jude* or that all-embracing, distracting sort, comprehending irrelevancy, which Mr. Huxley finds in the *Odyssey* as in the literature of today. In tragedy, on the other hand, it is the 'supertruth' of Mr. Huxley, or the 'higher reality' of Goethe, narrower than the material of our present literary art but more concentrated, more poignant but more stimulating. In tragedy it is, as in any good piece of realism, a new world, but depending much less on its breadth and its likeness to the world about it than on its steep intensity. In tragedy we are not reminded of the world about us except enough to be lost in its own. In our serious drama, in our literature generally, the world about us engrosses us, presses in upon us; the tragic machinery, the superstitions and conventions, whereby it was kept afar, has broken down; and perhaps tragedy may never fit in with contemporary subjects — among the Greeks and the Elizabethans themselves, as in the *Oedipus* and *Hamlet*, it was generally not made to do so! Perhaps our stories of contemporary life must still keep fairly within the limits and confines of fact and psychology. But the free and untrammelled converse and contention of the passions are too high a prerogative and solace for the spirit of man irrevocably to surrender. Other conventions and fictions will arise, have indeed, as we have noticed, in a measure already done so. And if there be no other way open, the old familiar legendary stories, with their bold contrasts and sharp simplifications, their large masses and ample improbabilities, may still be treated anew, as they have been of late in Hauptmann's *Arme Heinrich* and D'Annunzio's *Francesca*, and were by the Greeks and Elizabethans from the outset.

Appendix

APPENDIX TO 'HAMLET THE MAN'

NOTE A (to p. 126, etc.)

Mr. Wilson's Critical Method: The Influence of the Old Play; Hamlet's Treatment of Polonius and Ophelia; The Obtuseness of the Court

FOR fuller and more specific criticism of Professor J. D. Wilson's *What Happens in Hamlet* (1935), see Mr. L. C. Knights' review in the *Criterion*, April 1936, Professor Hazelton Spencer's discussion, 'What did *not* happen in Hamlet,' before the Modern Language Association, December 1936, and articles of my own, *Modern Philology*, August 1937, 1939, and *Shakespeare-Jahrbuch*, 1938, pp. 66–73. I pay this critic so much attention because he has such abundance of scholarly material, such positiveness and definiteness, liveliness and ingenuity in the application of it, that more than many other critics he has led readers astray.

Treating the tragedy as if it were an enigma, not only for our day but for its own, Mr. Wilson, in the process of solution, or of reconstruction, seizes upon single words or phrases, whether there already or as a result of his own emendation, and attributes to them undue importance, or, in this connection, improbable meanings. The interpretations (discussed in my articles) of the words 'loose' and 'nunnery' whereby Hamlet is made to take Polonius for a bawd and Ophelia for a prostitute, are as unlikely as the Prince's reproaching himself for 'cursing like a very drab, a *stallion* (male whore)' instead of *scullion*. (The point, as Professor Spencer says, is not sexual irregularity but vituperative volubility.)

And in the process of reconstruction Mr. Wilson, though making much of history, neglects the traditions and requirements of Elizabethan dramatic art, and slights, when it is not to the advantage of his theories, the circumstance of the familiarity of the story, already on the stage. That Shakespeare was rewriting and rearranging is the fundamental explanation of the critical difficulties, and in particular, as Mr. Santayana and others before him have said, of the delay and the antic disposition. That the motive of the latter could with impunity be omitted is entirely owing to the circumstance that the situation had been employed not only in the old *Hamlet* but in other Elizabethan revenge tragedies, and had been highly acceptable to the audience. Cf. the *Jahrbuch* article above mentioned, pp. 71–72.

As for Polonius and Ophelia, a familiarity with the old story, such as is still derivable from Quarto I, is what is necessary to a full understanding of

Hamlet's treatment of either in Act II, scene ii, and afterwards. See the above-mentioned articles, *Modern Philology*, August 1937, pp. 37–39, and *Jahrbuch*, 1938, p. 73. In Quarto I the position of the nunnery scene (now in III, i) immediately after the entry in II, ii, 'poring upon a book,' and before he is 'boarded' by Polonius alone, which seems to be its original position, gives Hamlet the provocation needed in the 'boarding' colloquy. It is only after Polonius has been spying and Ophelia lying, as in Quarto I, that there is any point, when he is accosted, to his immediately calling the counsellor a 'fishmonger,' or bawd — before, Polonius was the opposite! — or even to his 'harping on my daughter' and bidding him not let her 'walk in the sun.' The earlier stage entrance, provided by Mr. Wilson, whereby the Prince overhears, but merely 'loose my daughter to him,' a thing which, in Quarto II, indeed, Polonius is to do not till considerably later, would, even if that word were so wicked, be a meager and insufficient dramatic explanation or preparation — more so even than 'no traveller returns' (in a subordinate clause of a sentence in which the hero is speaking only of 'the undiscovered country' and of suicide) as a supposed indication that he no longer believes in the honesty of the Ghost. Moreover, such mistaken suspecting, for which there is no evidence in either Quarto, would lower Hamlet's intellectual prestige as a romantic hero. In shifting the nunnery scene for climacteric tragic effect Shakespeare has, as I show in the first-named article, here lost a comic one; but in Quarto II the comic effect is not wholly lost, as in Mr. Wilson's text it is. Hamlet, only playing mad, does not really think the old fellow a bawd, and Polonius, whether perceiving the *double entente* or not, is confirmed in both his impression and his hypothesis. 'Still harping on my daughter! Yet he knew me not at first; he said I was a fishmonger. He is far gone, far gone.' He does not see, as the audience do, that the Prince is not far gone and knows him 'excellent well.'

Also the obtuseness of the King, Queen, and Court at the 'Murder of Gonzago' was more acceptable at the Globe partly because of the familiarity of the situation. This is not, as Mr. Wilson thinks, a complicated and psychological but a simple and purely theatrical one, an experiment from the point of view and for the benefit not of the Queen or the Court but only of Hamlet, Horatio, and the audience, an endurance test under which Claudius finally succumbs. The *motif* itself is legendary — 'I have heard that guilty creatures at a play' — and there is no psychology of any sort in the matter of the Queen and Court's failure to catch the drift at the end or in the King's failure to catch it earlier and his betrayal of himself when he does. Their failure is made more credible by Hamlet's throwing dust in the eyes of the audience on the stage as he harps on woman's frailty and the marriage instead of the murder; and there is no failure on the part of the audience in the house! In Shakespeare's most explicit manner, there is comment before the experiment, during it and after it is over. There is no riddle, but a problem plainly put and solved. To appreciate Mr. Wilson's play-within-the-play, however — by which he tests the Queen's guilt as well as the King's and gives the Court to understand that he himself is threatening to poison his uncle — the audience would have had to be made up of students or detectives, of Mr. Wilsons, if they were not to be perplexed by Hamlet's huge satisfaction at the outcome. As they were, little troubled by psychological scruples, they would have appreciated, if only through its familiarity, the stage effect and simple emotional situation; would have remembered that Horatio alone has been given the tip, and that the Court here, as in the banquet scene in *Macbeth* (though, like the Greek Chorus at times, apparently wanting in perception or courage), serves the purpose of reflecting and measuring, through his final loss of self-control, the King's inner perturbation and commotion; and would not have been disappointed because at the close of his performance Hamlet did not forthwith stab the King and proclaim his crime, or else plot to that end with Horatio. For all the hero has undertaken to do is to test the King's guilt, much story, they know, being yet to come.

NOTE B (to p. 133) — 'HUMORS'

SEE Miss Lily Campbell's *Shakespeare's Tragic Heroes* (1930); Professor O. J. Campbell's acceptance of her 'convincing evidence,' in 'Jaques,' *Huntington Library Bulletin*, October 1935, p. 80, etc.; recent articles, referred to by Miss Campbell, by other investigators of the school; my articles 'Recent Shakespeare Criticism,' *Shakespeare-Jahrbuch*, 1938, and 'Jaques, and the Antiquaries,' *Modern Language Notes*, February 1939. For a proper and effective protest against the similar treatment of Chaucer see *Publications of the Modern Language Association*, 1915, pp. 236–371, 'Chaucer and the Seven Deadly Sins,' by J. L. Lowes.

NOTE C (to p. 156) — THE GHOST A DEVIL OR DEMON

CF. my *Hamlet* (1919), pp. 47–49, for the orthodox Protestant opinion, which took ghosts to be devils because of its denial of a Purgatory; and for the situation of such a doubt on the part of the seer of ghost (or god) elsewhere in Shakespeare and in Renaissance drama, as in the *Odyssey* and in Euripides, with, of course, no psychological repercussions (*Orestes*, 1668–69 and *Electra*, 979; *Odyssey*, V, 356–57). Orestes suspects that the god may have been a demon; Odysseus, that it may have been another than he seems, with evil purposes. Not that these parallels or others noted in the text above, as p. 154 note, are examples of 'influence.' It is rather a matter of tradition — or else of the simple identity of human nature and art, a matter of the dramatists' thinking and working like the ancients, without their being aware. It's the natural question — angel or devil? — when the spirit appears or vanishes, as to Rinaldo (*Orl. Fur.* 42: 65).

Mr. Wilson (*What Happens*, Chap. III) has worked up a case for the ghost scenes as a reflection of a contemporary controversy, making Marcellus a representative of the pre-Reformation attitude, Horatio a disciple of the sceptical (and Protestant) Reginald Scot, and Hamlet betwixt and between. But immediately Horatio is converted to belief; by the ghost's words, and then by the Mousetrap, Hamlet is too; his father, moreover, quite evidently, *is* in Purgatory; consequently, if Shakespeare is supposed to have an eye to the prejudices and partisanship of his spectators, he at once loses his accustomed artistic impartiality and himself becomes a partisan, not to say a dogmatist and propagandist, antagonistic to the majority of his audience! Doubt of the ghost's reality is part of the technique of Shakespeare (cf. *Julius Caesar* and *Macbeth*), of other Elizabethans, and of the great Spaniards, as of story-writers in our day, for the purpose of making the supernatural a thing intangible and apart. (See my *Shakespeare Studies*, 1927, Chap. V, 'The Ghosts.') Tirso, Lope, and Calderón, of course, never heard of Scot. This importing of a controversial, *actuel*, or timely interest into Shakespeare, to which present-day historical criticism is prone, interferes with the emotional. The ghost-or-devil situation is so traditional as in itself to be wholly acceptable; while this poetical, unorthodox Purgatory and the repeated references to shriving, sacrament, and extreme unction are so because appropriate at an early period, and on foreign soil, like the priests, friars, and confessions in the English 'histories,' or *Two Gentlemen of Verona, Measure for Measure,* and *Romeo and Juliet.* If there were any controversial interest it would be from the Catholic side, and then there is small room for Mr. Wilson's *Protestant* priest at the end.

NOTE D (to p. 188) — MR. WALDOCK'S 'HAMLET'

SINCE finishing the chapter I have come upon Mr. A. J. A. Waldock's *Hamlet* (Cambridge, 1931), which, though mainly negative in its results, and not quite so original as it appears, is exceptionally sensible:

> This is what is so very strange, that it should be difficult, or should have become difficult, to grasp the central drift of a play that has always been popular and successful . . . (p. 7).

Unfortunately, it is not of the slightest consequence how very reasonably all such considerations are urged, *if the play does not urge them* . . . (p. 23).

Delay does not exist in a drama simply because it is (as it were) embedded in it. The delay that exists in a drama is the delay that is displayed . . . (pp. 80–81).

And cf. pp. 9, 21, 26, 35, 68, 70–71.

Index

INDEX TO NAMES AND TITLES

(Topics of discussion may be found by the *Table of Contents*. Unless dealt with frequently or at length, plays are indexed only under the author and characters under the play. More important references are in italics.)